THE EAST MOVES WEST

THE EAST MOVES WEST
India, China, and Asia's Growing Presence in the Middle East

GEOFFREY KEMP

BROOKINGS INSTITUTION PRESS
Washington, D.C.

The East Moves West may be ordered from:
Brookings Institution Press,
1775 Massachusetts Avenue, N.W., Washington, D.C. 20036
Telephone: 1-800/537-5487 or 410/516-6956   Internet: www.brookings.edu

Library of Congress Cataloging-in-Publication data
Kemp, Geoffrey.
The East moves West : India, China, and Asia's growing presence in the Middle East / Geoffrey Kemp.
    p.   cm.
Includes bibliographical references and index.
Summary: "Details the growing interdependence of the Middle East and Asia and its likely ramifications. Particular attention is given to India and China, which have a strong interest in trade—especially in oil and natural gas—with the Middle East and Central Asia"—Provided by publisher.
ISBN 978-0-8157-0388-4 (hardcover : alk. paper)
1. Middle East—Foreign economic relations—India. 2. India—Foreign economic relations—Middle East. 3. Middle East—Foreign economic relations—China. 4. China—Foreign economic relations—Middle East. 5. Petroleum industry and trade—Political aspects—Middle East. 6. Gas industry—Political aspects—Middle East. I. Title.
HF1583.3.Z4I45 2010
337.5056—dc22   2010007516
9 8 7 6 5 4 3 2 1

Printed on acid-free paper

Typeset in Sabon

Composition by Cynthia Stock
Silver Spring, Maryland

Printed by R. R. Donnelley
Harrisonburg, Virginia

CONTENTS

ACKNOWLEDGMENTS

THROUGHOUT THE LONG GESTATION of this book, I have been assisted by a number of first-class Nixon Center interns who have been diligent, hardworking, and imaginative. I am especially grateful to Oliver Barry, Alexandra Booth, Jason Campbell, Justin De Rise, Rachel Dyke, Bryan Egan, Maria Fort, Michael Geremia, Kevin Grossinger, Stephanie Lei Haven, Mary Ismail, Andrew Kalaris, Sacha Kathuria, Paul Kiernan, Erin Kuhls, Thomas A. Lewis IV, Christine Linskey, Sarah Lippit, Fatima Mazhar, Whit Miller, Thomas Moore, Michael Murphy, Bethany Natoli, Thiru Paranthaman, Read Parham, Caroline Reder, and Arooj Sheikh.

I have benefited from the counsel, wisdom, and editorial suggestions of my colleague Drew Thompson, director of the Nixon Center's China Program. Rebecca White at the *National Interest* made early editorial suggestions. I am especially grateful for the guidance and practical editorial advice from Robert Faherty, Mary Kwak, Eileen Hughes, Janet Walker, and Susan Woollen at the Brookings Institution Press.

Dave Merrill has worked with me for many years on maps, and his products are well displayed in this book. Dimitri Simes and Paul Saunders of the Nixon Center have been a constant source of support. Jon Alterman included me in an interesting conference on China and the Middle East in Abu Dhabi in 2007, and I have learnt a great deal from John Garver. I owe a special debt to Abdulaziz Sager, chairman of the Gulf Research Center in Dubai, who has co-hosted two workshops on Asia and the Middle East with the Nixon Center. My former assistant, Steven Brooke, was responsible for early drafts of the chapters. Most of all I owe a debt to Indre Uselmann, who has been responsible for the organization and internal editing of the manuscript. Her dedication, editing skills, and attention to detail have been invaluable.

Finally, the work on the book was supported by an initial grant from the Smith Richardson Foundation, and supplementary contributions were made by the Ford Foundation and the Carnegie Corporation of New York.

PART ONE

INTRODUCTION

CHAPTER ONE

THE GROWING ASIAN MIDDLE EAST PRESENCE

ASIAN COUNTRIES HAVE TRADED with their western neighbors for centuries. Today, however, as a result of the emergence of China and India as world economic powers and the growth of other Asian economies, the ties between Asia and the Middle East have increased to an unprecedented extent.[1] The signs can be seen everywhere. All around the Arabian Gulf, hotels, banks, schools, and shopping centers are managed by Asian expatriate workers, who also provide most of the region's manual labor. Without Asian labor, the oil-rich economies of the Gulf would collapse. Many of the vast construction projects in Doha, Abu Dhabi, Dubai, and other city-states are supervised by South Korean companies. Most of the automobiles and trucks on the street are Japanese or Korean. The endless procession of tankers that sail from the huge ports of the Gulf carrying oil and liquefied natural gas is destined increasingly for the Asian market. Infrastructure projects, including new roads, railways, seaports, airports, gas and oil pipelines, and undersea communication lines, are expanding in both the Middle East and Central Asia, making access between the two regions easier and cheaper.

These trends suggest that, absent a protracted global recession, the Asian presence in the Middle East will continue to grow significantly over the coming decade. However, the strategic implications are far less clear. To what extent will major Asian countries such as China and India be drawn into the complicated, volatile geopolitics of the Middle East? What roles will they take on? How will intra-Asian rivalries play out? And how will

Asia's new powers interact with the countries that traditionally have dominated the region—notably the United States? With the exception of Indian and Chinese purchases of military technology from Israel, and Asian arms sales to the countries of the Gulf, the big issues of war, peace, and security in the Middle East have largely remained outside Asia's domain. Will that always be the case? Those are the questions that drive this book.

THE KEY ASIAN PLAYERS

Asia's involvement in the Middle East affects a huge swath of countries, including Pakistan, Indonesia, Malaysia, Thailand, Singapore, Sri Lanka, Bangladesh, the Philippines, Australia, New Zealand, and, more indirectly, the countries of Central Asia. All are influenced in some way by the scramble for Middle East energy, the huge amount of money that Middle East oil and gas producers have received and invested, and efforts to seek alternative energy supplies and supply routes. However, four countries merit particular attention owing to their economic and potential military prominence: India, China, Japan, and South Korea.

Over the next thirty years, the economies of India and China are expected to surpass that of the United States in size (although as a result of population growth, their per capita GDP will remain relatively low), giving their governments increased regional and global clout.[2] As India and China grow, Japan will be left behind. Nonetheless, Japan is likely to remain a key Asian power, given its close ties to the United States and its growing assertiveness in its relationship with China. Moreover, Japan's energy needs will keep it tied to the Gulf. Similarly, South Korea, while even smaller than Japan, is already deeply engaged in the Middle East, especially in the energy sphere. Lacking domestic oil reserves, South Korea is the world's fifth-largest importer of oil and the eleventh-largest importer of liquefied natural gas.[3] In addition, South Korean construction companies have been hired to build oil refineries, petrochemical plants, offices, and infrastructure across the Middle East. Although South Korea's relations with the region have focused on energy imports and construction, efforts have been made to pursue cooperative relations in other sectors as well.

INDIA

The Indian subcontinent has had close commercial ties with the Gulf for centuries, and India today has managed to cultivate good working relationships with all the countries in the Middle East, including Israel. While economic interests have provided the basis for many of those relationships, India has also taken on a modest military role. The Indian government has participated in Middle East peacekeeping operations since 1956, when it contributed troops to the United Nations Emergency Force (UNEF), which was established following the Suez crisis. Currently 672 Indian solders make up part of the United Nations Interim Force in Lebanon (UNIFIL), and India has provided two of UNIFIL's last four commanding officers, although the government has stated it does not want to become involved in military operations.[4] In addition, India has been increasing its bilateral military ties with all of the small countries in the Gulf.

To date, India has not been able to demonstrate significant power or influence in the region. It was humiliated in 1990–91, when Saddam Hussein invaded Kuwait and hundreds of thousands of Indian workers were stranded in the country. When the workers were released, the Indian government had no way to get them out and had to lease transport aircraft from Europe to mount an evacuation. Because of such frustrations as well as its proximity, India is likely to establish a stronger, more assertive presence in the Gulf over the coming decades.

CHINA

For a short period in the fifteenth century, China was the dominant power in the Indian Ocean, but over the centuries that followed, it had little to do with the Middle East. After the Communist Revolution in 1949, China tried to cultivate close relationships with revolutionary groups in the Arab world, but its efforts were violently opposed by Arab nationalists. In the wake of the Sino-Soviet split and China's eventual rapprochement with the United States in 1972, China changed course and sought instead to establish cordial relations with Middle Eastern governments. In particular, it became more directly involved in the geopolitics of the region through arms sales, notably to Saudi Arabia, Iran, and Iraq, during the 1980s.

More recently, China has followed India's example by becoming engaged in Mideast peacekeeping. China's participation in UNIFIL began officially on April 9, 2006. In addition to three observers, the first forces stationed included a 182-member engineering battalion, including minesweeping, engineering and logistics companies, and a field hospital. The first Chinese casualty occurred on the night of July 25, 2006, when Lieutenant Colonel Du Zhaoyu was among four UN peacekeepers killed by an Israeli air strike that hit a clearly marked UN outpost in southern Lebanon.⁵ Two months later, the Chinese government decided to increase its troop numbers in UNI-FIL to 1,000; in addition, China stated that it would provide Lebanon with roughly $5 million in aid.⁶

Considerable uncertainty remains regarding China's future presence in the region, particularly in the military arena. China is a long way from the Gulf. If its maritime reach expands into the Indian Ocean and its overland reach grows through Central Asia and Pakistan, it, too, could become a major strategic player in the Middle East. But those are significant "ifs."

Dimensions of Asia's Middle Eastern Footprint

The scale of the Asian powers' involvement in the Middle East can be measured in multiple ways, including by the amount of energy flowing east to Asian markets, the value of Asian exports to the Middle East, financial investment by Asian firms in the Middle East and by Middle Eastern firms in Asia, the number of tourists traveling in both directions, and the number of Middle Easterners enrolling for higher education in key Asian countries (see map 1-1).

Energy

Any review of the Middle East–Asia connection must begin with the issue of energy. Asia's need for fossil fuels is the determining factor in its growing interaction with the region, especially with the Gulf. Vast amounts of money are being exchanged as Asian energy consumption and energy imports grow and income from Middle Eastern oil is invested in infrastructure projects both in and outside the region.

Oil.   The Middle East and the Caspian basin contain approximately 850 billion barrels of oil—65 percent of the world's estimated 1,300 billion barrels of proven oil reserves.⁷ At approximately 30 million barrels a day, the region accounts for 33 percent of worldwide oil production. Within the Middle East, oil production is concentrated largely in Saudi Arabia, Iran, and Iraq, which accounted for just under 20 percent of world production in 2005. In 2008, the three countries produced 10.8, 4.1, and 2.4 million barrels a day, respectively. The U.S. Energy Information Administration (EIA) and the International Energy Agency (IEA) predict that by 2030, those countries could be producing 12.8, 4.7, and 5.6 million barrels a day,

MAP 1-1

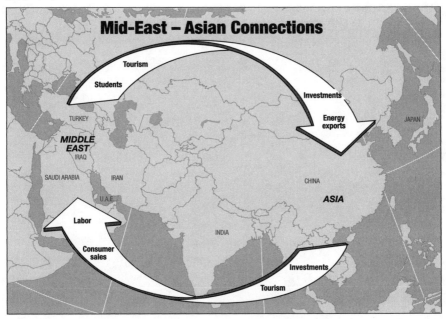

respectively, for a total of 23 percent of world production. By then, the Middle East as a whole is expected to account for 39 percent of world oil production. While the 6 percentage point increase in its share may appear modest, it means that the region will account for more than half of all new production from the present to 2030, when it is projected to produce 18.7 million additional barrels a day, or 56 percent of the total global increase of 33.4 million barrels a day.[8]

Japan, India, and especially China will consume much of that increase. The Asian market already consumes 23 million barrels a day, representing 30 percent of world demand, and two-thirds of Asia's oil imports come from the Middle East (see map 1-2). In 2006, Japan was the largest Asian consumer of Mideast oil, importing 4.19 million barrels a day, followed by China (1.84 million) and India (1.43 million). However, in the next 25 years China and India are likely to overtake Japan to become Asia's top oil consumers. As map 1-3 indicates, by 2030 oil flows to China will increase to 10.5 million barrels a day and those to India will increase to 4.5 million. Japan's Mideast oil flows will drop by 50 percent, to 2 million barrels a day. Furthermore, by 2030 the method of delivery will have shifted slightly.

Map 1-2

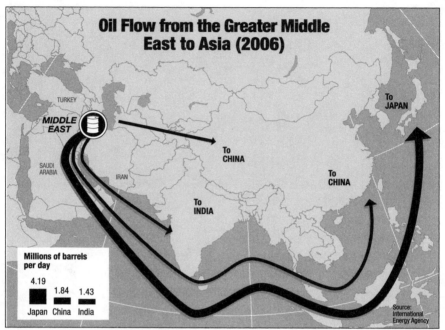

Source: International Energy Agency.

As oil pipelines throughout Central Asia begin to operate at full capacity, China will switch increasingly to land-based delivery.

Of course, such long-term predictions rest on a multitude of assumptions. Iraq is expected to have increased production from 2.1 million barrels a day (in 2007) to 5 million barrels a day by 2030. However, the country's future remains uncertain. Similar concerns could be raised about Iran, where continuing disputes with the United States over Iran's nuclear program have prevented Iran from securing the infrastructure funding that it requires to increase production. China and India also are expected to increase their production of oil significantly, but they will not produce anywhere near enough to meet their growing demand for fuel. China produced 3.9 million barrels a day in 2007 and is expected to produce 4.1 million barrels a day by 2030. India produced 900,000 barrels a day in 2007 and is expected to produce 1.3 million barrels a day by 2030.

Natural Gas.   The Middle East and Caspian basin also contain 45 percent of the world's proven reserves of natural gas, with approximately 6,200

MAP 1-3

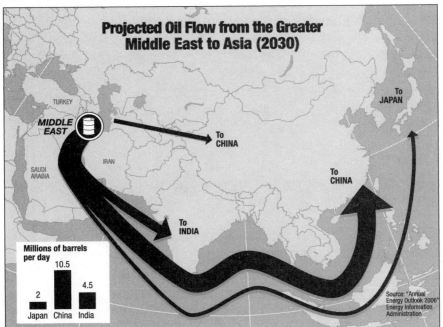

Source: *Annual Energy Outlook 2006,* Energy Information Administration.

trillion cubic feet; yet in 2007 the region accounted for only 20 percent of worldwide natural gas production. Although Iran possesses the world's second-largest supply of natural gas reserves and 15 percent of the world's total proven reserves, with 27 trillion cubic meters, it currently supplies only 6.2 billion cubic meters annually, ranking only 25th worldwide. It is an understatement to say that capacity for growth exists in this sector.

According to the International Energy Agency, the Middle East exported 1.6 trillion cubic feet of natural gas in 2004. Of that, 78 percent went to East Asia, 20 percent to Europe, and 2 percent to North America. Map 1-4 shows the amount of natural gas received by China, India, and Japan. The IEA predicts that in 2030 the Middle East will export roughly 8.2 trillion cubic feet of natural gas, of which 43 percent will go to Asia, 41 percent to Europe, and 15 percent to North America.[9] As with oil flows, by 2030 China will overtake Japan as the top importer of natural gas from the Middle East and Caspian basin. However, as shown in map 1-5, all three Asian giants will demand increased quantities of natural gas by that time.

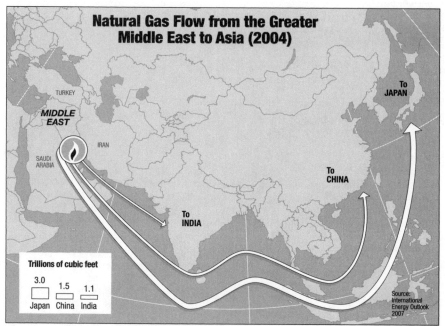

Source: *International Energy Outlook 2007,* Energy Information Administration.

Underlying Assumptions. The preceding projections assume strong economic growth in Asia in the coming decades. As their vast populations ascend into the middle class, China and India are best poised to realize those projections, providing huge post-recession growth to the global economy. However, growth is also likely in Korea and Japan and in the developing economies of Southeast Asia, including Malaysia and Indonesia, which are still recovering from the Asian financial crisis of the late 1990s. If the fallout from the 2008 financial crisis is contained and the growth of these economies continues, demand for energy in South and East Asia will rapidly exceed the region's energy production capacity.

In the coming decade, the main Asian oil importers will likely diversify their energy sources in an attempt to reduce their dependence on Middle Eastern oil and natural gas. Wealthier countries, including China, Japan, India, and Korea, will invest in research and development of alternative sources of energy, such as nuclear power. It is unlikely, however, that the region will be able to substantially reduce its dependence on imports. Instead,

MAP 1-5

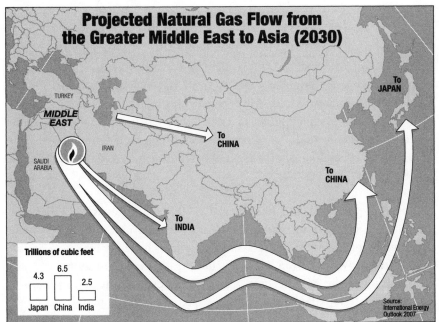

Source: *International Energy Outlook 2007,* Energy Information Administration.

the rising economies of Asia will increasingly look outward for new supplies of energy—a dynamic already well documented in the rush to engage Africa seen in China, India, and Japan. Yet no other region can match the capacity of the Middle East and the Caspian basin.

OTHER DRIVERS OF THE ASIAN PRESENCE

While the need for energy may be the major reason for Asia's interest in the Middle East, four other factors help account for the growing economic, political, and cultural ties between the two regions: immigrant labor, non-energy trade and investment, tourism, and educational exchange. In each category there has been an increase in activity that shows no signs of abating.

Immigrant Labor. The growing presence of Asian workers in the Persian Gulf is a key fact of life in the region. The Asian population is estimated at 8,568,400, but that does not take into account illegal immigrants. Some Asians work as agricultural laborers, oil plant workers, and service employees; others occupy prestigious jobs in banking and education. Some are newly arrived in the region; others come from families that have been in the Middle East for many generations. The majority come from Bangladesh, India, Indonesia, Nepal, Pakistan, the Philippines, Sri Lanka, and Thailand. They work mainly in Saudi Arabia, the United Arab Emirates, Kuwait, and Iraq, although small populations of Asians also work in Israel, Jordan, and Iran.[10] Why so many Asians? Most come from relatively close by in South Asia. Many are unskilled laborers prepared to work for low wages, while others are well educated and offer skills that are in high demand, including the ability to speak English, the language of business and tourism across the Middle East.

Non-Energy Trade and Investment.   Trade and investment between the two regions have increased, as Middle Eastern investors have sought new outlets for their petrodollars and Asian firms have pursued new opportunities for growth.[11] From 2003 to 2007, trade between the major Asian economies and the Middle East grew 269 percent, from $141 billion to $379 billion. (Maps 1-6 and 1-7 display changes in trade patterns between Asia and the Middle East.) Japan's trade with the Middle East increased by 195 percent ($70 billion to $137 billion); China's, by 366 percent ($30 billion to $109 billion); Korea's, by 243 percent ($34 billion to $82 billion); and India's, by 759 percent ($7 billion to $51 billion). During the same period, India's trade with the Middle East jumped from 9 percent of India's overall trade to 23 percent. Similarly, Korea's trade with the Middle East increased from 6 percent to 11 percent of Korea's overall trade. Typically, consumer goods, ranging from automobiles and televisions to clothing and jewelry, account for a significant share of Asian exports to the Middle East, while energy products make up the lion's share of Asian imports.

Middle Eastern investment in Asia and Asian investment in the Middle East also have grown, but precise figures are difficult to obtain. The emerging markets of China and India in particular have a great advantage in attracting investment because they can produce more goods at a lower cost than other countries. The combination of high GDP growth, cheap skilled labor, and growing markets makes Asia especially appealing to foreign investors.

More information is available on Asian direct investment in some Middle Eastern countries. In 2003, Chinese foreign direct investment (FDI) stocks in

MAP 1-6

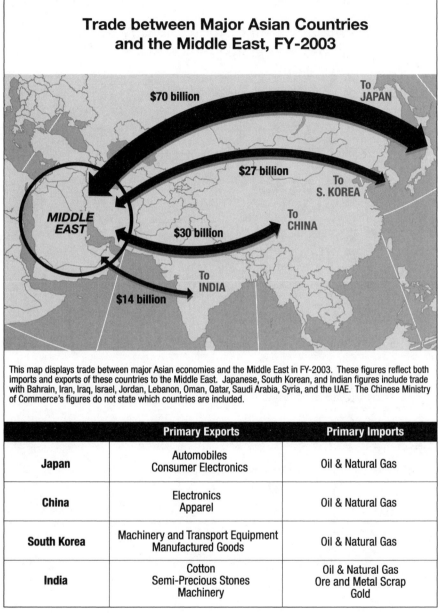

Trade between Major Asian Countries and the Middle East, FY-2003

This map displays trade between major Asian economies and the Middle East in FY-2003. These figures reflect both imports and exports of these countries to the Middle East. Japanese, South Korean, and Indian figures include trade with Bahrain, Iran, Iraq, Israel, Jordan, Lebanon, Oman, Qatar, Saudi Arabia, Syria, and the UAE. The Chinese Ministry of Commerce's figures do not state which countries are included.

	Primary Exports	Primary Imports
Japan	Automobiles Consumer Electronics	Oil & Natural Gas
China	Electronics Apparel	Oil & Natural Gas
South Korea	Machinery and Transport Equipment Manufactured Goods	Oil & Natural Gas
India	Cotton Semi-Precious Stones Machinery	Oil & Natural Gas Ore and Metal Scrap Gold

Sources: Ministry of Commerce, People's Republic of China: Ministry of Commerce, Government of India; Kita.org (South Korea); Customs Agency of Japan.

MAP 1-7

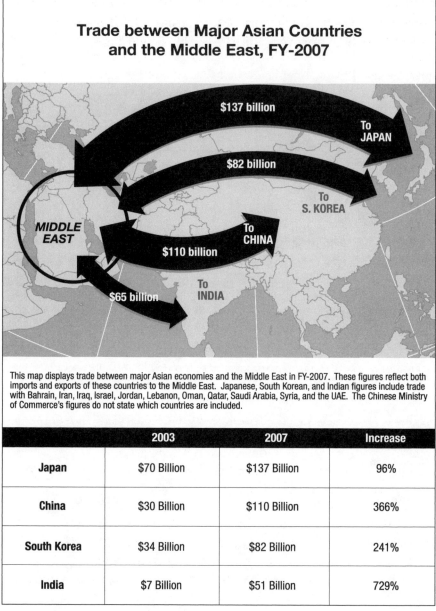

Trade between Major Asian Countries and the Middle East, FY-2007

$137 billion

To JAPAN

$82 billion

To S. KOREA

MIDDLE EAST

To CHINA

$110 billion

$65 billion

To INDIA

This map displays trade between major Asian economies and the Middle East in FY-2007. These figures reflect both imports and exports of these countries to the Middle East. Japanese, South Korean, and Indian figures include trade with Bahrain, Iran, Iraq, Israel, Jordan, Lebanon, Oman, Qatar, Saudi Arabia, Syria, and the UAE. The Chinese Ministry of Commerce's figures do not state which countries are included.

	2003	2007	Increase
Japan	$70 Billion	$137 Billion	96%
China	$30 Billion	$110 Billion	366%
South Korea	$34 Billion	$82 Billion	241%
India	$7 Billion	$51 Billion	729%

Sources: Ministry of Commerce, People's Republic of China: Ministry of Commerce, Government of India; Kita.org (South Korea); Customs Agency of Japan.

Saudi Arabia and the United Arab Emirates (UAE) were $240,000 and $31 million respectively. By 2008, those figures had grown to $620 million for Saudi Arabia and $375 million for the UAE. China's FDI stocks in Iran also have increased significantly, from $22.15 million in 2003 to a peak of more than $122 million in 2007. Increased Asian investment in the Middle East is not restricted to China, however. In 2000, Japan's FDI stocks in Saudi Arabia and the UAE stood at $714.53 million and $26.98 million, respectively. By 2007 those numbers had grown more than threefold for Saudi Arabia (to $2.564 billion) and almost tenfold for the UAE (to $251.62 million). [12]

In addition, there has been significant cross-regional investment in infrastructure. When King Abdullah of Saudi Arabia visited Asia in 2005 and China's president, Hu Jintao, visited Riyadh the following year, joint projects outside the oil sector were at the top of the agenda. [13] Asian countries have already signed contracts worth $500 billion to complete infrastructure projects in the Middle East, and the Gulf states may invest as much as $250 billion in East and Southeast Asian infrastructure projects and real estate development.

Tourism.   Tourism between Asia and the Middle East also has been on the rise, complementing the growth in diplomatic and economic relations between the two regions. Before the 2008 financial crisis, some analysts believed that by 2020, $3 trillion would be invested in leisure and tourism and supporting infrastructure in the Gulf states alone. Travel promoters expected the region to add 200 new hotels, 100,000 new rooms, and airport capacity to handle an additional 300 million Asian passengers, contributing to the creation of 1.5 million jobs. [14] Before the crisis, income from tourism to thirteen countries in the Middle East—including Egypt, Iran, Saudi Arabia, Turkey, and the UAE—was projected to increase from $150 billion in 2006 to $280 billion in 2020. [15]

Asian companies have begun to invest in construction of hotels and resorts in the Middle East. In May 2007, the Hotel JAL chain, the first Japanese operator to enter the Middle East, opened a 257-room hotel in the UAE. The company also announced plans to open additional five-star hotels in Dubai and Bahrain by 2011. Similarly, the Indian hotel chain Flora Group Hotels opened its sixth property in Dubai in 2008 and unveiled plans for three new properties in the region. Air traffic between Asia and the Middle East also is growing. For example, Air Arabia is building a strong network of flights between India and the Gulf region. The Sharjah-based airline began flights to India in March 2005 with service to Mumbai. Within two and a half years, it had expanded to offer more than fifty-five weekly flights to nine cities in India, which account for nearly 25 percent of Air Arabia's destinations.

Both the growth in commercial ties between Asia and the Middle East and the emergence of a large Asian expatriate community have fueled the increase in interregional travel. In addition, since 9/11 perceptions of hostility toward Muslims in Western countries have contributed to the growth of Asia–Middle East tourism. Asian countries, especially Malaysia and Thailand, have lured travelers from the region with the promise of not only acceptance but also special services for Muslim guests, such as halal meals.

Higher Education.   In recent years, growing numbers of students in the Middle East have been turning to Asia for higher education as well as to traditional destinations such as the United States and the United Kingdom. Saudi Arabia and the other Gulf states, in particular, have shown increased interest in the educational opportunities that Asia offers. For instance, a 2005 survey found that half of UAE residents regarded India as the best option for their children's higher education.[16] Several factors are driving the trend, including lower costs, less stringent visa requirements, and the growing economic and political ties between Middle Eastern and Asian nations.

The cost of obtaining a higher education in long-established study destinations, such as the United States and the United Kingdom, is much higher than in Asia. Overseas students in those countries pay more than $12,000 annually, on average, for undergraduate tuition; some Asian schools charge only half as much.[17] Because India, China, and South Korea are increasingly improving the quality of their domestic higher education, lower cost does not necessarily reflect inferior quality. In addition, the cost of living is lower in Asia than in the West, making it easier for international students to make ends meet.

People-to-people contact between the Middle East and Asia also is changing as a result of burgeoning cultural and educational exchange programs. In March 2007, for example, the governments of India and Bahrain established a cultural exchange program with the goal of building stronger bilateral relations through cooperation in the arts, education, and media events. Similarly, the Japanese government has sought to increase cultural and educational exchanges with Middle Eastern countries. Japan has established public information and cultural centers in Cairo and Tehran, and, through the Japan Foundation, it has planned cultural exhibitions, delegations, and theatrical performances in a variety of countries. In the years since 9/11, the foundation also has worked to promote greater understanding of Middle Eastern culture and traditions in Japan. Its efforts have included programs on Islam, Iran, and Iraq, as well as invitations to Middle Eastern artists to perform in Tokyo.

THE MIDDLE EAST AND EXTERNAL POWERS

Despite the growth in economic and cultural ties between the Middle East and Asia, the region remains dominated, as it has been for the past century and a half, by Western powers. From the 1850s to the 1950s, Britain, France, and, to a lesser extent, Italy held sway in North Africa, the Levant, and the Gulf. That era came to an end with the 1956 Suez crisis, which began with Egypt's decision to nationalize the Suez Canal, which precipitated a French, British, and Israeli invasion over the vehement opposition of the United States. In the wake of the crisis, Britain and France saw their importance rapidly diminish, and the U.S.-Soviet rivalry emerged as the predominant external influence in the region. Soviet support for anti-Western Arab regimes—such as the Egyptian, Syrian, and Iraqi governments—and the growing U.S. military relationship with Israel became cornerstones of the new dynamic. In addition, the United States increasingly extended its hand to the countries in the Gulf, particularly Saudi Arabia and Iran until the fall of the Shah.

With the collapse of the Soviet Union at the end of 1991, the strategic map of the Middle East changed again. The United States seemed to stand astride the region as the world's only superpower—or "hyperpower," in the words of one French politician.[18] However, that triumphalism was called into question by the September 11, 2001, terrorist attacks on the United States, which in turn led the United States to topple Afghanistan's Taliban government in 2001 and to invade Iraq in 2003.

Today, U.S. forces are deployed all the way from the Sinai desert through the Arabian Peninsula, Persian Gulf, Arabian Sea, and Indian Ocean as well as Afghanistan. U.S. troops are involved in combat in Iraq and Afghanistan, and the U.S. Navy controls large stretches of water from the Red Sea to the

Strait of Malacca. However, the country's involvement in two wars has become highly costly, in both lives and dollars, and increasingly unpopular at home, raising doubts about how long the United States can sustain its presence in the region. The questions about U.S. involvement became especially acute with the emergence of the worldwide financial crisis in 2008.

The financial crisis also diminished U.S. prestige by calling into question the validity of its economic model, which had been eagerly pursued on the Arabian Peninsula, the richest part of the Middle East. Overnight, optimistic growth projections for the Gulf were put on hold as the housing bubble in Dubai burst and investment virtually stopped. Since then, investment and development have resumed, although at a more cautious pace. But the financial crisis has strengthened the critics of the so-called "Anglo-Saxon" model of economic growth. As *The Economist* put it:

> The economic downturn has also opened the door to a seemingly alternative ideology to the West's liberal-market approach. So, goodbye "Washington Consensus" (in favor of open markets and limited government involvement in business) and hello to what is being called the "Beijing model" or "China model." Instead of placing one's trust in the market, the future of economic growth is seen to be coming from a more muscular state hand on the levers of capitalism.[19]

If all these factors coalesced to bring about a U.S. retreat from the region, would any Asian powers fill the vacuum? On that point, there is no consensus. Some writers acknowledge Asia's economic and cultural expansion into the Middle East but argue that domestic factors in India and China will limit their ability to play the role now held by the United States. Others maintain that, to the contrary, China is likely to take a more aggressive approach to the Middle East and develop close relationships with countries like Syria and Iran. Still others focus on the growing relationship between India and the United States, arguing that it may serve to counterbalance Chinese ambitions.[20] However, most analysts agree that while there may well have been a "unipolar moment" in the 1990s when the United States was the sole superpower, that moment has gone and new patterns of international relations are evolving.[21] The new dynamics must take into account not only growing ideological challenges to the West but also the reemergence of more traditional balance-of-power politics as the Asian nations become world players.

PLAN OF THE BOOK

This book brings together and explores the issues essential to understanding Asia–Mideast dynamics and their strategic implications. The first part outlines the main features of the Asian presence in the Middle East and explains how they fit into the overall foreign policies of the key Asian powers. It closely examines the roles that India and China currently play in the Middle East and notes the more limited but significant involvement of Pakistan, Japan, and South Korea. (Taiwan, North Korea, Australia, and the Southeast Asian countries also play roles, but they are not examined in detail here.) It also devotes special attention to the links between Asia and Israel.

Against that backdrop, the second half of the study focuses on developments that affect the entire region. It describes in detail the many large-scale infrastructure projects that are bringing Asia and the Middle East closer together. In addition, it considers the strategic implications of Asia's growing footprint in the Middle East and the challenges that it poses for the region and for the United States. It analyzes the major strategic issues facing the Middle East, Asia, and the United States—including maritime security, military competition, nuclear proliferation, terrorism, extremism, and energy security—and discusses ways in which leading Asian countries can contribute to the policing of this vast region. Finally, the conclusion examines key factors that may bring about very different outcomes for the Asian presence in the Middle East, the role of the United States, and the region as a whole.

PART TWO

THE KEY ASIAN PLAYERS

CHAPTER TWO

INDIA'S RISE AND THE GREATER MIDDLE EAST

INDIA HAS LONG PLAYED an important role in the Middle East. When Britain ruled the Indian subcontinent, it exercised hegemonic power over much of the Middle East, especially following World War I and the breakup of the Ottoman Empire, and it did so from Bombay, not Cairo. Many of the civil servants who implemented British policy were Indians, and most of the soldiers who enforced it were Indian volunteers serving in Britain's Indian Army. It therefore is unsurprising that many erudite Indians share the nation's amnesia about its past participation in the wars of the British Empire, especially those in the Middle East. Yet as the "jewel in the crown" of the empire, India became intensely involved in nearly all major armed conflicts or wars in which Britain was a participant—a record that has important implications for present and future relations between India and the Middle East.

During World War I, more than 1,000,000 Indian troops were sent to fight or serve as noncombatants with the allies on every major front of the war. More than 100,000 Indian battle casualties were recorded, including 36,000 fatalities. India's material and financial contributions to the war were significant as well, including the shipment of over $80 million in military stores and equipment and nearly 5 million tons of wheat.[1] Similarly, during World War II, the forces and logistical support that India supplied to the Middle East campaign were extremely significant. At the end of operations in Iran on September 5, 1941, General Archibald Wavell wrote in his

23

dispatch that "the Middle East Command owes a deep debt of gratitude to India. During the period of nearly two years while I was Commander-in-Chief, I never made any request for men or material that was not instantly met, if it was within India's resources to do so."[2] By 1945 Indian troops and officers had participated in major military campaigns across the Middle East and had been instrumental in the defeat of German forces in the Western Desert, the Vichy French forces in Syria, the pro-Nazi government in Iraq, and the Shah of Iran's forces in the 1941 invasion of Persia.

When Britain abandoned the subcontinent in 1947, leaving behind two warring, weak states, India and Pakistan, the role of the subcontinent in regional affairs diminished dramatically. Preoccupied with their own security and huge economic challenges, neither India nor Pakistan was able to exert much influence on its westerly neighbors. Today, that is beginning to change.

As an emerging great power, India has once more become a more important political player in the Middle East. With its economy projected to grow at a rate of 7 percent to 9 percent over the next two decades, despite some negative fallout from the 2008 recession, India is under pressure to secure long-tem access to oil and natural gas resources in the Persian Gulf and Indian Ocean littoral.[3] In addition, Indian firms and policymakers are pursuing opportunities in investment, sale of consumer goods, tourism, and even education throughout the region. Also significant is the low-level but potentially important military-to-military contact between India and the Gulf states, a factor that could, over the years, become a feature of the overall Gulf security environment. Security could be enhanced if as a result of the wars in Iraq and Afghanistan, the United States seeks more support from friendly regional powers in keeping the peace in that vital corner of the world.

India has been very successful in nurturing good relations with all of the key Middle Eastern countries. In recent years, India has been able to work closely with Muslim countries while also developing important military connections with Israel, including the purchase of advanced Israeli military technology. India also has been successful in establishing good relations with Muslim countries that have remained closely tied to Pakistan. One reason was India's image during the post-independence period as a benevolent, third-world, anticolonialist country with strong views on the dangers of bipolarity and the danger of a superpower confrontation between the Soviet Union and the West during the height of the cold war. In reality, India was far more partisan than its image implied. It fought a war with China in 1962, for which it readily accepted U.S. military aid, and it also nurtured close military ties with the Soviet Union until the latter's demise. Nevertheless, those actions had no negative impact on its ties to the Middle East.

Within the Middle East, India's relations with the six Gulf Cooperation Council (GCC) members have been the most obvious and intimate, though until recently Indian–Saudi Arabian ties were cool in comparison with those between India and the five smaller Gulf states, Oman, the United Arab Emirates, Qatar, Kuwait, and Bahrain. The reasons for those ties are varied. First is geography. Mumbai is closer to Dubai than Cairo, Amman, or Damascus, and only 967 miles separate Mumbai and Muscat (map 2-1). Despite their proximity, many in the West mentally separate India from the Middle East. Yet to India, the region is "West Asia"—historically, logically, and physically close to the subcontinent. As India's Minister of Commerce and Industry put it at the second India-GCC Industrial Conference in Muscat, in March 2006:

> India and the Member States of the Gulf Cooperation Council have historic ties that go back not merely decades, but centuries. It is significant that the earliest contacts between the Gulf States and India were based on trade, with dhows and ships crossing the Arabian Sea. Indeed, the Gulf region is part and parcel of India's "economic neighborhood."[4]

Then there are the demographics. Approximately 4.5 million Indian citizens currently work in the GCC countries—mostly in the UAE, Bahrain, Saudi Arabia, and Qatar—making them the largest expatriate community in the region (see map 2-1).[5] Remittances from those workers are an important contribution to the economies of Indian states—in 2003 remittances contributed as much as 22 percent to Kerala's GDP, and in 2007 the amount sent home totaled approximately $7.3 billion.[6] Most important, however, the workers are essential for the economic growth and well-being of the Gulf states. Ali Bin Abdullah al Kaabi, the UAE's minister of labor, was quoted in August 2007 as saying, "God forbid something happens between us and India and they say, 'Please, we want all our Indians to go home'. . . . Our airports would shut down, our streets, construction."[7]

A primary example of the vitality and centrality of Indian expatriates is the degree to which Indian culture has penetrated the Gulf. During the middle of October 2007, Abu Dhabi played host to the first-ever Middle East International Film Festival. While the star-studded gala showed movies

Map 2-1

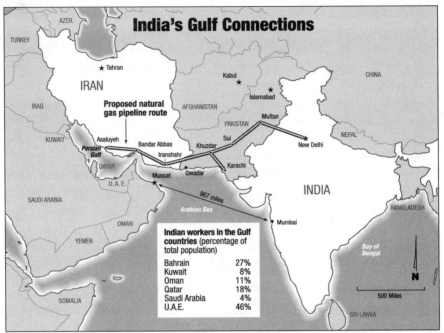

India's Gulf Connections

Indian workers in the Gulf countries (percentage of total population)	
Bahrain	27%
Kuwait	8%
Oman	11%
Qatar	18%
Saudi Arabia	4%
U.A.E.	46%

from numerous cultures, from American to Spanish to original Middle Eastern films, an entire showcase was devoted to Bollywood, the major Indian film industry. More important, however, was the strong showing of Bollywood A-listers who attended the festival, including Irfan Khan, Shiney Ahuja, and Donkona Sen Sharma. Prominent Bollywood actress Bipasha Basu served as the emcee at the closing night awards gala. The presence of the Indian entertainment elite is just another instance of the growing Indian influence within the GCC countries.

The mutual dependence of the Gulf states and India with respect to security, given their increasing interdependence regarding labor and energy, has also drawn them closer together. That mutual interest is becoming more apparent in the military sphere, where embryonic bilateral ties are emerging. It is premature to regard those developments as an alternative to the U.S. military presence that today provides ultimate security for the Gulf. However, it is not too early to think about the possible evolution over the next decade or so of closer GCC-Indian military ties. India's growing investment in the Gulf parallels its improved relations with the United

States, the Gulf's current guardian. For most of the cold war period, relations between the world's two largest democracies were cool. India, one
of the leaders of the nonaligned movement, objected to military alliances
such as NATO, CENTO, SEATO, and the Warsaw Pact. Indian politicians
resented the statement of President Eisenhower's secretary of state, John
Foster Dulles, that neutralism was "immoral."[8] Although the United States
sided with India during its war with China in 1962, bad blood persisted.
Tensions between the two were exacerbated in 1965 when the United
States and Britain imposed a joint arms embargo on India and Pakistan
and again in 1971 when the United States sent the USS *Enterprise* nuclear
aircraft carrier into the Bay of Bengal at the time of the Indo-Pakistani
war. However, with the end of the cold war in the late 1980s, relations
improved dramatically.[9]

INDIA'S ECONOMIC DEVELOPMENT

The first Gulf War, the catalyst that underlay India's decision to radically
reform its economy and adopt a more free-market approach to development, proved to be critical in shaping future relations between India and
the Gulf states. India depended on Iraq and Kuwait for 40 percent of its
oil imports, and the first impetus for reform was the shock of increased
fuel bills from higher prices for oil.[10] The loss of remittances from Indian
emigrant workers in the Gulf, which constituted a major source of India's
foreign exchange, was felt even more acutely. It was estimated that one
Gulf worker could support twenty people at home, and some states, such
as Kerala, which contributed large numbers of workers, were hit especially
hard. By the time that the Gulf War broke out in 1991, remittances were
approximately 7 percent of India's GDP.[11] Plus, there were the costs of
repatriating and resettling the workers, all of which had to be borne by the
Indian government itself. With approximately 150,000 Indian nationals
stranded in the area of hostilities, the Indian government was eventually
forced to airlift most of them from Kuwait after the invasion in August. In
addition, the trade embargo on Iraq led to a loss of export markets.[12]

Beginning in 1991, India underwent a period of trade policy liberalization
that increased the prominence of the GCC countries in its foreign trade and
provided a friendlier trading environment conducive to promoting India's
trade interests in the region.[13] Following the reforms, India embarked on a
period of economic growth that has yet to significantly slow down.

Economic Growth

India has the second-fastest-growing economy in the world, with a GDP growth rate of 9.3 percent in 2007 and 7.3 percent in 2008.[14] Some even speculate it will be the fastest-growing economy in Asia by 2020.[15] While much of India's growth can be attributed to increased consumption from increased agricultural production, the manufacturing sector is gaining momentum. There has been a surge in workers with skills in advanced computer and software development, and dotcom companies have been growing fast. Exports of software and high-tech goods increased in recent years. In 2008, total U.S. imports of Indian products were valued at $25.7 billion.[16]

Although there is controversy about the precise number, the Indian middle class is estimated to account for 300 million of a total population of more than 1 billion.[17] All estimates reveal a new class of Indian consumers that is very large in absolute terms and that has had a huge impact on the economy. The GDP per capita in 2006 was $3,800—more than twice the 1999 figure of $1,800.[18] Since the numbers seem deceptively low by Western standards, it is easier to think of them in terms of simple purchasing power (purchasing power parity)—of the types of consumer goods that a family can afford on its base salary.

Increased purchasing power makes the Indian middle class a significant factor in Indian economic and political life. Economic reforms have produced an orgy of consumer spending; the reduction in customs duties for imported goods and increased competition for domestic goods have driven down the relative prices of consumer items while improving quality and choice. Middle-class Indians, long deprived of the luxury goods enjoyed by their Western counterparts, are on an extended buying spree.

That has been paralleled by another important phenomenon: the slow but steady erosion of India's socialist ethos, long the pillar of the country's economic philosophy, which has led to a radical change in Indian attitudes and aspirations. For years, Indian socialism had stigmatized consumerism and wealth, while crippling income tax rates provided a further incentive to hide riches. Following the arrival of private satellite and cable television channels (both foreign and domestic), middle-class Indians were exposed to previously unavailable international programming illustrating the comfort and convenience offered by consumer goods. Expectations have risen, in tandem with the reduction of interest rates, an increase in credit and leasing (or "hire-purchase") facilities, and an increasing number of dual- or multiple-income households. Meanwhile, income levels have risen as more and more Indians are hired by foreign companies on foreign salaries. Moneymaking is now a major preoccupation; the acquisition of material goods is a close second. That is good news for the Indian economy.

Equally significant, more than half of India's population is under 24 years of age.[19] Born long after Gandhi's fiery *swadeshi* rhetoric brought India its independence in 1947, and after the subsequent wars with Pakistan and China, this new breed of moneyed, ambitious, and mostly young Indians has no philosophical ties to socialism. They also are the major force behind the retreat from economic isolationism toward notions of the free market and entrepreneurship; furthermore, they believe that India is destined to be a great power, and they are not shy about saying so. Traditional professions like medicine, law, and the civil service, which had been the preferred route up the socioeconomic ladder, are now being passed over in favor of careers in financial markets and business.

The most striking aspect of the new middle-class phenomenon, however, is that its ranks are increasingly being swollen by India's 750-million strong "rural underclass," which is also modernizing as it experiences an increase in income. Alarmists have long argued that the economic reform process in India is far from irreversible because the new middle-class consumers remain a minority that will inevitably be outvoted by the underclasses, which are increasingly disaffected by how hard life has become under liberalization. Traditionally the bastion of socialist support, the rural poor have been hit hardest by the steep increases in basic food prices caused by runaway inflation and the end of certain subsidy programs. While the burgeoning middle class frantically acquired its cars, cable TV service, and satellite dishes, alarmists noted the negative impact on the masses.

In fact, most indications are to the contrary. There are signs of the trickle-down effect of consumerism in the villages, where 75 percent of India's population resides (less than 11 percent of the population lives in cities).[20] The "need to climb up the ladder," according to an *India Today* survey, "is increasingly cutting across the rural-urban divide."[21] The only difference seems to be that the rural masses still consume basic, less technologically advanced goods.

Thus, while Westernized urban Indians may be busy acquiring fax machines, air conditioners and cellular phones, the rural underclasses are still acquiring black-and-white television sets and VCRs, albeit one per village rather than one per household. In its economic survey, *India Today* identified a burgeoning "aspiring class" of about 670 million people, mostly poor and rural;[22] it is this "aspiring class" that is constantly moving upward, into the middle class. Thus, a two-tier society that was once divided simply into a small class of "haves" and a huge class of "have-nots" has gradually been redefined into a multiple-tier society—one of "haves," "have-lesses," "aspiring to haves" and "have-nots." The increases in their purchasing power—whether massive or minute—will lead to increased consumption in India, in terms of both consumer goods and energy.

While India's economy might not be growing at the rate of China's, its oil consumption is still increasing rapidly. India's economic growth can be attributed to both the agricultural sector and intense growth in manufacturing and services. One result has been increased demand for automobiles. India's archaic and inefficient infrastructure was long seen as a major hurdle to industrial growth, and its poorly maintained road network is struggling even more thanks to the added strain of the surge in traffic that followed the 1991 reforms.

In addition to stimulating a boom in foreign investment and in the construction industry, the added demand for cars will certainly translate into increased demand for gasoline, inevitably putting even more pressure on the country's already limited hydrocarbon supply. Transportation is second only to electric power generation in hydrocarbon use. Moreover, demand for gasoline is inversely related to fuel efficiency, and Indian cars tend to rank rather low in that regard when compared with their foreign counterparts. All such domestic pressures will turn India's eye to the Persian Gulf.

However, all optimal forecasts must be balanced against the impact that the global economic meltdown—along with a domestic credit squeeze and falling demand—is having on India's economy. Global deleveraging and moves to reduce risk exposure have had a serious impact on India. Real GDP growth is expected to be 7 percent in 2009, down from 9 percent in 2008.[23] Duvvuri Subbarao, the governor of the Royal Bank of India, furthered that point in saying that "the outlook on real GDP growth has been affected further and the downside risks to growth have amplified because of slowdown of industrial activity and weakening of external demand as reflected in decline in exports. Service sector activities are likely to further decelerate in the second half of 2008–09."[24]

India also faces high inflation, large government deficits, and rising interest rates. Foreign investment in India's stock market has dwindled, the rupee has fallen, and the stock market fell more than 40 percent in 2008.[25] A study by investment bank Credit Suisse reported that thirty-four projects funded by a total investment of about $190 billion faced an average delay of 19 months, resulting in a 30 percent cost overrun.[26] That can be directly attributed to the devaluation of India's currency and the withdrawal of foreign investors, which have also had quite an effect on India's export market. Although less dependent on trade than its regional competitors, India's export market fell into a recession and capital flows dried up in 2008.

ENERGY NEEDS

As the pace of consumption and industrialization in India grows, no issue reflects the challenges more than the energy crisis and the debate about how to solve it. A burgeoning population combined with rapid economic growth has propelled India to become the world's sixth-largest consumer of energy.[27] Well before economic reform started in the 1990s, daily power cuts (brownouts) were common in most major urban areas, especially in the sweltering heat of summer. For many years, the majority of Indians tolerated the discomfort; it was part and parcel of a national ideology that called for India to be self-sufficient in virtually all staples of life, even if it meant inefficiency.

Today, the Indian middle class not only consumes more electricity, it also has become much more dependent on electricity for day-to-day living. A brownout today can mean that the air-conditioning stops, the water filtration system backs up, the computer crashes, and the fax and telephone recording machines stop. The Indian elite today is no different from its Western counterparts in that it wants the perks and comforts of modern living, most of which are based on high per capita energy consumption.

The increased demand for electricity and gasoline for industry, agriculture, and the growing middle class is paralleled by the failure of India's national energy programs to meet that demand. Present installed electrical generation capacity in India is 149 megawatts, generated primarily by coal (53 percent), hydropower (24 percent), natural gas (11 percent), nuclear power (2.5 percent), renewable energy (8.5 percent), and diesel (1 percent).[28] India will have to double its electrical generation capacity in the next decade if it is to keep up with projected demand.

Until recently, the energy sector in India was a huge public sector monopoly, operated and heavily regulated by the state. Individual state electricity boards (SEBs) ran government-owned power plants, where overstaffing, inefficient operations, and artificially controlled prices created huge distortions in the energy market. Government subsidies have kept prices low in order to mollify rural voters—farmers in some states receive virtually free electricity. Power plants operate at about 60 percent of their revenue-earning capacity; the other 40 percent is lost in transmission and distribution because of shoddy equipment, theft through jumper cables, inadequate billing procedures that result in nonpayment, or ad hoc subsidies to users by corrupt local officials.[29] That is no small matter: according to a 2007 World Bank report, the total value of SEBs' system losses equaled 1.2 percent of India's GDP in 2005.[30]

In 2004, India consumed 435 kilowatts of electricity per capita per year; comparable consumption in the United States is 13,066 kilowatts.[31] Now consumption increases are putting pressure on the generation and supply systems, an especially noteworthy fact because India's economy is extremely energy intensive and as growth in GDP takes place, the demand for energy increases at a high pace.[32] Given the reality of only small additions to the production of domestic energy and the absence of alternatives to oil, India's already major imports of oil and natural gas will increase.

Another indicator of higher energy consumption is the growth in sales of automobiles, trucks, and two-wheelers. Demand for energy in India's transportation sector is predicted to grow at an average rate of 4.4 percent a year[33] and is forecast to account for about 70 percent of oil demand in the future. Current vehicle ownership per capita in India is 195 people per car (the comparable U.S. figure is 1.3 per car).[34] With India's middle class expanding rapidly, that number is predicted to grow. In a decade or less it may be possible to drive on an expressway to virtually all of its major cities. To those who recall the horror of road travel in India only a few years ago, that would be a dramatic development that would increase the appeal of driving and therefore the number of cars in what is one of Asia's most populated countries. No matter how individual energy cases are resolved, what is abundantly clear is that India's energy crisis can only get worse with increased consumer demand.

ENERGY SUPPLIES

Coal. India is the world's third-largest coal producer, after the United States and China, and domestic supplies are enough to satisfy most of the country's demand for coal. Coal currently is India's largest source of energy, accounting for approximately 55 percent of the country's energy consumption.[35] India produces most of the coal that it consumes, with production at 393 million short tons and consumption at 421 million. Yet India's coal poses two major problems: first, it is of poor quality and creates serious pollution and huge amounts of slag as it burns; second, transporting coal increases demand on the already overused and undercapitalized railway system. If coal use is to grow commensurately with the anticipated demand for fuel, major new investments in both transportation and environmental protection will be required. Coal production also tends to be inefficient, largely because the government controls the vast majority of the industry, making higher-quality and cheaper coal imports more appealing to the domestic market.

Oil. India's second-largest source of energy is oil, which accounts for 36 percent of current national energy consumption.[36] India, which is estimated to have 5.6 billion barrels of proven oil reserves,[37] produces approximately 900,000 barrels a day but consumes approximately 2.6 million barrels. As a result, India's net oil imports are around 1.7 million barrels a day—about 70 percent of overall consumption.[38]

Imported oil is likely to remain an important source of energy as demand increases, despite Indian government attempts to increase the productivity of domestic oil reserves. India has been investing in domestic exploration and production, but its efforts are not likely to reduce its dependence on oil imports. Indian oil consumption is likely to grow significantly over time, with one projection suggesting that it will hit 2.9 million barrels a day by 2010.[39] The Energy Information Administration predicts that by 2030 Indian oil consumption will reach 4.5 million barrels a day, while domestic production will be only 1.9 million barrels a day.[40] Given that India already imports 45 percent of its oil from the Middle East, and that the region is predicted to produce more than half of new oil capacity through 2030,[41] it is highly likely that India will remain dependent and even increase its dependence on oil imports from the Middle East by reason of necessity, if not merely proximity.

Natural Gas. Natural gas, which India currently uses to produce approximately 9 percent of its energy, is another potential prime energy source.[42] While in India natural gas is not as plentiful as coal, the country still has significant natural gas reserves. With approximately 38 trillion cubic feet of proven reserves, India has the world's twenty-fifth-largest supply of natural gas.[43] Although the majority of the reserves are found off

Mumbai and Gujarat on India's western coast, recent but still unconfirmed discoveries off India's east coast could add as much as 26 trillion cubic feet to India's reserves. India's domestic supply ensured that it did not become a net importer of natural gas until 2004, when it imported 93 million cubic feet from Qatar.[44] India has shown a keen and persistent interest in importing natural gas, having explored the possibility of doing so from Iran by a pipeline through Pakistan or by tanker, and it also has considered a pipeline from Turkmenistan through Afghanistan and Pakistan. Moreover, India has looked into receiving Central Asian oil and gas from the Turkish-Israeli Medstream pipeline project.[45] India also has competed with China to gain natural gas supplies from Myanmar, although that source would likely serve to supply India's underdeveloped northeastern provinces rather than replace a potential deal with Iran.

Other Energy Sources. Nuclear power is another option to satisfy India's growing energy demands. In 2006, India received 1.6 percent of its power from nuclear energy.[46] Until 2005, the United States prevented the growth of the nuclear industry in India through its policy of embargoing all nuclear sales to countries that were not signatories of the Nuclear Non-Proliferation Treaty. That policy changed with the U.S.-India nuclear deal, which ended the embargo, but India's place in international nuclear commerce is not yet ensured. India is negotiating a safeguards agreement with the International Atomic Energy Agency (IAEA) to allow for international trade to supplement its nuclear industry; should such an agreement be signed, it would pave the way for completion of nuclear cooperation agreements with the United States as well as with France and Russia. Nuclear energy also is appealing to India because it holds the world's largest reserves of thorium, a radioactive material that can be used in yet unproven "fast breeder reactor" technology to create material for further nuclear plants.

India also uses hydroelectric power for electricity generation. In 2007, hydropower accounted for 24 percent of India's electricity.[47] Any further expansion of hydropower production in India will likely prove difficult due to environmental issues and the need to overcome conflicts with Nepal and Bangladesh over the control of waters flowing from the Himalayas. India also imports hydroelectricity from Bhutan, and a World Bank report has estimated that Myanmar has the potential to export 1.2 megawatts of hydroelectricity to India.[48]

INDIAN INFRASTRUCTURE PROJECTS

India cannot maximize its economic potential with its antiquated domestic infrastructure. The country has a vast network of national highways covering more than 40,742 miles, but most are poorly paved and crumbling.[49] The longest highway runs from Varanasi to Kanyakumari, the southernmost point of the Indian mainland, a distance of about 1,472 miles. While the network of highways accounts for only 2 percent of the roads in India, more than 40 percent of passenger and cargo vehicles combined regularly use them,[50] leading to massive congestion, not to mention degradation of the roads. Traffic jams can become so bad that it takes more than five hours to drive fifty miles. In rural communities, which account for almost 70 percent of India's population, villages lack access to all-weather roads and are cut off during monsoon seasons. The problem is especially drastic in the north, as most of the states are cut off from the country's major economic centers.

As a result, the Indian government has launched a national project to upgrade the highways (see map 2-2).[51] Included are the Golden Quadrilateral (GQ) project and the North-South–East-West (NS-EW) Corridor project, which had not been completed by December 2009. The Golden Quadrilateral project will connect India's four largest cities—New Delhi, Kolkata (formally Calcutta), Chennai, and Mumbai—with four- to six-lane expressways that will form a semi-quadrilateral shape. Throughout northern India, the NS-EW highway will connect Silchar in the east to Porbandar in the west. In addition, the northern city of Srinagar will connect with Kanniakumari at the southern tip of India.[52] There also are plans for a New Delhi–Chandigarh expressway, though it is expected that the Mumbai-Vadodra and the Delhi-Jaipur stretches will be among the first to be built. Map 2-2 shows the completed and planned portions of the Golden Quadrilateral and the North-South–East-West projects as of July 2007.

India has the third-largest railway system in Asia, the fifth-largest railway system in the world, and the fourth-most-heavily-used system in the world.[53] India maintains a Golden Quadrilateral railway system similar to the highway system, linking the four metropolitan cities of New Delhi, Kolkata, Chennai, and Mumbai. This system is said to carry 65 percent of India's freight traffic and 55 percent of its passenger traffic.[54] While in the past the trains have been characterized as poorly serviced, slow moving,

MAP 2-2

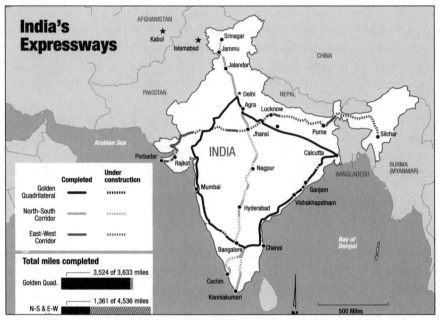

Source: Government of India, National Highways Development Project Status as of September 2008.

and filthy, the railways have begun a turnaround. The poor condition of the highways has led to increased traffic on the rail system, which has become one of India's lifelines. The government intends to continue the buildup in railways, including a track connecting Kashmir with the Himalayan foothills.

India has twelve major and 185 minor and intermediate ports along its extensive coastline. The ports are major export hubs—especially for trade in refined petroleum products, iron ore, and coal—and during the 1990s, port traffic more than doubled. Between 2004 and 2005, around 521 million tons were traded through Indian seaports, a number that is expected only to grow, possibly reaching 900 million tons by 2012. To meet the growing trade demand, the government plans to upgrade infrastructure and connectivity between the ports through the National Maritime Development Program, which will provide much-needed improvements in capacity and efficiency.

With sixty airports, eleven of which are international facilities, India has had difficulties coping with increased air traffic. Between April and June

2006, domestic passenger traffic grew 48 percent and international passenger traffic grew 16.3 percent.[55] The four major airports, corresponding to the four metropolises of the Golden Quadrilateral, have been stretched thin due to the increase. The strain is most visible in Delhi and Mumbai, which together account for around 50 percent of the nation's air traffic. The government has considered privatizing and expanding the two key airports.

While India has made a concerted effort to address its huge infrastructure shortfalls, it cannot compare with the progress made in China. The democratic government of India cannot ride roughshod over its citizens the way that its Chinese counterpart can, but that is also its great strength as a major democratic power. It is against the backdrop of rapid economic growth, major energy shortages, and a search for a better life by more than 1 billion people that the economic, political, and strategic elements of India's "westward" interest in the Middle East, especially the Gulf, must be examined. What follows are summaries of the major developments in India's relations with the GCC countries, Iran, Afghanistan, and Uzbekistan.

INDIA'S RELATIONS WITH SAUDI ARABIA

Indo-Saudi ties are based primarily on trade. Historically, that trade involved spices traveling across the Arabian Sea or over the desert by caravan, but now its primary component is petroleum. India and Saudi Arabia also share cultural connections due to India's large Muslim population and the 1.6 million Indians who work in Saudi Arabia.[56] In addition, thanks to the colonial structures of the erstwhile British Empire in the Middle East, India played a major role in Saudi Arabia in the first half of the twentieth century.[57]

DIPLOMATIC TIES

India and Saudi Arabia first established diplomatic relations in 1952. Relations between the two countries were fairly good in the 1950s, and their heads of state exchanged visits in 1955 and 1956.[58] India's first prime minister, Jawaharlal Nehru, spoke in 1956 before a large crowd in a stadium in Jeddah, the first time a foreign leader had been allowed to do so.[59] However, India's orientation toward the Soviet bloc during the cold war and Saudi Arabia's traditionally close relations with Pakistan prevented their relationship from achieving lasting progress. Relations improved in the early 1980s. In 1981, India's prime minister, Indira Gandhi, received a visit from the Saudi foreign minister, and she reciprocated by visiting

Saudi Arabia the following year.[60] Their visits laid the foundation for future growth through the creation of the Joint Commission for Economic, Trade, Scientific, Technical, and Cultural Cooperation.[61] However, once again progress was thwarted by cold war tensions arising from India's and Saudi Arabia's differing views of the Soviet invasion of Afghanistan. The Afghan conflict remained a point of contention throughout the 1980s, with Saudi Arabia supporting the mujahideen and subsequently the Taliban and India supporting the Northern Alliance as a means to combat Pakistani influence in Afghanistan.

In the wake of the cold war and the first Gulf War, India began to focus on economic development, and Indo-Saudi relations began to improve again in the mid-1990s. Visits and exchanges on scientific and economic matters, which restarted in the early 1990s, included a visit in 1994 by Manmohan Singh, who was India's finance minister at the time.[62] The improvement in Indo-Saudi relations was grounded also in the GCC-India Political Dialogue, which began in September 2003 and involved the external affairs minister of India and the ambassadors from the GCC countries.[63] Then, in 2005, India participated in the Counter Terrorism International Conference held in Riyadh. The willingness of Riyadh to host the conference played a crucial role in alleviating Indian concerns about Saudi complicity in the financing of Islamist groups in Kashmir. Another symbolically important and unprecedented event was King Abdullah's visit to India in January 2006, when he was the guest of honor at India's Republic Day, a privilege usually reserved for India's closest—and domestically noncontroversial—allies. The recently crowned Saudi monarch brought with him a 200-member delegation and, according to Indian analyst Subhash Kapila, a personal desire to establish a strategic partnership and special bond with India. Both sides broke protocol to show the warmth of the relationship. Prime Minister Singh met King Abdullah at the airport to see him off, and King Abdullah personally signed the Delhi Declaration in contravention of Saudi tradition, which usually calls for a royal representative to sign.[64]

The Delhi Declaration is a wide-ranging document that included a mutual agreement to deepen and broaden economic ties while cooperating in combating international crime and ensuring the stability of the oil trade.[65] King Abdullah also suggested that India should have observer status in the Organization of the Islamic Conference.[66] While Pakistan blocked that effort, it showed a significant diplomatic tilt toward India on the part of Saudi

Arabia. The Saudi foreign minister arrived shortly after King Abdullah's visit and, building on the head-of-state discussions, reached substantive agreements on cooperation in combating terrorism, avoidance of double taxation, promotion of investment, and cooperation in the fields of youth and sports.[67]

The high rate of diplomatic contacts has continued over the last few years. In November 2006, India and Saudi Arabia signed an agreement to cooperate in the fields of hospital consultancy and management, which includes an effort to recruit Indian doctors and paramedical staff for Saudi hospitals, import Indian pharmaceuticals to the kingdom, and train Saudi nurses in India.[68] In February 2007 an Indian parliamentary delegation headed by the speaker of the Lok Sabha—India's lower house of parliament—visited Saudi Arabia.[69] During 2008 there were reciprocal visits by their foreign ministers intended to broaden the economic relationship between the two countries and encourage cross-border investment.[70] The trip to Saudi Arabia in April 2008 of External Affairs Minister Pranab Mukherjee produced an agreement on relaxing visa restrictions for people traveling on business as well as a preliminary agreement on an Indo-Saudi fund for infrastructure investment.[71]

ECONOMIC RELATIONS

The central plank of the economic relationship between India and Saudi Arabia has been energy exports, but reciprocal foreign investment makes diversification of the relationship likely in the future. The bilateral trade relationship has grown significantly since the mid-1990s, with the demonstrable increase in Indian energy imports acting as the primary driver of growth. In FY 2007 India bought roughly $12.4 billion of petroleum from Saudi Arabia, amounting to around 26 percent of India's overall petroleum imports.[72] In the same year, trade in oil or oil products made up roughly 77 percent of Indo-Saudi trade.[73] The figure does not include the $3 billion in remittances that Indian workers in Saudi Arabia sent back to India.[74] Furthermore, non-oil bilateral trade also increased, from $1.3 billion to roughly $3.5 billion (more than 250 percent) from FY 2002 to FY 2007. And in FY 2007 Saudi Arabia was the twelfth-largest importer of Indian goods.[75]

Over the past few years, India and Saudi Arabia have sought to broaden their trade relationship through increased investment and partnerships. In that vein, Saudi Arabia has indicated that it is considering setting up a dedicated fund for investing in India with an eye toward infrastructure,[76] and

India expressed interest in investing in the Saudi petroleum sector as part of an energy security plan.[77] Many of India's world-class information technology firms have invested or set up subsidiaries in Saudi Arabia's Knowledge Economic City at Medina.[78] The last few years have seen a number of Indo-Saudi trade fairs in a variety of areas, ranging from the fashion industry to the automotive and health care industries.[79] According to the Saudi Arabian General Investment Authority (SAGIA), more than 190 Indian companies have obtained licenses to set up either fully owned or joint venture projects with Saudi nationals over the past two years.[80] Cooperation has spread even to the skies—the two countries agreed in January 2008 to expand air service between Saudi Arabia and India, increasing permitted passenger traffic from 8,500 to 20,000 a week.[81]

More broadly, India has been negotiating a free trade agreement with the GCC for a number of years.[82] One possible reason for the delay is the objections of India's petrochemical industry, which feels that it would suffer under the agreement. Gulf countries provide their petrochemical industry with subsidized feedstock, giving them an advantage by greatly reducing their operating costs.[83] Both countries are optimistic about the prospects of the bilateral trade relationship, and some in India predict that bilateral non-oil trade will double, reaching $7 billion by 2010.[84]

Defense, Labor Relations, and Education

Nascent cooperation between India and Saudi Arabia on defense also is emerging, a somewhat remarkable development considering that not too long ago some in India saw Saudi Arabia as being in league with Pakistan and speculated that the two might cooperate in case of war against India.[85] Indian warships visited Saudi Arabia a number of times over the past decade, most recently in May 2009; the Indian Navy also began a wide-ranging initiative to engage the GCC countries beginning in 2004.[86] Saudi Arabia has expressed interest in joint training, discussions on perspectives for peace and stability in the Middle East, and naval cooperation in the Arabian Sea and the Gulf.[87] Though no major progress has occurred thus far, defense cooperation has been a regular subject of discussion between India and Saudi Arabia.

The two countries also have found common ground in counterterrorism efforts. Their cooperation was first formalized as part of the Delhi Declaration in January 2006 and then strengthened when the two concluded a memorandum of understanding (MOU) on January 25, 2006, agreeing to work toward a comprehensive Convention on International Terrorism as well as greater information sharing.[88] However, it is unclear how substantive Indo-Saudi counterterrorism cooperation has become, because its primary activities, intelligence and information sharing, are necessarily conducted behind closed doors.

The sizable Indian diaspora residing in Saudi Arabia, which has been a driving force in the improvement of Indo-Saudi relations, also has the potential to do damage. Indians are a key fixture in Saudi Arabia's labor force (accounting for 20 percent of the country's 7 million expatriates),[89] and while the Saudi government insists that it protects the rights of Indian workers, many Indian nationals working in the kingdom have complained that Saudi employers have not paid their salaries or have kept them in uninhabitable quarters, or both.[90] Furthermore, Indians, along with other foreign nationals, often are subjected to discrimination by Saudi locals in general. In an attempt to address those issues, the Indian government passed the 1983 Immigration Act, which regulates recruitment agents in India and aims to help ensure the welfare of Indian workers abroad. The government has already put laws into place to protect Indian women from being forced into prostitution by not allowing Indian women less than 30 years of age to travel overseas for employment.[91] Negotiations to amend and strengthen the law have been proceeding since 2003; an amendment is perpetually expected "in the near future."[92]

Another focus of Indo-Saudi cooperation is education. India and Saudi Arabia are finalizing a program for Saudi students to pursue postgraduate and doctoral studies, particularly at technical institutions in India.[93] Although the overall number of Saudi students in India is still quite low— only about 600—anecdotal evidence indicates an increasing interest in India as an educational destination for Saudis.[94]

SAUDI TIES WITH PAKISTAN

Historically the Indo-Pakistani conflict has been a problem in relations between India and Saudi Arabia, since Saudi Arabia until recently sided with Pakistan on the issue of Kashmir in forums such as the Organization of the Islamic Conference. Saudi-Pakistani defense cooperation in years past also was a barrier to the relationship.[95] India had expressed concern about Saudi funding being diverted to Islamist groups tied to Pakistan that carried out acts of terrorism in India, especially in Kashmir. Saudi Arabia also supplies oil to Pakistan at a discount rate, and rumors have persisted that Saudi interests underwrote the Pakistani nuclear program and missile purchases.[96] On the whole, Saudi Arabia's historically close ties to Pakistan should not prevent Indo-Saudi relations from moving forward. In fact, India sees Saudi Arabia as a strategic ally that can act as a significant counterweight to Pakistan in the Islamic world.[97] The only area in which Saudi-Pakistan ties are likely to prove problematic is in defense cooperation, because India would be concerned about transfer of technology to Pakistan. If the more Islamist-leaning sections of the Saudi royal family ascend to power in the medium to long term, then Saudi Arabia would be more likely to nurture closer ties with Pakistan and limit geopolitical cooperation with India.

The growth of Indo-Saudi relations from 2003 on have been predicated on converging economic interests, the desire of high-level officials to see the relationship improve, and Saudi action on areas of Indian concern. Saudi Arabia's decision to host the Counter Terrorism International Conference in 2005 was especially significant in that regard. In the last few years, Saudi Arabia has also taken an even-handed stance on conflict between India and Pakistan, encouraging dialogue and urging both countries to settle their differences peacefully.[98] The dynamics of regional and global demand should ensure growth in the economic aspect of the Indo-Saudi relationship, but domestic and regional factors could prevent closer geopolitical cooperation. Widespread outbreaks of communal violence in India also could put a temporary brake on the growth of the relationship. However, barring a major global economic collapse, Indo-Saudi trade relations should experience growth even if other aspects of the relationship lag behind.

INDIA'S RELATIONS WITH THE SMALL GULF STATES

There is no better barometer of India's close ties to the region than its relationships with the geographically small but economically important Gulf states—Oman, Qatar, the UAE, Bahrain, and Kuwait. The Gulf states have historical connections to India through trade and migration, and their current economic relationship is booming. India's trade with the six Gulf Cooperation Council states (excluding oil) totaled $86.9 billion in FY 2008–09, surpassing India's trade with the European Union ($80.6 billion), the ASEAN (Association of Southeast Asian Nations) countries ($44.6 billion), and the United States ($40.6 billion).[99] Looking to the future, Indian leaders have expressed a desire to continue the rapid expansion of trade, attract Gulf investment for major infrastructure projects, and broaden their Gulf state relationships beyond economics. In a May 2008 speech in Abu Dhabi, India's external affairs minister, Pranab Mukherjee, called for a "transformation" of India's relations with the Gulf states beyond that of a buyer-seller relationship to a more "substantial and enduring partnership."[100] With India's thriving economic relationship with the Gulf, continuing demographic ties and nascent defense cooperation, such an evolution may already be under way.

INDIA AND OMAN

While India has historic connections to all the Gulf states, its ties to Oman are especially deep. Historical artifacts found in Oman have dated the relationship back to the time of the Harappan civilization of the Indus Valley—more than 1,000 years before the founding of Rome.[101] Muscat and Mumbai are separated by just under 1,000 miles, and the monsoon winds of the Arabian Sea have allowed for seasonal trade for millennia. Omanis and Indians have visited each other's countries as navigators, merchants, scholars, and pilgrims through maritime trade channels, and Islam probably was brought to India through the same channels.

Diplomatically, India and Oman established ties in the early years of India's independence, but the relationship has taken time to develop. India opened a consulate in Muscat in 1955 but did not open an embassy until 1973. India maintained a diplomatic presence in Oman throughout the 1960s and 1970s, although many countries withdrew their diplomats because of domestic insurgencies and the autocratic tendencies of Sultan Taymur, who was ousted in 1970.[102] Relations took a turn for the better in 1993 following a visit from India's prime minister, Narasimha Rao, and since then landmark steps have been taken in the relationship. India and Oman concluded an MOU on combating crime and terrorism in 1996—the first of its kind between India and a Gulf country. India and Oman also are founding members of the Indian Ocean Rim Association for Regional Cooperation (IOR-ARC), a trade and investment cooperation organization.[103]

The navies of India and Oman began to cooperate on joint defense in 1998. The Indian navy began holding bilateral exercises with its Omani counterpart in 2004, and they have continued annually since then. The countries expanded their defense cooperation through a memorandum of understanding in 2005, which led to the establishment of the joint Military Cooperation Committee in 2006. Visits between military leaders occur frequently. In a March 2006 visit to Oman celebrating fifty years of diplomatic relations between the two countries, Admiral Arun Prakash of India remarked that "the sea has great potential but it also poses threats in the form of piracy, terrorism, and human trafficking" and called for greater cooperation between their navies on that front.[104]

The economic relationship between India and Oman is widespread and diverse. Oman hosts around 570,000 expatriate workers (roughly 17 percent of its population), of whom Indians account for about 550,000, making them the largest expatriate group in the country. Like most of the foreign workers in Oman, the majority of Indians are blue collar workers, although there are significant numbers of Indian professionals as well, including approximately 2,000 doctors.[105] Oman also hosts India's largest overseas joint venture—the $969 million Oman India Fertilizer Company (OMIFCO) at Sur, which creates fertilizer from natural gas feedstock. Economic cooperation is nurtured by the India-Oman Joint Commission, which began meeting in 1995 to promote cooperation in filmmaking, IT training, tourism marketing, health care, and energy.[106] In 2004, India was the sixth-largest source of Oman's imports. Since the 1990s, India and Oman also have been discussing building an undersea pipeline to supply India with natural gas; the project was shelved because it was considered infeasible, but in October 2009, the two countries resumed negotiations on the matter.[107]

Oman's oil fields are not as productive as those of its Gulf neighbors, but energy still plays an important role in the Omani-Indian relationship. Indian petroleum imports from Oman made up roughly 20 percent of Indo-Omani trade over the last five years, even though they accounted for only 0.34 percent of India's oil imports in 2007.[108] Of course, another significant factor in the economic relationship—OMIFCO—depends on Oman's natural gas. OMIFCO provides India with a reliable, long-term source of urea fertilizer and offers Oman a permanent market for its production. India agreed to provide technical expertise and skilled personnel for maintenance and operations.

Beyond those realms, Oman and India are working toward greater private sector cooperation in pharmaceuticals, metals, and information technology. Omani developments like the Shadeed Iron and Steel project, for example, require a great deal of iron ore, and Oman is considering India as a primary source.[109] Furthermore, India is a large investor in Oman. Indian investment built an IT park there, the Knowledge Oasis in Muscat. Omani colleges are increasingly affiliated with their Indian counterparts, particularly in the field of information technology, and there is room for continued growth. Oman wants to benefit more from its bilateral relationship with India by acquiring expertise in microfinancing, vocational training, biotechnology, and nonconventional energy resources.[110] Likewise, Oman is investing in India. Bank Muscat acquired a 26 percent share in India's Centurion Bank.

India and Qatar

India and Qatar were connected historically by trade routes. Qatar has been an important way station on the journey to India since the time of the Roman Empire,[111] and Bombay was a central sorting and marketing location for pearls from the Gulf.[112] Until the late 1960s, Indian currency and stamps often were used in Qatar.[113]

Today, the economic relationship between India and Qatar focuses on trade, energy, and labor.[114] Qatar's population is under 1 million, but it hosts roughly 300,000 Indian workers, primarily from southern India,[115] who are employed in a variety of sectors in the Qatari economy, including medicine, engineering, services, civil service, business, and labor.

The two countries remain close partners in the hydrocarbon sector,[116] with India's current top priority being liquefied natural gas (LNG) from Qatar.[117] In January 1998 they signed an MOU for cooperation in the gas, oil, and industrial sectors, and in 1999 a sale-and-purchase agreement for supplying LNG was finalized. Under that agreement Qatar, which holds the world's third-largest gas reserves, promised to export 7.5 million tons of LNG to India annually for the following 25 years. The first shipment arrived in 2004. The long-term goal is for India to fuel 20 percent of its energy needs with natural gas by 2025, a large increase from the 11 percent fueled by natural gas today.[118] With respect to importation of LNG, India offered Qatar a 12.5 percent stake in Indian energy company Petronet LNG. The Doha Bank of Qatar and India's Industrial Bank Limited also have teamed up in a global strategic alliance to promote trade and broaden their opportunities abroad.

In 2001, Qatar hosted the WTO Conference, which initiated the Doha round of trade negotiations. Qatar took the opportunity to name India one of its top trading partners, and a new area for exchange, shipbuilding, emerged between the two countries. In 2002, a contract was signed to build, equip, and launch a 55-ton tanker berthing assistance tug.[119] By 2005, economic relations were burgeoning. Qatar was exporting 5.1 percent of its products to India and had concluded agreements with the UAE to export gas by pipeline to India.[120] The two countries have embarked on many joint endeavors over the last 20 years. They signed a development and production sharing agreement for the Najwat Najem offshore oil field in Qatar's waters. An agreement worth $1.2 billion was signed with Qatar Steel Company to set up a $3 million joint venture integrated steel plant in Qatar. In addition, the State Bank of India along with two other Indian banking services currently provides three prominent exchange houses in Qatar with services to manage remittances to India.[121] In November 2008, a plan was announced for Qatar to invest $5 billion in India's energy sector.[122] Qatar also helped to establish the Asian Cooperation Dialogue in 2002, ensuring that bilateral relations will continue.[123]

On a smaller scale, many Indian companies currently operate in Qatar, including those in consultancy, construction, engineering, and heavy industry.[124] India was the first non-Arab country to establish a labor contract with Qatar since so many Indian citizens are in the work force there.[125] On November 21, 2007, India and Qatar signed an additional protocol enhancing the terms of their previous 1985 labor agreement in order to provide better working conditions for Indian workers in Qatar.[126] The protocol was meant to close the loopholes that existed in the 1985 agreement. Both nations would be required to ensure the welfare of the Indian community in Qatar, stop illegal practices, and eliminate mistreatment by employers as well as ensure that wages are paid.[127]

Indo-Qatari cooperation extends beyond energy and commerce. The Qatari armed forces are interested in using Indian training facilities, and on occasion Indian navy ships make goodwill visits to Qatar.[128] In a formal agreement signed in 2003, the two committed themselves to cooperate in the war on terror. The Qatari government also is seeking to broaden Indian investment in health care, information technology, and education.[129]

In April 2000, Qatar and India met to set up a high joint commission to be co-chaired by the foreign ministers of the two countries. Three years later, the Indian prime minister met with the foreign ministers to discuss more security-related issues. Two years after that meeting, in 2005, the countries signed an air services agreement intended to ease travel between the two nations and discussed security and defense issues further, which led to the dispatch of a multidisciplinary delegation from Qatar to India.[130] Although these new fronts of cooperation are important to the relations between the two, the main focus for both countries remains the energy sector.

INDIA AND THE UNITED ARAB EMIRATES

Much like its relationship with the other Gulf states, India's relationship with the United Arab Emirates has been driven primarily by economics. The two countries have been connected by the trade routes of the Arabian Sea for millennia, and archeological evidence proves that contact occurred between what are now the emirates and the Harappan civilization of the Indus Valley as far back as 2500–2000 BCE. Within the first three centuries CE, an extensive trade network had been established, through which prized clothing and spices from India and dates and pearls from the UAE region were exchanged.[131] India had close trade relations with Abu Dhabi even before the UAE was formed in 1971. Those relations carried over to the current relationship between India and the UAE, which was grounded in the oil boom of the 1970s, when the Gulf's need for labor led many Indians to travel to the UAE. Indo-Emirati relations improved greatly in the 1990s, when Dubai's boom—and the UAE's continuing need for labor—coincided with India's economic reforms and paved the way for burgeoning trade opportunities.

Due to their geographical proximity, India and the UAE have long-standing cultural and economic ties, but India's cold war alignment with the Soviet Union and its conflict with Pakistan have proved to be historical problems in its relationship with the UAE as well as in its relationships with most of the Arab world. India and the UAE exchanged state visits in 1975 and 1976 as well as in 1981 and 1982.[132] In 1982, the UAE also helped India procure materials from West Germany for India's nuclear weapons program.[133] India-UAE relations were affected by lingering tensions from cold war alignments and the UAE's relationship with Pakistan until the 1990s, but they improved throughout the decade as the economic needs of India and the UAE increasingly coincided.

Recent years have seen a number of high-level visits between the two countries. In 2003 and 2004, the president of India, A. P. J. Abdul Kalam, visited the UAE, and in March 2007 his Emirati counterpart, Sheikh Khalifa Bin Zayed al Nayhan, visited India—a visit that produced a number of MOUs designed to increase economic cooperation and reduce obstacles to investment between the two countries.[134] India's external affairs minister, Pranab Mukherjee, visited the UAE in May 2008, when he called not only for deepening of the economic relationship but also for broadening it beyond a simple buyer-seller interaction.[135] His visit, which was to help fulfill India's 2008 initiative to reenergize its relations with the Middle East, showed a high-level desire to improve relations on both sides as well as the UAE's desire to see India, China, Japan, and Korea take a more active role in regional security issues and efforts to achieve a broader Middle Eastern peace.[136]

India is one of the UAE's main trading partners. As of March 2007, the UAE was the fifth-largest exporter to India, supplying 8 percent of India's petroleum imports, and the second-largest destination for India's exports, behind the United States, with total imports one-third higher than those from China.[137] In 2007, bilateral trade between India and the UAE accounted for 66 percent of the GCC's total trade with India,[138] increasing from $12 billion in April 2006 to $20.6 billion in March 2007. That increase is especially significant when one considers that Indian energy imports from the UAE increased by only $1 billion over that period, meaning that non-energy bilateral trade grew by 40 percent from FY 2006 to FY 2007.[139] India's trade with the UAE accounts for one-third of India's trade with the Middle East.

Over the last few years the trade boom has been the product of wide-ranging business engagements between the two countries—on both the government level, with agreements on taxation and technical cooperation,[140] and the business-to-business level. For example, in 2004 the UAE and the Indian Chambers of Commerce formed a joint business council aiming to promote cooperation in information technology, oil and gas, health care, infrastructure, and tourism.[141] It is estimated that more than 3,300 Indian companies have opened offices or manufacturing units in the UAE, with more than 600 located in the Jebel Ali free zone.[142] The economic relationship includes more than bilateral trade, however, as the total trade figure of $20.6 billion omits the remittances sent home by Indian workers in the UAE.

India also is actively seeking Emirati investment as part of its efforts to improve domestic infrastructure. With $626 million invested, the UAE was the top direct investor in India among Middle Eastern countries from 2000 through February 2008. The great majority of that investment has taken place very recently—of the $626 million, $508 million (81 percent) has occurred since June 2006.[143] India is hoping to receive much more investment from the UAE in the future, as evidenced by its request for $92 billion for the Delhi-Mumbai industrial corridor alone.[144] In March 2007, Indian and Emirati firms signed a real estate deal worth more than $20 billion, which included plans to build two large townships in the booming outskirts of New Delhi.[145] With both Emirati and Indian economies growing, bilateral trade between the two countries seems likely to continue its swift expansion, especially if the proposed India-GCC free trade agreement comes to fruition.[146]

Currently, 33 percent of the UAE's population and 50 percent of its workforce are Indian—about 1.4 million people.[147] Roughly 25 percent are unskilled workers, 50 percent semi-skilled or skilled workers, and 25 percent professionals and business people. Although the majority of the community is engaged in trading, the recent diversification into manufacturing has attracted many companies from India, especially in the UAE's free trade zones. There are about 100 cultural and literary associations in the UAE and more than fifty schools that follow an Indian curriculum.[148] Although Indian laborers are an essential component of the UAE's economic progress and provide a great impetus for the bilateral relationship, they also are a potential point of contention due to complaints of poor labor conditions. In order to make travel for guest laborers easier, Indian airlines began launching daily flights from Mumbai to Dubai in March 2006.[149] India and the UAE concluded a memorandum of understanding to allow service from the northern emirate of Ras al-Khaimah to India in May 2008.[150]

India and the UAE began taking steps toward cooperating on defense in the 1990s, but substantive progress did not occur until 2003, when they signed the first defense cooperation agreement between India and a GCC country.[151] The agreement led to the creation of the India-UAE Joint Defense Cooperation Committee, which met for the first time in 2006.[152] The navies of both countries held joint exercises in 2003, and they inaugurated naval staff talks in January 2007 following a series of high-level naval visits dating back to 2004.[153] The UAE's army chief also visited India in 2006, and a small number of UAE military personnel have been attending training courses in India since 2003.[154] In addition, India has been participating regularly in the annual defense trade show International Defense Exhibition and Conference (IDEX) in the UAE.[155] Furthermore, India and the UAE have been cooperating in the area of counterterrorism. In recent years, Emirati authorities have captured and swiftly extradited a number of high-profile terror suspects to India. The fact that several of those deportations occurred without invoking the extradition treaty in place between the two demonstrates their high level of mutual understanding concerning counterterrorism efforts.[156]

Despite close military ties with India, historically the UAE has maintained ties with Pakistan. That relationship has grown significantly over the past few years, and the UAE currently is Pakistan's third-largest foreign investor.[157] In the spring of 2008, negotiations attempting to hold together

Pakistan's coalition government were held in Dubai. It therefore is easy to see why *Gulf News* felt motivated to state that the period from 2006 to May 2008 represented a new "zenith" for the relationship.[158] Pakistan and the UAE also signed a new defense cooperation agreement in May 2008 that builds on their establishment in 1996 of a joint defense consultation group and their history of training exchanges.[159] More than 860,000 Pakistani nationals reside in the UAE, and while that number is about half the size of the Indian community, it is still significant.[160] Nonetheless, because the UAE has sought to maintain an even-handed policy between India and Pakistan since the late 1990s, the close relationship between the UAE and Pakistan should not have a significant chilling effect on the UAE-India relationship.

INDIA AND KUWAIT

As they were in the past, trade and economics are at the heart of the India-Kuwait relationship today. Maritime trade between the countries was well established by the fifteenth century, and under British rule, Kuwait was a depot for mail en route to India.[161] Until 1961, the Indian rupee was legal currency in Kuwait, and more than 500,000 Indians reside there today.[162]

Over the last few years their diplomatic relationship also has been productive. From 1999 to 2003, one of its main focuses was the Indian community in Kuwait. During that period, diplomatic initiatives on cultural cooperation and increasing air services have helped strengthen ties between the two countries.[163] In April 2007, the two countries signed the Memorandum of Understanding on Labour, Employment, and Manpower Development.[164] In August 2004, India and Kuwait completed legal agreements to cooperate on counterterrorism and signed an extradition treaty.[165] They also have issued joint positions on several regional issues, such as their June 2006 endorsement of the Arab Peace Plan of 2003 and their statement of support for the Palestinian people.[166] Kuwait historically has taken an even-handed stance concerning the Indo-Pakistani Kashmir dispute, focusing on the need for dialogue between the two sides.

Indo-Kuwaiti trade has grown threefold since 2003 and reached $6.6 billion in 2007. Over the last five years, petroleum imports have made up roughly 80 percent of Indo-Kuwaiti trade. In fact, Kuwait supplied 10 percent of India's petroleum imports in 2007—to the tune of $5.7 billion.[167] India and Kuwait have been in negotiations since 2004 about lowering trade barriers as part of a potential India-GCC free trade agreement. If the agreement is completed, their economic relationship may have a chance to broaden.[168]

India also has sought Kuwaiti investment and assistance in developing India's petrochemical industry, including chemical production and downstream refining. In 2006, India and Kuwait began negotiations on a joint venture to improve India's refineries. Although thus far Kuwaiti investment in India has focused mostly on infrastructure projects, the Kuwait Fund for Arab Economic Development has provided India $270 million in low-rate loans for projects in sectors such as industry, utilities, and agriculture.[169] Kuwait also has assisted with efforts to improve access to electricity in rural areas by modernizing the conducting and distributing networks to decrease cost and increase quality.[170] In addition, Kuwait has increased cooperation with Indian firms in the realm of science and technology, especially information technology and biotechnology,[171] as reflected in the increase in the number of Indian experts in those fields working in Kuwait.[172]

India and Bahrain

India and Bahrain, like most of the Gulf states, have historical connections due to the fact that both were once under British rule. Since Bahrain became independent in 1971, relations with India have been good, but they have not reached any great level of significance. India opened an embassy in Bahrain in 1973, and since then their relationship has focused on economic issues, resulting in a number of agreements and exchanges of delegations.[173] India does not rank among Bahrain's top trading partners, as bilateral trade between the two countries has not risen above 3 percent of Bahrain's overall trade in the last five years.[174] Nonetheless, India is important to Bahrain's economy because 290,000 Indian blue- and white-collar workers live in Bahrain, making up nearly 30 percent of its total population.[175] Yet concerns over worker conditions and human trafficking could lead to diplomatic incidents between the two countries.

India and Iran

Ties between the Indian and Iranian civilizations can be traced to ancient times, as far back as 3,500 years. Although Indian and Iranian diplomats often tout their countries' historical connections, relations between the two were unstable for much of the twentieth century and have continued to be inconsistent over the last decade. Although Iran and India established diplomatic ties in March 1950, Iran's decision to join the Baghdad Pact in 1955 stunted the growth of the relationship because India, which was attempting to keep cold war tensions from reaching into southern Asia, opposed military blocs.

Indo-Iranian relations improved in the early 1960s, but Iran aided Pakistan in its 1965 war with India, preventing long-term gains. However, India's decisive victory over Pakistan in 1971 led the Shah to pursue closer relations with India, which he saw as a rising regional power.[176] The early 1970s saw improvement in the relationship, as Iran and India exchanged state visits and concluded a number of agreements, including one in 1974 on nuclear cooperation.[177] However, Iran's 1979 Islamic Revolution proved a further obstacle to growing ties despite the fact that India was among the first states to recognize Khomeini's government. For much of the 1980s, theocratic Iran did not display a desire to improve relations with secular India. Similarly, New Delhi was wary that Iran would export militancy to India's sizable Shi'a Muslim population. But, thanks to India's desire to secure energy supplies and pursue economic opportunities in Central Asia, and the opposition of both countries to the Taliban in Afghanistan, Indo-Iranian ties improved in the 1990s.

While the two countries initially differed in their reactions to the Soviet invasion of Afghanistan, the rise of Sunni Islamist forces in Afghanistan, especially the Pakistan-backed Taliban, provided a unifying force. Pakistani support for Sunni Islamists in Afghanistan led to a deterioration of Pakistani-Iranian relations and put Pakistan in cooperation with one of Iran's regional enemies—Saudi Arabia. India and Iran both supported sections of the Afghan Northern Alliance in the fight with the Taliban and have cooperated in varying degrees in the reconstruction of Afghanistan.

Indo-Iranian relations picked up steam when the reform-minded Mohammed Khatami became president of Iran in 1997. India's motive in its initial opening toward Iran was to diversify its energy supplies: in 1991 Iraq and Kuwait supplied two-thirds of India's oil, and therefore the outbreak of the first Gulf War led to an abrupt drop in India's oil supply.[178]

The rapprochement between Iran and India also was predicated on overlapping economic interests in Central Asia. During the cold war, Indian producers were denied a direct route to Central Asian markets by Pakistan, but the Soviet Union gave Indian goods preference in the region through a roundabout trading pattern. After the fall of the Soviet Union, Indian leaders began to see passage through Iran as an alternate route. In 1995, India signed an agreement with Turkmenistan and Iran to develop transport infrastructure between the Gulf and Central Asia. India has assisted Iran with the modernization of its port at Chahbahar, and the two sides have discussed plans to build a railroad connecting the port to Zaranj in southwestern Afghanistan.[179] In addition, India, Iran, and Russia are cooperating on the North-South corridor project, the goal of which is to create a maritime-railway link between Mumbai and St. Petersburg through Bandar Abbas, Iran, that would shave more than 6,000 miles off the current maritime route. Proponents of the plan expect up to $10 billion in freight traffic annually once rail links are complete.[180] While most analyses of Indian participation in work at the Iranian ports have focused primarily on the possibility of India gaining a naval base in the Gulf to the west of Pakistan, commercial motives should not be discounted.

Iran's shift toward India during the 1990s was the product of a broader diplomatic strategy that became official in 1997—the country's "look east" policy, which was aimed at reducing dependence on Western countries.[181] Indian analyst B. Raman has argued that Narasimha Rao, India's prime minister from 1991 to 1996, deserves credit for the Indo-Iranian rapprochement. Rao thought that "there was more in common between secular India and Shi'a Iran than between secular India and an increasingly Wahhabized Arab world."[182] In line with that view, Rao visited Iran in November 1993, reciprocating the 1992 visit of Iranian foreign minister Ali Akbar Velayati to India.[183] President Khatami's actions after his election further bolstered Rao's argument, as Khatami's "dialogue of civilizations" portrayed a more inviting Iran, one with which India could do business, and hinted at the prospect of a less revolutionary regime.

Following in the diplomatic footsteps of leaders like Rao and Khatami, the most important event in the growth of the relationship was the April 2001 visit of India's prime minister, Atal Behari Vajpayee, to Tehran, which resulted in the signing of the 2001 Tehran Declaration. The agreement committed both countries to accelerating their cooperation on the proposed pipeline to supply natural gas to India through Pakistan.[184] Building on that groundwork, in 2003 Khatami traveled to India, where he had the high honor of being named the guest of honor at India's Republic Day celebrations. While that was primarily a symbolic gesture, Khatami and Vajpayee made some more tangible progress, agreeing to further cooperation in a number of fields, including science, energy, trade, and defense.

ECONOMICS AND ENERGY

India is the world's sixth-largest consumer of energy and Iran is the fourth-largest supplier, so it is unsurprising that the energy sector is an important part of their relationship.[185] Regular bilateral meetings between Indian and Iranian officials focusing primarily on energy supply issues have occurred since 2003. The talks have included discussions of a proposed liquefied natural gas pipeline from Iran to India through Pakistan and an alternative plan to supply LNG to India by tanker.

The initial project, first proposed in 1996 and recently estimated to cost $7 billion, has been very controversial. First, it would require cooperation and trust between India and Pakistan. While many in India recognize the common Indo-Pakistani interest in the pipeline project, the Indian strategic community has never been in favor of the proposal. In their opinion, the route of the planned pipeline ends up giving Pakistan too much leverage over India's energy security. Buying gas at the Pakistan-India border is being advocated as a better alternative.[186] Second, the United States, in accordance with its policy of attempting to diplomatically isolate Iran, has opposed the project.[187] U.S. pressure on India not to move forward with the project has been the source of some confusion in New Delhi. Given the geographical realities involved, India's section of the pipeline will be built only after the Iranian and Pakistani sections are completed. Therefore, while the United States may be able to exert enough pressure to delay the project, it is Pakistan, not India, that is central to finalization of the deal.[188] Third, as oil prices have risen, the price of the pipeline's natural gas cargo has become an issue.

Despite those and other hurdles, the Iran-Pakistan-India pipeline idea has proved resilient. Many in India see the relatively cheap energy that the pipeline would supply as crucial to the continued growth of India's economy.[189] The deal first appeared to be a realistic possibility in January 2005, when Iran agreed to guarantee the supply through Pakistan to India.[190] The election of Mahmoud Ahmadinejad as president of Iran in the summer of 2005, however, raised concerns that international finance might shy away due to his hard-line conservative political stance.[191] Doubts about India's commitment to the deal increased when Murli Deora, seen as friendly to the United States, was appointed oil minister in January 2006.

The proposal was further complicated when a pricing dispute emerged in July 2006. Because the Iranian government had not ratified the agreement, it felt that the pricing could be changed and suggested the much higher price of $7.20 per million British thermal unit (BTU) instead of the $4.25 per million agreed on when oil prices were cheaper.[192] The pricing dispute is a serious hurdle. India was irked by Iran's insistence on changing what New Delhi thought was a finished part of the deal. Indian officials also are contemplating a number of other pipelines from Burma and Central Asia through Turkey and Israel because of political instability in Pakistan.[193] In June 2009, Iran and Pakistan signed an agreement to begin construction on their sections of the IPI pipeline without India.[194] Despite the signing of the bilateral agreement, the Indian, Pakistani, and Iranian governments are still trying to push the project forward; given India's expansive energy needs, their plans may not be mutually exclusive.[195]

Iran and India also have discussed supplying liquefied natural gas by sea but have failed to reach an accord. Iran agreed in 2005 to supply India with 5 million tons of LNG a year for twenty-five years beginning in 2009.[196] The deal also included assistance by the Gas Authority of India Limited in building LNG terminals in Iran to allow exports. The construction of the plant, however, would require American components, which could end up violating the terms of U.S. sanctions against Iran.[197] In 2006, the deal encountered further problems when Iran asked for a higher price than had been agreed on previously. As of November 2009, the deal is still in limbo and is unlikely to go through because of disagreement over the price of the natural gas.[198] Despite Iran's bounty of fuel resources and India's need for them, diplomatic problems, concerns over Iran's reliability as a supplier, and financial disputes have prevented any agreements from coming to fruition.

DEFENSE COOPERATION

Defense cooperation has been another important part of the Indo-Iranian relationship. In the 1990s, India assisted Iran with upgrading its Russian-built military equipment, including adapting batteries for its Kilo-class diesel submarines to warmer conditions and providing avionics upgrades for its MiG-29 fighters.[199] Since 2000, India has conducted joint patrols or exercises with the majority of the navies of the Indian Ocean littoral. The 2003 meeting between Khatami and Vajpayee on India's Republic Day produced the Road Map to Strategic Cooperation, which presents goals for fulfilling the cooperation envisioned in the New Delhi Declaration.[200] In March 2003, India and Iran held their first joint naval maneuvers in the Arabian Sea, coinciding with U.S. preparations for the Iraq War. They also indicated a shared belief that the then-nascent conflict over Iraq should be settled by diplomatic means. Newspaper reports have suggested that India sought Iran's opinion as well as that of other states bordering Iraq when deciding whether to send troops to Iraq in the summer of 2003.[201]

Iran and India also held joint naval exercises in 2006, paralleling President Bush's trip to the region.[202] C. Christine Fair has argued that the timing was intentional—that India wanted to send a "reassuring signal to Tehran that India's foreign policies [would] not be dictated by Washington."[203] The exercises may also have sent a message to the United States, where they were noted with great concern, especially in Congress, but they were not in and of themselves remarkable. Washington also has expressed concern about reports of India assisting Iran with its satellite and space program, assistance that the United States fears could have the undesirable effect of advancing Iran's ballistic-missile capability.[204]

A number of reports have mentioned more direct Indo-Iranian cooperation in the realm of defense, such as Tehran's acquiescence to Iran-based Indian intelligence operations and even potential Indian military bases in Iran. Donald Berlin, a researcher at a Department of Defense–sponsored think tank, argued in 2004 that the "unusually large Indian consulate" in Zahedan, Iran, likely contained an intelligence station that would allow India to monitor western Pakistan electronically.[205] India's assistance in upgrading the Iranian port of Chahbahar has led many to infer that Indian warships would be based there in order to outflank Pakistan's China-assisted Gwadar port, seemingly pitting rising power against rising power.

In truth, the port projects are comparable. Both make sense from an economic perspective—Chahbahar would allow India and Iran better access to Central Asia, and Gwadar could serve as a transshipment point and provide better access to China's western provinces. Yet their strategic location on vital sea-lanes gives them obvious potential for military use. Some sources have suggested that Iran had agreed to allow India to base its forces in Iran in case of war with Pakistan. While that claim was denied by India and has not been substantiated, it would mark a significant shift in Indian strategy, which in the past has focused primarily on the plains of Punjab and on blockading Karachi. Indian forces in Iran would imperil Pakistan's western border and outflank ships based at Gwadar, forcing the Pakistani military to divide its assets and alter its current defense posture, which focuses primarily on its eastern border.[206]

Iran-Pakistan Relations and India

Just as some facets of Iran-Indian defense ties have been threatening to Pakistan, Iran's relationship with Pakistan has placed a strain on Indo-Iranian relations. Iran was the first nation to recognize Pakistan in 1947. The two countries established formal diplomatic relations in May 1948 and signed the Treaty of Friendship a year later.[207] Iran and Pakistan also were founding members of the Baghdad Pact, which in theory committed Pakistan to Iran's defense, and Iran provided Pakistan with military and financial aid during its 1965 war with India. However, the balance of power in the region began to shift following India's 1971 defeat of Pakistan, which prompted Iran to seek closer relations with India.

Relations between Pakistan and Iran began to decline further in the late 1970s. The Islamic Revolution in 1979 left Pakistan in a bind; Islamabad had been close to the Shah and tried to mediate internal disputes on his behalf.[208] While both countries found common ground in their opposition to the Soviet invasion of Afghanistan, Iran was displeased by Pakistan's close cooperation with the United States, which supplied anti-Soviet forces in Afghanistan with weapons through Pakistan in the 1980s. Nevertheless, relations were fairly good in the 1980s, if for no other reason than that Iran was preoccupied with Iraq.[209]

However, the shifting balance in international alignments brought on by the end of the cold war pitted Iran and Pakistan against each other, just as it pulled India and Iran closer together. The rise of the Pakistani-sponsored Taliban in the mid-1990s resulted in a proxy battle in Afghanistan, with Iran supporting segments of the Taliban's opponent, the Northern Alliance. The Afghan war indirectly inflamed preexisting ethnic and communal conflicts in Pakistan between Shias and Sunnis, which had further deleterious effects on Iran-Pakistan relations, especially after the killing of an Iranian diplomat in 1991. Even worse, Tehran nearly went to war with the Taliban in 1998 after ten Iranian diplomats were executed by the group in Mazar-e-Sharif.[210] Since the late 1990s, Pakistan has sought closer relations with Iran to prevent Tehran from moving too close to India.[211]

The fall of the Taliban in 2001 allowed relations to improve, and President Khatami's visit to Islamabad in 2002 resulted in a bevy of bilateral agreements and a mildly pro-Pakistani stance on Kashmir.[212] It is alleged that Pakistan, or at least Pakistani scientists, have transferred nuclear knowledge and technology to Iran. However, relations between Iran and Pakistan lack the depth of engagement found between India and Iran.

INDO-U.S. RELATIONS AND IRAN

India's relationship with Iran, which has been a subject of concern in Washington for some time, could affect its relationship with the United States. Increasing international tensions surrounding Iran's nuclear program and U.S. efforts to seek closer ties with India have improved Indo-U.S. relations. The most public sign of that improvement is the U.S.-India Nuclear Cooperation Agreement, which the U.S. Congress approved on October 1, 2008. The agreement, which the two governments had been working on since the release of a joint statement by President Geroge W. Bush and Prime Minister Manmohan Singh in July 2005, has been described as a potential turning point in the U.S.-India relationship. Indian opposition parties, however, have decried the agreement, arguing that it would tie Indian foreign policy to that of the United States.

Many in the United States have insisted that India pass a loyalty test on Iran before it can be regarded as a real strategic partner of Washington's. Every such demand, however, has been met with increased pressure in New Delhi to demonstrate the independence of India's foreign policy in the region.[213] When India voted to refer the issue of the Iranian nuclear program to the UN Security Council in September 2005, most commentators assumed that India had caved in under U.S. pressure, especially since India had opposed broad U.S. sanctions against Iran in 2004.[214] The perception that India had buckled enraged India's leftist parties, who made up a small but crucial part of the United Progressive Alliance coalition, led by the Indian National Congress party. India's leftist parties, especially the Communist Party of India (CPI), have ardently supported the India-Iran-Pakistan pipeline deal and sought to sink India's nuclear deal with the United States, even voting with India's Hindu conservative parties in a failed attempt to bring down the UPA government.

Despite its support for an IAEA vote demanding more transparency on Iran's nuclear program, India has maintained a fairly neutral stance. India has long maintained that it does not see further nuclear proliferation as serving its national interests, a position that stems as much from India's desire to project itself as a responsible nuclear power as from the very real danger that proliferation would pose to its own security.[215] In 2006, Prime

Minister Singh affirmed that Iran "must have all the rights that go with being a member of the NPT and it must also fulfill all obligations." That would allow Iran to enrich uranium, but only if Iran has abided by its NPT commitments.[216] India has generally emphasized the importance of solving the dispute through negotiations.

RECENT DEVELOPMENTS

While some analyses of Indo-Iranian relations portray a positive trend, the relationship was strongest when Khatami's reformist government ruled Iran. India enthusiastically supported Khatami's "dialogue of civilizations" in the hope of encouraging the development of a truly post-revolutionary Iran.[217] However, the election of Mahmoud Ahmadinejad in 2005 and the evolution of a more hard-line Iranian stance reversed that trend and slowed the growth of the relationship.[218] The result is what one Indian analyst has called a "period of drift" in Indo-Iranian relations,[219] which are said to be underdeveloped compared with India's relations with other Middle Eastern countries.[220] While the relationship may have been drifting for the past few years, the Indian public has retained a more positive impression of Iran than the world at large.[221]

FUTURE OF THE RELATIONSHIP

The growth in India-Iran relations has been predicated on economic and strategic logic. The question of which is more important is central to any prediction about what is to come. On the economic side, India's increasing need for energy would seem to be a reason for future closeness, but neither of the major energy proposals between Iran and India has come to fruition. Moreover, India receives a much greater proportion of its energy from Arab states in the Gulf than it does from Iran.[222] Similarly, defense is not likely to be a steady driver of the relationship, as India's cooperation with the GCC states and Israel in that area has been much more robust than with Iran.[223] Indo-Iranian defense cooperation has either decreased or continued extremely quietly since the 2006 naval exercise. The "drift" some Indian analysts have noted in Indo-Iranian relations from 2005 to 2007 would seem to argue for the former, but the absence of evidence of continued ties does not preclude intelligence sharing or other cooperation behind closed doors. India's relations with Iran are further complicated by the fluid nature of India's relationships with Pakistan and Afghanistan. As a neighbor of both countries, Iran directly influences India's immediate security calculus; India's policy toward Iran therefore must be managed in conjunction with its policies toward Pakistan and Afghanistan.[224]

Such uncertainty leads to diverging analyses of the future of the relationship. First, it is possible that India has been pursuing cooperation with Iran in sensitive areas such as defense, including the suggested intelligence station at Zahedan, but is doing so quietly to avoid international criticism, most notably from Washington. That interpretation is bolstered by the April 2008 statement of M. K. Narayanan, India's national security adviser, that there is a "great deal taking place between India and Iran which is not on the public realm."[225] That would posit a continuing growth in Indo-Iranian economic relations and subtle growth in other sectors, including defense or strategic cooperation.

The second analysis suggests a future relationship grounded deeply, and almost solely, in trade and cultural relations, without significant strategic interaction. That is based on the idea that India privately and subtly reassessed its policy toward Iran after Ahmadinejad replaced Khatami and Iran began to shift away from the reformist to more conservative forces. Part of the overall "drift" in the relationship is related to Iran's conservative shift and obstinacy in pipeline pricing disputes, which, when combined with nuclear developments and India's IAEA vote against Iran (whether due solely to U.S. pressure or internal factors as well), has caused India to slow or cease strategic cooperation. While Indo-Iranian relations picked up new momentum in late 2007 and early 2008, it has been limited to economic issues such as cooperation on railroad projects and energy supplies.

In either case, India and Iran's economic ties should continue to grow. For the foreseeable future, energy supply and Iran's role in facilitating Indian trade with Central Asia will be the unglamorous but consistent bedrock of the Indo-Iranian relationship.

INDIA, AFGHANISTAN, AND UZBEKISTAN

India has important relations with the Central Asian states. Its activity in Afghanistan and Uzbekistan is especially noteworthy, in part because it brings India directly into contact with Pakistan, Russia, and China.

Since the defeat of the Taliban in 2001, India and Afghanistan have enjoyed a growing relationship built on mutual diplomatic and economic interests. India is a large provider of aid to Kabul, having contributed more than $750 million for humanitarian purposes since 2001.[226] India has helped rebuild Afghan infrastructure, which has been in extreme disrepair since the Soviet-Afghan war of the 1980s. New Delhi government officials also have engaged in a long-term educational campaign to train their counterparts in Kabul.[227]

The increased political and economic ties between India and Afghanistan come after a decade of sour relations stemming from Afghanistan's Taliban regime. With a more democratic government in Kabul, India hopes to promote regional stability while also minimizing Pakistan's influence in Afghanistan. Because of the notoriously porous border between the two countries, Islamabad has long held considerable sway over Afghan affairs.[228] From Pakistan's perspective, a friendly client government in Kabul is a good way to limit India's expanding orbit of influence while promoting Pakistan's regional prominence. By peeling Kabul away from Islamabad, India can reduce Pakistan's influence while also strengthening its own regional economic ties.

Pakistan, of course, sees India's thrust into Central Asia as a serious affront to the traditional regional dynamic.[229] The Taliban, after all, had been based in and supported from western Pakistan. With NATO's ongoing rebuilding effort in Afghanistan—and the entire international community watching—Islamabad has had little opportunity to prevent Kabul from restoring its traditionally close ties to India. Even as New Delhi's foreign policy concerns expand in India's rise to prominence on the world stage, Pakistan's concerns are still dominated by the perception that India is an existential threat.

India and Uzbekistan share historical ties that go back to the fourteenth century, when they traded along the ancient Silk Road, but their relationship did not grow significantly until Uzbekistan gained independence from the Soviet Union in 1991.[230] Nonetheless, India and Uzbekistan do have historic connections in the twentieth century; Tashkent, Uzbekistan, for example, was the site of the Soviet-moderated talks between India and Pakistan in the wake of their 1965 war.

India had trade relations and some diplomatic ties in Central Asia throughout the cold war, but since Uzbekistan was part of the Soviet Union until 1991, their formal diplomatic relationship did not begin until the late 1980s. India opened a consulate in Tashkent in April 1987, and it was upgraded to an embassy in 1992, not long after Uzbekistan gained its independence.[231] Indo-Uzbek relations grew quickly, with reciprocated state visits in the early 1990s and a variety of agreements on cultural and trade issues.[232] India and Uzbekistan have focused on their economic relationship, including cooperation agreements on energy resources and a multilateral agreement with Iran and Afghanistan to open more efficient trade routes between India and Uzbekistan.[233] When Prime Minister Singh visited Uzbekistan in 2006, India and Uzbekistan signed MOUs relating to oil, gas, and mining. During that visit, Uzbekistan also declared its support for India's bid for a permanent seat on the UN Security Council.[234]

India and Uzbekistan also have limited cooperation in security matters. In 2006, the two agreed to cooperate in counterterrorism operations, energy security, and regional security in Central Asia.[235] Of course, both countries have important interests in the ongoing conflict in Afghanistan. In addition, India, which has been working to acquire greater influence in the region, opened an air base in southern Tajikistan.[236] India and Uzbekistan also have planned to stage joint military exercises and to cooperate in maintaining weapons and support equipment, which should be helpful because both operate Russian-made equipment.[237] India also purchased IL-76 transport aircraft and one IL-78 refueling tanker from Uzbekistan between 2003 and 2004.[238] India's security relationship with Uzbekistan should increase if India is admitted as a full member of the Shanghai Cooperation Organization (SCO), where it currently has observer status.

Most of India's exports to Uzbekistan have been pharmaceuticals, with tea, machinery, packaging materials, plastic items, surgical items, and consumer goods constituting the remainder of Indo-Uzbek trade. Uzbekistan's exports include aircraft and machinery. Uzbekistan became an Indian Technical and Economic Cooperation (ITEC) partner country in 2003.[239]

SUMMARY

India has strong and growing ties with key Middle East countries, especially in the Gulf. It has a unique relationship with Israel, which is described in chapter 5. To date, it has managed to avoid being drawn into the vortex of regional conflicts and has been able to maintain good relations with virtually all states in the region. India's expanding influence and its shift toward perceiving itself as a great power, which involves accepting higher security responsibilities, encounters resistance from those who wish to maintain India's anti-imperialist tradition.[240] Therefore, while policymakers have begun to accept the realities of its growing influence in the region, India shows no overt desire to play a more assertive role, certainly not to the point of taking sides in the region's many unresolved disputes or of becoming a strategic ally of the United States.

Nevertheless, despite its low-key diplomacy, a number of issues could eventually force India to flex its muscles and become a more active player in Middle East geopolitics. The large number of Indian expatriates working in the Gulf could eventually become a source of friction between India and the host countries in various areas, from the treatment of low-paid workers in the rich Arab states to more sensitive issues like rights to citizenship for Indians who have lived in the Gulf for generations. The tensions could grow especially if the boom times in the Gulf wind down as a result of the global recession and fewer workers are needed. At a strategic level, there clearly are a number of long-term questions that Indian planners must be concerned about—India's role in the event of an escalation of conflict in the Gulf, U.S.-Iran-Arab Gulf disputes, and the possibility that in the years ahead China, in cooperation with Pakistan, might begin to project its presence into the Indian Ocean. Under those circumstances, speculation about more active U.S.-India-Japan maritime cooperation could intensify, although at present any such speculation certainly is premature.

CHAPTER THREE

CHINA'S RETURN TO THE GREATER MIDDLE EAST

FOR SIX CENTURIES, CHINA'S westward voyages of exploration were a visible manifestation of China's superpower status. At its peak in the fifteenth century, the Chinese fleet included as many as 300 vessels and 30,000 men, and, commanded by a Muslim from Central Asia, Admiral Zheng He, it traveled as far west as modern Tanzania. The admiral's last expeditions reached Mecca and modern day Iran. Yet, after his last expedition in 1432, China, having reordered national priorities to focus on domestic issues and the landward threat from Central Asia, abruptly halted its naval explorations. As a result, China had little contact with or influence in the Middle East for centuries afterward. However, soon after achieving independence in 1949, the People's Republic of China began to show interest in the Middle East, in particular by trying to work with Arab revolutionary groups. Those efforts, which were vigorously opposed by the nationalists who controlled most of the states in the region, were never successful. However, since China's emergence as a major economic power and the corresponding growth in its need for energy resources, its traders and diplomats have increasingly followed Zheng He's footsteps.

Unlike India, which historically has had a comfortable relationship with the Middle East, especially the Gulf, China is considered a relative outsider in the region. Despite that, China has productive and deepening relationships with many states in the Greater Middle East, including Pakistan, Iran, Israel, Saudi Arabia, and the Gulf states. Although during the 1980s arms sales to Iran, Iraq, and Saudi Arabia were Beijing's primary link to the Middle East, more recently China has become a major importer of goods from the region, most notably petroleum, as well as military technology from Israel. One of the sources of China's current popularity in the region is that China is a good customer—the country needs what Middle Eastern countries are seeking to export. Its voracious appetite for resources and its other economic needs match the economic profiles of the countries in the region. China also maintains a strictly business approach to its relationships with its trading partners—refraining, for example, from public comment on their domestic policies—which greatly appeals to states like Saudi Arabia.[1] That approach also has allowed China to maintain good relations with states in the region that are nominally opposed to each other.

How long Beijing can maintain its light diplomatic footprint, however, remains an open question. Although China's relations with the Middle East are good, it is unclear how Beijing's influence will develop in the future—at what point might its interests in the Middle East force China to play a more assertive role? In examining China's emerging role in the greater Middle East, many different elements of the relationship are relevent. In the short term, the focus must inevitably be on China's diplomatic and economic interactions, especially with the major energy producers as well as Egypt and Israel. But over the longer run it is necessary to take into account China's growing physical links with the countries of Central Asia, especially Pakistan. If China's westward development is sustained, it will open up new road, rail, and pipeline routes that eventually will directly influence trade, politics, and commerce in the Middle East.

THE GREATER MIDDLE EAST AND CHINA'S FOREIGN POLICY

Although China's early efforts at direct engagement in the Middle East through arms sales raised a lot of eyebrows and garnered a lot of attention, they did not serve long-term Chinese interests.[2] Once it became clear that China's ideological conflict with the West was less important to its leaders than its need to build the nation's economy and engage in international trade with the rest of the world, a new pattern of engagement emerged. Since the beginning of this century, China has embarked on a charm offensive, using a "soft power" approach in its efforts to engage with and gain political influence in various regions of the world. A cornerstone of the new approach is China's assurance that it is not seeking ideological domination and that it has no territorial ambitions or desire to nurture client states. The Chinese assume that their country's economic development and international trade are not a threat to their neighbors or to the world. Instead, China's "soft power" should appeal to the rest of the world by offering an alternative to the "hard power" of the United States and its parallel pretension of global hegemony.

As the Chinese economy has continued to grow, the nation's foreign policy goals have inevitably become linked to the need to raise the living standards of the huge Chinese population, thereby dampening the prospects of social disaffection arising from poverty and lack of jobs and sustaining the legitimacy of the regime. As a result, enhancing sustainable economic growth, particularly in the energy field, has become the cornerstone of China's foreign and domestic policy. At the same time, it faces the continuing challenge of what to do about Taiwan, which China regards as part of its national territory. Its policy has been to squeeze Taiwan's international space by eliminating Taiwan's remaining diplomatic relationships. Acceptance of the "one-China" policy by other countries has been a precondition for Chinese investment, and in that way China has used its economic clout to outbid Taiwan in diplomatic relationships. Though the policy has been successful in many respects, Taiwan has remained a key mutual security concern of the United States and Japan.

Because of its need to expand its economic reach, China has put a high priority on maintaining regional stability. It has worked to ease border disputes and downplay maritime claims. However, it has not been altogether successful; many disputes still remain. In 2003 China began to refer to its "peaceful rise," suggesting that it did not want to compete with the United States in any direct military sense. However, that is not to say that China has not had strong concerns about U.S. pretensions of supremacy; indeed, its goal has been to limit U.S. ability to interfere around the world by seeking multiple international partnerships with other countries and institutions. It has not sought formal alliances, preferring to create a framework of less direct international agreements. It also has focused on working with new multinational institutions such as the Euro-Asian Council for Standardization, Metrology, and Certification (EASC), the Shanghai Cooperation Organization (SCO), and the Forum on China-Africa Cooperation (FOCAC).

One of the presumed advantages of China's soft-power approach is that it focuses on no-strings aid to and investment in countries that it does business with and does not demand the "good governance and human rights" associated with Western assistance. The Chinese view has been that this approach gives them a competitive advantage because it is less intrusive. Furthermore, since many of the entities that engage in Chinese overseas investments are state-owned, they can operate without the constraints that burden U.S. and European corporations concerning transparency and corruption. The assumption is that over time, China can establish strong economic relations with its economic partners by focusing on longer-term goals instead of short-term profits. However, the negative side of this approach is that by its very nature, state ownership of assets often results in a lack of self-discipline and the likelihood of engaging in less profitable agreements that ultimately do not pay dividends.

China's soft power approach has many limitations. The win-win strategy takes a narrow focus on only those issues on which the parties can immediately agree. The lack of transparency in China's dealings with many countries raises doubts regarding China's claims that its dealings with them are innocuous and that it does not wish to interfere in their domestic affairs. The fact that China initially refused to take a strong stand against the behavior of the Sudanese government in the matter of Darfur raised strong protests in the Western countries against Chinese investment policies. In short, while China's reliance on its economic clout together with its hands-off approach to other countries' internal matters has served its interests and allowed China to avoid direct confrontation with the United States, doubts remain about the sustainability of that approach, particularly in areas such as the greater Middle East and Africa, which are so ridden with unresolved and emotional conflicts.

While it is clear that China has shown a remarkable ability to be friendly with every political entity in the Middle East—including the Israelis, the Palestinians, and the Iranians—sooner or later, as its involvement grows, it will be drawn into the politics of the region. It therefore remains an open question whether China's peaceful rise and its soft-power strategy will ultimately succeed.[3]

This chapter first reviews some of the key energy and infrastructure issues that increasingly affect China's relations with the countries of Central Asia and the greater Middle East. China's growing relations with Iran, Saudi Arabia, the smaller Gulf states, and the key countries of Central Asia are then summarized.

ENERGY NEEDS AND SUPPLIES

The transportation sector provides the clearest indication of demand for oil. Although in Asia that sector currently accounts for only a small portion of the region's total energy consumption, the number of cars in China has been growing by 20 percent a year, and with a population of 1.3 billion and increasing migration to cities, that rate is not likely to decline.[4] There are some predictions that by 2030 China will have more cars than the United States and import as much oil as the United States does today.[5] In addition, major infrastructure projects will lead to growth in the transportation sector and therefore in demand for oil. For example, China has embarked on massive interstate highway projects as part of its efforts to encourage development in its vast western provinces.

COAL

China possesses the world's third-largest coal reserves, after those of the United States and Russia. China is the world's leading producer and consumer of coal, which accounts for 69 percent of the nation's total energy production. China is hoping to diversify its use of this abundant fuel by opening coal-to-liquid production plants.[6] Most of China's coal is located in the north, particularly in Shanxi province, although dirtier deposits with higher sulfur and ash content exist in the south as well. The production difficulties caused by the dirtier content of southern coal have dovetailed with China's effort to increase efficiency and achieve economies of scale by closing small operations and moving toward large, state-run operations, so northern production should become increasingly important.[7]

OIL

China has proven oil reserves of 16 billion barrels, more than Qatar's reserves.[8] Of course, China's domestic consumption is much greater than that of the small Gulf states. China became a net oil importer in 1993, and by 2006 the gap between its consumption and domestic production was roughly 3.5 billion barrels a day.[9] China's oil consumption has increased 8 percent annually since 2002.[10] In 2008, China was the world's second-largest national consumer of petroleum products, with total demand of 7.9 million barrels a day.[11] The U.S. Energy Information Administration (EIA) predicts that China will produce 4.9 billion barrels a day by 2030 but that production will fall well short of projected Chinese consumption of roughly

15 billion barrels a day. The EIA and the International Energy Agency (IEA) predict that in 2030 China will remain the second-largest national consumer of oil and that its consumption will come very close to, if not exceed, the combined consumption of the European OECD countries.[12]

The Middle East accounted for 44 percent of China's oil imports in 2006, with Saudi Arabia and Iran being two of China's largest sources of oil.[13] In 2008 China's primary suppliers of oil were, in order, Saudi Arabia, Angola, Iran, Oman, Russia, Sudan, Venezuela, Kuwait, Kazakhstan, and the United Arab Emirates (UAE).[14] As noted above, Chinese demand for oil imports will have a significant effect on the international market as China's share of worldwide demand rises from 7 percent in 2003 to 25 percent in 2030 and increases in Chinese demand account for 25 percent of worldwide growth in demand from 2003 to 2030.[15] In the scenario projected by the IEA, Chinese dependence on Middle Eastern oil is unavoidable. To get an idea of the scale of Chinese demand, the projected increase in China's consumption amounts to 83 percent of projected new production in South America and Africa. Rough calculations based on EIA projections indicate that China will get, at a minimum, one-third of its oil from the Middle East in 2030.

NATURAL GAS

Historically, natural gas has not been a major source of energy in China because most of China's reserves are in its Western provinces, far from the more developed coastal areas. However, natural gas use has increased in recent years, and it is projected to grow quickly to meet the needs of China's expanding economy. In the past natural gas was used in China primarily to create fertilizer, but it is gaining much wider use as a cleaner way to produce electricity. Chinese consumption of natural gas doubled from 1999 to 2005. In 2004 China consumed 1.3 trillion cubic feet of natural gas, only 3 percent of China's overall fuel mix.[16] Estimates of China's natural gas reserves vary from as high as 83 trillion cubic feet to as low as 56 trillion cubic feet, although most estimates tend toward the higher figure.[17] Through 2004 Chinese natural gas production met and slightly exceeded consumption;[18] most predictions expect this trend to continue, with domestic production accounting for a large portion of Chinese natural gas consumption. The IEA predicts that China will consume 6 trillion cubic feet of natural gas in 2030 (360 percent of 2004 consumption) and that roughly one-third of that (2 trillion cubic feet) will be imported, half from the Middle East and Central Asia.[19] China has expressed specific interest in importing natural gas from Iran as well as by pipeline from Kazakhstan, Turkmenistan, and Uzbekistan.[20]

OTHER ENERGY SOURCES

China also aims to expand its energy production through nuclear power and hydroelectric energy. China is the world's second-largest producer of hydroelectric power, after Canada, and its hydroelectric power makes up 6 percent of its total energy consumption. China produces its hydroelectric power at a series of dams, of which the gigantic Three Gorges Dam is the most famous. Three Gorges, by itself, is projected to produce 22.5 gigawatts of energy annually, and China is adding a further 15.8 gigawatts of hydroelectric capacity on the Yellow River, through a dam to be completed in 2010.[21] Nuclear power accounted for only 1 percent of China's overall energy use and 2 percent of its electricity generation in 2004. China has commenced an ambitious program to add 30 gigawatts of greenfield nuclear power generation by 2020, yet even that would account for only 4.5 percent of its total supply of electricity.[22]

INFRASTRUCTURE PROJECTS WITHIN CHINA

Modernizing its highways, railways, and sea- and airports is essential to China's economic growth and its ability to trade with the rest of the world.

HIGHWAYS

Over the past few years, China has been working steadily to develop its highway system. Before 1993, very few modern highways existed in the country; since 2000, however, the government has increased construction, adding about 3,000 kilometers (1,864 miles) of expressway a year to the pre-existing network (in 2010 the total network covered approximately 40,389 miles).[23] The expressway network, known also as the National Trunk Highway System (NTHS), is now the world's second largest, trailing only that in the United States. That is an extraordinary development. According to the World Bank, more than 27,000 miles of expressways were built in China from 1996 to 2006, the bulk of which make up the NTHS, now connecting all provincial capitals and cities with populations of 500,000 or more.[24] The Jingzhu expressway, which runs from Beijing to Zhuhai, is China's longest. Plans for the National Expressway Network were approved in 2004. The new system, also called the 7-9-18 Highway Network, will comprise some

52,000 miles of roadway, including the NTHS.[25] Map 3-1 shows the existing and planned highways and expressways in China in 2008.

Moreover, the government of China plans to continue building expressways over the next three decades, ultimately connecting all provincial capitals and cities. There is, of course, inequality between modern and rural China. Most rural roads are not well paved—often they are simply mud tracks—but the government has promised to construct more than 112,000 miles of new rural highways.[26] In addition to those projects, China invested $10 billion in Beijing's transportation infrastructure in preparation for the 2008 Olympics, including city expressways, subway systems, and an intracity light-rail system.

RAILWAYS

China has one of the busiest railway networks in the world. Well-functioning rail lines, which are vital for continued growth, are another key component of infrastructure development. In the past decade, passenger traffic on China's rail system grew by 70 percent, while freight traffic increased by 60 percent.[27] Furthermore, the volume of China's railway traffic is the highest of any country's, amounting to a quarter of the world's total traffic.[28] In 2005, there were approximately 46,875 miles of track. The Chinese rail system comprises about twenty principal domestic railway routes. Most of the existing rail lines, however, are single-track, which can lengthen trips by a few days to weeks or more. The government has begun to double the number of railways in order to alleviate scheduling conflicts between passenger and freight trains on heavily used tracks. According to the World Bank, by 2020 China's rail system will boast 100,000 kilometers (62,000 miles) of track.[29] In 2008, in time for the Olympics, China opened the new Beijing-Tianjin intercity rail line, with top speeds of 350 kilometers (217 miles) an hour, making it one of the fastest conventional trains in the world.[30]

SEAPORTS AND AIRPORTS

China has twelve major shipping ports that handle more than 100 million tons of cargo a year. Those ports, as well as smaller sea and river ports, handle most of China's vast volume of imports and exports.[31] To put that in context, by 2010, around 35 percent of the world's shipping is expected to originate in China.[32] The port of Shanghai already is the second largest by container volume in the world, after Singapore. Four of the world's top ten container ports are in China. Due to high volume and projected growth,

Map 3-1

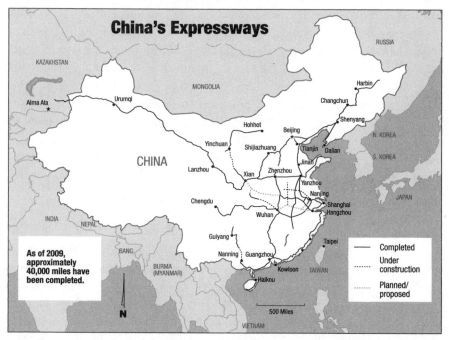

the Chinese government plans to distribute seaports along the coast, which would be of great importance to the national transport networks and the expansion of foreign trade. In 2005, China invested almost $5 billion in port-related infrastructure in order to increase capacity at all ports in the country. Shanghai, one of the most important ports, is undergoing significant upgrading in order to automate more procedures, minimize loss of goods and time, and help customs officials collect more accurate tariffs. If implementation of the plan succeeds, it will likely be applied in other Chinese ports.

Air travel is the fastest-growing transportation sector in China, and in 2008 Beijing had the eighth-busiest airport in the world.[33] From 1995 to 2006, air passenger traffic increased from 51 million to 160 million passengers, while cargo increased from 1 million to 3.5 million tons. By the end of 2005, there were 142 commercial airports in China, 25 of which were larger-scale facilities and 57 of which were international.[34] In addition, China's General Administration of Civil Aviation estimated that the aviation industry will have grown 14 percent by 2010, with a fleet of 1,600 aircraft. By that time, China also will have 48 new airports and hopes to have 220 of them by 2020. Beijing has also expressed the desire to implement a modern air traffic control management system. China plans to spend $17.5 billion overall on airport improvements from 2006 to 2010.[35]

If the number of infrastructure projects outside China being developed with Chinese help are taken into account, China's westward thrust can be seen as having major potential to bring China closer to the Middle East using transit routes through Central Asia and Pakistan.

CHINA'S RELATIONS WITH IRAN

China and Iran have a long history of trade and diplomatic relations, dating back to their precolonial empires. In fact, the roots of the Sino-Iranian relationship are found in pre-Islamic times, when the Han people of China established commercial relationships with the Parthians and then with the Sassanids. The shared historical experiences of the two countries further unite them. Both were major regional powers that found their empires carved up and their autonomy challenged when Western colonial powers came into dominance, and they often are referred to as having a similar victim mentality as a result. China and Iran's 2,000-year history of cultural and economic ties along with more than 500 years of Western domination brought not only trade and war but also a common experience that currently forms a significant part of their relationship.

THE SILK ROAD

Before Islam made its debut in the Middle East and Central Asia in the seventh century, Zoroastrianism was the religion of the Persian Empire which adopted many of the cultural practices of surrounding and conquered lands.[36] Persia's relations with its Gulf neighbors and Central Asia were most impressive, and they were especially apparent in its trade along the Silk Road, which originated in the first millennium BCE. By the time Islam emerged as a religious force, the route had spread from its origins in Xian, a city in Shaanxi Province in China, all the way to lands in the Mediterranean.[37] (Persia was not called Iran until 1935.)

The road, central to the development of international trade, was of utmost importance to Persia. During the rule of Emperor Mehrdad II, from 123 to 88 BCE, the Parthian empire, which controlled Persia at the time, and China, under the rule of the Han Dynasty, signed their first trade agreement. Iran, which was developed enough to have customs offices on its borders, profited from the trade going through the region.[38] In addition to silk, valuables such as silver, gold, and porcelain; horses; and intangible assets like science and religion moved eastward along the Silk Road. Like Buddhism before it, Islam spread along the Silk Road in the seventh and eighth centuries, eventually becoming a popular movement in Central Asia, which would later see the rise of the nations of Kazakhstan, Uzbekistan, Azerbaijan, Kyrgyzstan, Turkmenistan, and the area of China known as Xinjiang or Chinese Turkistan.[39] Another link between China and Iran is that throughout the rise and fall of the various Iranian empires, nobles of both empires often intermarried. Even today there is an atypically high prevalence in China of the inherited blood disease thalassemia, which, although it is often found in the Middle East and India, is uncommon in the rest of Southeast Asian nations.[40]

When the Silk Road began to crumble after the fall of the Mongols and the rise of the Ming Dynasty, the populations on the route gradually began to adopt more regional or nationalistic identities. The cultural barriers between the Islamic people of Persia and the Buddhists of China, as well as natural barriers such as the mountains and deserts of Central Asia, discouraged trade. Meanwhile, nations encouraged isolationism, which led to xenophobia among their populations, and trade and communications along the Silk Road dwindled.[41]

COMMON EXPERIENCES: COLONIALISM AND LOSS OF AUTONOMY

After Marco Polo traveled the Silk Road in the thirteenth century, Western interest in the region began to increase exponentially. For approximately 500 years after 1450, both China and Iran endured constant threats and invasions from Western nations eager for land and riches. The sea routes provided the nations of the West with a faster way of transporting the goods of the East. The Portuguese—who, thanks to their improved navigation techniques, were the pioneers—were trading with China as early as 1511. Eventually, they displaced the states of the Gulf region as the primary traders in spices. [42] Other major world powers began to move into Asia and the Gulf region, most notably the British, the Russians, and later the Germans and Americans. The Central Asian nations were slowly taken over by the Russians, and by the beginning of the nineteenth century, the Russian empire had expanded to the border of Iran, where Uzbekistan and Turkmenistan are today.[43] China later lost territories to the imperial expansion of the West, including Hong Kong, a number of offshore islands, and dominions in modern Korea and Vietnam.[44]

Such common experiences served to connect Iran and China, especially during the twentieth century, when the end of colonialism left nations across the globe in chaos. They helped build a common mentality, one that has been described as a "desire to reclaim status and influence on the world stage."[45] According to John W. Garver, a scholar in the field of international affairs, "The spirit of Sino-Iranian ties means that Beijing seeks cooperation with Iran as a way of making the world whole after the humiliation of ancient non-Western nations at Western hands in the modern era."[46] After several millennia of trade, intermarriage, cooperation, social and political contact, and common experiences during the colonial era, China and Iran have hopes of regaining international status. Both are attempting to rebuild their shared domination of the East, lost during the European conquests of the sixteenth century. Thanks to their economic, political, military, and energy resources, they have reestablished themselves as strong forces in the Persian Gulf and in the East. The precise goals of the Sino-Iranian relationship are somewhat unclear. Despite some struggles during the mid-twentieth century, the two nations have begun a new strategic partnership that is important to both regions and viewed warily by the other major powers of the world, especially the United States.

ECONOMIC TIES

China is one of Iran's top trading partners. Total trade between the two countries rose from $3.1 billion in 2001 to $6.1 billion in 2004, to $9.2 billion in 2005, and to a staggering $27 billion in 2008.[47] Exports from Iran to China account for 62 percent of that trade, 90 percent of which is in oil. China imports 14 percent of its oil from Iran;[48] in 2006 alone, China's crude imports from Iran rose to 74,000 barrels per day.[49] In 2006, China overtook Japan as Iran's largest trading partner, with bilateral trade volume amounting to nearly $14.5 billion. Sino-Iranian trade volume continued to soar in 2007, increasing 38 percent and topping $20 billion.[50] Those figures become even more impressive when one considers that they do not even include China's sizable weapons sales or the goods smuggled into Iran via the United Arab Emirates.

INVESTMENT IN INFRASTRUCTURE

More than 100 Chinese firms operate in Iran, primarily in dam and ship construction, steel production, the energy sector, and seaport and airport development.[51] Investment projects involve small ventures like fish canneries, sugar refineries, and paper mills, but they also include major projects such as the construction of Tehran's subway system and the completion of a new $3 billion oil refinery.[52] However, Chinese infrastructure investment in Iran pales in comparison with its investment in neighboring Pakistan. Of the Pakistan projects, the development of the port of Gwadar is of particular interest to Iran because it has the potential to reduce the influence of Iran's port at Chahbahar and displace Iran as a pathway to Central Asian markets.[53]

ENERGY DEALS

China and Iran have signed several big energy deals that promise to bring the two countries even closer together. In January 2001, Sinopec entered into an agreement with the National Iranian Oil Company (NIOC) to undertake a joint oil exploration venture in the Zavareh-Kanshan oil block in Iran. Sinopec, which was designated head of operations, is responsible for the design, purchase, and construction of the project. The deal specifies that the NIOC can send its oil by pipeline to the nations around the Caspian Sea. The two firms also signed an agreement to upgrade two NIOC refineries.[54]

In March 2004, China's state-owned oil company, Zhuhai Zhenrong Corporation, signed a 25-year deal to import 110 million tons of liquefied natural gas (LNG) from Iran. In October of that year, China signed a preliminary agreement to buy oil and natural gas from Iran and to develop Iran's Yadavaran oil field. Reports differed on the specific numbers involved, but the deal was estimated to be worth between $70 and $100 billion. China will buy approximately 250 million tons of oil from Iran over the next 25 to 30 years, and Iran will export approximately 150,000 barrels of crude oil a day once Sinopec has developed the Yadavaran field.[55] The two countries rushed to finalize the deal in February 2006 amid the escalating argument over Iran's nuclear program. According to the final deal, Sinopec will develop the Yadavaran oil field, and beginning in 2009, China will buy 10 million tons of LNG a year for 25 years. The field is capable of producing 300,000 barrels a day, although Sinopec may set the daily export amount lower. Sinopec has a 51 percent stake in the field, India's Oil and Natural Gas Corporation (ONGC) has a 29 percent stake, and either Iranian firms or a foreign company such as Shell will own the last 20 percent.[56]

On January 18, 2006, Iran's North Drilling Company (NDC) and China Oilfield Services (a Hong Kong–based company) signed an oil exploration agreement that includes the repair, management, and maintenance of the

Alborz semi-floating platform in the Caspian Sea. The platform, which was inaugurated in July 2009, is designed for waters as deep as 1,000 meters.[57] It will enable Iran and China to explore the deep waters of the southern Caspian Sea, a key advance since Iran previously was unable to reach oil fields deeper than 295 feet. Exploration will most likely take place in the area known in Iran as Alborz and in Azerbaijan as Alov. However, the five countries surrounding the Caspian have not agreed on how to divide the area, so its legal status has yet to be settled. The deal is valued at $33 million over three years.[58]

TECHNOLOGY ASSISTANCE

Weapons. Tehran has become the largest market for Chinese arms exports, valued at $200 million over the 2001–04 period.[59] Since the mid-1980s, both China and Russia have supplied Iran with missiles and missile technology, with China being Iran's major source of missile guidance equipment.[60] Beijing has sold Iran anti-ship and surface-to-surface cruise missiles, including several hundred Silkworm missiles, and China and Russia have aided Iran in the development of the Shahab 2 and Shahab 3 long-range ballistic missiles.[61] In April 2006, Tehran revealed that it has a radar-guided version of the Chinese C-701 anti-ship missile and that it also has tested the Noor anti-ship missile, a version of the Chinese C-802. The sale of advanced weapons systems and their subsequent reappearance in the hands of Iranian-backed terrorist groups such as Hezbollah has been widely condemned by the international community.[62] The United States has placed sanctions on several Chinese and Russian companies for their sale of missiles and missile technology to Iran in breach of the Iran Nonproliferation Act of 2000.[63]

Nuclear Technology. China has a history of assisting Iran with the development of nuclear capability. Beginning in 1985, China trained nuclear technicians in Iran, helped build Iran's primary research facility, and also agreed to provide Iran with subcritical or zero-yield nuclear reactors, all under International Atomic Energy Agency (IAEA) safeguards. In 1991 and 1992, the two countries made plans for Iran to buy three Chinese reactors: a 20-megawatt research reactor and two 300-megawatt pressurized water reactors. China cancelled the plans for the research reactor, but later came under fire from the United States for its assistance in building enrichment and conversion facilities in Iran. In 1997, Beijing assured Washington that it would no longer assist Iran with its nuclear program.[64] In May 2006, the BBC reported that Chinese assistance in some way helped Iran develop its current nuclear capabilities, but Beijing claimed that its aid was provided in accordance with the Nuclear Non-Proliferation Treaty and reported completely to the IAEA.[65]

Stance on Iranian Nuclear Proliferation.   While China has worked with the United States, Germany, France, and the United Kingdom to stop Iran's nuclear program, it, along with Russia, opposes the use of sanctions or force to resolve the issue and reiterates Iran's NPT-recognized right to develop nuclear power for peaceful uses. China has resisted supporting tougher UN Security Council (UNSC) sanctions against the Iranian nuclear program, consistently pushing for dialogue rather than penalties. Beijing argues that it is the IAEA's responsibility to build a case against Iran, not the UNSC's.[66] China has been performing a delicate balancing act, weighing its desire to expand its lucrative energy deals with Iran against the need to avoid alienating itself from those countries most worried about Iran's nuclear ambitions, including the United States, the European Union, the Arab Gulf states, and Israel. China does not want to be seen as condoning proliferation or otherwise at odds with the United States and Europe because it fears increased scrutiny and constraints on its broader global commercial activities. Therefore China, along with Russia, voted in March 2006 with the United States and the European countries at the IAEA to report Iran to the Security Council. Given the energy deals between Beijing and Tehran, that came as a surprise to Iran, though it is unclear to what extent Iran may be "using" China to fight for low or no penalties.[67]

In the March 2006 debate over Iran in the UNSC, China and Russia fought with the other members over the wording and strength of the statement. Despite the best efforts of John Bolton, the U.S. ambassador to the United Nations, to come up with a strong and binding agreement to impose tough economic sanctions on Iran, the Security Council issued a statement that ultimately only referred the issue back to the IAEA for another report on Iran's suspension of uranium enrichment. China and Russia made sure the UNSC statement was nonbinding and did not include a quote from the UN charter that stated that "the Security Council is responsible for international peace and security," fearing Security Council members would use the quote to support sanctions or military strikes.[68] In June 2008 the need to resolve the dispute over Iran's nuclear program became more pressing when

Mohamed ElBaradei, the director general of the IAEA, announced that Iran would need only "six months to a year to acquire a nuclear weapon," in contrast to the three to eight years that he had previously claimed.[69]

On February 2, 2009, ElBaradei, speaking on the issue of Iranian nuclear proliferation, revised those estimates: "Even if I go by the CIA and other U.S. intelligence, the estimations are that even if they go through all these scenarios, we're still talking two to five years from now."[70] The IAEA conceded in a November 2008 report that Iran has managed to enrich uranium only to less than 5 percent uranium-235, an amount consistent with the development of a nuclear power plant.[71] Nuclear arms production requires enrichment of above 90 percent uranium-235.

SUMMARY

China has growing stakes in Iran, especially in the energy sector. It has been a consistent opponent of UN sanctions against Iran on the nuclear issue. However, despite China's and Iran's common historical experience of Western colonialism, China has been careful not to overplay its hand in challenging the United States on the key issues that plague U.S.-Iran relations, most notably nuclear activities, terrorism, and antagonism toward Israel and efforts to derail an Arab-Israeli peace. There is little to suggest that Iran could count on China for anything more than rhetoric if a serious crisis between the United States and Iran were to arise.

CHINA AND THE ARAB COUNTRIES

China has developed close bilateral ties with key Arab countries, especially in the Gulf and the Horn of Africa, and it also has established formal ties with all Arab states belonging to the Arab League. In January 2004, during President Hu Jintao's meeting with the Arab League in Cairo, the Sino-Arab Cooperation Forum was founded to promote Sino-Arab economic ties and cultural understanding and to maintain "mutual respect."[72] While the creation of the forum attracted a great deal of attention from the Arab and Chinese media, the West seems to have seen little significance in the high-level meetings between China and the Arab League.

Since the inaugural meeting, China and the Arab League have met five more times, in the Middle East and China.[73] The forum is used primarily to deepen economic ties, particularly in energy.[74] In 2005, more than 1,000 entrepreneurs and government officials attended a conference promoting investment in areas such as finance, energy, and machinery.[75] The forum resulted in more than $400 million in trade agreements and a Chinese pledge to build a power station in Sudan.[76] In 2006, Arab and Chinese representatives pledged to increase bilateral trade to $100 billion by 2010.[77] During the most recent forum, in May 2009, both sides emphasized their shared cultural values, such as the wish to build a just world, and Arab-Sino scientific cooperation.[78]

The Arab League and China have also sought to use the forum to deepen their cooperation on political issues. The 2006 forum concluded with a joint communiqué pledging to expand cooperation on anti-terrorism efforts.[79] In a significant recognition by China of Hamas's legitimacy, a senior member of Hamas attended the meeting, over U.S. and Israeli objections.[80] Discussions at the 2007 forum returned to the Arab-Israeli issue, and the two sides reiterated their belief in the rights of Palestinians and the need for a peaceful resolution to the conflict.[81]

China and the Arab League appear to be satisfied with the progress made at meetings of the Sino-Arab Cooperation Forum. In 2009 China's assistant foreign minister, Zhai Jun, and Sudan's ambassador to the Arab League, Abdel-Moneim Mabrouk, praised the "fruitful achievements" of the forum since its founding, and Zhai remarked that China and the Arab countries, both in a critical stage of development, should foster even closer ties.[82] Given the forum's record of success and their shared interests, it is likely that China and the Arab League will continue to use the forum to foster closer economic and political bonds. However, given the Arab League's long history of ineffectiveness in advancing pan-Arab causes, the forum must be seen primarily as perhaps necessary but not very substantial political window dressing.

CHINA AND SAUDI ARABIA

Saudi Arabia and China established diplomatic ties in 1990 and have since seen impressive growth in their economic and political relationships. Before 1990, pragmatic cooperation formed the backbone of Sino-Saudi relations; in fact, the countries' defense relationship began when Saudi Arabia bought intermediate-range ballistic missiles from China in the late 1980s, before they had diplomatic relations.[83] Economic ties centering on energy resources have been the primary driver of the relationship, although political ties have become increasingly close in recent years. High-level diplomatic contact has increased, with King Abdullah bin Abdul Aziz visiting

China in January 2006 and President Hu Jintao returning the visit in April of the same year[84] and again in February 2009.[85]

Saudi-Chinese Trade.   Trade between the two states has grown significantly, increasing 59 percent in 2005 and hitting $14.5 billion in the first eleven months of that year. In 2007, bilateral trade between the two reached $25 billion for the year.[86] The growth in trade has allowed Saudi Arabia to overtake Angola as China's largest source of oil, despite the fact that Angola and other West African nations offer sweet crude, which most of China's refineries are able to process, rather than sour crude (oil with a high sulfur content), which Saudi Arabia produces.[87] The Saudi company SABIC (Saudi Basic Industries Corporation) alone exports $2 billion in petrochemicals to China yearly.[88]

Because of the increased trade between the two, Saudi Arabia has emerged as a major investor in China. Saudi Arabia's Aramco Overseas Company has invested $750 million of the total $3 billion needed for the construction of a petrochemical complex in southeastern Fujian Province that will process 8 million tons of Saudi crude oil. In addition, several members of the Organization of the Petroleum Exporting Countries (OPEC), including Saudi Arabia and Kuwait, intend to build a new refinery in Guangzhou, the capital of Guangdong province, involving a total investment of $8 billion.[89] The Saudis are eager to invest in such projects to secure their status as a major oil provider to China, and their contribution is expected to continue to grow with the anticipated dramatic increase in China's demand for energy over the coming years. In 2005, Saudi Arabia accounted for approximately 17 percent of China's oil imports, or about 440,000 barrels a day.[90] Although China continued to import just over 17 percent of its oil from Saudi Arabia in 2007, the number of barrels imported increased by 332 percent, to 1.9 million barrels a day, reflecting the growth of China's demand for energy.[91]

Fueled by that increase in oil consumption, trade between the two nations has increased significantly. In April 2006, China's commerce ministry announced that Sino-Saudi trade volume hit $2.7 billion in the first two months of 2006, a 43 percent increase from the same period in 2005.[92] It is not just oil-related companies that are contributing to the growth in trade; major Saudi companies such as SABIC, SAGIA (Saudi Arabian General Investment Authority), and Saudi Arabian Airlines have established offices in China in recent years.[93] China also invested $1.1 billion in Saudi Arabia in 2006 after investing only negligible amounts since 2000.[94] In 2009 China

Railway Company won a bid to build a $1.8 billion monorail in Mecca to move pilgrims around.[95]

Saudi Arabia and China's Strategic Oil Reserves. Four aboveground oil storage facilities have been or are planned to be built in China, in Zhenhai and Zhoushan in Zhejiang Province, in Qingdao in Shandong Province, and in Dalian in Liaoning Province. The facilities initially will have 10 to 12 million tons of storage capacity; after the second phase of development, they will have 28 million tons of storage capacity. In summer 2006, China began building underground oil storage facilities. The first of several planned facilities is being built in Zhangjiang in Guangdong Province, a location chosen for its port infrastructure and for its proximity to two refineries, Maoming and Dongxing. The Zhangjiang storage facility, expected to be complete by 2010, will hold 7 million cubic meters of oil; construction will cost $287.5 million.[96] These strategic oil reserve depots, which are for both civil and military contingency use, are located near major Chinese navy bases, both for their protection and for use during wartime. Zhoushan, Zhenhai, Qingdao, Dalian, and Zhangjiang are all major navy bases.

In the long run, China hopes to have a reserve of 800 million barrels—larger than the United States has ever possessed (the largest U.S. reserve was 700.7 million barrels, in August 2005). Saudi Arabia can choose either to sell China oil for its storage facilities or to fill the reserve with Saudi oil that still belongs to Saudi Arabia. The second approach would give Saudi Arabia more flexibility and a large storage facility in the second-largest oil market in the world.[97] Saudi oil certainly will not supply the entire reserve because China can (or should) store only so much Saudi crude oil, the sour nature of which does not suit China's refineries.[98] That being said, China is planning to build a strategic oil reserve filled primarily with Saudi oil. Sweet crude is normally used for producing gasoline and kerosene, which is efficient and more productive than cracking high-sulfur crude. Heavy, sour crude is used for bunker fuel (fuel used to power ship and aircraft engines) or for energy production.

Sinopec—China's second-largest oil producer—and Saudi Aramco signed a deal in 2007 to upgrade a refinery along with ExxonMobil in Fujian Province. The $3.5 billion upgrade will allow the refinery to process heavier Saudi crude oil. The deal includes plans to distribute diesel and gasoline from the refinery in Fujian.[99] ExxonMobil and Saudi Aramco will each have a 25 percent stake in the refinery.[100] In 2006, Saudi Aramco began engineering work with Sinopec on a second refinery in the port city of Qing-dao.[101] In May 2008 the first delivery of 2 million barrels of Saudi crude oil arrived at the facility; two months of testing were to follow before major commercial operations began.[102] Once fully operational, the facility will be able to refine 200,000 barrels a day of Saudi crude oil, along with hydro-refining kerosene and gas oil and undertaking other processes.[103]

During Hu Jintao's April 2006 visit to Saudi Arabia, there was discussion of a $5.2 billion joint Saudi-Chinese project to build a refinery and petro-chemical complex in China. SABIC would build the petrochemical complex and the Chinese company Dalian Shide would build the refinery.[104] Since Hu's visit, negotiations between the corporations appear to have stalled.

In May 2006, SABIC confirmed it was in negotiations with Sinopec for an approximately $1 billion petrochemical plant (ethylene complex) in China.[105] In June 2008, it was announced that costs would be in the region of $2.5 billion for the petrochemical facility, to be located in the northern Chinese city of Tianjin. The Tianjin facility is expected to produce 4 million tons of petrochemical products, 1.2 million of which will be ethylene.[106] While Saudi Arabia is looking to gain access to China's wholesale oil prod-ucts market, Sinopec wants to build a refinery in Saudi Arabia that can pro-cess up to 12 million metric tons. China is also drilling for gas in the Saudi desert following a March 2004 gas drilling deal between Sinopec and Saudi Aramco. In April 2006, Sinopec and Saudi Aramco signed agreements that strengthened their cooperation in gas exploration.[107]

Military Cooperation.   As mentioned, Sino-Saudi defense relations began in the 1980s before the two nations had diplomatic ties. In response to the U.S. refusal to sell Saudi Arabia long-range fuel tanks for its F-15 fighters, Saudi Arabia brokered a deal with China to acquire between fifty and sixty nuclear-payload-capable CSS-2 intermediate-range (1,864 miles) ballistic missiles capable of reaching central Libya to the west, southern Russia to the north, and India to the east.[108] Upon learning of the transaction, the Reagan administration reprimanded the Saudis and demanded access to the missiles in order to inspect them, a demand that the Saudis adamantly refused.[109] The United States was concerned because the missiles originally were designed to carry nuclear warheads. Both China and Saudi Arabia made assurances that those particular missiles would carry a conventional payload, but the limited accuracy of the missile made that claim somewhat dubious. The missile's circular error probability (CEP)—the diameter of the circle within which half of the missiles are expected to land—of 1 to 1.5 miles makes it an inadequate conventional weapon.[110] As one commentator put it, "The Chinese in essence hoodwinked the Saudis into buying an antique missile system worthless without its nuclear warhead."[111]

The missiles were delivered to Saudi Arabia in 1988, but there has been no documented evidence of similar transactions since then.[112] Nonetheless, there is speculation that the Sino-Saudi strategic relationship has continued to grow. One expert, Robert Mullins, estimates that since the early 1990s China has based at least 1,000 of its military advisers at Saudi missile installations.[113] Press reports have suggested that Beijing has approached Riyadh with offers to sell more modern missile systems, such as the 373-mile range CSS-6 and the 1,118-mile range CSS-5 solid-fueled missiles, as well as the 3,418-mile range CSS-3 intercontinental ballistic missile, which is essentially a longer-range version of the CSS-2.[114] Considering that the original deal for the CSS-2 missiles is thought to have been in the range of $3 to 3.5 billion, it is apparent that China would be interested in doing business with Saudi Arabia again, especially since the Chinese, as one of the world's few suppliers of such technology, can demand a cash transaction.

In addition to the bilateral military relationship between China and Saudi Arabia, there are reports that the Saudis have reached an agreement with Pakistani authorities to station nuclear weapons on Saudi soil in the event that Iran develops a nuclear bomb. The weapons, which would be fitted with a new generation of Chinese-supplied ballistic missiles, would probably be under Pakistani control.[115] If the reports are correct, what has happened, in essence, is that Saudi Arabia has funded Pakistan's missile and nuclear programs through the purchase of military technology from China. If so, Riyadh could be covertly buying its own nuclear capability from China, using Pakistan as a conduit.[116]

CHINA AND THE SMALL GULF STATES

Although China's relations with the small Gulf states are not as extensive or as intimate as India's, China has nevertheless made remarkable progress in developing agreements and business ties with them. In July 2004, China and the Gulf Cooperation Council (GCC) agreed to begin talks on a free trade agreement. China has an obvious stake in the region's oil, and the agreement would provide a huge market for Chinese manufacturing companies. The GCC states have an interest in gaining access to Chinese goods such as clothing, fabrics, electronics, and telecommunications products.

Although the United States would never refuse to support the agreement, Washington is wary of the negotiations, which could drive a wedge between the United States and the GCC states with which it has lucrative alliances.

Completing a free trade agreement with the GCC states is of special importance because more than 40 percent of China's oil comes from the GCC's six member states. China and the GCC held their third round of talks July 19–22, 2006, and while no agreement was reached, both sides urged that the talks move forward and hoped to conclude negotiations in early 2010.[117] In May 2008, China's foreign minister, Yang Jiechi, commented on the ongoing negotiations: "The two sides have been conducting the FTA talks, and we both are willing to accelerate the negotiation process so as to reach a deal based on mutual benefit as soon as possible."[118]

China and Oman. Trade between China and Oman has been important to both countries. A number of Chinese porcelain pots have been found in Oman dating back to the third millennium BCE, indicating that Chinese goods had found their way to the Middle East.[119] In the tenth century, Arab culture began to spread across the Asian continent as far as the eastern portions of China as Muslim conquerors brought Islam and trade to the region.[120]

Since the two countries established formal diplomatic ties in 1978, their relationship has been stable and growing.[121] According to Chinese statistics, China-Oman trade volume was $1.51 billion in 2002. Exports to Oman were valued at $60 million and imports at $1.45 billion.[122] At the China-Oman trade fair held in the autumn of 2005 in Beijing, Maqbool bin Ali bin Sultan, the Omani minister of commerce, industry, and mining, said that trade between the two countries reached $4.5 billion in 2004.[123] China was the main importer of Omani crude oil in 2004, accounting for 40.3 percent of exports.[124]

A number of high-level exchanges between the two nations have occurred over the years, facilitating further economic agreements. In 2002, delegations from the two countries met to discuss cooperation on national infrastructure construction in Oman and foreign relations.[125] Celebrating the twenty-fifth anniversary of official ties in 2003, diplomats from both countries held a meeting in which they traced their friendly relations back 2,000 years to the time of the Silk Road. One year later, in August 2004, the Omani government and Sinopec signed an energy accord for development of the southern part of Oman, solidifying plans to explore crude oil and natural gas blocks in the area. Sinopec is expected to spend $22 million in energy exploration, with the option of increasing $29 million more in investment.[126]

In December 2005, Oman Oil Company entered a share subscription agreement to purchase 8 percent of issued shares of China Gas Holdings Limited, the company's first direct investment in China. Since then, the two companies have continued to expand their areas of cooperation. In 2006, China Gas received a rare import-export license to help facilitate Omani investment in liquefied natural gas.[127] In May 2007, China Gas and Oman Oil set up a 50-50 joint venture for Chinese energy imports.[128] China Gas's primary engagements are in investment, operation, and management of city gas pipeline infrastructure, along with distribution of gas, operation of oil stations, and development of oil- and gas-related technologies.[129]

China and Qatar.   Qatar supports a free trade policy and is an active member of the GCC. Asia is the main market for Qatari products, and China is one of its top buyers of energy products. In May 2005, Qatar began talks with China to sell LNG to the China National Offshore Oil Corporation (CNOOC), China's top offshore oil and gas producer. Qatar, which is home to the world's third-largest gas reserves, plans to export 77 million tons globally by 2012. In total, China is expected to import approximately 20 million tons of LNG a year by 2010.[130] Qatar Associated Fertilizers Corporation exports the largest amount of commodities to China.[131]

In 2005, Qatar celebrated the first anniversary of the Qatar Airways route to Beijing by increasing the number of flights offered in order to accommodate the growing demand for travel between the two nations that has resulted from increasing economic ties. By April 2008, Qatar Airways was offering twenty flights a week to Chinese cities, including Shanghai, Hong Kong, and Guangzhou.[132] Diplomats have claimed that the additional connections will build and strengthen solid trade and commercial relationships between China and Qatar.[133] In June 2006, China and Qatar also agreed to expand military cooperation. They will look into joint military exercises and exchange of military equipment, along with the possibility of having China train Qatar's armed forces.[134]

China and the UAE.   The United Arab Emirates and China established diplomatic relations on November 1, 1984, and they have since developed their bilateral relationship through a number of high-level exchanges and accords, including the following: the Sino-UAE Agreement on Cultural Cooperation in 1989, the Agreement on Medical and Health Technical Cooperation between the Ministries of Health of China and the United Arab Emirates in 1992, the Protocol on China's Sending Doctors to the United Arab Emirates in 1992, the Protocol on China's Further Sending Nurses to the United Arab Emirates in 1992, the Sino-UAE Agreement on Judiciary Extradition in May 2002, and the Sino-UAE Agreement on Information and Cultural Cooperation in 2002. China and the UAE have cooperated in the field of aviation as well, signing the Sino-Sharjah Bilateral Aviation Agreement in 1980 and the Sino-UAE Agreement on Civil Air Transportation in 1989.

In September 2005, the Chinese Foreign Ministry urged the UAE to end official contacts with Taiwan. Chinese officials stated that the UAE had allowed then-Taiwanese leader Chen Shui-bian to pass through the country and carry out political activities, violating its stated commitment to the one-China policy.[135]

The growth of economic ties between the two countries has increased since the mid-1980s. In 2002, bilateral trade volume was $3.4 million, with China exporting $3 million and importing $445,000. In 2003, the UAE was China's second-largest Middle Eastern trading partner. The major exports to the United Arab Emirates were textile products, clothes, industrial and metallic products, handicrafts, and machinery, while China's major imports from the Emirates were aluminum, chemical fertilizer, petroleum, and polyethylene. The countries have a history of labor-service cooperation, which has developed in recent years into service contracts in the industrial and retail sectors, construction, and medical care centers.[136]

China is a major trading partner of the UAE, and China's presence in the Middle East is especially notable in Dubai, one of the UAE's most economically active cities. The most visible aspect of China's presence is the Dragon Mart, a huge shopping and trading hub encompassing showrooms, restaurants, warehouses, office areas, and a business center.[137] The complex, which opened in 2004, covers an area of 82 square miles (in the shape of a dragon), making it the largest Chinese commercial center outside China. Dragon Mart also serves as a de facto cultural exhibit for China in the UAE, offering visitors, whether Chinese or Middle Eastern, a unique experience and a glimpse into Chinese culture and traditional products.

China and Kuwait.   China and Kuwait established diplomatic ties on March 22, 1971, making Kuwait the GCC country with the longest diplomatic relationship with China.[138] A demonstration of the closeness of that relationship came in 1991, when Kuwait sought to sign a security agreement with China similar to the ten-year agreement that it had signed with the United States earlier that year.[139]

Like all countries that recognize China, Kuwait has pledged its support for the one-China policy and for any efforts that China undertakes to guard its national sovereignty, including preventing Taiwan, Xinjiang, or Tibet from declaring independence. Kuwait has also stated its support for China's efforts to solve the North Korean nuclear issue.[140] In return, China has pledged support for Kuwait's efforts to ensure its independence, sovereignty, and territorial integrity.[141]

In 2002, bilateral trade between China and Kuwait totaled $727 million.[142] Of all the GCC states, Kuwait has been the largest supplier of preferential official loans to China. From 1982 to the end of 2001, the Kuwait Fund for Arab Economic Development gave China $620 million in favorable loans.[143] During the Kuwaiti prime minister's visit to China in 2004, the two countries promoted two-way investment and trade, furthering that connection. Three agreements were signed, on economic and technology cooperation, oil and natural gas, and environmental protection.[144] In April 2004, China and the GCC agreed to implement a free trade policy. The Chinese premier and the Kuwaiti prime minister jointly met with the delegation of finance ministers from the six member countries of the GCC; before the meeting, the ministers held separate talks and signed an agreement on bilateral economic and technical cooperation.[145] The National Bank of Kuwait, the largest Kuwaiti bank and the most highly rated in the Middle East, also opened a branch office in Shanghai in 2005, and Kuwait was the largest single investor in the 2006 initial public offering (IPO) of the Industrial and Commercial Bank of China (ICBC). Ahead of the event, the Kuwait Investment Authority stated its intention to buy up $720 million worth of shares in the project;[146] as a result, Kuwait owns roughly 3 percent of ICBC shares (the offering was a record $21.9 billion).

The economic and commercial counselor at the Chinese embassy in Kuwait claimed that bilateral trade between China and Kuwait hit $2.7 billion in 2006, a large increase from $1.6 billion in 2005, which was attributed mostly to the oil industry.[147] Sinopec, which has imported crude oil from Kuwait since the signing of a long-term supply agreement in 1998, has also been in talks with Kuwait about setting up more projects in upstream and downstream oil sectors.[148] Kuwait Petroleum Corporation (KPC) opened an office in Beijing in early 2005, stating that it was in talks with every one of China's large oil companies on furthering cooperation. KPC still hopes to participate in the long-term development of China's oil industry through joint ventures in the realms of crude oil refining, petrochemicals, and infrastructure, and Kuwait has vowed to increase its oil exports to China and daily crude production capacity to 4 million barrels by 2020.[149]

In December 2005, Kuwait entered into negotiations to build an $8 to $9 billion refinery and petrochemical plant with an expected daily capacity of 300,000 barrels in southern China.[150] This deal, which was the biggest Chinese joint venture with a foreign entity in the petrochemicals industry to date, was finalized in 2006.[151]

Also in 2006, China sought assistance from Kuwait to invest in downstream infrastructure, including oil refineries and petrochemicals, with the goal of boosting domestic capacity.[152] The project, however, has been stalled, due to environmental concerns over the plants' proposed location. In May 2009, Sheikh Ahmed al-Abdullah, the Kuwaiti oil minister, visited China to discuss the matter, but the issue remains unresolved and talks are ongoing.[153]

CHINA AND CENTRAL ASIA

China is taking a more proactive role in Central Asia. It has been close with Pakistan for many years, funding or supporting various infrastructure projects as a means of fostering a strategic alliance within reach of the Persian Gulf. It also has taken the initiative to help settle border disputes among several of the Central Asian states and has formed an organization that will further diplomatic ties with those states. China stands to benefit as its sphere of influence expands into the region.

When the Central Asian states became independent in 1991, China focused its attention on developing security, political, and financial ties with the region. China played a leading role in the 1991 development of the Shanghai Five, which was formed to settle border disputes between China, Russia, Tajikistan, Kazakhstan, and Kyrgyzstan. The Shanghai Five later expanded to become the Shanghai Cooperation Organization (SCO), whose current activities include undertaking joint military training between member states, facilitating stable economic relationships in the region, and broadening cultural ties between its members.

Through the SCO and its bilateral ties with the individual states of Central Asia, China has made significant progress in its quest to gain greater influence in the region. From 1992 to 2005, total trade between China and Central Asia increased from approximately $465 million to $7.7 billion.[154] China has also made a great deal of progress in securing its oil- and natural gas–related financial assets in the region. In fact, Chinese national oil companies (NOCs) have had greater success acquiring energy assets in the region than any other Asian nation, and since the companies are state controlled, they have been the benefactors of amicable government foreign policy toward Central Asia.[155] China has used its diplomatic muscle to facilitate business transactions by supporting the bids of Kazakhstan and Uzbekistan for membership in the World Trade Organization (WTO), offering lucrative aid packages, and supporting security crackdowns by repressive Central Asian regimes.[156]

CHINA AND UZBEKISTAN

The relationship between China and Uzbekistan has centered on security issues and the development of Uzbekistan's natural gas reserves, the eighteenth-largest in the world.[157] Furthermore, that dissident and separatist organizations are operating in both countries provides opportunities for greater political and military cooperation in matters of security. China has also signed many energy agreements with Uzbekistan, beginning with the 2004 contract between the China National Petroleum Corporation (CNPC) and Uzbekneftegaz, Uzbekistan's national oil company. Important infrastructure development projects also are under way between the two nations.

Diplomatic and Security Cooperation. China and Uzbekistan both face domestic opposition from Islamist groups. China's foremost concern has been Uighur separatists in Xinjiang province. The stateless Uighurs are a Muslim-Turkic group located in pockets throughout Central Asia that historically have sought to establish a separate Uighur state in Xinjiang province.[158] For over a decade, Islamic militants have orchestrated terrorist attacks against Chinese troops and civilian targets and sought to undermine political and social stability. Riots in July 2009 killed many hundreds of Han Chinese and Uighurs and led to a state of emergency.

Since 1991, China has pressed the Central Asian governments to crack down on Uighur-led separatist activities within their states. Uzbekistan, which has a large Uighur population, has been especially compliant in repressing the group's activities, prohibiting any Uighur political organizations. Following Uzbekistan's admission into the SCO, Uzbek president Islam Karimov prohibited all pro-Uighur and anti-Chinese messages within Uzbekistan, viewing any such message as harmful to Sino-Uzbek relations.[159]

Furthermore, Uzbekistan is receiving Chinese political and military support in combating its own Islamic insurgency, the Islamic Movement of Uzbekistan (IMU). The IMU launched an insurgency against the Uzbek government in 1991, after President Karimov refused to acquiesce to IMU demands to impose Islamic sharia law. In response to numerous attacks from the IMU, Karimov instituted a crackdown on all opposition groups. His government is especially suspicious of Islamic organizations preaching anything other than the state-sanctioned version of Islam.

Tashkent and Beijing became increasingly alarmed when it was discovered that militant Uighurs were training at IMU bases in Uzbekistan. Cooperation between the two organizations has spawned fears in China that if the IMU succeeds in toppling the Uzbek government, the Uighurs not only will receive greater material support from Uzbekistan but will be further emboldened in their efforts to establish an independent state in Xinjiang.[160] In 2000 and 2001, China gave Uzbekistan $1.3 million in military aid, including sniper rifles, bulletproof vests, and other material assets. After releasing a joint statement in 2004 condemning terrorism, extremism, and separatism, China announced that it would give Uzbekistan an additional $2.5 million in humanitarian assistance.[161] China and Uzbekistan have also held joint military exercises through the SCO. The latest of those, which occurred in August 2007, involved some 6,500 troops from SCO member states in a nine-day exercise focused on counterterrorism drills; it took place in the Xinjiang region in China.[162]

China and Uzbekistan also have also been building close diplomatic ties. In addition to supporting measures against terrorist organizations, both governments have supported controversial actions taken by the other. In 2005, China threw its support behind Karimov after the brutal suppression of a popular uprising in the Uzbek city of Andijan. China continues to support Karimov's claim that only 187 civilians were killed in the government's response to the uprising, despite Western estimates that place the number of dead at 750.[163] Furthermore, China supports Uzbekistan's refusal to allow an international investigation into the event. Following the uprising, Karimov drew sharp criticism from the U.S. government and other Western leaders. Repeated U.S. demands for an investigation led Uzbekistan to urge

China and the other SCO countries to call for the removal of U.S. troops from Karshi-Khanabad airbase in Uzbekistan, an important asset for U.S. efforts in Afghanistan. U.S. forces formally withdrew from the airbase in December 2005.

In November 2007 China's premier, Wen Jiabao, met with Karimov in Tashkent. During the meeting Karimov reiterated his support for the one-China policy, pledging to support Chinese efforts to combat the Uighur national liberation movement and the Chinese stance on the issue of Taiwan and Tibet. Wen also stated that only countries within Central Asia should participate in ensuring its security and stability.[164]

Trade and Investment.   Uzbekistan's primary trade partner is Russia, with total trade equaling $4 billion in 2007, but China, with total trade exceeding $1 billion, is becoming a more important player. Some in the Uzbek government claim that Chinese officials have repeatedly expressed a desire to become Tashkent's top trade partner, displacing Russia.[165] Whether or not that is Beijing's true motivation, China is clearly attempting to enhance its trade status in Uzbekistan. In 2007, total direct Chinese investment in Uzbekistan was estimated at about $500 million; however, several additional projects have the potential to increase that to $1 billion.[166]

Uzbekistan's largest cash crop is cotton. Due to limited domestic production of textiles, Uzbekistan exports over 75 percent of its cotton yield each year.[167] While Europe is the primary destination, China has gradually increased its imports. Disagreement on the exact figure of Uzbek exports to China makes it difficult to estimate trade growth. In 2003, for instance, Uzbekistan claimed that only 4 percent of total exports to China were cotton, while Chinese officials assert that cotton accounted for 84 percent of imports from Uzbekistan.[168] Furthermore, imports from China by Uzbekistan are minimal compared with those by other Central Asian nations due to restrictive and protectionist trade practices by the Karimov government.[169] However, many expect that Sino-Uzbek cooperation in energy development will lead to better bilateral trade relations. The construction of a new railroad linking Uzbekistan, Kyrgyzstan, and China will facilitate trade as well.

China is far more interested in Uzbekistan's natural gas reserves than its cotton. Natural gas reserves in Uzbekistan are estimated to measure 66.2 trillion cubic feet, stemming from fifty-two gas fields in the country. Uzbekistan also has a small amount of oil (about 600 million barrels in proven reserves), which traditionally was used only for domestic consumption; however, the China National Petroleum Corporation has become increasingly interested in tapping that resource.

The first energy agreement between the two nations was signed in 2004, when CNPC signed contracts with Uzbekneftegaz. A year later the two companies signed a joint venture worth $600 million. In 2006 Uzbekneftegaz signed another deal, with the China National Oil and Gas Exploration and Development Corporation, worth $210 million for onshore exploration. CNPC also receives a 20 percent share in a production sharing agreement (PSA) for natural gas deposits in the Aral Sea with Lukoil, Petronas, and the Korea National Oil Corporation.[170]

International aid has also been an important component of Chinese-Uzbek relations. China provides financial assistance to Uzbekistan in the form of soft and interest-free loans. In 2008 the Export-Import Bank of China provided a $7.8 million loan through a credit line established for Central Asia by the SCO, and China has provided a total of $380 million to Uzbekistan for social and public utilities through the same line of credit.[171] Finally, Uzbekistan provided a small sum of humanitarian aid, in the form of tents, mattresses, pillows, and food, after the May 12, 2008, earthquake that devastated China's Sichuan province.

Infrastructure Development. China is currently engaged in several promising projects in Uzbekistan, including the construction of new gas pipelines, telecommunications infrastructure, and a railroad that will connect Uzbekistan, Kyrgyzstan, and China. In 2008, Uzbeknefetgaz and CNPC announced a joint venture to build a natural gas pipeline from Turkmenistan through Uzbekistan to China. The venture, named Asia Trans Gas, will include the building of a 330-mile pipeline that will carry approximately 30 billion cubic meters of natural gas from Turkmenistan to China.[172] The first section of the pipeline will be completed by December 31, 2009, with operations beginning in January 2010. The project, which will update Uzbekistan's poor pipeline infrastructure, will also break the monopoly that Russia currently holds on Turkmenistan's natural gas reserves.[173] China has also promised $35 million to develop natural gas infrastructure and update facilities already in Uzbekistan.

Telecommunications is another area of cooperation and infrastructure development between the two nations. In 2005, the responsible ministries of both nations concluded an agreement on telecom cooperation.[174] Since then numerous Chinese companies have teamed with their Uzbek counterparts in projects to develop telecommunications infrastructure. The Chinese telecom company Alcatel Shanghai Bell signed agreements in 2004 to digitize television broadcasting ($5.85 million), modernize and extend telecommunications networks ($4 million), and construct 400 ground components for satellite systems. Furthermore, one of China's largest telecom providers, Huawei Technologies, upgraded the telephone network of Uzbektelecom in 2005 and 2006, at a cost of $12.5 million.

Negotiations on a proposed railway system linking Uzbekistan, Kyrgyzstan, and China are in the final stages. After years of political gridlock, all sides now recognize that a rail link would improve the flow of trade in Central Asia. Construction of the railroad will have to overcome technical difficulties and challenging terrain as well as regional rivalries among the former republics of the Soviet Union. If completed, however, the railway would allow the Central Asian states to gain from China's rapid economic growth.[175]

CHINA AND KAZAKHSTAN

Kazakhstan's vast natural resources have attracted Chinese business interests since the end of the 1990s. With estimated oil reserves of 100 billion barrels (30 billion barrels of proved reserves)[176] and 85 trillion cubic feet of natural gas, Kazakhstan has some of the largest unexplored and untapped energy reserves in the world.[177] While China seeks to capitalize on those reserves, it is unlikely that it will dominate the Kazakh energy sector any time soon due to competition from the United States and Russia. Furthermore, Kazakhstan's president, Nursultan Nazarbayev, seems content to pursue a "multivector" policy that "skillfully balances the major powers' interests in the region" and diversifies investment in the energy sector.[178] That will prevent any one country or company from dominating the energy sector and exerting too much influence over Kazakhstan.[179]

While China's main interest in Kazakhstan is its energy reserves, it has also sought to establish political, economic, and infrastructure ties there. Their "strategic partnership," established in 2005, has received widespread coverage in the international media. Ranging from transnational infrastructure projects to bilateral diplomatic exchanges, strategic ties between the two nations are rapidly expanding. Currently, China is one of Kazakhstan's largest trade partners, and it is becoming an important external player in Kazakh affairs.

Political Ties.   Kazakhstan and China were founding members of the Shanghai Five. Their early relationship, characterized by border disputes and Kazakh nuclear disarmament, was mainly political and played out within the framework of the Shanghai Cooperation Organization, the successor to the Shanghai Five. Early political agreements between the two included a 1995 Chinese security guarantee to Kazakhstan in exchange for nuclear disarmament, a border demarcation agreement in 1998, and an agreement on the use and protection of shared rivers along the China-Kazakh border in 2001. Those agreements paved the way for increased cooperation in the areas of economics, trade, and energy.

The most important development in bilateral relations was the 2006 China-Kazakhstan Cooperation Strategy for the Twenty-First Century, which outlines future cooperation in the spheres of politics, economics, security, culture, and international affairs. The document included a preliminary agreement for Chinese funding of an oil pipeline in Kazakhstan worth $292.8 million.[180]

Kazakhstan and China have also participated in joint military exercises under the auspices of the SCO. In 2006, SCO counterterrorism exercises were held in Kazakhstan's eastern Almaty region. Although militant Islamist activity is negligible in Kazakhstan, its leadership is paranoid about the possibility. China has used that fear to secure Nazarbayev's cooperation in fighting what it calls the "three evils"— extremism, terrorism, and separatism.[181] Furthermore, Nazarbayev looks to the Chinese for support in repressing opposition groups under the guise of combating terrorism, support that is not forthcoming from his Western allies and friends. However, it should be noted that Kazakhstan has conducted a series of joint exercises with NATO forces called Steppe Eagle, which are based on peacekeeping operations, and it has deployed a small contingent of troops to Iraq.[182] Kazakhstan is pursuing a multivector policy in security cooperation as well as in its energy sector.

Trade and Investment.   Since the late 1990s, China has sought to increase its economic ties with Kazakhstan. Increases in bilateral trade, the development of a tax-free trade center along the border, and Chinese investment in the Kazakh energy sector characterize recent economic relations between the two countries. Kazakhstan is China's largest trading partner among the former Soviet states of Central Asia.

China is Kazakhstan's third-largest trade partner, accounting for 15 percent of Kazakhstan's total trade in 2006.[183] In 2005, total bilateral trade hit $6 billion.[184] Kazakh exports to China include steel, oil, wheat, and meat. To facilitate trade, in 2006 China and Kazakhstan began construction of the China-Kazakhstan Korgas International Border Cooperation Center, located in a zone that will cover 4.63 square kilometers in Korgas, Kazakhstan, and Xinjiang province, China.[185] Goods and services traded at the center will benefit from import duty and tariff exemptions, promoting economic and trade cooperation between the two countries.[186] Both countries aim to increase bilateral trade to $15 billion by 2015.[187]

Energy Acquisitions.   Chinese companies both cooperate and compete with U.S., Indian, Russian, and European oil companies for partial or complete ownership in energy development projects in Kazakhstan. In 1997, China's CNPC acquired a 60.7 percent stake in the Aktobe oil field in northwest Kazakhstan. That was China's first large acquisition of a Kazakh oil asset and marked the beginning of plans to construct a pipeline from Atasu, Kazakhstan, to Xinjiang province.[188] Since then, China has done its best to secure access to and ownership of Kazakh oil reserves, an effort that included CNPC's 2003 purchase of the North Buzach oil and gas field. PetroKazakhstan, a Canadian-based company and Kazakhstan's largest supplier of refined products, is the largest company that CNPC has purchased. In August 2005, after a long bidding period, CNPC was awarded the company for $4.18 billion.

PetroKazakhstan's oil fields, which are located in central Kazakhstan, lie along the path of the Kazakhstan-China oil pipeline. The fields have proven reserves of only 340 million barrels, and many experts say China overpaid for the company.[189] At $55 per share, CNPC's pledge was 21 percent more than the market price at the time. Bidding such a high price for PetroKazakhstan signals China's willingness to pay for influence and resources in the region. In February 2006, CNPC was forced to sell 33 percent of its holdings back to Kazakh state-owned KazMunaiGas and establish a joint venture between the companies as part of the original purchase deal for PetroKazakhstan.[190]

Energy Infrastructure Projects.   Plans for a Kazakhstan-China oil pipeline began in 1997, after China acquired a large share in the development of the Aktobe oil field. The first phase of the project, completed in 2005, resulted in the first pipeline to connect the two countries, stretching from Atasu, Kazakhstan, to the Alataw Pass in Xinjiang province. With a capacity of 20 million tons a year, the pipeline is an important asset to China, providing it with a major artery for overland energy delivery.[191] Since the pipeline does not traverse a third country, it provides a safe and stable source of energy that will be less susceptible to interruption than the Strait of Malacca, which carries roughly 80 percent of China's oil imports. China, which fears that the strait could one day be closed to Chinese shipments, has been aggressively attempting to diversify its sources of oil to reduce its reliance on that strategic choke point. The pipeline also will provide energy directly to China's western provinces, rural areas that have not seen the benefits of China's recent growth and that suffer from energy shortages.

In 2007, China and Kazakhstan agreed to begin the final phase of the project, which will connect the Atasu-Alataw pipeline to the Caspian Sea. The final stage, which will be complete in 2011, will stretch 3,000 kilometers across Kazakhstan, from the Caspian Sea to Xinjiang province in China. Once the new section is open, Kazakh oil exports to China through the pipeline will increase from 85,000 to 200,000 barrels per day.[192]

CNPC and KazMunaiGaz have also developed plans to build a natural gas pipeline that will run from the Turkmenistan-Uzbek border through Kazakhstan and into China. The first phase of the Turkmenistan-Kazakhstan-China pipeline, which will be completed in 2009, will have an annual capacity of 10 billion cubic meters. In 2012, the second phase of the project will be complete, increasing annual capacity to 30 billion cubic meters. In total, the pipeline will run 1,100 miles and cost $7.31 billion. According to KazMunaiGas, "This project would help transport gas to China and diversify Kazakhstan's gas export routes."[193]

Other Infrastructure Projects. In September 2006, China opened twenty-two new passenger and cargo roads between China and Kazakhstan, for a total of sixty-four highway routes between the two countries (thirty-three for passengers, thirty-one for cargo). Kazakhstan is the Central Asian republic most connected with China.[194] In June 2006, the World Bank announced that it would finance a $2.5 billion road project connecting Asia and Europe that will run through Kazakhstan. The project is part of a larger venture to upgrade a 2,800-kilometer corridor from the Sino-Kazakh border to Kazakhstan's border with Russia. The upgrades are expected to boost Kazakh trade and infrastructure connections with China and other Asian nations.[195]

In May 2008, a new passenger rail extending 1,898 kilometers between Kazakhstan and China officially opened. One round trip is offered every

week from the Kazakh capital to the capital of Xinjiang province. Furthermore, in 2004 the Kazakh rail company, Temir Zholy, announced that it
would build a 2,450-mile rail system running from Urumqui, China, through
Kazakhstan, Turkmenistan, Iran, and Turkey to Hamburg, Germany. The
project, now under way, will be complete in 2010; its cost is estimated at $5
billion to $7 billion.[196]

CHINA AND TURKMENISTAN

Like those of many other Middle Eastern and Central Asian states, relations between Turkmenistan and China date back to the Silk Road. Historically, Turkmenistan had been occupied by groups of nomadic herders,
and their lack of unity allowed Imperial Russia to invade the territory and
officially assume control in 1894.[197] Russia maintained tight control on the
country, and after the Bolshevik Revolution of 1917, Turkmenistan was
named one of the fifteen Soviet republics. With the collapse of the Soviet
Union on October 27, 1991, Turkmenistan declared its independence.[198]

During the "colonial" years and the first few years after independence,
Turkmenistan was virtually dependent on Russia for trade routes. Turkmenistan is one of the top fifteen gas producers in the world, but until very
recently Russia held a monopoly on gas and oil pipelines in the country and
exerted strong control over the Turkmen energy sector.[199] Although China
established official relations with Turkmenistan in 1992, trade between the
two was minuscule at the time. Diplomatic visits between heads of state
have helped strengthen ties between the two; however, in comparison with
Uzbekistan and especially Kazakhstan, interaction between China and Turkmenistan has been lacking. Reasons include the strong hold that Russia has
maintained over the country and former president Saparmurad Niyazov's
eccentric and erratic personality. Niyazov's death in 2006 sparked renewed
interest in Turkmenistan from Asian and Western actors. While discussions
have covered topics ranging from politics to economics to telecommunications, the focus of bilateral relations is the transport of and trade in oil and
gas.[200] Both China and Turkmenistan see the strategic, economic, and security benefits of strong bilateral relations.

Political Ties.   Turkmenistan, which declared a policy of neutrality in
1995, is the only Central Asian country that is not a full member of the
Shanghai Cooperation Organization, although it is likely to be the next
state admitted. However, it is unknown when the next round of accessions

will occur. China and Turkmenistan have maintained an ambivalent political relationship. In April 2006 Niyazov visited China for the first time in eight years, bringing a contract for a China-Turkmen pipeline that supposedly would be complete in 2009. The agreement also included a Chinese low-interest loan to Turkmenistan for the purchase of Chinese drilling equipment.[201] Since Niyazov's death, the new president, Gurbaguly Berdimuhamedov, has been working to build stronger ties, advocating cooperation to defeat terrorism, separatism, and extremism. China is intent on maintaining stable and peaceful borders, and Turkmenistan has agreed not to support Uighur separatist movements. Turkmenistan worries that helping Uighur separatists would have spillover effects in the country and upset peaceful conditions. The Turkmen government has promised to support China in all cases involving separatism, including the case of Taiwan, and recognizes the People's Republic of China as the only legitimate government within the country.

Economic Ties. Turkmenistan has large oil and natural gas reserves, and since establishing diplomatic ties in 1992, China has grown closer to Turkmenistan in hopes of gaining access to those resources. Turkmenistan's oil and natural gas must travel through Russian pipelines to reach export markets, and there is speculation that the Turkmen government has grown increasingly frustrated with the control that Russia exerts on the Turkmen energy sector. While Turkmenistan has proven oil reserves of 600 million barrels and the fourteenth-largest natural gas reserves in the world,[202] estimated at 100 trillion cubic feet (tons per cubic foot), it has been forced to sell its oil through Russian pipelines, diminishing its control over prices.[203] Russian pressure was illustrated in 2003 when Turkmenistan was forced to abandon pipeline options that did not include Russia.[204]

Saparmurad Niyazov went to great lengths to attract Western oil companies to the region in hopes that they would build pipelines that would be independent of Russia.[205] However, foreign investment in Turkmenistan remained stagnant during Niyazov's reign due to his authoritarian, corrupt, and erratic nature. The election of Berdimuhamedov in 2006 sparked renewed interest among outside players in the Turkmen energy sector. The new regime has shown modest improvement in terms of political and economic transparency, signaling a friendlier business environment.[206] Growing anger over Russian control is likely to push Turkmenistan away from Russia and closer to other nations, including China.[207] In 2007 Berdimuhamedov reported that "the country is ready to make concerted efforts with China in pushing forward even greater cooperation in areas including energy, culture, education, and medical services."[208]

Bilateral trade between the two nations has been minimal, despite the proximity of the two states.[209] In 2002, total trade volume was $87.52 million, of which Chinese exports were $86.78 million and imports $0.74 million, according to the Chinese General Administration of Customs.[210] A 2005 ranking of Chinese trading partners placed Turkmenistan at 130th, just behind Mozambique.[211] However, foreign investment by Chinese firms in Turkmenistan has been gradually increasing. From 1992 to 2002, only two projects in Turkmenistan received Chinese investment. As of July 2005, China had invested in thirty-seven projects in Turkmenistan worth a total of $383 billion. In 2005, the Chinese Oil Engineering and Building Company was granted the rights to work in oil pits located in the western part of Turkmenistan, which are estimated to produce around 2.3 million barrels of oil in a year.[212]

In 2006 a $125 million contract was signed by Turkmenistan and CNPC, granting the latter the right to drill twelve boreholes, up to 5,000 meters deep, in eastern Turkmenistan.[213] In July 2007, China signed a contract agreeing to import 30 billion cubic meters of natural gas annually for 30 years.[214] Under the agreement, China promised to assist in constructing a natural gas pipeline connecting Turkmenistan and China; construction of the pipeline, which began in August 2007, is slated to be complete by 2009.[215] China and Turkmenistan are also working closely together to establish an oil pipeline between the two countries. While specifics are not yet available and no pricing decisions have been made, the two countries did sign a "general agreement on realization of construction of a pipeline" in 2006.[216] The export of oil through the pipeline—which will run from the Turkmen border area through Uzbekistan, cross into the southern part of Kazakhstan, and finally make its way into China—is scheduled to begin in December 2009.[217] The deal is said to be of special importance to China because the pipeline not only fulfills its desire to ease dependence on coal and oil but also extends its influence into Central Asia, in competition with Russia.

SUMMARY

China is securing a foothold in the greater Middle East, especially in Iran, Saudi Arabia, and the countries of Central Asia. China, like India, has been successful in expanding its political and economic ties with key Middle Eastern countries without having to "take sides" in the various unresolved regional conflicts or openly challenge the dominant, but highly controversial, role of the United States as hegemon. However, as its presence in Sudan demonstrates, China runs the risk of becoming deeply embroiled in regional issues, and it is the object of much international criticism for its seemingly hardheaded mercantile approach to local politics.

Like India, China has been cautiously evenhanded in dealing with the Arab-Israeli conflict and balancing the competing overtures of the key Gulf States, especially Saudi Arabia and Iran. It sold arms to Saudi Arabia, Iraq, and Iran during the Iran-Iraq war, and it has been a major purchaser of military technology from Israel. This multifaceted approach has not stymied its military relations with the Arab countries, but it has caused significant angst in Washington, particularly given the reality that the United States and China could eventually come into conflict over the independence and security of Taiwan.

It is said the Chinese have a very Westphalian concept of sovereignty, which is to say that they strongly believe in the sanctity of territory and reject external interference in domestic politics. That explains their extreme sensitivity to interventionist policies, particularly those of the United States. For instance, in the Middle East the Chinese regard the U.S. determination to change regimes in Afghanistan, Iraq, and possibly Iran as misguided and dangerous, and they believe that part of the problem of the Middle East derives from the U.S. penchant to interfere. In addition, the Chinese argue that the United States dominates the region and that, in the last resort, it can control oil supplies. China, however, does not want to confront the United States on that issue. On the other hand, the unpopularity of U.S. policy in the region does give China and other Asian powers the chance to play a bigger role, in part to balance U.S. influence. China sees itself as a rising power, but one that has to be careful about taking too strong a position on international affairs, particularly if they touch on local issues.

Probably the only country to the west of India in which China has strong commitments is Pakistan. In fact, Pakistan has sometimes been referred to as "China's Israel"—which is to say that no matter what action the Pakistani government takes, China will back it, because of China's need to check India's power. However, today China, the United States, India, and Pakistan have a growing common interest in limiting the power of radical groups, particularly the Taliban. In sum, while the Chinese role is certainly growing and becoming more important, it is very unlikely that China will directly challenge U.S. power and influence.

In the context of the Middle East, China has no interest in a serious confrontation with the United States and has no intention of replacing Washington as security guarantor of the region, let alone the capability to do so. Maybe in a decade or so China will have a more robust capability to project power, but as the above overview suggests, China's current preoccupation with the Gulf countries is commercial and, for that reason, it seeks cooperation with both them and the United States. However, when one examines China's relations with Central Asia and Pakistan, a more "hands on" policy is at play, given their geographic proximity, direct access to alternative energy routes, and mutual concerns about Russian dominance, Islamic extremism, and fear of separatism. Given the growing physical ties between China and its westward Asian neighbors, it is realistic to assume that those links will eventually have a more direct impact on Iran than the Arab Gulf. But that day is a long way off. While the prospect gives rise to interesting geopolitical speculation, for the near term China's political role in the Middle East and Gulf remains low level. The Chinese are well aware of the benefits of having a strong U.S. presence in the Indian Ocean and the Gulf, even though they know that this trump card could be used against them if relations between China and the United States descended into all-out confrontation.

CHAPTER FOUR

PAKISTAN, JAPAN, AND SOUTH KOREA: MIDDLE EAST CONNECTIONS

IN ADDITION TO INDIA and China, most other Asian countries have growing Middle East connections. This chapter focuses on Pakistan, Japan, and South Korea. A more exhaustive study would recognize the impact that Singapore, Malaysia, and Indonesia—whose cooperation is vital to secure the maritime straits through which much of the trade between the Middle East and Asia passes—have had on economic, political, and cultural ties with the Middle East.[1] Taiwan and Australia also are important players in the economic arena. Australia, in particular, is a significant Asian maritime power and a key ally of the United States and Japan. North Korea's relevance is related to its weapons technology transfers, many of them illegal, to Pakistan and Iran.

Pakistan, Japan, and South Korea play different roles in the Middle East. Pakistan's borders with China and India and its proximity to the Persian Gulf make it a critical player in the geopolitics of the region, irrespective of its economic potential. On the other hand, Japan and South Korea are far removed from the Middle East. Their importance stems primarily from their economic activities, both as purchasers of Middle East oil and natural gas and as significant trading partners with the Middle East and the rest of the world.

PAKISTAN

To understand Pakistan's close ties with the Middle East and China, it must be remembered that since its creation in 1947 the state has been preoccupied with survival. Pakistan's ruling elites have long viewed their huge neighbor, India, as an existential threat. Much of the animosity between the two stems from their half-century-long dispute over the Kashmir region in Northeast Pakistan (Northwest India). British India was partitioned in 1947 on the principle that the Muslim-majority areas of the subcontinent were to become a new nation, Pakistan.[2] While Kashmir's population was predominantly Muslim, many of its Hindu rulers elected to join the newly created India, and a violent territorial dispute began, with the two nations fighting wars over the region in 1947 and 1965. The conflict has been furthered by religious tensions between Muslims and Hindus within India and the perception among Pakistani elites that India has never truly accepted the principles on which partition was based.[3] Pakistan fears that India, if given the opportunity, would not hesitate to eliminate the Pakistani state. Yielding or compromising over the fate of Kashmir is therefore viewed as politically disastrous by the Pakistani leadership.[4]

In 1971, civil war broke out between West Pakistan and predominantly Bengali East Pakistan, which demanded autonomy. After West Pakistan invaded East Pakistan, 10 million Bengalis fled to India. India intervened and defeated the Pakistani army. East Pakistan became the independent state of Bangladesh in December 1971.

Indo-Pakistani relations continue to be complicated by Pakistan's relationship with Islamic extremists. During the 1980s, President Zia-ul-Haq supported Islamic militancy in conjunction with the U.S.-funded effort to expel the Soviet Union from Afghanistan. In addition, the Pakistani army and Inter-Services Intelligence (ISI) have a history of training and financing Islamic jihadists to strike in the India-controlled portion of Kashmir.[5] Indeed, India's traditional argument assumes that Pakistan's leadership has consistently viewed terrorism as a primary means of pressuring India to discuss Kashmir.[6] Only a year after both Pakistan and India detonated nuclear devices, a conflict between India and Pakistan broke out in 1999 in the Kargil district of Kashmir. Pakistani soldiers infiltrated the Indian side of the "line of control," which has served as the de facto border between the two countries. After brief fighting, Pakistan was forced to withdraw its forces. However, the crisis demonstrated the dangerous nature of the Kashmir conflict and raised concerns that a full-blown Indo-Pakistani war could involve the use of nuclear weapons. Another major crisis came in November 2008, when ten gunmen attacked the famous Taj Mahal hotel in Mumbai, India, killing some 170 people. The attackers allegedly were connected to the Pakistan-based Islamic extremist group Lashkar-e-Taiba, and India has accused the ISI of being involved in planning the attack.[7]

Although the United States has been a strong supporter of Pakistan since its creation, their relationship has suffered serious setbacks over the years, triggered by U.S. concerns about Pakistan's many years of undemocratic rule, its nuclear weapons program, and its support in the 1990s of the Taliban in Afghanistan. Since the end of the cold war, Pakistan, in turn, has been troubled by growing relations between the United States and India and U.S. laws penalizing Pakistan for its nuclear activities and restrictions on U.S. arms sales to the Pakistani armed forces.

Pakistan's ambivalence about the extent of the U.S. commitment to its security has led its leaders to seek strong military relations with Saudi Arabia and China. In the case of the Saudis, Pakistan has offered military services in exchange for financial and political support. Its relationship with China, which has been much deeper, has resulted in significant Chinese military and economic assistance, including help to develop its nuclear program.

Since 2001, the U.S. offensive against the Taliban has created a dilemma for Pakistan's leadership. Groups with extensive historical ties to Pakistan's security services, such as Jaish-e-Muhammad, have been labeled terrorist organizations by Washington.[8] As Pakistan faces increasing pressure from the United States to counter domestic Islamic extremism—which could threaten the Pakistani state itself—it must consider the consequences of eliminating one of its most effective tools against India. In July 2009, Pakistani officials stated that "[Pakistani leaders] still consider India their top priority and the Taliban militants a problem that can be negotiated."[9]

Pakistan became a center of Islamic fundamentalism when thousands of Islamic fighters, returning to their homes following the Soviet withdrawal from Afghanistan, brought with them a populist form of *takfir*, a fundamentalist ideology that stretches across much of the Islamic world. Pakistan itself has become a reluctant host to a wide range of Islamic fundamentalist organizations, including the Taliban and al Qaeda, whose leaders found a new hideout there.[10] And while the Pakistani state has largely ceased funding for religious *madrassas*—indeed, in 2009 the Pakistan army launched an intense offensive against the Taliban in western Pakistan—ideological links to Saudi Arabia and the Gulf states have ensured a steady flow of financial support from private and public sources alike.[11]

That Islamic connection to the Gulf has helped provide funding for madrasas, in which, lacking a secular alternative, Pakistani children

memorize the Koran daily. A number of the schools espouse a jihadist ideology, helping more radical organizations recruit followers, and provide
training for fighters from across the Gulf and the wider Muslim world.[12]
The one Gulf country that has shown no interest in supporting radical Sunni
groups such as the Taliban is Iran, where the majority are Shi'a Muslims.
Pakistan's ambivalent relations with Iran remain an important factor in the
overall strategic balance in the region. For many years Iranian officials worried about the possible "Talibanization" of Pakistan; however, Pakistan's
leaders also have come to the conclusion that the Taliban pose a huge threat
to them. On that question, then, Pakistan and Iran not only have common
interests but also share them with India and the United States, which regard
the Taliban as a serious threat to the entire region.

With respect to Israel, Pakistan, at both the state and popular levels,
historically has used opposition to the Jewish state to endear itself to the
Arab world. In 1955 Pakistan signed the Baghdad Pact for the purpose
of regional defense, but with the understanding that Israel would not be
invited to join because to do so would be to recognize the Israeli state.[13]
More locally, fierce opposition to Israel's existence has been a cornerstone
of the ideology of radical Pakistani Islamists. Lashkar-e-Taiba has claimed
that it plans "to plant Islamic flags in Delhi, Tel Aviv, and Washington,"
while another fundamentalist group, Harkat, has argued that "Jews and
peace are incompatible."[14] Conspiracy theories abound regarding the reach
and scope of Jewish power in the imperialist West. In the past, such vehement opposition to Israel has strengthened Pakistan's relationships with
Arab states, but there is suggestive evidence that it is on the decline, at least
among the Pakistani elite.

MILITARY LINKS WITH SAUDI ARABIA AND THE GULF

Pakistan has had a long history of military connections in the Middle
East. Throughout the 1980s, Pakistan signed lucrative military personnel
contracts with many Gulf states, significantly bolstering its defense budget.
Troops deployed in the Gulf received up to four times their normal wages,
and the Pakistani military has sent advisers, specialists, and entire brigades
to the region frequently.[15] Between 1983 and 1987, Pakistan deployed some
20,000 troops to Saudi Arabia to protect the royal family from threats from
both Arab states and Israel.[16] In 1991, following Saddam Hussein's invasion
of Kuwait, Pakistan dispatched roughly 6,000 soldiers to join the multinational force defending the Saudis from any spillover of hostilities. The

deployment triggered popular resistance on the domestic front, as many Pakistanis disapproved of the decision to enter into a conflict between Muslim states.[17]

Pakistan was also deeply involved in the U.S. effort to end the Soviet occupation of Afghanistan from 1979 to 1989. In the largest covert war in history, Washington, Saudi Arabia, and Islamabad coordinated the transfer of vast sums of money and arms and provided training to the mujahideen on the border between Pakistan and Afghanistan.[18] The effort not only gave Pakistan a huge influx of Saudi money and weapons but also provided President Zia-ul-Haq with a pretext for strengthening Pakistan's military and Inter-Services Intelligence. Always mindful of its enemy to the east, Pakistan has consistently used foreign military aid earmarked for anti-Soviet and counterterrorism operations to bolster its conventional forces in order to guard against possible aggression from India.[19] Cooperation on Afghanistan also laid the groundwork for further Saudi military and financial support. In 1981, the Saudis facilitated Pakistan's purchase of F-16 fighter jets from the United States by underwriting an initial $300 million down payment for the deal.[20]

PAKISTAN AND THE SMALL GULF STATES

Although Pakistan's relations with the Arab Gulf states pale in comparison with India's, for reasons of history, geography, religion, and culture Pakistan too has a well-established presence in the Gulf. Over the years, the United Arab Emirates (UAE) has emerged as one of Pakistan's major economic and trading partners. Pakistanis make up the second-largest expatriate group in the country, with one estimate putting their number at over 1 million.[21]

After the first Gulf War in 1991, Pakistani military personnel were involved in mine clearance in Kuwait,[22] and Kuwait was the first country to send aid to mountain villages in Kashmir after the earthquake of 2005, offering the largest amount of aid, $100 million, for reconstruction. Oman is the Arab country geographically closest to Pakistan, and the Omani population includes a minority of Baloch, who are one of Pakistan's key ethnic groups.[23] It is important to note that Gwadar was part of Oman before it was transferred to Pakistan, on December 8, 1958.[24] Pakistan is Bahrain's fourth-largest principal trade partner after the United States, Japan, and Saudi Arabia. The defense forces of Pakistan and Bahrain also have strong relations, strengthened by visits of delegations and consultations with defense officials from both countries.[25] Pakistani investors have purchased property in Bahrain's real estate market. Pakistan has offered defense and military cooperation to Qatar, along with other Gulf Cooperation Council states; the two countries have also staged joint naval exercises.[26] In addition, Pakistan and Qatar are working on a joint gas pipeline project. [27]

PAKISTAN'S ECONOMIC CHALLENGES

Apart from its preoccupation with internal conflict, Afghanistan, and relations with India, Pakistan has severe economic problems. It needs more fossil fuels, and the Middle East is a natural source. Like India, Pakistan has been experiencing severe energy shortages; the frequency and duration of power outages throughout the spring and summer of 2009 led to violent riots in Karachi and Peshawar.[28] The ongoing energy crisis has multiple causes, both systemic and external, with high transmission losses[29] and lack of investment in additional power plants being two of the most serious problems.[30] Between 2003 and 2007, Pakistan's average GDP growth rate was more than 6.5 percent,[31] boosting demand for energy, which could not be met with the existing infrastructure. That has had adverse effects on the country's economy, including the important manufacturing and textile sector.

The Pakistani government had been heavily subsidizing the cost of electricity to households, but both end users and the government began to fall behind on payments as a result of the global economic slowdown. That led to "circular debt" in the power sector: the power companies were not receiving the expected government subsidies and consequently had difficulty paying for fuel, which resulted in so-called "load shedding"—lengthy and repeated brownouts and blackouts.[32] Pakistan's total production capacity is roughly 20,000 megawatts, by some estimates as much as 3,000 megawatts short of demand.[33] Oil and natural gas supply about 80 percent of the country's total energy; the remaining 20 percent is supplied mainly by hydroelectric power, with coal, liquefied petroleum gas, and nuclear power contributing only a small percentage.[34]

In June 2009, Qatar agreed to export an annual 1.5 million tons of liquefied natural gas (LNG) to Pakistan, roughly half the amount that Pakistan had aimed for when starting negotiations.[35] After India dropped out of the IPI pipeline negotiations in 2008, Pakistan also reached a bilateral deal with Iran to import gas overland, but it will take years to build the pipeline, provided that the United States does not succeed in pressuring Pakistan to cancel the deal.[36] Other forms of energy, including renewable resources, have considerable development potential, but they will not be able to deliver soon. To generate more hydroelectric power, Pakistan would have to build additional dams. The country has only seventy-one dams of more than 15 feet in height, compared with 4,050 in India and 26,000 in China.[37] The Pakistani government aims for all renewable energy sources combined to account for 7.4 percent of the energy mix by 2030.[38]

PAKISTAN'S INFRASTRUCTURE

Pakistan's infrastructure needs massive investment to modernize, but updating it to meet ever-growing demand will take many years. New expressways now link Islamabad and Lahore in the north and Gwadar and Ratodero in the south, and extensions are under construction to link Peshawar and Multan to the system in the north and Dadu to Karachi in the south. The National Highway Authority of Pakistan reports that there are about 5,937 miles (9,555 kilometers) of national roads in Pakistan,[39] which account for only 3 percent of the entire road network in the country.[40] The government is expected to expand the national highway system to accommodate the emerging economy. Map 4-1, which shows all existing and planned expressways throughout Pakistan, indicates that transportation infrastructure in Pakistan is lacking compared with that in China and even India. Most rural areas do not have access to any major highway system and must rely primarily on dirt roads for transportation.[41] The World Bank estimates that inadequate transport infrastructure costs Pakistan between 4 percent and 5 percent of GDP each year. Pakistan has increasingly looked to China for assistance in infrastructure development, including the upgrading of its antiquated railroad system.

Pakistan has around 5,000 miles (7,791 kilometers) of railways (see map 4-2).[42] The busiest routes link Peshawar and Karachi, Lahore and Sialkot, and Faisalabad and Khanewal. Passenger traffic accounts for 50 percent of the railway's total revenue and freight traffic for the other 50 percent. During fiscal year 2005, Pakistani railways carried a total of about 78 million passengers.[43] There are two new major proposed railways; one would link Gwadar and Quetta,[44] and the other would extend to Kashgar, China.[45] Both of the projects (shown in map 4-3), are supported by the Chinese government, which is also financing a deep-sea port in Gwadar.

Pakistan's primary transit resources are located in Karachi, but the government is building large port and airport facilities near Gwadar in the west; those cities, along with Port Qasim, are Pakistan's three major seaports.

Map 4-1

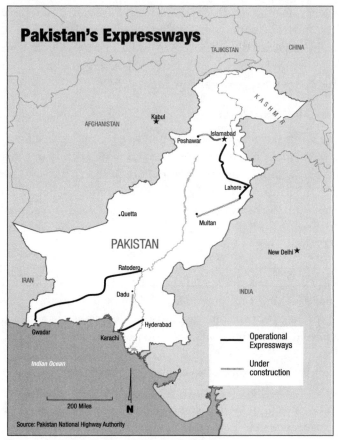

Pakistan's Expressways

Source: Pakistan National Highway Authority.

The primary port, Karachi, which has a capacity of 525,000 TEU (twenty-foot equivalent units) a year, handles approximately 75 percent of national trade.[46] It is undergoing an expansion that will increase its capacity to 700,000 TEU a year, roughly half the amount that Dubai's smaller port—Port Rashid—handles annually.[47]

Pakistan has ninety-one airports with paved runways, the largest being Jinnah International Airport in Karachi, which accommodates 6 million passengers a year. Smaller international airports are located in Lahore, Islamabad, Peshawar, and Quetta, and a jumbo-jet-capable airport is being constructed at Gwadar in Balochistan with Chinese assistance. The most important ongoing project between the two nations today is the construction

MAP 4-2

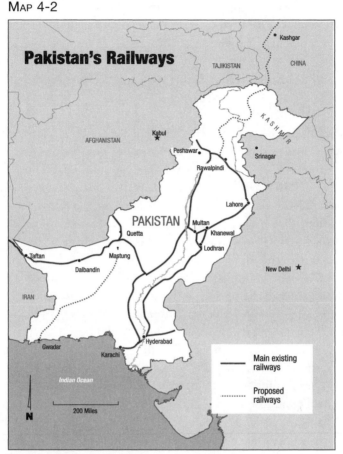

Source: Pakistan Railways.

of the port complex at the naval base at Gwadar on the Arabian Sea, the centerpiece in Pakistan's "dream of becoming a regional transport and energy hub."[48] While Gwadar is located in a remote area, it is intended to be a transit point for goods bound for western China and for Central Asian oil and gas.[49] The Pakistani government also hopes that Gwadar can compete with Dubai, Jeddah, and Salah, Oman, as a transshipment hub for goods making the passage from Asia to Europe. Gwadar's location gives it a chance to compete in that market—loading ships there instead of Dubai could save roughly 700 nautical miles of travel—but many hurdles remain before Gwadar can reach its envisioned level of productivity, including political instability in Balochistan and Afghanistan. Construction of the port began in

March 2002 after China agreed to provide $198 million of the $248 million necessary for phase 1 of the project.[50] China also has invested $200 million in building a coastal highway that will connect the port to Karachi. The second phase of the construction, which will include nine more berths and terminals, all to be financed by China, will cost $256 million.[51]

PAKISTAN-CHINA RELATIONS

Historically, Pakistan has been China's closest ally, a relationship based on geography and strong strategic and economic ties that has been described as "deeper than the seas and higher than the mountains."[52] Diplomatic contacts began in 1950 when Pakistan officially recognized the People's Republic of China (PRC), becoming the first Muslim state and the third noncommunist state to do so. Formal diplomatic relations were established a year later.[53] In the 1950s, Pakistan and China both were nominal members in the Non-Aligned Movement, but Pakistan's military ties with the United States and the PRC's vitriolic opposition to the United States soured that relationship. Relations began to improve in the late 1950s and deepened in the early 1960s. Indo-U.S. relations, which strengthened under John F. Kennedy, concerned Pakistan, which therefore sought to develop ties with China as a strategic alternative. That shift was evident in 1961, when the Pakistani government supported the restoration of China's seat in the United Nations.[54] U.S. military aid to India following the 1962 war between India and China and its arms embargo on India and Pakistan during the 1965 war further alienated Pakistan. Its leaders concluded that they could not trust the United States to help secure their interests vis-à-vis India; accordingly, they pursued a strategic relationship with China.

The strategic basis of the Sino-Pakistani relationship was a shared need to provide a check on India, a common neighbor and Pakistan's primary foe. Sino-Pakistani engagement has limited India's strategic options and forced it to occupy a defensive posture since 1962. While that remains an important, if not essential, consideration, the relationship has broadened greatly over the last forty years to include extensive trade ties. Pakistan also provides China with a bridge, metaphorically speaking, to the Middle East, as China's close, long-standing relationship with a Muslim country eases its engagement with the predominantly Muslim region.

The Sino-Pakistan relationship gained momentum after the end of the cold war. Former Pakistani prime minister Nawaz Sharif visited China in 1991, and former Chinese president Jiang Zemin undertook the first

Chinese state visit to Pakistan in December 1996, which resulted in the announcement of an "all around cooperative partnership into the 21st century."[55] Relations since then have continued to improve steadily. In 2005 China and Pakistan signed a Treaty of Friendship and Cooperation, which states that "neither party will join any alliance or bloc which infringes upon the sovereignty, security and territorial integrity" of the other.[56]

Military cooperation is a major part of the China-Pakistan relationship. China supported Pakistan militarily and economically during its two wars against India, in 1965 and 1971, and remains Pakistan's primary source of arms. Chinese-built equipment—including Pakistan's main tank, the T-96, and its air force's F-7 and JF-17 fighters—makes up most of Pakistan's front-line systems.[57] In May 2006 China and Pakistan finalized a $600 million agreement to modernize Pakistan's navy and maritime infrastructure; the deal included four F-22P frigates, maritime electronics systems, and upgrading of the Karachi dockyard.[58] China also supplied Pakistan with M-11 short-range ballistic missiles in the late 1980s,[59] and it is helping Pakistan build a new deep-water port and modern airport at Gwadar in western Pakistan.

China has played its most significant role in the development of Pakistan's nuclear program. China supplied Pakistan with the design of a 25-kiloton nuclear weapon and enough nuclear material for two weapons in the early 1980s and supplied nuclear reactor components in the mid-1990s.[60] While A. Q. Khan's illicit procurement networks were essential for the development of Pakistan's nuclear weapons program, China has contributed $150 million to the development of the Chasma reactor complex in central Pakistan over the last ten years.[61]

Economic Cooperation with China.   China-Pakistan bilateral trade amounted to $7 billion in 2008, up from $6.5 billion in 2007. In 2008, the balance of trade was heavily in favor of China, with $6 billion in Chinese exports to Pakistan and only $1 billion in Pakistani exports to China.[62] After two years of negotiation, China and Pakistan reached a free trade agreement (FTA) in November 2006 that is to come into effect in two segments. The first—covering livestock, vegetable products, minerals, and textiles—went into effect in July 2007; the second phase—covering investment and other goods—is scheduled to come into effect in 2012.[63] The agreement should benefit both countries, as more than 70 percent of Pakistan's exports to China in 2005 were cotton yarn or cotton fabric, with the remainder comprising leather goods, minerals, and seafood. The completion of the

FTA has only increased optimism about Sino-Pakistani trade; China has set a bilateral trade target of $15 billion a year—more than double the current level.[64] Pakistan also hopes to position itself as a trade corridor for goods between China and western Asia.

Since the 1960s, China has invested at least $5 billion dollars in Pakistan, mostly for infrastructure.[65] The goal is to improve trade routes through Pakistan to increase Chinese access to Central Asia, Iran, and potentially the wider Middle East. For China, Pakistan offers a shorter route for goods to reach its western provinces; for Pakistan, the routes allow for transport of supplies in case of an Indian blockade.[66] While transporting goods through Pakistan poses logistical difficulties—not least that Pakistan's infrastructure is not yet sufficient to support the trade—completion of such a corridor would shorten the distance goods would have to travel from the Gulf to western China by some 1,243 miles. The corridor would also provide quicker access to the 65 million people of the Central Asian states,[67] and it could carry pipelines that would allow some Chinese oil supplies to travel overland, avoiding the chokepoint of the Malacca Strait. The Pakistani government has enthusiastically supported the idea of Pakistan as an energy corridor since 2006. While the Chinese government has not formally endorsed the idea, it has gained some backing from Chinese experts.[68] Map 4-3 presents the major transportation infrastructure projects supported by China in Pakistan.

Efforts to create infrastructure links between northern Pakistan and western China began in the early 1960s when the China-Pakistan relationship was in its early years. Chinese and Pakistani engineers finished construction of the Karakoram Highway, linking northern Pakistan to Kashgar, China, in 1978.[69] While the highway is an impressive achievement, it needs further improvement because it is passable only from May to October. Improvements to try to make the highway an all-weather road and installation of a parallel railroad track along the highway's route are being discussed. A parallel track, however, could cost as much as $5 billion to complete, over ten years.[70] China also is building a 56-mile highway link connecting the Chinese side of the Karakoram Highway to the Russian-built network that already connects the five Central Asian republics. This regional highway network will allow the Chinese-assisted port at Gwadar to serve Central Asian markets as well as China and Pakistan.[71] China also is investing in the wholesale improvement of Pakistan's railways and has invested in Pakistan's energy sector (including investments in hydropower projects and a

MAP 4-3

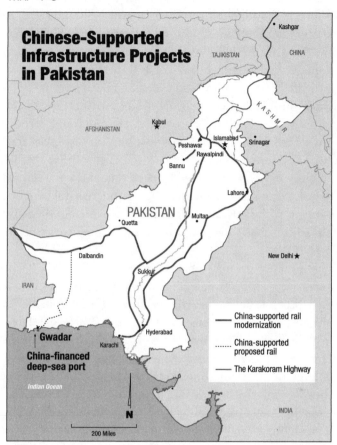

Chinese-Supported Infrastructure Projects in Pakistan

$150 million investment in nuclear power facilities at the Chasma complex)[72] and mining sector in hopes of securing nearby sources of commodities such as gold and copper.[73]

The Importance of Gwadar and the Problem of Balochistan.   China and Pakistan's relationship is multifaceted, but its potential for the greatest growth may depend on the success of the new port at Gwadar. For Pakistan, Gwadar provides a chance to obtain revenue as a transit point for Central Asian and Chinese goods and to promote economic development in western Pakistan. One Pakistani naval officer has argued for a bright future, noting that Dubai was not much to speak of before Port Rashid began operating in

1976.[74] China would gain another trade route to its western provinces and a potential strategic foothold in the Indian Ocean. All of those factors indicate that Gwadar should serve as a point of convergence in the China-Pakistan relationship. Yet Gwadar has also led to some short-term consternation due to the ongoing unrest in Balochistan. That unrest, and Islamist militancy in general, is the main irritant in China-Pakistan relations.

The Gwadar port is located in the Pakistani province of Balochistan—the largest and poorest of Pakistan's provinces. Despite rough terrain and high levels of poverty, Balochistan contains vast natural resources and produces 45 percent of Pakistan's natural gas needs.[75] Historically, the Baloch have felt that the province was ill-treated by the Punjabi-dominated federal government, which takes the province's resources but has not provided funding for development. Although natural gas was discovered in Balochistan in the 1950s, Balochistan never had gas for local use nor was it given royalties until the mid-1980s.

Baloch nationalist groups rebelled in 1948, 1958–59, 1962–63, and 1973–77, seeking a separate Balochi state or better treatment within Pakistan, but each time the Pakistani army suppressed the revolts.[76] The conflicts in Afghanistan, first in the 1980s and then after 2001, also have inflamed tensions in Balochistan. The Soviet invasion of Afghanistan resulted in an inflow of refugees to the province, which changed the ethnic and religious balance as large numbers of Sunni Pashtuns moved in among the secular-leaning Baloch. Similarly, Balochistan's rugged territory proved to be a useful haven for al Qaeda and Taliban sympathizers fleeing Afghanistan in 2002—especially after rigged elections in 2002 allowed the pro-Taliban party Jamiat Ulema-e-Islam (JUI) to take control of the regional government.[77] Those factors combined with lingering dissatisfaction with the central government led to a new round of fighting in 2003.

Over the last few years, the conflict in Balochistan has resulted in attacks on natural gas infrastructure, government forces, and foreign workers operating in the area. Since 2004, Chinese nationals in Balochistan have become regular targets. In May 2004, three Chinese officials were killed by a car bomb en route to Gwadar and eleven other officials—nine Chinese and two Pakistanis—were injured. In October, two Chinese engineers were kidnapped in Balochistan, and one was later killed.[78] The Baloch insurgents have also attacked a wider range of infrastructure and government targets, delaying the progress of the Gwadar complex. In January 2005, an attack disrupted the Sui gas field, resulting in eight deaths and a daily electricity shortfall of 470 megawatts. The conflict escalated significantly at the end of 2005, when the Balochistan Liberation Army (BLA) attacked participants in a meeting that President Musharraf was attending in Quetta, wounding a general. In response, a "humiliated" Musharraf ordered an extensive offensive against "anti-development groups" with helicopter gunships and other heavy weapons. The campaign resulted in hundreds of civilian casualties and the death of Baloch leader Nawab Bugti.[79] Bugti's death led to a counterescalation that included militant attacks on natural gas pipelines in Nasirabad and Loti and the Pirokh gas field.

The Pakistani media and to a lesser extent the government have enthusiastically spread the idea that the Baloch insurgency is sustained by foreign assistance. Naturally, India is the first suspect in this case, by providing funding through channels in Dubai. More fanciful press reports have claimed that some combination of the UAE, Britain, Russia, and the United States are funding the Baloch insurgents. Even if the current conflict has an international dimension, it is clear that its roots are essentially local, like those of the rebellions in Balochistan before it.[80]

The development of the port will bring a great deal of investment to the Gwadar region and create a large number of jobs.[81] The region could also expect significant transit revenues from the planned Iran-Pakistan-India natural gas pipeline. Yet many Baloch lack the skills and training—not to speak of the government's trust—necessary to take advantage of the potential construction boom.[82] As construction has ramped up, Baloch leaders have expressed resentment that they have been excluded from decisionmaking and that the port's development contracts were encouraging Punjabi and Sindhi labor instead of Baloch.[83] Therefore, while the development of the province could eventually help ameliorate the conflict in Balochistan, its short-term effect has been—and likely will continue to be—intensification of the conflict.

Violence in Balochistan and concerns over the safety of Chinese nationals in Pakistan have generally been a source of tension in bilateral relations between China and Pakistan. Chinese workers have been targeted for a variety of reasons. In Balochistan, the primary reason is that they are seen as outsiders; others have been targeted as agents of moral corruption, while the plight of China's Uighur Muslim minority is another possible motivation. Pakistan has reacted quickly to attacks on Chinese nationals, notably by stepping up the security of Chinese personnel in Balochistan.[84]

Chinese nationals also have been threatened beyond Balochistan in recent years. On June 23, 2007, religious militants abducted seven Chinese nationals, six of whom were employed by a massage parlor in Islamabad. The militants claimed the parlor was a front for prostitution, which they vowed to eliminate as part of their anti-vice campaign. The Chinese government deviated from its usual diplomatic and courteous stance, publicly demanding that Pakistan ensure the well-being of Chinese citizens in Pakistan. While this view is confined to a few observers, some have speculated that Chinese pressure to clamp down on militants was a significant factor in Musharraf's tough response in the Lal Masjid (Red Mosque) crisis in summer 2007.[85] Weeks later, on July 8, 2007, three Chinese businessmen were killed execution-style in a town in northwestern Pakistan, resulting in another public Chinese condemnation. Despite the violence, Sino-Pakistani relations appear to be too strong for militants to destroy single-handedly, as recent economic and infrastructure agreements attest.

Future Prospects.   Close relations with China are the cornerstone of Pakistan's strategic foreign policy. To quote Gilles Boquerat, a historian of South Asian diplomacy, Pakistan is "a very interesting pawn" in China's broader Asian strategy and a potential corridor for Chinese access to the Middle East.[86] China's need for the energy resources of the Middle East, Central Asia, and Africa will likely bring it to extend its influence to the Indian Ocean, increasing Pakistan's value as a strategic ally. Yet beyond trade in Central Asia, the interests of China and Pakistan do not necessarily converge, although Pakistan has been responsive to Chinese concerns about potential militancy among China's Uighur population.

Militant attacks on Chinese interests in Pakistan will likely lead to public spats, but the China-Pakistan relationship should remain close, barring high-profile or widespread attacks that could goad the increasingly nationalistic Chinese public. However, in order for Pakistan to serve as a major transport corridor, the security situation in Balochistan, the North-West Frontier Province (NWFP), and the Federally Administered Tribal Areas must improve. Pakistan is likely to pursue continuing its strong relations with China, as the United States appears to be a temperamental friend. It should also be remembered that Pakistan's most important power bloc—the military, and the army especially—highly values Pakistan's relationship with China as a constraint on India. Some have suggested that a substantive Indo-Chinese rapprochement could diminish Pakistan's importance to China. While that is possible—India and China exchanged positive diplomatic gestures in 2008[87]—the border dispute between India and China remains unresolved and it is not clear whether their interests in the Middle East and South Asia converge sufficiently to allow for such a shift. The China-Pakistan relationship has been a close one for more than forty years, and it will likely remain so.

JAPAN

Japan's political footprint in the greater Middle East is less apparent than those of China, India, and Pakistan. However, Tokyo is a key player in the energy field, and in the future it could have a more decisive role in the emerging power relationships among itself, China, the Koreas, and the United States. Japanese imports from the Middle East doubled between 2003 and 2007. Although those trade numbers are less significant than those for China and India, Japan will nevertheless be a competitor in the struggle for energy resources in the Middle East. How that will affect the overall balance of power within the Middle East remains unclear. Two scholars have noted that while "Japan is certainly re-emerging as a more confident partner, . . . it could also become more erratic, demanding, and unpredictable."[88]

After years of being labeled a "free rider" and a practitioner of "checkbook diplomacy," Japan began to emerge as a more robust U.S. ally during the 2001–06 tenure of Junichiro Koizumi. His successor, Shinzo Abe, was expected to continue that policy, but his short tenure in office has raised questions about Japan's foreign policy in the future. The issues on which Japan is expected to show more assertiveness include diplomatic relations with key Asian neighbors, especially China and the two Koreas; greater cooperation with the United States on defense issues, including ballistic missile deployments; and greater willingness to use Japanese military assets to support international military and peacekeeping operations. Evidence of a shift was seen in Japan's decision to send noncombat troops to Iraq and Afghanistan, which contrasts with its inaction, aside from providing financial support, during the 1990–91 Gulf War. On September 16, 2009, the Democratic Party of Japan (DPS) secured a historic victory over the entrenched Liberal Democratic Party (LDP). The new prime minister, Yukio Hatoyama, went out of his way to assure the United States that the Tokyo-Washington alliance was "the cornerstone" of Japan's foreign policy.

Japan has engaged in a campaign for a permanent seat on the UN Security Council, and as the second-largest contributor to the UN's budget, it can make a good case. However, the five permanent members currently cannot agree on an expansion plan. The United States, Mongolia, Cambodia, India, Indonesia, Malaysia, and several other Asian countries back a Japanese seat, while China, South Korea, and North Korea strongly oppose it.

Japan's post–WWII constitution allowed only for a national self-defense force and forbade the use of military force to solve international disputes. Former prime minister Junichiro Koizumi expanded the definition and capabilities of the self-defense force to include a role in international humanitarian missions. The resulting changes, including cooperation on missile defense and intelligence as well as the removal of some 8,000 U.S. troops from Japan, have been closely coordinated with the U.S. military. Japan's cabinet has endorsed a bill that would elevate the Defense Agency to a ministry, putting it in a more prestigious and visible position that may attract greater funding.

China's dramatic military expansion over the last two decades has been, in part, a cause of recent shifts in Japanese military policy. For the past eighteen years, China has increased spending on its military by double-digit percentages each year. Information on its expenditures is incomplete, and there are still discrepancies between Chinese government claims, U.S. and Japanese government suspicions, and independent studies on actual Chinese military spending. Japan has questioned China's expansion, asking for more specific statistics and a more complete explanation of the rationale for it.[89] The annual white papers released by Japan's Defense Agency refer to the need to monitor Chinese military expansion, ask for increased Chinese transparency, express apprehension regarding a China-Taiwan conflict, and question China's need for a blue-water navy.[90] In December 2005, the Japanese foreign minister, Taro Aso, described China's military expansion as "beginning to pose a considerable threat."[91]

As a signatory of the Nuclear Non-Proliferation Treaty, Japan operates its nuclear facilities in full compliance with requirements for safeguards and inspections. However, Japan's concerns over the nuclear program of the Democratic People's Republic of Korea's (DPRK) and China's military expansion have prompted international concern that Japan might eventually develop nuclear weapons. Its formidable nuclear power infrastructure could certainly support a weapons program.

Although China and Japan enjoy very profitable economic ties, four strategic issues have a negative influence on their diplomatic and political relations. First, China continues to resent Japan's failure to apologize fully for the atrocities it committed during World War II. Second, there is an unresolved dispute between the two over ownership and rights in the East China Sea and Senkaku Islands. Third, Japan fears China's military expansion. Fourth, the probability that North Korea will refuse to end its nuclear weapons program increases the risk that Japan will develop nuclear weapons. (These issues are explained in more detail in chapter 7.)

After years of frosty relations, Japan and India have begun a rapprochement. One reason is simple economics: Japan has investment capital and excellent industrial skills, which India needs. India is also one of the largest emerging markets in Asia and has a growing, affluent middle class that wants the sorts of products that Japan produces. Although Japan has lent India considerable sums of money in the past, it has been reluctant to invest and engage in partnership deals. In 2005, Japan and India entered into a new public-private partnership to develop, among other projects, a $100 billion infrastructure corridor between New Delhi and Mumbai that "will allow multi-modal, high axle load freight trains, with a fully computerized traffic control, to run from one end of the country to another. The project will be under Japan's 'Special Terms for Economic Partnership' (STEP) scheme."[92] As India and China continue to grow and the nature of their relationship remains unclear, India and Japan are likely to develop stronger ties. Japan's relations with the Middle East, although primarily economic, cannot be separated from its close ties with the United States and its wish to be regarded as a strong supporter of internationalism and the rule of law. Brief summaries of Japan's relations with Iran, Kuwait, Saudi Arabia, the UAE, Oman, and Qatar follow.

JAPAN AND IRAN

Japan's relations with Iran have gone through a number of iterations in recent years because of U.S. pressure and Japan's own concerns about Iran's behavior. Nonetheless, their relations go back many centuries, and today the two nations exhibit an enduring economic and diplomatic interdependence. The Silk Road Exhibition, which opened in Tokyo in December 2006, demonstrated the historical commonalities and interconnections between Iran and Japan. Energy imports are the central pillar of Japan's economic relationship with the countries of the Middle East, and Iran is no exception. Japan imports roughly 90 percent of its oil from the Middle East, and Iran supplies 12 percent of Japan's total oil imports, which account for 10 percent of Iran's production.[93] That being the case, it is easy to see why Japan would want to maintain good relations with Iran and would be reluctant to cut off purchases of Iranian oil. Japan's bilateral trade with Iran amounted to $5.8 billion in 2002—$5 billion of which was for Japanese imports of oil. In 2008, Japan's bilateral trade with Iran was $20.5 billion, of which $18.5 billion was for Japanese imports of oil.[94] The growth in their economic relationship is attributable to other trade as well, though trade in petroleum products remains central.

When Japan lost its concessions to the Khafji and Hout oil fields in Saudi Arabia in 2000 (Japan was their largest importer at the time), it was forced to immediately look elsewhere. In November 2000 Iran's former president Mohammad Khatami visited Japan, the first official to visit since the Islamic Revolution.[95] The Japanese hoped the visit would enhance energy relations between the two countries and promote new oil agreements with the Iranians. The Japanese government regards Iran as an integral regional geopolitical stronghold due to Iran's oil reserves and its central and politically influential position in the oil-rich Persian Gulf and Caspian regions.

In February 2004 a Japanese consortium led by Japanese oil company Inpex and the Iranian government signed a concession worth $2 billion dollars that would allow the Japanese to develop the Azadegan oil field. The United States criticized Japan for strengthening economic relations with Iran, especially after the September 11 attacks, but Japan felt that abandoning Iran due to international pressure would damage their long-standing cordial relations.[96] Fearing that Tehran would lose interest in its offer, Japan went ahead and signed the deal despite U.S. objections.[97] Japan was concerned about securing oil reserves, and the Azadegan oil field was viewed as key to diversifying Japan's strategic oil supply.[98]

The election of ultraconservative Mahmoud Ahmadinejad as president in June 2005 shocked much of the international community, including the Japanese. Japan's plans to develop Azadegan were slowed as tensions rose between President Ahmadinejad and the Bush administration, especially after the Iranian president's inflammatory rhetoric and demands that Iran be seen as an equal great power.[99] However, Japan's economic interests in the Middle East seemed to outweigh its political concerns. In December 2005, a $122 million joint venture petrochemical project in Iran, of which the Japanese trading company Itochu Corporation became the major beneficiary, was approved by the Multilateral Investment Guarantee Agency of the World Bank.[100]

In November 2006, the Azadegan agreement was dissolved. Japan's Inpex Corporation's holding in the oil field was reduced to 10 percent from 75 percent, and Iran's National Oil Company renounced its status as operation manager. The breakdown jeopardized Japanese plans to ensure energy security through increasing the stakes of Japanese-owned companies in foreign energy assets.[101]

JAPAN AND KUWAIT

In December 1961, Japan and Kuwait established diplomatic relations. During a meeting in Tokyo in 2004, the Kuwaiti and Japanese foreign ministers backed the goal of peace and stability in the Gulf region and agreed that further efforts needed to be made toward the reconstruction of Iraq.[102] In their discussions the ministers also stressed the importance of respecting the sovereignty and territorial integrity of countries in the region. Both nations expressed hopes that through cooperating on the aforementioned issues they would further deepen bilateral ties.[103]

In May 2007, Japan's prime minister, Shinzo Abe, visited Kuwait on the third leg of his Middle East tour. His visit was the first of its kind in twenty-three years, and he was accompanied by a delegation of more than 150 businessmen. During his time there, Abe visited a Kuwaiti air base where elements of Japan's air self-defense force were stationed.[104]

Compared with Japan's relations with other Gulf states, the economic relationship between Japan and Kuwait is less significant, yet Japan is Kuwait's largest purchaser of oil. Kuwait provides roughly 7 percent of Japan's oil imports,[105] and exports to Japan account for about 20 percent of Kuwait's total crude exports.[106] In 2002, bilateral trade between Japan and Kuwait amounted to about $5 billion,[107] with Japanese petroleum imports accounting for roughly 80 percent. By 2008, bilateral trade had increased to $17.3 billion, of which $15.1 billion was in Japanese imports. Kuwaiti imports of Japanese goods doubled from 2002 to 2007, but oil still dominates bilateral trade.[108] Japan's primary exports to Kuwait are cars, machinery, and electrical equipment. Meanwhile, Japan has aided Kuwait by means of ¥294 million ($3.25 million) in grants and ¥935 million ($10.35 million) in technical cooperation.[109] In addition, in 2007 Japan's Mitsui and Company secured a $1.5 billion order from Kuwait's Ministry of Electricity and Water to build a power and desalination plant 31 miles south of Kuwait City that will be able to generate 750,000 kilowatts of electricity and desalinate about 200,000 tons of water a day.[110] The plant is expected to be completed in the first quarter of 2010.

On May 1, 2007, Japan and Kuwait renewed their energy partnership, and Japan was assured a stable and steady supply of oil from Kuwait. In addition, they vowed to work together in reconstructing Iraq as well as in encouraging Iran to resolve the crisis over its nuclear ambitions.[111] At the first Japan-Arab Economic Forum, which was held in Tokyo on December 7–8, 2009, the two countries agreed to further strengthen bilateral relations and continue to promote a free trade agreement between Japan and the Gulf Cooperation Council (GCC) states.

JAPAN AND SAUDI ARABIA

Japanese contact with Saudi Arabia prior to World War II included the first pilgrimage to Mecca by a Japanese Muslim, Kotaro Yamaoka, in 1909, and a visit by Hafiz Wahab, the Saudi envoy to England, to Japan for the opening of a mosque in Tokyo in 1938. The following year, the Japanese envoy to Egypt, Masayuki Yokoyama, visited Saudi Arabia, where he had an audience with King Ibn Al Sa'ud.[112]

Japan and Saudi Arabia established diplomatic relations in June 1955. The Saudi embassy was founded in Tokyo and the Japanese embassy opened in Jeddah in 1958 and 1960 respectively. (The Japanese embassy moved to Riyadh in 1984.) Bilateral relations have been smooth, and through mutual visits by imperial and royal family members, they have even been strengthened. In 1960, Prince Sultan Bin Abdul-Aziz Al Saud became the first member of the Saudi royal family to visit Japan; later, in 1981, Emperor Akihito and Empress Michiko (then the crown prince and princess) visited Saudi Arabia.[113] In 1998 Japan and Saudi Arabia undertook two initiatives: first, the Comprehensive Partnership toward the Twenty-First Century, and then, the Japan–Saudi Arabia Cooperation Agenda, which focused on human resources development, the environment, health sciences and technology, culture and sports, and investment and joint ventures. In 2001, Japan's foreign minister, Yohei Kono, announced the Kono Initiative to strengthen Japan's relations with countries throughout the Middle East but especially with Saudi Arabia. The bolstering of relations would occur through promotion of communications with the Islamic world, development of water resources, and participation in diverse political dialogues, which have occurred annually since their initiation in 2001.[114]

Saudi Arabia is an essential trading partner for Japan and its largest trading partner in the Middle East. Japan's largest oil supplier, Saudi Arabia provides 28 percent of overall Japanese oil imports.[115] In 2002, Saudi-Japanese bilateral trade totaled $16.3 billion, three-quarters of which consisted of Japanese imports. By 2008, bilateral trade had grown to almost $60 billion, of which $8 billion was Japanese exports.[116] Japan's primary exports to Saudi Arabia are automobiles, machinery and equipment, and metals. While Japan has been avoiding giving financial aid to Saudi Arabia, it has provided some forms of expert assistance to maintain close ties (and to ensure that the supply of oil does not dry up). The Japanese Ministry of Foreign Affairs has stated that "since Saudi Arabia's per capita GNP is high, Japan does not extend funding assistance. But in view of their close economic relationship and Saudi Arabia's great need for technical assistance, Japan provides technical cooperation on a project basis; accepts trainees in sectors such as communications, broadcasting, mining, and manufacturing; sends experts to the country; and offers other forms of assistance."[117] Saudi Arabia and Japan also take part in a trainee-expert exchange to promote technical advancement; as of 2004, 1,750 trainees were sent to Japan and 757 Japanese experts were sent to Saudi Arabia.[118]

Trade between Saudi Arabia and Japan amounted to $22 billion in 2004, when a number of major deals were concluded, among them an $8.5 billion joint venture between Japan's Sumitomo Chemical Company and Saudi state-run Aramco Oil Company and the $1.8 billion joint venture between SABIC (Saudi Basic Industries Corporation) and Mitsubishi Corporation. Such partnerships demonstrated the strategic importance of relations between the two countries.[119]

In April 2006, Sumitomo Chemical and Aramco agreed to jointly construct an integrated refining and petrochemical complex, Petro Rabigh, some 120 miles from Jeddah, which was opened in November 2009.[120] Also in 2006, Japan and Saudi Arabia agreed to launch negotiations concerning a free trade agreement between Japan and the GCC, and Crown Prince Abdullah ibn Abd al-Aziz declared that his nation would continue to be a consistent supplier of oil to and a promoter of investment by Japan.[121]

JAPAN AND THE UAE

In 2007, the Japan Bank for International Cooperation (JBIC) signed an agreement with the Abu Dhabi National Oil Company (owned by the national government) in hopes of creating a strategic partnership. The JBIC is expected to invest billions of dollars to boost crude oil production in exchange for stable oil supplies; the oil company also signed an agreement to invest in Dubai's infrastructure and improve business opportunities for Japanese firms.[122]

The UAE is Japan's second-largest trade partner in the Middle East, behind Saudi Arabia. Bilateral trade between the Emirates and Japan grew to $57.2 billion in 2008, a 41.8 percent increase over the previous year's figure.[123] Japanese oil imports have been the dominant factor in the trade relationship, although Emirati imports have kept pace, at roughly 20 percent of bilateral trade, despite the burgeoning of Japan's oil imports. The UAE also is Japan's second-largest oil supplier, accounting for 25 percent of Japan's overall oil imports in 2007.[124] The Japan Oil Development Company (JODCO) and the Japan Oil, Gas, and Metals National Cooperation (JOGMEC) have made plans to fund a petroleum institute in Abu Dhabi.[125]

In recent years, Japanese firms have been increasingly involved in Dubai's private sector. In April 2007, Mitsubishi Fuso Truck and Bus Corporation (MFTBC) announced the establishment of a new distribution center in Dubai. The objective is not only to supply parts to distributors and customers in the Middle East but also to broaden its business in a region where its vehicle sales have increased in recent years.[126] In addition, Japanese companies such as Marubeni and Hitachi have been taking part in the building of Dubai's massive resort islands, which will be shaped like a palm tree and a map of the world.[127]

JAPAN AND OMAN

The historical relationship between Japan and Oman dates back to trade through the Silk Road of Central Asia. In the eighth century, after years of overland trade, Oman's naval capabilities allowed it to reach East Asia and the trade route shifted to the sea. In 1924, Japanese geographer Juko Shiga became the first of his nationality to visit Oman, where he was given an audience with Taimur, the sultan of Oman, and a decade later the sultan visited Japan.[128]

Japan recognized and established diplomatic relations with the Sultanate of Oman in 1972. Two years later, a goodwill mission from Oman visited Japan. In 2007, Oman established the Oman-Japan Friendship Association in Muscat; at the same time, the Japan-Oman Association, which had remained inactive for a number of years, was reopened.[129] The Oman-Japan

Friendship Association was very important in establishing relations before official diplomatic channels were in place. It was not until 1979 that Oman opened its embassy in Tokyo; a year later, the Japanese embassy opened in Muscat.

In the 1990s, the foreign minister of Japan visited Oman to discuss events in Kuwait and Iraq during the first Gulf War. There also were many cultural and sports exchanges between the two nations in the 1990s—Oman held a Japan Week in 1992, and Oman participated in the Asian Games in Hiroshima in 1994. Finally, the Directorate General of Tourism of Oman started its first overseas tourist bureau in Japan in 2001. The value of Japan's trade relationship with Oman is small when compared with the relationships that Japan has with the other Gulf states, but Japan is a major purchaser of Omani petroleum and has provided Oman with development financing. Bilateral trade has grown from $3.1 billion in 2002 to $9.6 billion in 2008. As with most of the Gulf states, the trade balance tips toward Oman's petroleum exports.[130] Japan is one of the largest importers of Oman's liquefied natural gas, having had a contract to purchase 700,000 tons a year for twenty-five years since 2000. It is also the largest importer of Omani oil, which accounted for 3.5 percent of Japan's imported oil in May 2007.[131] In 2008, Japan's exports to Oman, which consist mostly of electrical machinery and transport equipment, grew 54 percent over the previous year's figure, to $3.9 billion.[132]

Japan also has been a source of infrastructure development funding for Oman. The Japan Bank for International Cooperation participated in the $250 million financial plan for the Sohar Port project, extending a loan that has been used for building the port as well as the infrastructure and roads needed to support it. Japanese companies have also invested in the construction of the Oman LNG plant, a refinery, and a chemical fertilizer plant.[133] Japanese direct investment in Oman totaled 2 billion yen as of May 2007. Japan also gave 368 million yen in grants and 9.9 billion yen in technical assistance to Oman.[134]

JAPAN AND QATAR

Japan and Qatar, which established diplomatic relations in May 1972, agree on a number of issues, including Japan's campaign to secure a permanent seat on the UN Security Council, for which Qatar has expressed support.[135] In May 2007, Qatar asked Japan to provide technical assistance to develop nuclear energy for peaceful use.[136]

In 2005, Qatar was Japan's fourth-largest supplier of liquefied natural gas and accounted for 11 percent of Japan's total imports. Qatar will become the biggest supplier in the world of liquefied natural gas around 2010, and Japan is very interested in taking advantage of the energy security that Qatar could offer. Exports of LNG to Japan are slated to double by 2010. Japan is the world's second-largest importer of crude oil, and Qatar is Japan's fourth-largest crude oil supplier, with exports totaling 3.84 million barrels a day.

Qatar's minister of the economy made a nine-day visit to Japan in November 2006, where he assisted in the formation of the first Japan-Qatar Joint Economic Committee, which is aimed at boosting bilateral relations. Japan's Bank for International Cooperation also signed a business agreement with Qatar Petroleum to create a favorable environment for Japanese companies wishing to invest in energy resource development projects. Japan also launched negotiations on a free trade agreement with the GCC, of which Qatar is a member. Finally, the Doha Bank, a major private Qatari commercial bank, established a plan to promote two-way investment between the countries.[137]

In October 2006, a Japanese company claimed the right to build one of the largest independent power-producing projects in Qatar, valued at $2.3 billion. The firm stated that it would complete construction of the plant by April 2010 and manage it for twenty-five years.[138] In May 2007, the prime minister of Japan and the Qatari emir met to secure cooperation on stable energy supplies for Japan; cooperation was to be extended to the areas of education and culture as well.[139] In the same year, four Japanese firms agreed to join a Qatari refinery project. The project, the Japanese industry's first overseas refinery investment, was expected to cost $800 million, and gas production began in December 2009.[140]

Summary

Japan's relations with the Middle East have focused almost entirely on economic issues. Given Japan's great dependence on Mideast energy, that focus is appropriate and adequately sums up how Japan's role in the region has evolved. Japan remains highly sensitive to U.S. policy in the region. While its companies would like to do more business with Iran, Japan's foreign policy decisionmakers remain fearful of incurring U.S. wrath and therefore have pursued a very cautious policy on all the most sensitive Mideast issues, especially the controversial war in Iraq and Western pressure on Iran.

South Korea

South Korea's engagement with the Middle East has focused primarily on energy imports and construction, although there have been efforts to pursue more cooperative relations in other sectors.

Construction Projects in the Middle East

In the 1970s and 1980s, there was a significant community of South Korean construction workers in Saudi Arabia and other parts of the Middle East. As oil prices have risen over the past decade, benefiting Middle Eastern oil giants, construction projects have begun to reappear. South Korean construction companies are being hired to build oil refineries, petrochemical plants, offices, and infrastructure within the region, and their involvement in lucrative construction markets, especially in the Gulf states, is not to be underestimated. The Organization of Petroleum Exporting Countries (OPEC) earned a record $650 billion in petroleum export revenues during 2006, a 22 percent increase from 2005 and almost twice the amount earned in 2004. OPEC export revenues in 2007 were $675 billion, a 10 percent increase from 2006. According to a January 2010 report from the Energy Information Administration (EIA), export revenues reached $573 billion in net oil export revenues in 2009, a 41 percent decrease from 2008.[141]

According to MEED Group, new construction projects undertaken in the Middle East are worth about $1.7 trillion, and many Korean construction companies are benefiting. In August 2007, Korean-owned GS Engineering and Construction (GSEC) won a $1.8 billion contract for construction of a refinery in Egypt. GSEC's overseas revenue is projected to reach $3.15 billion in 2009; in 2004, it was only $545 million. In addition, Korean-owned Samsung Engineering (builder of the $4 billion Burj Khalifa Tower) states that its overseas orders rose by 87 percent to $2.5 billion; most of its overseas work is in Saudi Arabia. A South Korean firm entered a $40 billion bid to build a nuclear power plant in the UAE, and South Korean construction companies will have a prominent place at the Big 5 PMV, a construction and machinery industry conference held in Dubai.[142]

South Korea and Saudi Arabia

Diplomatic ties between South Korea and Saudi Arabia were officially established in 1962. In 1973, South Korea opened an embassy in Jeddah (it was moved to Riyadh in 1982), and the Saudi embassy in Korea was opened in 1974. The first summit between the two countries took place in 1980, when President Choi Kyu-hah visited the Saudi capital.[143]

Twenty-seven years later, in March 2007, South Korea's president, Roh Moo-hyun, became only the second Korean head of state to visit Saudi Arabia. President Roh's principal focus at the summit was the advancement of economic relations between the two countries, especially because Saudi Arabia is considered an important mediator and economic hub in the region. "The prospects of increasing bilateral cooperation between the two countries are bright," Roh stated in an interview.[144] Saudi Arabia is the single largest supplier of oil to South Korea,[145] and King Abdullah and President Roh agreed to strengthen cooperation in securing a stable supply of oil for South Korea. They also committed to increasing South Korea's construction orders in Saudi Arabia, which is the single largest construction market for Korean builders, with cumulative orders totaling $58 billion.[146] New construction projects include a new economic city, petrochemical and refinery facilities, desalination plants, power plants, and railroads. A Korean company also pledged to provide a training program for Saudi Arabian construction workers. In 2009, Korean construction firms already had won contracts worth $1.45 billion.[147] In addition, Aramco is the biggest shareholder in S-Oil, the third-largest Korean refinery and oil company.[148] The fifth-largest importer of crude oil in the world, South Korea called upon Saudi Arabia to play a constructive role in stabilizing oil prices.[149] In total, 30 percent of all South Korean crude oil imports come from Saudi Arabia.[150]

Although President Roh's primary aim was to enhance Korea's economic relations with Saudi Arabia, he and King Abdullah reached several informal agreements concerning the expansion of bilateral relations and cooperation in the information technology, education, and cultural sectors.[151] As part of a people-to-people exchange program, a number of prestigious Korean universities agreed to accept Saudi Arabian students sponsored by their government, and in March 2007, a group of eighty-four Saudi students traveled to South Korea to study. Officials plan to continue promoting Korean universities with the goal of attracting up to 500 Saudi students in the future.[152] The Korean-Arab Friendship Express Caravan toured Saudi Arabia in October 2008, highlighting traditional Korean culture and celebrating Saudi-Korean ties.[153]

SOUTH KOREA AND IRAN

In October 2007, South Korea and Iran celebrated the forty-fifth anniversary of the establishment of diplomatic relations between them, although they have engaged in informal trade for centuries, since the time of the Silk Road. In modern times, economic cooperation between the two countries has been steadily increasing, especially since Iran adopted a "Look East" policy, similar to Saudi Arabia's, under which Iran looks to East Asian nations for new opportunities instead of focusing on trade partnerships currently dominated by Western nations. South Korean products are selling very well in the Iranian marketplace, and South Korean companies have invested more than $10 billion in Iranian projects, mostly in the energy sector. The relationship between Iran and South Korea revolves around Iran's large reserves of oil and gas, which can help South Korea meet its energy needs; in addition, Iran can use South Korea's technological expertise to develop its industrial sector. In 2007, the two countries signed a memorandum of understanding (MOU) on the establishment of a joint investment committee.[154] Bilateral trade totaled $12.5 billion in 2008.[155]

The two countries also are making an effort to forge cultural connections. In October 2007, the South Korean embassy sponsored a benefit concert in Tehran to raise funds for Iranian children suffering from heart disease, and the embassy hosted a similar concert in Tehran in May 2009 to benefit Iranian children suffering from cancer.[156] Interestingly, a South Korean television series, *Jewel in the Palace,* has been the most popular show broadcast in Iran.[157] Tensions over Iran's nuclear weapons program have put some political distance between Iran and South Korea. Although there was an embargo on some South Korean products after Seoul backed the October 2005 IAEA resolution against Iran's nuclear program, it was lifted after Korean representatives went to Tehran to discuss the matter. In a January 2006 meeting between South Korea's foreign minister, Ban Ki-Moon (now the UN secretary-general), and Iran's deputy foreign minister, Mehdi Safari, Ban Ki-Moon emphasized his support of international efforts to stop the proliferation of nuclear weapons but also stated that Seoul hoped that the issue could be resolved through dialogue instead of by referring it to the UN Security Council. South Korea also called for Iran to facilitate the import of South Korean products, suggesting that the multilateral nuclear issue should be kept separate from their bilateral economic connections.[158] Iran's foreign minister, Kamal Kharrazi, echoed that sentiment when he maintained that "Tehran and Seoul must think about a balanced and comprehensive expansion of their relations in the framework of the two countries' lofty interests without being swayed by external impacts."[159] In November 2008, South Korea's foreign minister, Yu Myung-Hwan, took a more forceful stance, stating that Iran should demonstrate the peaceful purposes of its nuclear program to the international community.[160] South Korea is also concerned about Iran's role in North Korea's nuclear program. As former foreign minister Ban Ki-Moon has stated, "The resurgent disputes over [Iran's] nuclear program may have a negative impact on global efforts to resolve the North Korean nuclear crisis."[161]

SUMMARY

South Korea, like Japan, is focused mainly on its economic ties with the Middle East, especially its lucrative construction projects and its energy deals. It will likely continue to play a low-key role on matters concerning geopolitics and diplomacy. Its foreign policy priorities relate to its relations with the United States, China, Japan, and Russia and on how to aid in the efforts of those countries to settle the North Korea problem. To the extent that North Korea has military relations with Middle Eastern countries such as Iran and Syria, South Korea will respond by strengthening its support for international efforts to rein in North Korea's dangerous behavior. If at some point in the future the two Koreas were to be reunited, there would be a new and probably powerful Korean footprint in East Asia that could eventually increase the Korean presence in the energy-rich Middle East.

CHAPTER FIVE

ASIA AND ISRAEL

IN VIEW OF THE extreme polarization concerning the Arab-Israeli conflict found in many Western and most Muslim countries, it is significant that the Asian countries with majority non-Muslim populations have cooperative and friendly relations with Israel and that Israel has good relations with several Muslim countries in the Caucasus and Central Asia. It therefore is useful to summarize Israel's relationships with key Asian countries in a separate chapter. The most interesting have been the close ties between the Israeli defense technology sector and India's and China's defense establishments. Those ties not only reflect the mutual benefit that all parties perceive in their relationships but also demonstrate the ease with which both India and China also sustain good relations with countries and entities that are extremely hostile to Israel.

INDIA AND ISRAEL

While India and Israel now cooperate in a wide range of areas, India's "Nehruvian" policies kept the two countries apart for more than 40 years. In the 1930s and 1940s, Gandhi, Nehru, and most of the Indian National Congress, which had a significant Muslim membership, opposed the creation of a Jewish nation and the partition of Palestine and eventually voted against Israel's admission to the United Nations. Most of the leaders in congress disagreed with the idea of a state based on confessional allegiance, a system of governance that allocates political power proportionally to religious groups. India and Israel took small diplomatic steps in the early 1950s—India recognized Israel in 1950, and Israel opened a consulate in Mumbai in 1953—but relations and cooperation remained at a low level and the two countries did not establish full diplomatic relations until after the end of the cold war, in January 1992.

Indo-Israeli ties remained at a low level throughout the cold war for both ideological and practical reasons. India's large Muslim population was, of course, a factor. But apart from India's opposition to the idea of Israel as a religious state, India was very active in the Non-Aligned Movement, which had a large Arab—and anti-Israeli—contingent. In addition, India purposefully directed its gaze toward the Arab states in the hopes of preventing Pakistan from gaining their support by making Kashmir into a Hindu-Muslim issue and, as today, of securing a stable supply of energy. Furthermore, Jawaharlal Nehru, India's prime minister until 1964, was a close friend of Egypt's Nasser, who was an implacable foe of Israel.[1] While India and Israel periodically cooperated on mutual interests, such as Israeli aid to India during the 1962 war with China or proposed plans to destroy the Pakistani reactor at Kahuta in the 1980s,[2] their public relationship often was acrimonious, especially after the 1967 Arab-Israeli War, which put India's allies in direct conflict with Israel. In fact, in 1975 India publicly supported and funded the Palestine Liberation Organization and voted for the UN resolution to equate Zionism with racism.[3]

IMPROVED POLITICAL RELATIONS

The decline of the Soviet Union forced India to reevaluate its foreign policy. That led to an opening of the Indian economy and a desire to trade with high-tech states, including Israel. The new approach to foreign policy, combined with the new initiatives to end the Arab-Israeli conflict in the wake of the 1991 Gulf War and the push by the opposition Bharatiya Janata Party (BJP) to exchange ambassadors, argued for an opening toward Israel. Accordingly, the two countries established full diplomatic relations in 1992.[4]

For nearly a decade afterward, commercial trade in arms and other goods thrived and ties were quietly strengthened. Diplomatic progress was visible in 1996, when Israel's president, Ezer Weizman, led a business delegation to India, and in 2000, when the Indian and Israeli foreign ministers exchanged visits.[5] It was, however, the highly symbolic September 2003 visit of Prime Minister Ariel Sharon to India that indicated how far bilateral ties had come. Sharon's visit laid the groundwork for Indo-Israeli military exercises and agreements in the fields of the environment, health, illicit traffic in drugs, visa waivers for diplomatic service personnel, and an educational cultural exchange program.[6] In the same year, India and Israel issued the Delhi Statement on Friendship and Cooperation, in which they agreed to cooperate closely on counterterrorism and called on the international community to take "decisive action" against cross-border terrorism and money-laundering operations to finance terrorism.[7]

DEFENSE COOPERATION

A BJP-led government rose to power in India in 1998, opening the door for strategic cooperation between India and Israel. The BJP saw Israel as a potential ally against what it perceived as a Muslim threat to India; nevertheless, India deepened its ties with Saudi Arabia and Iran during the BJP's administration from 1998 to 2004. Defense collaboration and arms sales picked up in January 1999 when the United States withdrew the sanctions that it had imposed on India in the wake of New Delhi's 1998 nuclear test. In the late 1990s India purchased unmanned aerial vehicles, artillery, and radar systems from Israel. The emerging Indo-Israeli relationship was codified in 2001 with the creation of the Joint Defense Cooperation Group, which meets annually to solidify defense deals and military ties and coordinate the security relationship.[8]

India has become Israel's largest arms market, overtaking Russia in 2009. India has purchased a wide range of technically advanced equipment and weapons from Israel, including antimissile radar and electronic warfare components for the Indian navy and air force, for a total of more than $5 billion since 2002. Indian procurement of such advanced components has worried the Pakistani government, which in response initiated a brief opening to Israel in 2005.[9] While the sales revenue is very important to Israel's defense industry, which needs exports in order to remain financially solvent, some analysts have wondered whether Israel would push to get more out of the relationship. Many observers, for example, have suggested that it is in Israel's interest to locate logistical naval bases in the Indian Ocean with India's consent—and perhaps assistance. Israel currently has no bases with easy access to the Indian Ocean aside from the port of Eilat on the Red Sea. However, pursuit of a strategic presence in the Indian Ocean may prove difficult. Historically, India has not allowed foreign forces to be based in its territory, and allowing Israel such access would be politically problematic given India's large Muslim population. On the other hand, India recently signed an agreement to allow Singaporean forces to train in India, so while the prospect is unlikely, it does not seem out of the realm of possibility.

India's cooperation with Israel also extends into the realm of nuclear politics and policy. On September 17, 2008, at IAEA headquarters in Vienna, a vote was cast for a resolution urging all Middle Eastern states to abandon efforts to make nuclear bombs. The only state that voted against the IAEA resolution was Israel, which accuses Iran and Syria of pursuing nuclear weapons. Tehran and Damascus voted for the resolution, and India abstained in support of Israel along with United States, Canada, and Georgia.

COUNTERTERRORISM

Counterterrorism efforts represent one of the strongest collaborations between the two countries. India's and Israel's intelligence agencies had been quietly cooperating on topics of mutual interest since the 1960s, but their partnership took off in the late 1990s as the countries' broader economic and diplomatic relationship improved. Cooperation was formalized in 2001, when India and Israel formed the Indo-Israeli Joint Working Group on Counter Terrorism, which began meeting in 2002.[10] The two exchange information regarding Islamist terrorist groups, and Israel is helping India fight terrorism in Kashmir by providing logistical support. It has been speculated that the level of intelligence sharing between these two countries might be more than that between India and the United States.

Both India and Israel have an unfortunately rich history of experience with counterterrorism and counterinsurgency operations and likely have much to learn from each other. India has been largely unsuccessful in dealing with the Islamist-Kashmiri insurgency over the past two decades, and it faces simmering discontent in many of its eastern provinces; similarly, Israel struggles against groups such as Hamas and Hezbollah, which continue to pose a threat to Israeli security. It is easy to see how cooperation on such matters could benefit both countries, as they could learn from each other's mistakes as well as successes. India stands to benefit primarily from Israel's technological proficiency with border monitoring; Israel could benefit from India's approach to counterinsurgency, which "stresses the impossibility of military victory against guerrillas, emphasizes the political resolution of insurgencies, and places severe limitations on the use of military force in counterinsurgency operations."[11] While Israel's conflicts differ from those facing India, such exchanges of ideas and practices have helped both countries.

ECONOMIC COOPERATION

Since diplomatic relations between Israel and India began to improve in the early 1990s, economic ties have grown swiftly. Bilateral trade saw a sixfold increase in the ten years after diplomatic relations were fully established, making India Israel's second-largest trading partner in Asia in non-military goods. Diamonds alone account for 65 percent of the total trade. Technology and communications also have been growth sectors. Investment in collaborative science and technology projects doubled from $0.5 million in 2003 to $1 million in 2005, with an increased interest in the field of nanotechnology.[12] India and Israel also have been cooperating on their respective space programs, and in 2003 they signed a memorandum of understanding for the late-2008 launch of an Israeli telescope on an Indian space vehicle.[13] Prospects for future cooperation in the field are good, as India's geography makes it a more favorable launching pad for satellites than Israel's. India has proved its reliability in this regard, launching an Israeli spy satellite into space on January 21, 2008, via an Indian space rocket at the Satish Dhawan Space Centre in Sriharikota, Andhra Pradesh. The satellite has greatly enhanced Israel's intelligence-gathering capabilities against Iran, Syria, and Lebanon.[14]

Agricultural cooperation also has been important. India and Israel established a research and development farm in 1998 with the aim of sharing technology to improve agricultural efficiency and quality. Experts from Israel have traveled to West Bengal to offer a course on international marketing for agribusiness in which they discussed developing new products for international markets, using post-harvest technology, packaging fresh produce, analyzing costs, and developing name brands.[15] Israeli companies also are looking toward dairy management as an area of cooperation, hoping to develop methods to reduce the impact of dairy farms on the environment and to overcome water scarcity while increasing farm production. Codifying such efforts, the two governments signed the three-year Work Plan for Cooperation in the Field of Agriculture, which is expected to lead to more "practical cooperation," particularly in the areas of technology sharing and in collaborative projects.[16]

FUTURE PROSPECTS

In an increasingly globalized world, India and Israel are becoming closer partners on a variety of issues, from commerce to defense. The two countries were kept apart by ideology and differing views of the Middle East until the early 1990s, but since then, pragmatic efforts to build on their common interests have ruled the day. On the whole, their relationship should continue to improve as its strategic merits and financial potential outweigh its domestic and regional political liabilities. Although the Indo-Israeli relationship was revived because of pragmatic concerns, the relationship is broader than a buyer-seller arrangement. The two countries share common interests beyond their commercial ties, including the threat of Islamic terrorism.

While Indo-Israeli relations are on an upward trend, a number of factors could prove complicating over time and damage the relationship. One factor is the relations of the two countries with third-party countries. India has displayed concern about Israel's willingness to export high-tech electronics and arms to China, an important regional competitor, and the possibility of sales to Pakistan, a long-time foe. Both Israel, which views Pakistan as an important non-Arab Islamic state, and Pakistan, which is concerned about India's exclusive ties with Israel, have made efforts toward forging new ties with one another. If and when Islamabad and Jerusalem establish an overt and more substantial relationship, the role of Israel in India's domestic politics could experience a significant shift. Similarly, Israel is concerned about India's ties with Iran. The Indo-Iranian relationship, however, seems unlikely to threaten Indo-Israeli ties in the near future. Another possible problem would arise if the United States replaced Israel as one of India's primary defense suppliers. Many U.S. companies no doubt wish to play that role, and the United States has bid to supply major naval and air assets to the Indian armed forces.

Indo-Israeli relations have become less controversial within India over the last few years as the Congress Party has by and large moved beyond historical opposition to form close ties with Israel, but India's leftist parties are still virulently opposed. In the future, attempts to secure the vote of India's large Muslim population and the potential need to include leftists in a coalition government, especially one with a narrow hold on power, could once again make Indo-Israeli ties a contentious issue in the Indian political debate.

CHINA AND ISRAEL

Although China and Israel have very little common history, Israel was the first country in the Middle East to recognize the People's Republic of China.

However, formal diplomatic relations were not established until 1992, after about a decade of private talks and consultations.

The focus of Sino-Israeli cooperation has been military relations. Israel and China began to engage in extensive military cooperation as early as the 1980s, even though formal diplomatic relations did not exist, and some estimate that Israel sold arms worth $4 billion to China during that period.

Seeking credibility and competitiveness in the international arms market, China had to turn to Israel to supplement its own military technology— particularly with arms and technology that it wanted but could not acquire from either the United States or Russia[17]—when Chinese arms exports experienced a downturn in the 1990s. The downturn was due in part to the Gulf War, in which advanced U.S. weapons and technology demonstrated their superiority over low-tech Chinese weapons. One of China's main buyers, Iran, noted the performance of the Chinese weapons used by Iraq and became apprehensive about buying similar weapons. Further problems occurred when the Sino-Pakistani K-8 jet trainer project performed poorly due to low-quality engine components and poor construction. The delay of the joint program between China and Pakistan to build the Super 7 fighter due to resource constraints also proved an obstacle. Chinese reliability—in terms not only of technology but also of capability—became a concern for Pakistan, too, suggesting that unless China changed its practices, it might need to find a market for its arms elsewhere.

China's shrinking buyer base, coupled with the inability of the Chinese to export cruise and some ballistic missiles and related technology due to nonproliferation agreements, has served to exacerbate the decline in the profitability of China's arms sales. In the 1990s, China also saw its naval exports drop as countries shied away from the Soviet-era ships that it was offering because of design and construction flaws as well as their lack of modern weapons systems and electronics.

Moreover, U.S. and EU arms embargoes deny China direct access to advanced military technology and U.S.-made weapons platforms, which are critical to its ambitious military modernization program. By purchasing arms from Israel, China is able to circumvent the embargoes and secure advanced military technology that would otherwise be unavailable. Israel, however, does not have total freedom in its military dealings with Beijing because of U.S. pressure to limit the extent of its cooperation with China. In July 2000, U.S. pressure forced Israel to cancel a Chinese order for

PHALCON airborne early warning systems. In 2004–05, the United States blocked a similar Sino-Israeli deal to upgrade Israeli-manufactured HARPY drones. In both cases, Washington intervened because it viewed the deals as contrary to U.S. national security interests.

Before the formal establishment of ties between Israel and China in January 1992, the countries had a long relationship based on the arms trade. A U.S. Arms Control and Disarmament Agency study estimated that China imported nearly $526 million in Israeli arms between 1984 and 1994.[18] In 2005, Israel and China decided to double total trade to nearly $5 billion by 2008, a show of good faith to ensure profitable mutual ties through scientific and technological cooperation. Bilateral trade exceeded $3 billion in 2007, and China is the third-largest exporter of goods to Israel, behind the United States and Germany.[19]

China's market for high-tech Israeli military products is growing, and Israel sees China as a major customer. According to a report from the U.S.-China Security Review Commission, "Israel ranks second only to Russia as a weapons system provider to China and as a conduit for sophisticated military technology, followed by France and Germany."[20] The shift to an interest in high-tech military systems and platforms may be a result of European suppliers positioning themselves to secure entry into the Chinese market if the European arms embargo is lifted, leading to increased competition.

Since the establishment of diplomatic relations, cultural exchanges also have been a major component of the bilateral relationship. Both sides recognize the importance of creating a strong foundation based on their different but ancient and rich histories, and in 2007, China launched a countrywide Festival of Culture in Israel to mark their 15 years of relations.

Chinese relations with Israel, however, do not operate in a vacuum. China's policy toward Iran, its public support for Palestinian militant groups, and its supply of arms to Israel's enemies have all been points of contention. China's vocal support for the Palestinian cause, however, is necessary to protect its economic ties with the Arab states in the face of Beijing's close military cooperation with Israel. In a show of diplomatic support, China invited the Palestinian foreign minister, Mahmoud al-Zahar, a member of Hamas, to the China-Arab Forum in 2006. While both Israel and the West condemned China's move to build ties with Hamas, a greater threat to the security of the region and especially to Israel is China's so-called "no questions asked" arms policy. In the pursuit of its own economic interests, China has been willing to sell arms to any country, despite links to terrorist groups or a proclivity to use the weapons to incite conflict. The 2006 war in Lebanon underlined the threat when Syria and Iran transferred legally purchased Chinese arms to Hezbollah for use against Israel.[21] Several sources reported that Chinese-made rockets were fired from Gaza into Israel in late 2008 and early 2009. Unnamed sources also indicated that Chinese-made rockets were sold legally to Iran and then transferred to Hamas.[22]

However, it should also be noted that the building of military cooperation and trade has also softened China's historical anti-Israel policy over Palestine and Middle East issues. China has now become a vital market for Israel's extensive military industries and arms manufacturers. Israel also has limited its cooperation with Taiwan in order to foster closer ties with China.

JAPAN AND ISRAEL

Japan recognized Israel in 1952, and Israel established a legation in Tokyo the same year. In 1955, Japan opened a legation in Tel Aviv. Both assumed the status of embassies in 1963. Israel and Japan maintain thriving scientific connections in the form of joint projects and academic exchanges among universities. With the thaw of the cold war and the end of the 1991 Gulf War, bilateral relations strengthened. Japan has been an important player in the peace process, holding summits between Palestinian and Israeli leaders and providing $833 million in aid to the Palestinians between 1993 and 2005.[23] Japan has taken on a positive role not only within the framework of multilateral peace negotiations but also in the areas of environmental and economic development and water resource management in Israel.

In 2002, bilateral trade between Israel and Japan amounted to $1.6 billion, with Israel benefiting slightly more. In 2008, Israel-Japan trade amounted to $3.1 billion, of which Japanese exports constituted more than two-thirds of the total.[24] Japan's primary exports to Israel are automobiles, machinery, electrical equipment, and chemical products. Israel's primary exports to Japan include polished diamonds, chemical products, machinery, electrical equipment, and citrus fruit. In conjunction with the Tokyo Diamond Exchange, the Economic Mission of Israel in Tokyo held a seminar in June 2006 about the Israeli diamond industry and opportunities for trade with Japan; exports of Israeli diamonds to Japan in that year accounted for 20 percent of total Israeli exports to Japan.[25] It was announced in June

2007 that the first delegation of Israeli builders would travel to Japan to assess prospects for engagement in the successful Japanese building market, the second largest in the world, which was valued at $500 billion in 2006.[26]

SOUTH KOREA AND ISRAEL

Israel and South Korea established full diplomatic relations in 1962. Israel's embassy in Seoul closed in 1978, allegedly for budgetary reasons; the true reason may have been South Korea's recognition of the PLO as the sole legitimate representative of the Palestinian people and Seoul's repeated calls for Israel to withdraw from the occupied territories.[27] The embassy finally reopened in 1992, and then foreign minister Ban Ki-Moon made a visit to Israel in 2005. With Ban Ki-Moon's appointment as the new UN secretary-general, South Korea has gained special prominence in the global arena, of which Israel is well aware. In January 2007, Tzipi Livni, then Israel's deputy prime minister and minister of foreign affairs, met with South Korea's prime minister, Han Meyong-Sook, during a tour of northeast Asia. Livni emphasized economic cooperation and commercial relations during her visit, and she also spoke at the Leadership Institute of Yonsei University.[28]

Economic ties are by far the strongest connection between the two countries. Bilateral trade exceeded $1.4 billion in 2004. In 2005, both sides "agreed to generate funds of $9 million over the next three years as part of their effort to work more closely in research and development in the private sector."[29] In addition, Israel's prime minister, Ehud Olmert, held talks with Chin Dae-jae, Korea's information and communication minister, to discuss the potential for enhanced cooperation in the information technology sector.[30] In 2006 alone, approximately 300 Israeli companies completed economic deals in South Korea.

Since 2005, there has been discussion of a possible free trade agreement between the two countries. The Israeli government has already conducted research on the issue, concluding that an agreement would be useful and effective. Olmert said that he "believe[s] that the Free Trade Agreement between Korea and Israel is something that can benefit both sides" while recognizing that it would have to be implemented gradually. There is a huge demand in Israel for South Korean automobiles and electronic items from Hyundai and Samsung, and Olmert suggested that those goods be the starting point for an FTA. South Korea and Israel also have discussed promoting bilateral tourism. In 2004, approximately 18,000 South Korean tourists visited Israel. Currently, nationals of both Israel and South Korea can visit the other country for a period of up to three months without a visa, which helps encourage the exchanges.[31]

SINGAPORE AND ISRAEL

Singapore and Israel have enjoyed close relations from the outset and have strong bilateral ties, in part because each country perceives itself as a regional economic powerhouse surrounded by much larger Islamic countries with which it has an uneasy relationship. Following its independence in 1965, Singapore appealed to the international community for technical assistance and military aid. Israel sent a mission to jump-start Singapore's economy and create, from scratch, Singapore's armed forces and its Ministry of Defence (MINDEF), the former modeled after the Israeli Defense Forces (IDF) in both doctrine and order of battle. Both have always perceived the right of existence of small countries to be of vital importance, and such shared values and perceptions have contributed to the formalization of bilateral ties. And indeed, Israel has had a political presence in Singapore since its earliest days, taking formal shape in 1968.

Other understandings include the necessity of developing broad international trade relations in order to overcome geographical limitations, a shared view that led to significant growth in mutual cooperation. Singapore is a hub for Israeli business and regional trade, while a growing number of members of both business communities seek opportunities for joint operations in biotechnology and in the IT and software industries, where both countries' comparative advantages are strongest.[32]

TURKMENISTAN AND ISRAEL

The decision by the government of Turkmenistan to allow Israel to open an embassy in its capital city, Ashgabad, was a major diplomatic victory for the Jewish state. Although the two countries established relations 17 years ago, not until May 2009 was Israel—despite several requests—allowed to open an embassy in the country. One of the reasons for Turkmenistan's hesitation is its relations with Iran, with which it shares a 992-kilometer border and engages in bilateral trade worth $1.2 billion a year. Turkmenistan's late president, Saparmurat Atayevich Niyazov, feared that allowing

Israel to open an embassy in the capital would sour relations with Tehran, whose friendship was important to him. However, on the death of Niyazov, Turkmenistan's enthusiasm for Tehran waned.

The opening of the embassy will strengthen Israel's presence in Central Asia and the Caucasus region. With Turkmenistan's increasing importance as a supplier in the international energy market, its companies will gain a bigger foothold in sectors such as construction, agriculture, and possibly defense. That is important for Israel, not just for economic reasons, but also for strategic ones. All of the Central Asian countries share borders with Iran. Israel could use the opportunity to expand its intelligence-gathering operations against Tehran. Furthermore, with the weakening of its ally in Georgia after the 2008 war against Russia, Israel was worried that its influence in the area may wane.[33]

AZERBAIJAN AND ISRAEL

Relations between Azerbaijan and Israel have been in good shape for a number of years, and Israel has an embassy in Baku. In May 1999, the U.S.-Azerbaijan Council sponsored a seminar to discuss relations between the people of Azerbaijan, Jews, and Israel. In April 2000, an Israeli trade delegation visited Baku to discuss ways of strengthening bilateral economic relations.

Many Azerbaijanis express the hope that friendship with Israel may help to resolve Azerbaijan's continued dispute with Armenia over their respective claims to the Nagorno-Karabakh region of the South Caucasus and thereby expedite Azerbaijan's integration with the West. The Azerbaijan-Israel Friendship Society facilitates and promotes bilateral diplomatic and business links. In October 2001, President Aliyev pledged to open an embassy in Israel and to send his foreign minister to visit the country; as of December 2009, that had not happened, although Azerbaijani-Israeli strategic cooperation continues to grow.

For many years, Azerbaijan has had a high rate of immigration to Israel due to the economic and political situation in the country. In 2002, 475 Jews made Aliyah (immigration to Israel) and 111 immigrated to the United States. The Azeri government gets regular updates from Israel regarding Azeri Jews in Israel, who face unemployment, crime, and other social issues as new immigrants in Israel.[34]

CONCLUSION

This short review of the connections between Asia and Israel is a useful reminder that the hyperbolic propaganda found in the Middle East and the West about the centrality of the Arab-Israeli conflict to Middle East stability does not seem to have had much impact on the practical decision by key Asian countries to do business with Israel. Israel has one of the Middle East's most robust economies, regulated by democratic institutions and a vigorously independent judiciary. It also has an advanced technology sector that is especially innovative in high-tech agriculture, medicine, information technology and, probably most important, aerospace and defense.

In sum, the most successful Asian countries regard Israel as a similarly successful country that they can do business with rather than a pariah to be boycotted. The Asians would like to see the Arab-Israeli conflict resolved because it would improve the chances for greater economic development throughout the region. But at this stage of their Middle East forays, the Asians have no interest in becoming heavy hitters in the exhaustive and frustrating search for Middle East peace.

PART THREE

STRATEGIC LINKAGES

CHAPTER SIX

INFRASTRUCTURE PROJECTS IN THE GULF AND CENTRAL ASIA

To GAIN MORE PERSPECTIVE on long-term trends in relations between Asian and Middle Eastern countries, it is important to examine other infrastructure projects that will make travel and trade between Asia and the Middle East by land, air, and sea easier and further facilitate commercial and political ties. If most of the projects are completed, their long-range impact on regional geopolitics and geoeconomics will be far-reaching.

This chapter examines two sets of infrastructure developments. First, the economic boom in the Arab Gulf has generated a number of important projects that relate directly to commerce with Asia, especially new airport, seaport, and tourist facilities. Second, improvements in both east-west and north-south land routes across Central Asia—together with the improvements in the internal road and rail networks of India, China, and Pakistan that already have been discussed—also will make access across Asia and into the Middle East much easier.

THE ARAB GULF

Thanks to large deposits of petroleum and natural gas and record high prices for those commodities until 2008, the Gulf states accumulated a vast amount of wealth and witnessed the doubling of their economies from 2002 to 2006.[1] With their new assets, they have begun massive construction and development projects estimated to be worth more than $3 trillion.

Map 6-1 summarizes a few of the major projects currently under way in the Gulf states. The most spectacular and most advanced developments are in the UAE, with Dubai clearly at the forefront. What is happening there is especially illuminating because Dubai's infrastructure projects are part of an audacious business plan that, if successful, could bring great change in the Gulf and have far-reaching economic as well as strategic consequences. Abu Dhabi, the UAE's capital, is a close second, and Doha, in Qatar, is rapidly expanding its own development. Saudi Arabia, Bahrain, and Kuwait also have major new projects; even Oman is seeking its own niche for tourism. All of the undertakings involved have important implications for the key Asian countries, providing investment opportunities, a huge labor market, and a growing tourism industry. But all have been set back by the slowdown in the global economy, and it is difficult to judge which will survive and thrive.

DUBAI

Dubai's economic growth in the 1990s was based on the policies of Dubai's ruler, Sheikh Maktoum bin Rashid al-Maktoum. Sheikh Maktoum's policies focused on using oil wealth to diversify Dubai's economy by creating state-run property firms and working to establish a local financial services sector.[2] He also set up Dubai as a free trade zone, helping the city to become a successful transshipment point in the international market. The 1990–91 Gulf War brought short-term problems to Dubai when international funding was held up due to political concerns, but foreign companies soon returned, attracted by Dubai's free trade zones.[3] Sheikh Maktoum aimed to make Dubai not just a destination but a brand name by establishing prominent international sporting events and focusing on the ultra-luxury goods and entertainment markets. Dubai's economy grew by 15 percent annually from 1996 to 2006, and its stock market saw 500 percent growth from 2004 to 2006.

In 2006 Sheikh Maktoum died and was succeeded by his brother, Sheikh Mohammed bin Rashid al-Maktoum. Sheik Mohammed's ambitions to make Dubai an international hub, a financial and tourist center comparable to Hong Kong and Singapore—which include plans to make Emirates Airlines the largest in the world—have been dampened by the global economic crisis that emerged in the latter months of 2008.

MAP 6-1

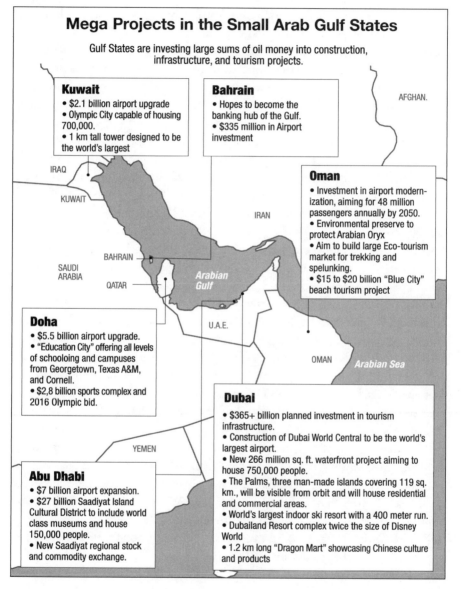

Mega Projects in the Small Arab Gulf States

Gulf States are investing large sums of oil money into construction, infrastructure, and tourism projects.

Kuwait
- $2.1 billion airport upgrade
- Olympic City capable of housing 700,000.
- 1 km tall tower designed to be the world's largest

Bahrain
- Hopes to become the banking hub of the Gulf.
- $335 million in Airport investment

Oman
- Investment in airport modernization, aiming for 48 million passengers annually by 2050.
- Environmental preserve to protect Arabian Oryx
- Aim to build large Eco-tourism market for trekking and spelunking.
- $15 to $20 billion "Blue City" beach tourism project

Doha
- $5.5 billion airport upgrade.
- "Education City" offering all levels of schooloing and campuses from Georgetown, Texas A&M, and Cornell.
- $2,8 billion sports complex and 2016 Olympic bid.

Dubai
- $365+ billion planned investment in tourism infrastructure.
- Construction of Dubai World Central to be the world's largest airport.
- New 266 million sq. ft. waterfront project aiming to house 750,000 people.
- The Palms, three man-made islands covering 119 sq. km., will be visible from orbit and will house residential and commercial areas.
- World's largest indoor ski resort with a 400 meter run.
- Dubailand Resort complex twice the size of Disney World
- 1.2 km long "Dragon Mart" showcasing Chinese culture and products

Abu Dhabi
- $7 billion airport expansion.
- $27 billion Saadiyat Island Cultural District to include world class museums and house 150,000 people.
- New Saadiyat regional stock and commodity exchange.

AFGHAN.

IRAQ

KUWAIT

IRAN

SAUDI ARABIA

BAHRAIN

QATAR

Arabian Gulf

U.A.E.

OMAN   *Arabian Sea*

YEMEN

Building Projects. Over the last few years Dubai has built and begun construction on a collection of awe-inspiring projects that are unlike anything else in the world, much less the Middle East. One notable example is the Burj al-Arab (Tower of the Arabs), a 1,053-foot building built to resemble the sail of an Arab sailing ship that claims to be the world's only seven-star hotel. Such opulence comes at a high price, however; the Royal Suite fetches roughly $28,000 per night. Dubai's largest construction projects involve the wholesale creation of new land out of the Gulf itself. The Palms are a set of three artificial islands in the shape of palm trees; they are surrounded by a crescent that covers more than 50 square miles, and the project is visible from space. Only one, the Palm Jumeirah, has been completed. Its 9 square miles are dedicated to luxury homes and resorts, retail properties, and entertainment districts. The second island, Jebel Ali, is to be formed from 16 square miles of reclaimed land in the Gulf and to host a variety of amusement parks, including Sea World, and luxury housing. When seen from above, a series of floating homes within the complex will spell out a poem in Arabic by Dubai Sheik Mohammed bin Rashid al-Maktoum.[4] The third and largest, Palm Deira, will be formed from 28 square miles of reclaimed land, making it the largest man-made island in the world, and will include luxury residential and commercial developments.[5] Dubai also has plans for a massive waterfront development project, including a district of luxury homes and hotels encompassing 266 million square feet and housing up to 750,000 people. The project also includes a series of islands in a crescent shape surrounding the western half of Palm Jebel Ali.

Dubai's Nakheel Real Estate Development Company, a government-owned firm, originally made plans to build "The Universe," a serpentine set of islands winding from Palm Deira toward Palm Jumeirah, between the current shore and "The World,"[6] a series of islands that resemble the shape of the seven continents. The plans for The World consist of 250 to 300 small islands intended for private residential use that are accessible only by helicopter or boat. Each island ranges from 250,000 to 900,000 square feet, separated from the others by 130 to 260 feet of water. If completed, The World, which is located 2.5 miles off shore, will be 5.4 miles in length and 3.6 miles in width. As of December 2009, the reclamation of the land had been completed but construction had stalled.

Since the economic crisis of 2008, the future of the islands, with the exception of Palm Jumeirah, is unclear. The crown jewel of the construction boom is the Burj Khalifa. It is the tallest structure in the world, and will encompass both commercial and residential space, including the flagship hotel of Giorgio Armani's new luxury hotel chain.[7] Emaar, the property development firm behind the Burj Khalifa, states that the tower will be "tangible proof of Dubai's central role in a growing world . . . an icon of the new Middle East: prosperous, dynamic, and successful."[8] The Burj Khalifa was formally opened amid great flourish on January 4, 2010. Originally called the Burj Dubai, it was renamed in honor of the president of the UAE, Khalifa bin Zayed. However, many other building projects have been suspended and thousands of construction workers have been laid off.

Air Travel Infrastructure. During the coming twenty years, the UAE has plans to spend $20 billion on the expansion and modernization of its airports, including the redevelopment of Abu Dhabi International Airport, the expansion of Dubai International Airport, and construction of Al-Maktoum International Airport, which is scheduled to open in June 2010.[9] In the first eight months of 2009, Dubai International Airport (DIA), the Middle East's busiest, handled nearly 27 million passengers (up from just over 25 million in the corresponding period of 2008) flying on 125 airlines to 210 destinations. Total passenger traffic is expected to top 46 million in 2010.[10] The aviation industry currently accounts for "at least 25 per cent of Dubai's GDP."[11]

The key to Dubai's plan to become a global hub is Al-Maktoum International Airport in the Dubai World Central trade project. Dubai hopes that Al-Maktoum International will become the largest and busiest airport in the world, handling up to 120 million passengers and 12 million tons of cargo annually.[12] If its plans are realized, Al-Maktoum International will be ten times the size of the current Dubai International Airport and Dubai Cargo Village combined. With Al-Maktoum's proximity to Jebel Ali, an enormous—and growing—manufacturing center and port, air and sea cargo shipping will be integrated, providing Dubai with an unmatched advantage, with the possible exception of Singapore and Hong Kong.[13] Upon completion, Al-Maktoum International will have almost twice the annual passenger throughput of airports such as London's Heathrow and Chicago's O'Hare.[14]

Dubai's efforts to become a global transport hub are also based on the fact that the successful and swiftly growing Emirates Airlines is based in Dubai. The airline, which was started in 1985, has grown more than 20 percent a year since its inception. It now pays the Dubai government dividends of more than $100 million every year on its $80 million initial investment.[15] Today, Emirates is the fourteenth-largest and fifth-most profitable airline in the world. Emirates aims to expand to 246 aircraft and has signed a contract for 120 Airbus A350s, 11 A380s, and 12 Boeing 777-300ERs—a $34.9 billion investment. Emirates, which is the largest customer for the Airbus A380 super-jumbo jetliner, is expected to carry 45 million passengers annually by 2025.[16] It also is rapidly expanding its routes, offering direct flights from Dubai to Los Angeles and Houston, and it is projected to be flying more than 100 aircraft to more than 100 destinations by 2010.[17] Despite massive investments, the airline is not just a sinkhole for reinvested oil wealth: Emirates reported a profit for the first six months of 2009 of 752 million UAE dirhams ($205 million), almost triple that for the corresponding period in 2008.[18] In the summer of 2008 Emirates announced the creation of its new low-cost carrier, FlyDubai, which began operation in June 2009.[19]

Quite apart from the downturn caused by the 2008–09 global recession, an open and fiercely debated question within the airline industry is whether the hub model chosen by Emirates and its main competitor, Etihad Airways, can stand up to a point-to-point model. Generally speaking, the hub model looks like a bicycle wheel; passengers move along the spokes of the wheel and connect to a central hub from which they can access a variety of destinations. This system maximizes efficiency and allows the airlines to operate out of more locations at a lower cost. In contrast, airlines in a point-to-point system fly passengers directly to their destination—an option that, although it is preferred by most passengers, increases airline operating costs and limits available destinations. While the hub model should yield lower costs, some point-to-point airlines have fared better than major hub carriers in recent years. Emirates might make a profit running a route from Athens to Singapore, but if Dubai's purpose is to make itself a world center, then within certain margins the cost advantage may be a moot point.[20]

Maritime Infrastructure.   Dubai's ports are the busiest in the Middle East, with the most traffic at Port Jebel Ali and Port Rashid. In 2005, the World Container Port League listed Port Jebel Ali and Port Rashid combined as the ninth-busiest in the world. Port Rashid was reconfigured in 2008 to become a terminal for cruise ships because its urban location has no space for expansion. The reconfiguration coincides with the rapid expansion of Jebel Ali. The ports were a transit point for 7.6 million twenty-foot equivalent units (TEU), the standard measure of a ship's or port's cargo capacity.[21] The next Middle Eastern port on the list, Jeddah, recorded only 2.8 million TEU in 2005. Jebel Ali recorded the majority of incoming traffic to the UAE, with 2006 figures of roughly 7.9 million TEU; Port Rashid accounted for 1.45 million TEU. Jebel Ali's numbers are only increasing. In 2007, the port had a throughput of 9.9 million TEU, and its current capacity of 11 million is scheduled to increase to 14 million by the end of 2009.[22]

To keep pace with that growth, the UAE has announced a $1.25 billion expansion plan for Jebel Ali through 2020.[23] As the world's largest man-made port, Jebel Ali already has state-of-the-art facilities such as gate automation, e-payment services, and the world's first simulator to train operators to use the port's giant tandem lift cranes.[24] That capability could prove to be an invaluable asset, as the neighboring emirate of Abu Dhabi has set itself the goal of becoming the largest producer of aluminum in the world.[25] Jebel Ali is also well-placed to handle the super-large container ships that run ferry routes from East Asia through the Suez Canal.[26]

Tourism. Dubai is building a number of tourist attractions including Dubailand, an amusement park planned to grow to twice the size of Walt Disney World that will encompass U.S. brand theme parks such as Six Flags, Universal Studios, DreamWorks Animation, and others.[27] The park is slated to include sports complexes and traditional theme park rides as well as the world's largest artificial ski resort, which features a 400-meter run with a 60-meter drop. The complex also will feature an arctic zoo as well as areas for sledding and snowball fights, a surely welcome respite from the Gulf region's heat.

Dubai, which is a destination and venue for major international events, especially in the northern hemisphere's winter months, is spending the most money to attract tourists. Located within four hours flying time of nearly 2 billion people (see map 6-2), Dubai plans to become the tourist destination of choice for many Asian and European travelers. Before the recession, the emirate expected a massive increase in tourism in the next few years; accordingly, investors spent more than $365 billion erecting the tallest towers, the most luxurious hotels, and the largest shopping malls in the world in preparation for the boom.

Dubai hosts the annual Dubai Desert Classic golf tournament, which began in 1989 and has since become one of the most popular events on the European Tour.[28] Dubai also is the venue for the Barclays' Dubai tennis championship, held every February and March. In addition, Dubai plays host to an annual international Rugby Sevens competition every December, and it is the starting point of the UAE Desert Challenge rally race every

November.[29] Dubai's most prominent sporting event is horse racing. The Dubai World Cup, which takes place every March at the conclusion of the Dubai racing season, features the richest purse in the horse racing world—$6 million, with $3.6 million going to the winner alone.[30] Dubai also hosts a prominent film festival every December, and it is an increasingly popular venue for business conferences.[31] In 2008, Dubai hotels hosted 7.5 million overnight visitors as well as more than 182,000 cruise ship passengers on day visits; its hotel occupancy rates were the second highest in the world, eclipsing Tokyo, Sydney, London, and Hong Kong.[32] The first three months of 2009 saw occupancy rates drop from nearly 90 percent to 73 percent as guests opted for shorter stays; however, the total number of guests continued to increase, to 1.62 million, during that time period, growing 3.7 percent.[33]

The recession has affected funding for Dubai's projects and depressed tourism generally. Thus Dubai has found itself to have overbuilt at the height of the boom cycle and left with too much capacity in the downturn. Estimates suggest that in order to fill all planned commercial and residential developments, Dubai must increase its population from the current 1.3 million to 4 million by 2020.[34] Dubai's development ventures have a high risk-reward ratio on the basis of their costs alone; their huge scope leaves them the most exposed to a decline in demand. In short, Dubai's building splurge was predicated on a historically high boom economy. While fundamentals—such as population growth and increased Asian, especially Chinese, demand for hydrocarbons—may well continue even in the face of the downturn and lower oil prices, it is likely that planned projects either will be downsized or will face similar overcapacity. Dubai's economic future is also vulnerable to disruption from regional instability or a terrorist attack. The fact that the British Foreign Office assessed the UAE to have a "high" risk for terrorism in June 2008 demonstrates that this is a valid concern.[35]

ABU DHABI

Unlike Dubai, Abu Dhabi has huge oil reserves and one of the largest sovereign wealth funds (SWFs) in the world. While not immune to economic downturns, it is better placed to sustain growth than any other entity in the Gulf. Abu Dhabi aims to strengthen and diversify its economy with an eye toward top-end industry and tourism in order to create jobs in the service and downstream energy sectors.[36] It has announced plans to spend $7 billion to expand its airport capacity to handle 40 million passengers a year by 2025. The first stage of expansion will allow the airport to handle

MAP 6-2

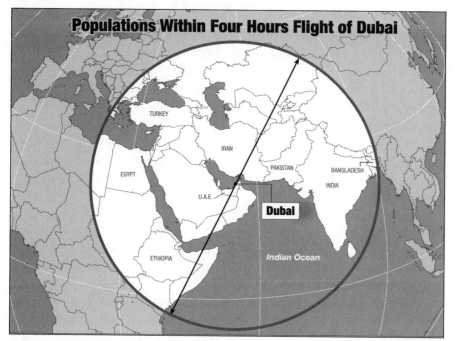

20 million passengers by 2010, up from 5.4 million in 2005.[37] Although a major waterfront real estate project is currently under way, the project that Abu Dhabi is counting on to turn it into a traveler's haven is a new cultural district, Saadiyat Island, which it hopes will make it a beacon of culture in the Gulf region.

Plans for Saadiyat Island include four new world-class museums as well as mixed commercial, residential, and leisure development. Saadiyat Island will be home to a new Guggenheim Museum for contemporary art—set to be the world's largest upon completion and the only one of its kind in the Middle East—as well as an outpost of the Louvre, in Paris. Plans also include a new maritime museum and a performing arts center that will house a music hall, concert hall, opera house, and two theaters, one seating up to 6,300 people.[38]

Abu Dhabi's tourist board insists that it is not trying to one-up Dubai but that it wants instead to complement Dubai's choices in entertainment. Abu Dhabi is relying on the idea that "cultural tourists are wealthier, older, more educated, and they spend more. From an economic view, this makes sense."[39] Abu Dhabi also plans to develop Saadiyat Island, which is half the size of Bermuda, as a luxury residential destination housing more than 150,000 people. The master plan envisages six highly individual districts including twenty-nine hotels, three marinas with combined berth space for 1,000 boats, a cultural center, two golf courses, civic and leisure facilities, sea view apartments, and elite villas. The new real estate will come in handy; Abu Dhabi expects continued population growth of 4.57 percent annually, with a total population of more than 1.75 million in 2010.[40] Abu Dhabi, like Dubai, is entering the international sporting events market. It has built a Formula One Grand Prix track, which held its first race in 2009;[41] that, along with other developments, has further increased claims that Abu Dhabi is trying to surpass Dubai.

Abu Dhabi has also broached the idea of building a new stock exchange, the Saadiyat Market, to comprise an international stock exchange, a futures and options exchange, a commodities exchange, and a clearing house. The market will be strategically located to access an estimated $1 trillion in regional assets, plus annual commodities trading of about $400 billion.[42] Its sphere of influence will include the key markets of the Middle East, the Gulf Cooperation Council countries, eastern and southern Africa, India, Pakistan, and Central Asia. Estimates have predicted that Saadiyat Market will create spin-off benefits to the region's economy in excess of $170 billion in its first 25 years of operation.[43] Basically, Abu Dhabi is looking to transform itself into an Arab version of Hong Kong or Singapore, although it is unclear how many companies will take part in an untried market.

Abu Dhabi also is investing a great amount in its energy sector, but not in hydrocarbons. While the UAE is projected to need 40 gigawatts of electrical power by 2020, domestic gas production will be able to supply only 25 gigawatts, and Abu Dhabi has responded by opening up ventures in nuclear and solar power. It also has announced plans for a sustainable development called Masdar City, which will be completely powered by renewable energy from the sun and an innovative hydrogen plant.[44] The solar facility will be a 100-megawatt concentrated solar power (CSP) plant, which uses parabolic mirrors instead of traditional photovoltaic cells to collect the sun's energy and generate heat.[45] The proposed hydrogen plant will break down natural gas into hydrogen and carbon dioxide and use the hydrogen for power while sequestering the carbon dioxide.

Abu Dhabi plans to build two nuclear power plants with French assistance under a France-UAE nuclear cooperation deal signed in January

2008.[46] In October 2009, the United States and the United Arab Emirates finalized an agreement to transfer U.S. nuclear technology to the UAE in a groundbreaking deal initiated by the Bush administration and implemented under President Barack Obama.[47] The nuclear pact has been highlighted as a model for peaceful nuclear cooperation among states.[48] The deal—under which the UAE will not enrich its own uranium or reprocess plutonium, relying instead on imported nuclear fuel[49]—will likely mean billions of dollars' worth of contracts for U.S. nuclear power companies.[50] Some in the U.S. Congress questioned the wisdom of transferring sensitive nuclear technology to the UAE, given its human rights record and its role as a hub for A. Q. Khan's black market nuclear network.[51] Despite those reservations, Congress authorized the agreement to proceed under section 123 of the U.S. Atomic Energy Act of 1954.[52]

QATAR

Qatar, which has huge natural gas reserves, also has an impressive development program under way to make itself into a more attractive tourist destination. A new $5.5 billion airport currently under construction should be able to accommodate up to 20 million passengers a year by 2010 and up to 60 million passengers a year by 2020.[53]

To attract the travelers needed to make Doha a regional hub, Qatar is developing golf courses, hotels, equestrian clubs, and luxury apartments, but it also is investing in the country's intellectual wealth. It has completed the already flourishing Education City, which provides free education for Qataris from kindergarten through university in world-class facilities and is intended to transform Qatar into the educational leader of the region. U.S. universities including Georgetown, Carnegie Mellon, Cornell, Texas A&M, Northwestern, and Virginia Commonwealth University have all established campuses in Doha. Like its neighbors in the UAE, Qatar also is trying to entice visitors with world-class sporting events. Doha spent $2.8 billion to build sporting facilities so that it could host the fifteenth annual Asian Olympic Games.[54] The event went off without a hitch, proving not just to Qataris but to the world that Doha could handle major sporting events. Qatar also bid for the 2016 Olympic Games but lost out in the second-to-last round of eliminations in June 2008.[55]

Despite all the investment and press attention, Doha's main expansion is not in tourism but in real estate. With the population of the city increasing by 60,000 between 2004 and 2006 because of the expanding energy market, there was a boom in real estate that caused dramatic increases in commercial and housing prices. Housing prices increased by 130 percent from 1996 to 2007;[56] moreover, office space shortages resulted in skyrocketing prices in the commercial sector.[57] The strong rate of growth has led to development of numerous residential projects, including Lusail City, which is being built north of Doha to house more than 200,000 people.[58] Doha also saw a boom in construction with the building of fifty new skyline-changing towers and thirty-nine new hotels that added about 9,000 new rooms for tourists. Nevertheless, whether Doha will be able to compete with Dubai and the other Gulf states in its efforts to become a regional hub is still an open question. The current economic downturn also raises doubts about the sustainability of Doha's real estate boom. Since October 2008, real estate prices have fallen by nearly 35 percent.[59] Although prices now appear to be stabilizing, as of the end of 2009, the supply of real estate still exceeded demand.[60]

KUWAIT

Kuwait also has ambitious development plans to help it compete with its Gulf neighbors. It expects to spend $2.1 billion to update its existing airport to accommodate 55 million passengers annually by 2030, a tenfold increase over 2007 traffic.[61] Kuwait is planning a 250-square-kilometer urban development in Subiya, opposite Kuwait City. Called the City of Silk, it will include hotels, spas, gardens, a nature reserve, and a skyscraper called Burj Mubarak al-Kabir, which, if built, will be taller than the Burj Khalifa. The City of Silk is the single largest real estate development in the Middle East.[62] The $132 billion project is expected to contribute nearly $15 billion to Kuwait's annual GDP by 2030 and to create 430,000 jobs for the area.[63]

In addition, Kuwait plans to develop a "future city" called Khabary near Fahaheel. The $1.8 billion project is intended to enhance Kuwait's status as a target for international investment and host for international events while regenerating the surrounding area. Wholly financed by the private sector, it offers a range of residential areas, hotels, retail space, and services, such as a specialized hospital; all are hoped to encourage international investors to pump money into the Kuwaiti economy.

BAHRAIN

While Bahrain has little oil compared with its super-oil-rich neighbors, it still harbors ambitious development plans. Bahrain has chosen to focus on banking, heavy industry, retail, and tourism to boost its economy, in addition to spending some $335 million to update its existing airport facilities.[64] Like the other Gulf states, Bahrain witnessed a boom in real estate development until the global recession in 2008.[65] Commercial development was accompanied by a surge in the construction of luxury apartments and villas. A center for Islamic finance and the main banking hub of the Gulf, Bahrain built the new Financial Harbor district to house its stock market, one of the oldest in the region.[66] A 240-meter World Trade Center offering offices and a shopping mall was completed in 2008 in Manama.[67] Located strategically near Saudi Arabia's rapidly growing eastern province, Bahrain hopes to attract a host of wealthy clientele as the state of the global economy improves.

Success will not come automatically, however. Bahrain's airport expansion program is impressive, but is outpaced by Dubai and the airlines of the UAE, Etihad and Emirates. Similarly, Bahrain faces direct competition from the UAE in its quest to be the financial hub of the region.

OMAN

Oman has chosen a different tack. Although, like other states in the area, it is investing petroleum revenues in its tourism sector, Oman aims to take advantage of its more diverse array of natural resources. The country does have some advantages over its neighbors. Oman's larger size and mountainous terrain allow it to aim for a regional niche market in ecotourism and adventure tourism. Oman has begun projects to preserve the wetlands and the grazing ground of the endangered Arabian oryx, and it also is opening up mountain trekking routes and a system of caves for avid adventurers. In addition, it is investing in its airports to increase capacity to 12 million passengers a year, and further development will increase throughput to 48 million by 2050.[68] Oman's more traditional "Blue City" project will create a major beachfront resort complex at an expected cost of between $15 and $20 billion. Although its projects are not on the same level as those of the other Gulf countries, Oman is hoping that adding to the tourism infrastructure now will pay off in the long term.

SAUDI ARABIA

While many Saudi projects are not as striking as those in Dubai or Abu Dhabi, ongoing construction in Saudi Arabia is, in total, immense. The kingdom, which has the largest construction market in the Middle East, attracted projects worth $410 billion in 2008.[69] Saudi Arabia's current building program is intended to foster economic growth in non–oil-based segments of the Saudi economy, provide necessary infrastructure and employment for Saudi Arabia's large indigenous population, and promote tourism along the Red Sea.

The challenges that Saudi Arabia faces—such as a disproportionately young population and the need to provide transport over vast, harsh stretches of land—are different from those of its small Gulf neighbors. With 38 percent of Saudi Arabia's population under fifteen years of age, as opposed to 20 percent in the UAE and 21 percent in Qatar, the first is an especially tough problem.[70] Accordingly, Saudi authorities have begun projects to construct education, health, and transportation infrastructure to cope with population growth of approximately 2 percent a year.

Much of the development is focused around Saudi Arabia's western Red Sea coast, especially the port of Jeddah, one of the main points of entry for pilgrims performing the pilgrimage to Mecca (hajj). With millions of visitors a year, the Saudi government plans to spend $1.5 billion to refurbish the Abdul Aziz airport in Jeddah.[71] To expand beyond its traditional hajj traffic, the Saudi government also is investing in tourism on the Red Sea— for example, in a planned $40 billion project to create three new tourist destinations there.[72]

A major expansion of the Saudi railway system is under way. Already the only country on the Arabian Peninsula with a large-scale rail system, Saudi Arabia aims to connect Jubail to Riyadh and Jeddah through a 600-mile link estimated to cost $5 billion.[73] The impact on commerce should be significant, as it will reduce border-to-border transit of goods by approximately 5 days.[74] It also has a contract with China to build a $1.8 billion monorail in Mecca.[75] In addition, Saudi Arabia and Egypt have discussed building a causeway across the Red Sea at Sharm Al-Sheik.[76] That project, which gained popularity after the tragic sinking of a ferry on the Red Sea in 2006, is projected to cost about $4 billion. Map 6-3 shows the current and future railway infrastructure in Saudi Arabia.

The Saudi government also has announced a plan to build six new "economic cities," four of which already are in development and projected to require a $72 billion investment. The cities will focus on specific industries; for example, the Prince Abdulaziz Bin Musad Economic City near Hail will center on agribusiness and construction, while the Knowledge Economic City near Medinah will focus on "knowledge-based industries with

MAP 6-3

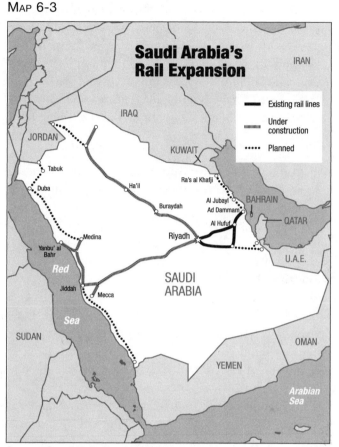

Source: Saudi Railways Organization.

an Islamic focus."[77] A new financial district in Riyadh also is being built, at a cost of $6.7 billion.[78]

Saudi Arabia's oil wealth allows it to finance many of the projects on its own, but it has received an influx of investment since 2002. According to the UN Commission on Trade and Development, Saudi Arabia received $12 billion in foreign direct investment (FDI) in 2005, and $38 billion in FDI during 2008, representing a huge increase over the $183 million the kingdom received in 2000.[79] Various factors contributed to the increase, including improvements in the business environment and increased opportunities for investment.

A primary factor in the shift was a major upsurge in Japanese investment in 2005. Japan's FDI in Saudi Arabia had been negligible from 2000 to 2004, but increased to over $516 million in 2005 and over $754 million in 2007.[80] While Saudi figures indicate only $83 million in Indian investment in Saudi Arabia from 2000 to 2006, the Indian embassy in Riyadh notes that a number of Indian firms have begun joint ventures since 2006 and predicts that India will account for $467 million in FDI over the next few years.[81]

FUTURE ECONOMIC PROSPECTS FOR THE GULF STATES

The building projects that the Gulf states are undertaking are impressive in scope, size, and content, but it is not clear that all or even most of them will be viable in the long term, given the fallout from the 2008–09 economic recession. The breakneck speed of investment in air transport is a telling example. Dubai, Qatar, and Abu Dhabi are all investing huge sums of money in hopes of becoming the main regional hub and a major global hub, but obviously only one can be the main one.

The soundest long-term investments are likely to be in basic infrastructure, for which there plainly is a need today, especially in Dubai, that is likely to increase in the future. Qatar's investment in education appears to be a wise move that should increase the productivity of its citizens generally and allow for creation of an economy that is less dependent on oil. Bahrain's pragmatic attempt to focus on financial services also is a logical move and should see success despite competition from Abu Dhabi. Oman's pursuit of a niche market helps set it apart from Abu Dhabi or Dubai, but its reliance on tourism generally leaves it vulnerable to a downturn. Dubai's development ventures feature the highest risk-reward ratio on the basis of cost alone, and their huge scope makes them the most exposed to a decline in demand.

In short, the megaprojects of the Gulf states have been predicated on a global boom economy. While fundamentals such as population growth and increased Asian, especially Chinese, demand for hydrocarbons will continue even in the face of the downturn, it is likely that the projects will be downsized now that the market has descended from its apex.

INTRA-ASIAN INFRASTRUCTURE AND ECONOMIC EXPANSION

Although the glamorous, yet risky, building projects in the Gulf attract worldwide attention, the more mundane infrastructure developments throughout Asia may have more strategic importance. This section reviews key transnational projects in Asia that supplement the domestic infrastructure programs in China, India, and Pakistan discussed in previous chapters.

China and, to a lesser extent, India are involved in numerous projects across Eurasia focused on the development of transportation and pipeline infrastructure. One of the most notable examples was the construction of the Karakoram highway between Pakistan and China. The highway, completed in 1986, stretches 1,300 kilometers, from Xinjiang province in China to Havelian, in the Abbottabad district of Pakistan.

SILK ROAD REDUX

Following the breakup of the Soviet Union, leaders throughout the region began to discuss establishing a new Silk Road to facilitate trade between Central Asia and its neighbors. However, progress has been slow. Outdated and poorly maintained domestic transportation systems, protectionist economic policies, and regional rivalries hinder the development of roads and railroads both across the region and within individual countries. Recently, outside players from Asia, Europe, and the Middle East have been actively encouraging the Central Asian nations to integrate their transportation networks and connect them to major transport corridors in China, India, Pakistan, Iran, and eastern Europe. Two main transportation corridors are envisioned for the new Silk Road: an east-west corridor that would ultimately connect China to Europe and a north-south corridor running from Russia to ports in Pakistan and Iran. According to development economists Martin Reiser and Dennis DeTray, a great deal of attention is "concentrated on unlocking the roads south from Central Asia, and providing access through the region to a new deep-water port currently being built at Gwadar in Pakistan, as well as to the existing port of Bander Abbas in Iran."[82] The payoff in trade along the corridor for the refurbishment of old roads and investment in new roads will be significant. Reiser and DeTray estimate that $5.6 billion in investment could increase total trade by 15 percent in the region.[83] (See map 6-4.)

Factors such as geography, topography, and population make Uzbekistan a favorite to host a major section of the new Silk Road. Situated at the geographic center of Central Asia, Uzbekistan is less mountainous than its Kyrgyz and Tajik neighbors, making the physical construction of both east-west and north-south roads less expensive and arduous.[84] In December 2007 the Asian Development Bank (ADB) announced that it would provide a $75.3 million loan to Uzbekistan to upgrade a key highway system that runs

MAP 6-4

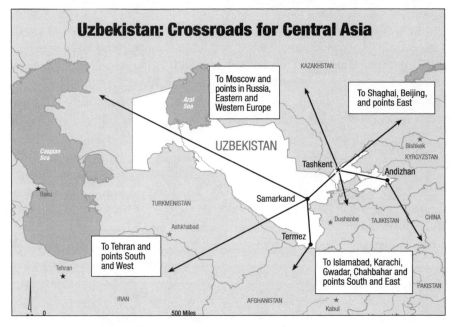

Uzbekistan: Crossroads for Central Asia

KAZAKHSTAN

To Moscow and points in Russia, Eastern and Western Europe

Aral Sea

To Shaghai, Beijing, and points East

Caspian Sea

UZBEKISTAN

★ Bishkek
KYRGYZSTAN

Tashkent ★

★ Andizhan

★ Baku

TURKMENISTAN

Samarkand

★ Dushanbe TAJIKISTAN CHINA

Ashkhabad ★

Termez

To Tehran and points South and West

Tehran ★

To Islamabad, Karachi, Gwadar, Chahbahar and points South and East

PAKISTAN

IRAN

AFGHANISTAN

★ Kabul

0   500 Miles

from the Uzbek-Kazakh border south to Afghanistan and Turkmenistan;[85] it will be a key section of the new north-south corridor.

The United Nations and the European Union also have been instrumental in the development of transportation corridors. In the early 1990s, the UN Economic and Social Commission for Asia and the Pacific endorsed the Asia Land Transport Infrastructure Development Project (ALTID) and the Trans-Asian Railroad (TAR) in hopes of facilitating interregional trade by integrating existing transportation infrastructure in Central Asia, the Caucasus, and eastern Europe. Likewise, in 1993 the European Commission launched the Transportation Corridor Europe-Caucasus-Asia (TRACECA) project, which uses EU funds to provide technical assistance for the development of an east-west corridor that runs from eastern Europe across the Black Sea, through the Caucasus, and into Central Asia.[86] EU-funded projects in Kazakhstan and Kyrgyzstan will connect China's Xinjiang Province to this corridor, enhancing trade opportunities between China and Europe.

China and India also are contributing to transportation infrastructure in greater Central Asia. While updating domestic infrastructure has been India's primary concern, New Delhi has reached out to some of its neighbors to improve energy and transportation infrastructure that will connect it to Iran and Afghanistan. India is supporting a project to create a 235-kilometer (146-mile) road from the Iran-Afghan border to Delaram, Afghanistan, where it will connect to major transport routes from Central Asia.[87] Another Indian-supported project will link the Chabahar port on the Oman Sea in Iran to an Iranian rail network that traverses Zaranj, Afghanistan, and connects to Central Asian and European roads. India is assisting in the expansion of Chabahar as part of the project. There is some speculation that India's involvement in the port of Chabahar is motivated by the aspiration to one day base Indian naval vessels there; however, Indian officials maintain that the port is strictly for commercial purposes.[88] India's involvement could also be a reaction to China's involvement in the Gwadar port in Pakistan.

Improvements in Indo-Iranian relations have been the driving force in bilateral infrastructure development as both countries seek to tap into the enormous commercial benefits that a north-south corridor would provide.[89] The Tehran Declaration, signed in 2001, solidified both nations' intentions to cooperate in the development of a north-south corridor in Eurasia to "permit the transit of goods from Indian ports to Iran's port of Bandar Abbas, or hopefully Chabahar."[90] In 2003 the New Delhi Declaration was signed, reaffirming, among other things, India and Iran's commitment to development of the corridor.[91]

China, meanwhile, is becoming increasingly involved in Central and Southwest Asia. Map 6-5 displays major Chinese-supported projects in the region, including the Karakoram highway and major railway projects. Beijing is relying on new Central Asian transportation routes to reduce its reliance on sea-based trade and to increase access to its energy-rich western neighbors. Chinese investments in the region include the rehabilitation of the Jinhezhi-Yining-Horgos route, which will reduce the distance between Urumchi, in Xinjiang province, and Almaty, Kazakhstan.[92] The development of a new rail line connecting Uzbekistan, Kyrgyzstan, and China also is under way.

Railways will be an important component of the new Silk Road. According to a report by the ADB, 88 percent of passenger and cargo traffic in the region currently is carried by rail.[93] The existing railway infrastructure in Central Asia runs from Moscow to Hairatan, Afghanistan. However, there are key gaps in the regional rail system, making long-term development difficult. For example, all trade transported by rail between Central Asia

MAP 6-5

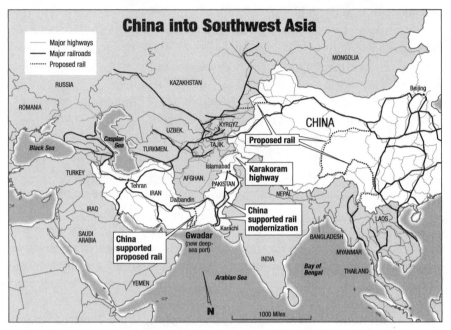

and China must pass through a single border crossing at the Druzba-Ala Pass along the Sino-Kazakh border, which creates a critical chokepoint that is easily overloaded.[94] Construction of new crossings that connect China's rail lines to Central Asian lines is being discussed, as is the expansion of rail systems along the north-south corridor. A major railway currently connects western Siberia, through Kazakhstan and Uzbekistan, to Turkmenistan and Tajikistan, and it could be expanded to connect to eastern Iran and Afghanistan.[95]

The development of a new Silk Road across Eurasia undoubtedly will also increase trade and regional integration. However, physical infrastructure represents only a small portion of the challenge of developing transport corridors. The protectionist economic and trade policies practiced by Central Asian leaders, particularly in Uzbekistan, will continue to hinder regional trade even if a new Silk Road is established. Regional rivalries and quarrels also prevent the linking of corridors across borders. For example, both Uzbekistan and Kazakhstan want to become the leading regional power in Central Asia, and competition between the two has impeded the integration of their transportation networks. Until Central Asian nations can put aside their regional rivalries and liberalize their trade sectors, the development of a new Silk Road will be for naught, even if the transportation infrastructure for such a road does eventually exist.

An important element of the transnational infrastructure projects under way in Central Asia is the Russian factor—the stake that Russia will have in the projects. Historically, Russia has been the dominant power across the region, and to this day it controls much of Central Asia's energy exports. However, the development of the new Silk Road will significantly change that dynamic—both hurting and helping Russia's position in the region.

Russia has been an advocate of the north-south corridor of the new Silk Road, which will provide it with the access to the Indian Ocean and the warm-water ports that it has always sought.[96] Increased opportunities for land-based trade with all countries in the region, transit revenues, and strengthened ties with Iran are just a few of the benefits that Russia could reap. The Russians therefore have been actively engaged in ensuring that their transportation networks are up to date and able to connect to wider regional networks. However, Moscow still has some reservations about whether the new corridor will ultimately diminish its influence over the region's energy resources. As the former Soviet territories in Central Asia look elsewhere for transit routes to help supply fuel to meet their growing need for energy, Russia fears that it will become economically irrelevant to the region once its monopoly on supply lines is broken.

Russian opposition to the new transport corridors focuses mainly on the east-west corridor, which bypasses Russia completely. When the TRACECA agreement was first signed in 1998, Russian observer delegates opposed the routes outlined in the agreement, contending that it would be cheaper and more reliable for the routes to traverse Russian territory.[97] The members of TRACECA disagreed. Russia's greatest fear is that its influence over the region will diminish in light of increased trade opportunities with the West. According to Russian analyst A. Bogaturov, the West (especially the United States) wants to make Central Asia and the Caucasus "an alternative energy belt."[98] While that claim may be exaggerated, there is no doubt that U.S. and European energy interests are attempting to break Moscow's energy monopoly in the region—an action that Moscow fears will affect its position as the main land-based transit corridor between Europe and Central Asia.

PIPELINES

As oil and natural gas imports rise, so too will the number of intra-Asian pipelines. Many pipeline projects reaching across Eurasia to China, India, and Japan are being planned. The majority will run through Turkmeni-stan and the other Central Asian countries, which possess large, untapped oil and natural gas reserves. A Turkmenistan-Afghanistan-Pakistan-India (TAPI) pipeline was proposed and brokered by the Asian Development Bank in 2002; however, negotiations have been delayed for numerous rea-sons, including the stalled Iran-Pakistan-India (IPI) pipeline talks and politi-cal instability in Pakistan. In April 2008, GAIL Limited, an Indian state-run firm, announced that the TAPI pipeline will be built by a consortium of national oil companies of the four states involved at an estimated cost of $7.6 billion. The United States, a vocal critic of the IPI pipeline, strongly backs the TAPI pipeline, which bypasses the Islamic Republic of Iran.[99]

Internal and regional infrastructure projects have been developed to improve energy efficiency and to deliver oil and natural gas to China. China has built a pipeline from the northwestern Xinjiang region to Shanghai to increase the flow of gas from the rural countryside to its main cities. The pipeline is one of a broad array of investments to bring Chinese resources in western provinces to the booming coastal cities, including "coal-by-wire" projects and hydropower projects that generate power in mountainous rural areas and "export" it to more prosperous urban jurisdictions. The pipeline eventually will connect with transnational pipelines traversing Central Asia.

Currently, China also is assisting in the development of various pipelines from Kazakhstan, Uzbekistan, and Turkmenistan (see chapter 3 for plans for the Kazakh-China pipeline). Maps 6-6, 6-7, and 6-8 show current and future oil and gas pipelines traversing Eurasia.

In 2008, the Uzbek and Chinese state-run energy companies, Uzbeknefte-gaz and China National Petroleum Corporation, announced a joint venture to build a natural gas pipeline from Turkmenistan through Uzbekistan and Kazakhstan to China. The venture, named Asia Trans Gas, will include a 330-mile pipeline that will carry approximately 30 billion cubic meters of natural gas from Turkmenistan to China.[100] Operations on the first section of the pipeline, completed in July 2009, will begin in January 2010, updat-ing Uzbekistan's poor natural gas infrastructure and breaking the monop-oly that Russia currently holds on Turkmenistan's natural gas reserves.[101]

MAP 6-6

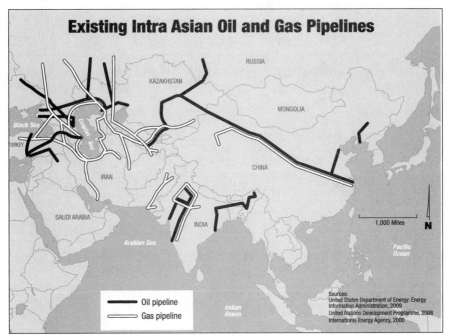

China also has promised $35 million to develop and update natural gas infrastructure already in Uzbekistan.

In 2012, the second phase of the project will be complete, increasing capacity to 30 billion cubic meters annually. In total, the pipeline will run 1,100 miles through Turkmenistan, Uzbekistan, and Kazakhstan to China, at a cost of $7.31 billion. According to KazMunaiGas, a state-run Kazakh energy company, "This project would help transport gas to China and diversify Kazakhstan's gas export routes."[102] Finally, China is interested in making arrangements with Iran to build an oil pipeline from the Caspian Sea to connect to the Kazakhstan-China pipeline.

SUMMARY

The infrastructure projects under way in the Gulf states and Asia will have a long-term impact on the future commercial and economic vitality of those regions. The Gulf states have recognized the need to diversify their

Map 6-7

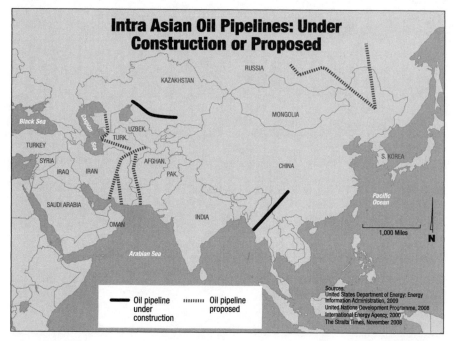

Map 6-8

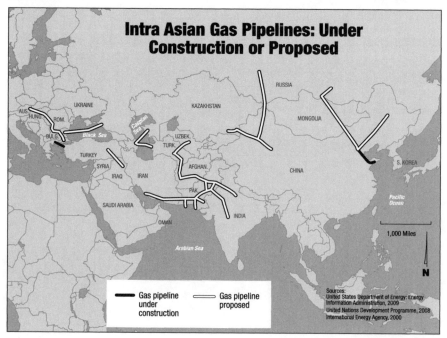

economies and, using their oil wealth, have invested in their tourist, banking, and educational infrastructure. While the accomplishments of the Gulf states seem dramatic, they can be easily overstated. The drop in oil prices and the subsequent economic recession in 2008–09 could reduce their significance in the short term.

The transnational transportation and energy infrastructure projects in Eurasia, if successful, could lead to significant economic rewards for Central Asia and eventually the Middle East and Southwest Asia. Furthermore, the development of new pipelines in the region will relieve some of China's and India's reliance on seaborne energy shipments—key because those shipments could easily come to a halt if the straits at Hormuz or Malacca are compromised by either a blockade or an attack. But once again, it is easy to overstate these accomplishments. Infrastructure development in Eurasia has been plagued by regional rivalries and could be derailed in the future. Conflict in Afghanistan, political instability in numerous governments in the region, or a showdown between the United States and Iran could all impede the progress of planned developments. While all of the projects will have important impacts if successful, whether development will continue at the current pace is uncertain given the geopolitical and economic realities.

CHAPTER SEVEN

STRATEGIC ISSUES AND THE MARITIME ENVIRONMENT: COOPERATION, COMPETITION, AND CONFLICT

THE PRECEDING CHAPTERS HAVE focused on the growing ties between the Middle East and Asia, including economic developments and infrastructure projects that it is hoped will facilitate mutual access in the decades ahead. However, such access is not certain; one has to take into account not only the unpredictability of the global economy but also the prospects for continuing military conflict and confrontation throughout the region.

Since most of the commerce between the Middle East and Asia goes by sea or air over long tracks of the Indian Ocean, the security of the maritime environment is a key factor in economic growth. As road, rail, and pipeline projects expand in Central Asia, the security of the land routes will become more important, but for the foreseeable future the bulk of energy supplies and consumer goods will be seaborne. Furthermore, most of the communications between Asia and the Middle East are increasingly dependent on undersea cable networks.[1]

For the next two decades, and probably longer, the basic security of the Gulf and the Indian Ocean will depend on the United States. Since the United States replaced Britain in 1971 as the guardian of the Gulf and Indian Ocean, the U.S. military presence "East of Suez" has grown steadily. In the 1980s, U.S. military relations with Saudi Arabia and the Gulf states intensified, leading to increased arms sales and the construction of huge new facilities, especially airbases. During the Iran-Iraq war, which lasted from 1980 until 1988, U.S. forces were actively engaged in maritime combat against Iran to protect Kuwait's fleet of oil tankers and to keep the strategic Strait of Hormuz open. It was expected that U.S relations with Iraq would strengthen with the end of the war; in fact, the reverse happened. In the fall of 1990, after Saddam's reckless invasion of Kuwait in August, the United States deployed nearly half a million troops to Saudi Arabia. After the brief war to liberate Kuwait in early 1991, U.S. and British forces maintained a no-fly zone over northern and southern Iraq. Although the United States reduced its forces in Saudi Arabia, it increased its presence in Kuwait and adjacent Gulf countries. The cost of sustaining the U.S. presence in the region during the 1990s has been estimated to be about $60 billion a year, although it is difficult to be precise since different accounting methods can be used to assign costs. After the terrorist attacks of September 11, 2001, and the war in Afghanistan, the United States invaded Iraq in 2003 to overthrow Saddam Hussein, leading to a second surge of U.S. forces in the region. Today the United States maintains a major military presence in both Iraq and Afghanistan. In the case of Afghanistan, Pakistan has become the critical logistical route for supplies.

Outside the war zones, the United States has military facilities in the British–Indian Ocean Territory (Diego Garcia), Djibouti, Egypt, Oman, Qatar, Bahrain, Saudi Arabia, Kuwait, and the UAE. It is anticipated that with the drawdown of U.S. forces in Iraq the U.S. presence will be strengthened in some of those countries, especially in the smaller Arab Gulf states. The cost of sustaining that presence will likely be at least as high as it was in the 1990s. If fighting intensifies in Afghanistan, the cost will be much higher.

While the United States may regard its military presence as benign and protective, adversaries, especially Iran, regard it as hostile. In their worst-case scenarios, some Chinese strategists point to the fact that while in peacetime the United States may protect the sea lines of communication (SLOC)—the primary maritime routes between ports—to everyone's benefit, it can also close them down in wartime. Thus if China and the United States ever entered into war over Taiwan, the United States would be able to exercise significant control over China's energy and raw material supplies as well as its vital export trade. Although India today is relaxed about the U.S. presence and is cooperating with the U.S. military establishment, that was not always the case. In the 1970s India regarded the United States as a threat, especially after the Nixon administration sent U.S. carriers into the Indian Ocean during the 1971 Indo-Pakistan war in what was regarded as a provocative "tilt" in favor of Pakistan.

Nevertheless, for many years to come U.S. maritime power will be crucial to ensuring stability and keeping sea lanes open for international commerce. The reality is that the United States is providing a service to the world's trading nations, which, if withheld, would either create a more dangerous environment or force other powers to take responsibility for securing sea-lanes, straits, and ports. Unless one assumes that another global superpower (for example, a future China) takes over from the United States, it is likely that a new group of powers, each with greater regional responsibility but not as dominant as the United States had been, would be charged with enforcement.

Here it is important to distinguish between the future security of the Persian Gulf, and its immediate surroundings, and the wider swaths of the Indian Ocean that stretch from East Africa to the Indonesian archipelago. The Gulf is a relatively small, narrow body of water along whose shores vast economic investments derived from the energy industry have resulted in an extraordinary concentration of wealth, trade, and migrant populations. It also is a region of extreme vulnerability and sensitivity to political and military developments between the littoral states. The United States is the dominant military power in the Gulf, challenged by Iran, an aspiring Gulf power in its own right. It is unlikely that any of the major Asian powers that are expanding their naval capabilities have any interest in moving into this small, crowded, and dangerous area. The nearby Asian countries, especially India and Pakistan, have increased their military cooperation with the Gulf states, but that is hardly a substitute for U.S. power.

The Indian Ocean is a different environment and warrants a different approach. In this vast region, the predominant role of the United States may come under scrutiny in the years ahead, because of three realities. First, the costs of sustaining the U.S. presence are huge, especially if the U.S. economy is in turmoil and the United States is conducting wars in both Iraq and Afghanistan, which through 2009 were commanding major defense commitments. Second, assuming that world trade eventually resumes its expansion, the region will become more prosperous and protection of sea-lanes will become more important and more costly. Third, in different ways both India and China are expanding their maritime reach and both have reasons to be concerned about each other's long-term strategic objectives. Japan's future maritime role also could be an important factor in the emerging Asian balance of power.

Some American writers have argued that the U.S. navy will face a decline in its influence, both relative and absolute, in the coming half-century.[2] That decline will be based on the rise of naval power in Asia, especially China; the growing sophistication and therefore cost of naval hardware; and, crucially, the fact that an increase in U.S. defense spending is unlikely due to the current demands of expeditionary warfare and public discontent with both defense spending in general and spending related to the current conflict. Others argue that the United States will dominate the seas of the world for the next 50 years, while China might achieve local dominance, but only with a crash program to rapidly expand its military machinery.[3] While U.S. forces have greatly decreased in number, they have orders of magnitude more capability due to guided munitions and the revolution in military affairs (RMA).[4] U.S. maritime power is most vividly displayed in its use of sea-based air and missile strikes against hostile targets. Sea control missions—those to exert hegemonic dominance—are equally important. They rarely garner publicity because they take place primarily in peacetime, when it is assumed that their mere occurrence deters would-be aggressors from interfering with seaborne commerce.

While the aircraft carriers and advanced submarines of the United States will ensure that Washington retains the ability to exert sea control in the long term, the modernization plans of the Indian and Chinese navies could lead to a multipolar balance of power in the Indian Ocean. Both the Indian and Chinese navies are conducting exchange and outreach programs beyond their normal areas of operation. Chinese forces have worked with Pakistan in the Arabian Sea, and India has participated with the United States and Japan in tri-nation naval exercises as far away as the Sea of Japan. Despite historical parallels to the rising naval powers of the early twentieth century, this combination of rising naval powers with overlapping areas of interest will not necessarily lead to conflict.

Rather, their overlapping interests could lead to further cooperation between navies on low-intensity security issues. The Indian Ocean itself presents a conundrum—it carries more than one-third of the world's seaborne trade, but is also beset by a variety of maritime conflicts and potential nonconventional challenges, such as piracy, maritime terrorism, and disasters requiring humanitarian relief.[5] The combination of the high value of goods traveling through the region and low-intensity challenges—especially piracy—invites, if not requires, cooperation among naval powers operating in the region. Yet the combination of the strategic value of the trade involved and existing political dynamics means that the main naval powers of the Indian and western Pacific oceans often are pursuing similar ends independent of each other.

Japan, India, and China have taken a number of security-related actions that demonstrate a willingness to take very small steps toward direct involvement in regional security, including arms transfers, peacekeeping efforts, and support of military operations in Afghanistan.

Peacekeeping operations have been an avenue for increased Asian military interaction. In particular, China and India have deployed units to the United Nations Interim Force in Lebanon (UNIFIL). China also provides observers to the United Nations Truce Supervision Organization (UNTSO) in the Middle East and previously contributed observers to the United Nations Iraq-Kuwait Observation Mission (UNIKOM). Historically, India has been one of the largest contributors of troops to UN peacekeeping missions—and the third largest, behind Pakistan and Bangladesh, since 2006.[6] In fact, India's peacekeeping role in the Middle East dates back to 1956, with the establishment of the United Nations Emergency Force. Japan has played a naval role in supporting U.S. military operations in Afghanistan— the first time the Japanese naval force has participated in combat operations since 1945.

In contrast, North Korea has played a more negative role in the Middle East, by sharing technical and intellectual know-how for the development of nuclear weapons programs with Syria and Iran.

This chapter discusses the emerging threat environment and presents a review of the efforts taken by the major maritime powers to work together to meet future threats and challenges. It then summarizes the most important unresolved conflicts between India, Pakistan, China, and Japan and suggests why those conflicts may, at the end of the day, work against the spirit of cooperation that should serve the interests of all the major maritime powers.

THE THREAT ENVIRONMENT

The juxtaposition of wealth and war is illustrated in map 7-1, which covers the greater Middle East. Here three key phenomena are in play. First, a Middle East war zone stretches from the eastern Mediterranean to the Hindu Kush, encompassing virtually all the major crises that face the

MAP 7-1

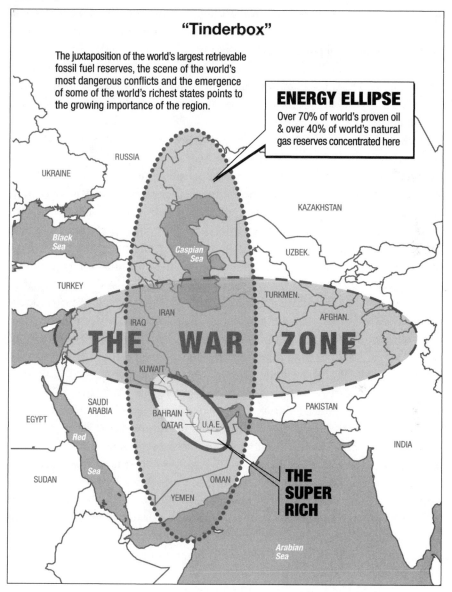

"Tinderbox"

The juxtaposition of the world's largest retrievable fossil fuel reserves, the scene of the world's most dangerous conflicts and the emergence of some of the world's richest states points to the growing importance of the region.

ENERGY ELLIPSE

Over 70% of world's proven oil & over 40% of world's natural gas reserves concentrated here

RUSSIA

UKRAINE

KAZAKHSTAN

Black Sea

Caspian Sea

UZBEK.

TURKEY

TURKMEN.

IRAN

AFGHAN.

IRAQ

THE WAR ZONE

KUWAIT

SAUDI ARABIA

PAKISTAN

EGYPT

BAHRAIN

QATAR

U.A.E.

Red Sea

INDIA

SUDAN

OMAN

THE SUPER RICH

YEMEN

Arabian Sea

international community today, with the exception of the problems with North Korea. The unresolved Arab-Israeli conflict manifests itself at three critical levels: Israel's ongoing battles with the Palestinians, particularly in Gaza; the possibility of renewed conflict between Hezbollah and Israel; and Israel's long-standing confrontation with Syria, including the occupation of the Golan Heights. The fact that Iran is deeply involved in arming and supporting Syria, Hezbollah, and Hamas escalates the traditional Arab-Israeli conflict.

Although the situation in Iraq has improved, it is far from stable. In recent years, Turkey has sent troops into northern Iraq to root out elements of the PKK, the Kurdish Workers Party. Serious issues remain to be settled in Iraq, including the future of the city of Kirkuk, which the Kurds wish to maintain as part of their own autonomous region. The concern over Iran is focused on its meddling in Lebanon, Gaza, Iraq, and Afghanistan and its efforts to develop nuclear weapons. Further east, the struggle for Afghanistan remains a key factor in U.S. policy, and while the Pakistani government has shown willingness to confront the Taliban, there is still a great deal of civil unrest in the country, including in the southwest province of Balochistan. India and Pakistan, both of which have nuclear weapons, have not resolved the crisis over Kashmir. Terrorist groups, including al Qaeda and its offshoots, are operating in many different regions, including the Horn of Africa, Indonesia, and the Philippines.

Second, an energy zone runs from southern Russia through Iraq and the Gulf countries. It contains most of the world's proven oil reserves and over 40 percent of its natural gas reserves. In the future, energy supplies will become an even more important factor in the geopolitics of the Middle East. As discussed earlier, economic growth in Asia will be the primary driver of increased demand and competition for those resources. Absent a prolonged global recession or a drastic shift away from oil to greater use of other forms of energy, the Asian countries will inevitably be drawn into the politics of the Middle East to prevent disruption of oil and natural gas production. Whether they will do so in cooperation or in competition with the United States is the key issue.

The third phenomenon, the growth of "super rich" countries in the Arab Gulf, is more recent. Building projects in those countries have attracted massive amounts of foreign direct investment—$32 billion in 2006, more than three times what they received in 2000 and more than double the $14 billion that they received in 2004.[7] However, there are any number of events that could bring the whole dream world down in ruins in a very short period of time. The financial crisis of 2008 and consequent slowing down of the global economy caused a dramatic drop in oil prices; until there is a global recovery, the credit crunch and investor panic will pose severe challenges for even the richest Gulf states. The most serious threat would be an interstate war. Everyone in the region remembers what happened to Kuwait when one of the most prosperous countries in the world was overrun, occupied, and trashed by Saddam Hussein's invading army in a matter of hours. The smaller Gulf states know such a threat could hypothetically reemerge from an ascendant Iraq or even a radicalized Saudi Arabia. Without the protection of the United States, Iran's navy could effectively shut down Gulf commerce in a short period of time.

Equally dangerous, the region harbors a number of radical terrorist organizations, which are mostly, but certainly not exclusively, Islamist. As demonstrated by the Mumbai attacks of November 2008, they are capable of inflicting mayhem on any of the major regional countries. Beyond these well-understood conflicts, a range of more exotic threats and challenges exists, including piracy, nuclear proliferation, and relief missions in the event of humanitarian disasters.

PIRACY

Despite a formidable U.S. and NATO presence in the Indian and western Pacific Oceans, piracy remains a serious problem. The International Maritime Bureau (IMB) defines piracy as "an act of boarding or attempting to board any ship with the apparent intent to commit theft or any other crime, and with the apparent intent or capability to use force in the furtherance of that act."[8] Several major factors have enabled piracy to flourish in recent years: legal and jurisdictional weakness within host states, favorable geography, regional conflict and disorder, underfunded law enforcement or inadequate security, permissive or corrupt political environment, cultural acceptability, and, of course, the promise of a quick and lucrative reward.[9]

Pirate attacks are especially prevalent in the Indian and western Pacific oceans because of the high volume of trade flowing through the waters. Map 7-2 shows the location of pirate attacks in that region from 2003 to June 2009. Counting the number of pirate attacks is a challenging process. Noel Choong, the head of the International Maritime Bureau's Piracy

Map 7-2

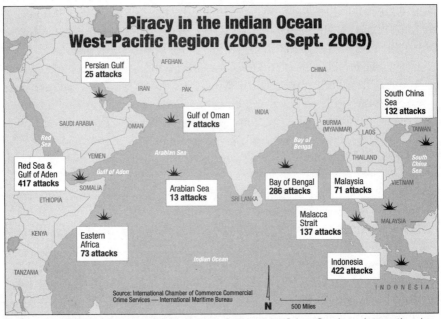

Source: International Chamber of Commerce Commercial Crime Services, International Maritime Bureau.

Reporting Centre, estimates that half of all pirate attacks go unreported. Jhonny Batam, a well-known pirate in the region, assumes that 75 percent of heists are inside jobs involving the ship's crew, often the captain.

In the past, many men relied on older seamen to teach them seamanship in order to avoid the expensive training and then obtained counterfeit credentials to land a job. However, the international shipping community has become more stringent, leaving many seamen unemployed; as a result, many have turned to piracy in order to support themselves.[10] That provides some insight as to why most attacks are not reported—shipping companies would rather write off smaller losses than suffer bad press and risk losing their insurance.[11] Similarly, some ports are assumed to fail to report incidents out of fear of ruining their reputations. In other instances, the witnesses are killed or intimidated into silence.[12]

Southeast Asian waters have posed a significant policing challenge for states with commercial interests in shipping and international trade. The Malacca Strait and surrounding waters in particular have always been a focal point for shipping because the most direct route between China, India, and the Middle East runs through them. Indeed, more than 30 percent of the world's trade and approximately half of the world's oil shipments pass through the Malacca Strait.[13] The strait's indispensability to trade, however, also provides ample opportunities for piracy and similar threats, as witnessed by the sharp rise in the number of attacks on ships traveling through between 2003 and 2006.[14]

One solution to the dilemma is to strengthen regional and international cooperative security arrangements in order to take a multilateral approach to combating piracy. The escalating number of piracy incidents in 1992 led to the establishment of the Piracy Reporting Centre in Kuala Lumpur, Malaysia. The center is part of the IMB, which is in turn part of the International Chamber of Commerce Commercial Crime Services (ICC-CCS) organization. The center focuses on raising awareness of piracy hotspots, provides detail on specific attacks, and further investigates incidents at sea and in port. In addition, the center is continuously working with national governments on a range of initiatives to decrease and ultimately eradicate attacks.[15]

Several transnational efforts have been made to reduce and eliminate piracy in the past decade. To illustrate the seriousness of the problem, the insurance division of Lloyd's of London classified the Malacca Strait as a war zone in June 2005. In response, Malaysia, Singapore, and Indonesia bolstered their security in their respective waters, and Lloyd's suspended the rating in August 2006.[16] East Asian nations such as Japan, South Korea, and China, which rely on oil shipments through the strait, are especially concerned. Although the security of the strait has always been the responsibility of the littoral states—Indonesia, Malaysia, and Singapore—it is not possible for any one nation to secure them. The Malaysian inspector general of policy has called for continued cooperation among agencies and governments in order to provide the region with better maritime security. The United States, for instance, has provided ten radar systems along the Indonesian island of Sumatra facing the strait.[17]

On June 14, 2007, U.S. president George W. Bush approved the Policy for the Repression of Piracy and Other Criminal Acts of Violence at Sea for immediate implementation. The United States, like the East Asian nations, feels that its interests are threatened by pirate activities and is trying to promote international solutions. The ICC-IMB reported that "this document establishes United States Government policy and implementation actions to cooperate with other states and international and regional organizations in the repression of piracy and other criminal acts of violence against maritime navigation."[18]

The results of such cooperative efforts have been dramatic. Although piracy increased on a global level from 2006 to 2009, it has decreased substantially in areas such as the Malacca Strait and Indonesia. Although there were 121 pirate attacks around Indonesia in 2003 and 46 pirate attacks in the Malacca and Singapore straits in 2004, by June 2009, there were only 3 and 4 four attacks in those regions respectively.[19] The surprising decline has been attributed to a number of factors, including the immediate effects of the 2004 tsunami, resolution of the conflict between the Indonesian government and the Free Aceh Movement in 2005, the introduction in September 2005 of joint air patrols by the littoral states, and a myriad of other regional collective security measures.[20] Those measures include the 2004 creation of the Trilateral Coordinated Patrol (MALSINDO), which coordinates the naval patrols of Malaysia, Indonesia, and Singapore, and the ratification by fourteen regional powers of the 2006 Regional Cooperation Agreement on Anti-Piracy (ReCAAP), which established the Information Sharing Center (ISC) in Singapore to produce regular reports on piracy in the region. Although those efforts have had shared success, they are still hampered by lack of resources, overemphasis on issues of regional sovereignty, and the absence of targeted attacks against the pirates' bases on land.

While instances of piracy have been decreasing in Asia, they have been increasing off the coast of Somalia at an alarming rate. Somalia is a failed state with a very long coastline that runs alongside one of the world's busiest shipping lanes. Because of Somalia's desperate poverty and almost complete lack of centralized political order, piracy has blossomed into a major business. Many of the pirates are former Somali fishermen who, amid the chaos, lost their traditional livelihoods to foreign fishing operations. Their booty has included oil tankers, ships carrying weapons, and cruise ships.

The issue became so serious in late 2008 that the international anti-piracy Combined Maritime Force (CMF) became actively involved. The CMF is a twenty-two-nation taskforce led by the United States that includes Britain, France, Germany, Denmark, Australia, the regional GCC states, and Pakistan, among others.[21] The CMF has around forty-five ships and fifteen maritime patrol aircraft, approximately a third of which are of non-U.S. origin.[22] China and India also have been prominent contributors. In spite of this international presence, however, piracy has continued to rise dramatically off the coast of Somalia, with 111 attacks in 2008 and more than 140 attacks in the first six months of 2009, which constituted almost 75 percent of the total attacks in the entire Indian Ocean for that period.[23]

Nuclear Proliferation

The proliferation of nuclear weapons in the Middle East and Indian Ocean region is probably the most frightening threat that has emerged in recent years. For all intents and purposes there is a full-fledged nuclear arms race under way between India and Pakistan. Though there are worries of Pakistan becoming a failed state, its nuclear forces remain firmly under the control of the Pakistani military. Pakistan is expanding production of its nuclear forces, which will inevitably elicit a response from India, which sees its nuclear capability as a deterrent against not only Pakistan but also China.

The debate about Iran's nuclear capacity is based in part on concern about the nature of the Iranian regime and the types of power play it might be able to make if it were a nuclear weapons power. But equally troubling is that if Iran becomes a nuclear weapons power, it will be only a matter of time before Turkey, Saudi Arabia, and Egypt join the nuclear club. Such an increase in nuclear forces, together with Israel's formidable existing nuclear force, will raise the anxiety level in the region even higher. The small states, such as the UAE, Kuwait, and Jordan, that cannot develop nuclear weapons because of their size or lack of money will seek closer military ties with the United States, which will have to provide for their protection. If the United States extends its nuclear umbrella further into the Middle East, it too will be drawn into conflict should nuclear weapons be used. Thus, whether the immediate issue is Iranian, Pakistani, Indian, Israeli, or Egyptian bombs, the bottom line is that proliferation could become far more dangerous.

Moreover, developments in the Middle East and South Asia cannot be decoupled in the long run from concerns in East Asia about North Korea. If there is one development that would tip Japan in favor of adopting nuclear weapons, it would be continued bomb and missile development by North Korea. If North Korea continues to behave as a rogue state, not only Japan but also South Korea might reexamine its nuclear weapons options, which would cause China to respond by increasing its own nuclear capabilities, which in turn would affect India, and so forth. Thus, nuclear proliferation in East Asia is linked to nuclear proliferation in South Asia and the Gulf and to the Arab-Israeli conflict.

Since any major conflict in the Gulf and Indian Ocean region will have a potentially disastrous impact on commerce, including energy supplies, it would seem obvious that it is in the interest of all the major players to avoid conflict. For that reason, the necessity of cooperating with regard to security, especially to contain nuclear threats and maritime threats such as piracy and local conflict that can interrupt energy supplies, is accepted by most of the key Middle East and Asian countries as well as the United States and Europe.

HUMANITARIAN RELIEF MISSIONS

In contrast to countering piracy and proliferation, a more uplifting role of peacetime maritime forces concerns humanitarian relief operations. The U.S. ability to employ its hard power for soft-power missions has improved its international reputation, especially among the Southeast Asian countries after the 2004 tsunami.

When the tsunami hit, the worst casualties were suffered by Indonesia, Malaysia, India, Bangladesh, Sri Lanka, and Thailand. A global emergency relief effort was launched, demonstrating the overwhelming superiority of the U.S. capacity to mount a large rescue operation over vast distances. Joining the United States were the maritime forces of India, Japan, Indonesia, Singapore, Britain, France, and Australia.[24] The Chinese navy was notably lacking from the international effort, although China did provide financial and medical support. After the U.S. navy hospital ship *Mercy* was dispatched on a humanitarian mission following the tsunami, the crew treated "almost 10,000 patients and performed close to 20,000 medical procedures."[25] More important, however, was the goodwill generated by the mission. A poll conducted after the mission reported that 38 percent of Indonesians had a favorable view of the United States, up from 15 percent before the tsunami.[26] Another poll found that 65 percent of Indonesians had either a "much more favorable" or "somewhat more favorable" view of the U.S. after the tsunami relief mission.[27]

Instead of directly inserting its air, land, and sea forces, China responded largely by using its military to fly donated supplies to civilian airports in China for delivery by civilian aircraft to Jakarta, Bangkok, Colombo, and Male in the Maldives. Its major commitments abroad included a medical unit from the People's Armed Police general hospital, which traveled to Indonesia, and a small team from a Beijing Military Area Command engineering unit that was deployed to Indonesia to undertake search-and-rescue operations.[28]

The reasons why China did not deploy more maritime forces are varied. First, China's navy does not regularly operate outside domestic waters and lacks the logistics infrastructure and the experience to support missions taking place beyond its borders. China has a tradition of isolationism, and it has long avoided involvement in other nations' affairs, only joining the UN special committee on peacekeeping in 1988. There also was concern that sending People's Liberation Army (PLA) forces would revive anxiety about "the China threat," both in the region and in the United States, potentially undoing China's considerable efforts to convince neighbors of its "peaceful rise."[29]

In recent years the Indian navy has become active in humanitarian operations. It provided humanitarian assistance to Sri Lanka in May 2003, when serious flooding struck the southern and central districts of the country.[30] It deployed a significant force following the 2004 tsunami, including thirty-two ships and more than twenty-five aircraft, across the Bay of Bengal and Indonesian coast, with more than half arriving within days of the disaster itself.[31] Even more impressive, in 2006 the Indian navy conducted simultaneous humanitarian operations in Lebanon and Fiji.[32] It also recently improved its capacity for humanitarian assistance by acquiring an amphibious transport vessel from the United States.

It will be many years, if not decades, before any of the Asian powers will be able to duplicate the magnitude of current U.S. maritime forces in the Indian Ocean and west Pacific. However, that could happen if two fundamental elements in the balance of power change. The first would be a unilateral decision by the United States to downgrade its maritime presence. The other would be a decision by China, India, or Japan or any combination of the three to dramatically upgrade their current maritime expansion programs through a vast infusion of money and personnel and a concerted effort to seek and obtain the access rights to port facilities and air bases necessary for power projection and sea-lane protection missions.

STRATEGIC COOPERATION: U.S.-ASIAN CONNECTIONS

U.S. strategic interaction with the key Asian powers takes place on several levels. Cooperation is closest between the United States and Japan, but the security dialogue between the United State and India is increasing. While the dialogue between the United States and China has progressed, it remains uneven. How these strategic relationships evolve will depend on many factors, including developments on the Korean Peninsula and China's relations with Taiwan. In addition, the greater Middle East poses many strategic challenges for all four powers, and how they handle them will have ramifications far beyond the region itself.

UNITED STATES AND INDIA

The United States and India have been expanding their cooperation on security and defense since the mid-1990s, and it has evolved into what could be a durable defense partnership. The stated goal of both countries is to support their common interests in security and stability, defeat terrorism, prevent the spread of weapons of mass destruction, and protect the free flow of commerce. On June 28, 2005, India's minister of defense, Pranab Mukherjee, and the U.S. secretary of defense, Donald Rumsfeld, signed a new and more expansive agreement on a framework for U.S.-India defense relations that has important ramifications for the long-term security of the Gulf and Indian Ocean, including broadening the range of U.S. naval operations and increasing cooperation in securing sea-lanes.

The 2005 framework states that the United States and India have entered into a new phase that reflects their common principles and shared national interests, including political and economic freedom, the preservation of democratic institutions, the rule of law, and enhanced security. Both parties outlined new ventures for their defense establishments, including participating in joint exercises and exchanges, collaborating in multinational operations (when in their common interest), and expanding interaction with other nations in ways that promote regional and global peace and stability. In the context of a strategic relationship, both the United States and India should strive to increase defense purchases from each other as a means to build greater understanding between their defense establishments. Due to the successful nature of the meeting, both parties agreed that the senior leadership from their national defense departments should hold continuous strategic-level discussions. The meetings allow both sides to exchange vital information and perspectives on international security issues while increasing mutual understanding and promoting shared goals and objectives.

Since the signing of the agreement, both countries have worked together to fulfill their goals. On July 27, 2007, officials signed a bilateral agreement for peaceful nuclear cooperation, which will govern civil nuclear trade and open the door for firms to participate in each other's nuclear energy sector, an agreement considered by some to be a historic milestone in the U.S.-India strategic partnership.[33] Known as the 123 Agreement, it offers benefits to both parties, including a more environmentally friendly energy source, greater economic opportunities, enhanced energy security, and more robust nonproliferation efforts.

Much of the agreement surrounds the supply of fuel to India. In March 2006, President Bush assured the Indian government of U.S. intentions to provide fuel. The 123 Agreement affirmed that promise and created the conditions necessary to allow India access to the international fuel market and also supported the creation of an Indian strategic fuel reserve. In addition, the United States granted and outlined its consent to India's reprocessing of safeguarded nuclear material, though that is dependent on the establishment of procedures to guide the reprocessing. For its part, India promised to put appropriate procedures in place to safeguard all civil nuclear material and equipment, and its leaders assured the United States that nuclear items would be used only for peaceful purposes.[34]

That agreement was only the first step. On October 10, 2008, India's external affairs minister, Pranab Mukherjee, and the U.S. secretary of state, Condoleezza Rice, signed the Indo-U.S. Civilian Nuclear Agreement, which allows full civil nuclear cooperation between the two countries as long as civil nuclear facilities meet the safeguards requirement of the International Atomic Energy Agency (IAEA). The agency granted an India-specific exception to the full scope of the requirement to allow for slightly less obstructed development of nuclear technology by India in exchange for the promise to meet certain other safety requirements. Military-to-military interactions between India and the United States, including air, land, and sea exercises, also have increased in recent years. Cope India is a bilateral air force exercise focusing on air combat in Indian territory that began in 2002. Expanding each year, in 2005 Cope India incorporated AWACS radar and control aircraft for the first time.[35] The Indian air force also participates in Red Flag exercises—a series of air combat exercises hosted by the United States that draws planes and personnel from various friendly nations around the world. In August 2008 frontline (as opposed to reserve) Indian planes and crews participated—Su-30 Flanker-C fighters and Il-78 Midas tanker aircraft.[36] The exercises have promoted goodwill and interoperability and—more significant—allowed

Indian and U.S. pilots to face off with top-of-the-line aircraft flown by other countries in the region.

The Indian navy also has conducted a series of exercises with the U.S. navy entitled Malabar, which have grown in complexity with each occurrence.[37] The Malabar series initially began with just a handful of participants from each side, but the 2005 exercises featured an aircraft carrier from both India and the United States. In 2007, they expanded to incorporate ships from Singapore and Australia.[38] The armies of the United States and India also have come together to conduct biennial field exercises known as *Yudh Abhyas* (Hindi for "training for war") since 2004. Each year, the exercise occurs once in each country, focusing on training in areas ranging from basic security cooperation to more detailed counterinsurgency tactics and jungle warfare.[39]

The Department of Defense has stated that it is the goal of the United States to help India meet its defense needs, including by providing assistance with important capabilities and technologies that India seeks, such as tactical radar technology. In the past, India typically turned to Israel and Russia for direct arms sales. In recent years, however, Washington has begun to make some sales to New Delhi. In 2002 the United States sold 12 Firefinder AN/TPQ-37 counterbattery radar units plus support equipment (a deal amounting to around $245 million) to India. Since signing the 2005 framework agreement, the Defense Department has worked to increase arms sales to India and remains committed to working with India on the issue. India also purchased an amphibious transport vessel that the United States was retiring for $50 million in 2007.[40]

Reaching into the private sector, Washington has sought to support U.S. corporate bids for production of India's multi-role combat aircraft—part of a fleet replacement program that could include more than 100 aircraft and total more than $10 billion. If either of the confirmed U.S. entrants—the F-16 and the F-18 Super Hornet—were selected it would greatly improve interoperability and mark a significant step forward in the defense relationship. The presence of forty-two U.S. defense firms at an Aero India show held in Bangalore in February 2007 was evidence of the willingness of U.S. companies to invest in building a long-term relationship with their Indian counterparts. High-level officials also have voiced that willingness. In 2007 R. Nicholas Burns, U.S. under secretary of state for political affairs, said that "our firms do not want to be merely suppliers to the Indian military, but also long-term partners during the modernization and development of India's defense industry."[41] Perhaps no one put it better than former U.S. ambassador to India Robert Blackwill when he said that "taken together, our defense cooperation and military sales activities intensify the working relationship between the respective armed forces, build mutual military capacities for future joint operations, and strengthen Indian military capability, which is in America's national interest."[42]

In addition, military sales to India will help the country in its efforts to combat separatist and terrorist threats, something that has always been a concern of the Indian government. In a 2006 press conference held in New Delhi, President Bush and Prime Minister Singh agreed that "terrorism has no place in democracy, and terrorism must be defeated for our children to be able to live in a peaceful world."[43] The countries committed themselves to work together to root out terrorism wherever it exists. The key to defeating the terrorists in the short term, according to President Bush, was good intelligence, leading both leaders to vow to make sure intelligence services increase information sharing in the future. Defense relations between India and the United States are the strongest that they have ever been. The Bush administration emphasized the need to build and foster stronger relations with India; India, for its part, sees a common interest with the United States in maritime security in the Indian Ocean.[44] An unspoken motive for some is that India will serve as a counterweight to China's growing presence in the Middle East and Central Asia. While changes in the national security environment will continue to shape the relationship between the United States and India, it is likely that cooperation will continue.

One problem is that as long as Pakistan plays such a vital role in the war against al Qaeda and the Taliban, the United States has to carefully balance its relations with Islamabad and New Delhi. The United States has to avoid giving the impression that it needs Pakistan only as long as the terrorist threat is serious and that once Osama bin Laden has been caught or killed, India will inevitably become more important than Pakistan to the United States. Some Indians have expressed worry that in its efforts to be evenhanded, the United States is letting Pakistan off the hook regarding the support that some within the Pakistani army still display for the Taliban. Secretary of State Hillary Clinton's visit to India in July 2009 was designed, in part, to redress that critical view.

UNITED STATES AND CHINA

Military relations between China and the United States have displayed
the greatest volatility of those between the United States and any other foreign nation, alternating between periods of intense engagement and increasing tension.[45] To examine the current status of the relationship, it is important to analyze bilateral developments in the 1990s and their subsequent
implications.

Following rapprochement with China in 1972, U.S.-China military
ties moved forward in fits and starts, but by the late 1980s, contacts were
extensive and wide-ranging. In addition to senior-level contacts, the United
States upgraded Chinese fighter aircraft avionics and supplied cutting-edge
weapons such as UH-80 Blackhawk helicopters. All such interactions ended
abruptly in 1989, after the June 4 Tiananmen Square massacre. Bilateral
military exchanges did not resume until Charles W. Freeman Jr., the assistant secretary of defense for international security affairs, visited China in
October 1993.[46] Initially the most pressing issue concerned maritime security—the Chinese navy was just beginning to transition into a blue-water
fleet that operated beyond Chinese territorial waters and began to enter
areas regularly patrolled by the U.S. navy. Also important was that both
countries thought that they could use bilateral military links to influence the
other's policies and learn from each other in a transparent way. The Defense
Department's 1998 East Asian Strategy Report (EASR) reflected that sentiment: "Dialogue and exchanges can reduce misperceptions between our
countries, increase our understanding of Chinese security concerns, and
build confidence between our two defense establishments to avoid military
accidents and miscalculations."[47]

U.S.-China relations were at their most cooperative and cordial in 1998–
99, but the relationship declined in following years. In January 1998, the
United States, in its most important bilateral confidence-building measure,
supported the establishment of the Military Maritime Consultative Agreement. In taking that step, Washington intended to promote a defense dialogue to avoid miscommunication between U.S. and Chinese naval and air
forces operating near each other. Then, during President Clinton's June 1998
visit to Beijing, the countries agreed to allow observers to attend the other's
military exercises; they also agreed to create another bilateral agreement stating that the two countries would not target strategic nuclear weapons at one
another. It was a symbolic and reassuring gesture, even though the agreement

was never enacted.[48] Despite the lack of an official stamp on the agreement, the direct communications link forged by the two presidents in May 1998 proved to be a significant development. It paved the way for a final bilateral agreement initiated in September 1998 by Defense Secretary William S. Cohen and Zhang Wannian, the vice chairman of the Chinese Central Military Commission, authorizing bilateral military exchanges to address environmental degradation, use of cleaner energy, and climate change.[49]

Despite the attempts at bilateral cooperation, several factors prevented the two countries from significantly improving their strategic relationship. The most evident obstacle was that both perceived a lack of reciprocity on the part of the other. From the U.S. perspective, it was providing China with detailed briefings, publications, and special access to many different military facilities, while the Chinese army made only symbolic gestures in return, such as taking U.S. officials to tourist sites and hosting lectures on general topics. China, on the other hand, argued that it could not fully reciprocate U.S. actions because both its funds and its technological military knowledge were lacking.

In addition, the United States and China remained suspicious of the other's true intentions and behavior, always fearing the worst. Chinese strategists argued that due to the overwhelming superiority of U.S. military power, China must rely on obfuscation to ensure that it maintains a credible deterrent. While Washington was preoccupied with the idea of Chinese exploitation of mutual contacts in order to acquire military secrets, Beijing was concerned that the United States wanted to bring an end to communism in China and transform the country into a Western-style democracy. China was also extremely troubled by U.S. military alliances with the other key Asian powers, especially Japan, and in particular by the Clinton administration's attempts to revive the U.S.- Japan security alliance.[50]

International events also have driven Washington and Beijing further apart. Taiwan remains a disputed subject between the two countries because the United States is militarily involved in the Taiwan Strait, poised to intervene on Taiwan's behalf with a carrier battle group operating in the area. In January 1999, a report compiled by the Cox Committee, in the U.S. House of Representatives, accused China of nuclear espionage, increasing tension between the two countries. The accidental bombing of the Chinese embassy in Belgrade in May 1999 by U.S. aircraft, along with the Cox Committee report, led to the mutual cutback of military dialogue,[51] and the bombing was a key factor in the abrupt termination of U.S.-China military cooperation that followed. Ten years later, Chinese leaders still refused to accept the U.S. claim that the bombing was a mistake, and mutual distrust over the bombing remains. Attempts to engage in defense cooperation again in 2000 also came up short. The arrival of the Bush administration in January 2001 and the April 2001 incident involving a mid-air collision between a Chinese fighter jet and a U.S. reconnaissance aircraft led the United States to sever all military ties with China, in particular because the twenty-four-member U.S. EP-3 crew was detained for several days.[52]

In December 2002, Chinese and U.S. officials met at the Pentagon to reengage in military and strategic dialogue, officially titled defense consultative talks. After the meeting, it was stated that the United States was interested in military-to-military exchanges that would increase mutual understanding in order to reduce the risks of miscalculation. China also assured the United States during the meeting that it was not providing missile technology to North Korea. Meanwhile, the United States emphasized that its missile defense program should not be seen as a threat to China.[53] In December 2008, the ninth round of the defense consultation talks was held.

U.S.-China security relations were dealt a further setback in January 2007 when it was reported that China successfully tested an anti-satellite weapon. The Chinese military used a ground-based missile to hit and destroy one of its own aging satellites orbiting more than 500 miles above Earth, thereby demonstrating China's ability to target regions of space that are home to U.S. spy satellites and space-based missile defense systems. The action provoked harsh protests from several countries with satellite programs, raising questions about China's willingness to ignore international opinion in pursuit of its military goals. However, one school of thought believes that there was very poor coordination between the People's Liberation Army and civilian authorities, with the PLA not appreciating the negative international sentiment that the test would generate. The PLA sought to keep the test secret and would not confirm it for several days after U.S. scientists leaked the news that it had taken place. U.S. National Security Council spokesman Gordon Johndroe stated that "the U.S. believes China's development and testing of such weapons is inconsistent with the spirit of cooperation that both countries aspire to in the civil space area."[54] Ashley Tellis, a scholar at the Carnegie Endowment for International Peace, went further, suggesting that Beijing had determined that a strong anti-satellite capability is essential to "counter the overall military capability of the United States" and to disable the "complex, exposed network of command, control, communications, and computer-based systems that provide intelligence, surveillance, and reconnaissance" to U.S. forces.[55]

Despite such gloomy scenarios, there is still reason to be optimistic about the long-term U.S.-China military relationship. At the annual Asia Security Summit Shangri-La Dialogue, hosted by the International Institute for Strategic Studies in Singapore in May 2008, the U.S. defense secretary, Robert Gates, commented that the two countries have increased their military-to-military contacts on all levels and that their blossoming economic and trade links would help forge a more trusting and positive relationship.[56] In 2009 Gates returned to Shangri-La, where he stressed that "we are working with China on common challenges—from economic matters to security issues such as regional areas of tension, counterterrorism, nonproliferation, energy security, piracy, and disaster relief. It is essential for the United States and China to find opportunities to cooperate wherever possible." Should the United States and China overcome their concerns and misconceptions about each other, both countries may eventually be able to engage in earnest and mutually beneficial strategic dialogue. The following statement, written by Defense Secretary William Perry in 1994, remains true today:

> China is fast becoming the world's largest economic power, and that combined with its UN P-5 status, its political clout, its nuclear weapons, and a modernizing military, make China a player with which the United States must work together . . . we must rebuild mutual trust and understanding with the PLA, and this could only happen through high level dialogue and working level contacts.[57]

UNITED STATES AND JAPAN

The U.S.-Japan alliance dates back to Japan's defeat in World War II and subsequent occupation by the United States and the Allies. For Japan, the basic foundation of the relationship has been the Yoshida Doctrine—that Japan would focus on economic reconstruction with the eventual aim of reclaiming great-power status while cooperating with, but not becoming dependent on, the United States.[58]

The U.S.-Japan strategic relationship initially was very one-sided. During the cold war, Japan was protected by the U.S. security umbrella, but over time, its economic growth and increased defense capacity allowed it to play a greater role in its own defense. By the 1980s, Japan took on a limited role in ensuring regional security. The 1952 U.S.-Japan Security Treaty provided the original legal basis for the U.S.-Japan strategic relationship and the U.S. military presence in Japan,[59] but that treaty was replaced in 1960. The second treaty reaffirmed the U.S. commitment to defend Japan; removed some of the features of the 1952 treaty that most intruded on Japan's sovereignty; and placed a greater emphasis on the potential role of the United Nations in resolving security issues that might threaten Japan.[60]

From the late 1960s forward, the United States encouraged Japan to take broader responsibility for its own security and to provide some assistance in regional affairs. President Nixon spelled the new policy out in the Guam Doctrine, announced in July 1969, which asked allies to take more responsibility for their own defense while maintaining the U.S. treaty commitments.[61] In 1978, Tokyo and Washington agreed on the Guidelines for U.S.-Japan Defense Cooperation, which defined the roles of U.S. and Japanese forces in repulsing a potential attack on Japan. Japanese forces were to serve as the "shield" in the immediate defense of their country; U.S. forces were to serve as the "sword," striking the oncoming forces in the short term, and to provide reinforcements in the long term.[62] Functionally, the guidelines outlined a substantial role for the Japanese self-defense forces while taking into account the constraints of Article 9 of the Japanese constitution, which prohibits offensive action. Japan's most notable contribution in the cold war period came after 1983, when it took responsibility for protecting sea-lanes 1,150 miles south of Japan.[63]

The end of the cold war brought a wave of uncertainty about the future of the relationship. The rapid decline of the Soviet Pacific fleet eliminated the primary threat that the United States and Japan had been hedging against. With that mutual interest gone, the relationship frayed, and the political controversy in Japan over the presence of U.S. servicemen on Okinawa and in other parts of the country further strained ties. The sternest test of the relationship came in 1994 with the crisis over North Korea's nuclear program, when disagreements over contingency planning "brought the alliance to the brink of collapse."[64] North Korea has continued to be a central factor in the U.S.-Japan relationship, as its unpredictable and threatening behavior and policies as well as China's military expansion have given Japan an incentive to continue cooperating closely with the United States. The relationship has also expanded to include cooperation in humanitarian and international peacekeeping measures.

In June 1997, Japan and the United States revised the Guidelines for Defense Cooperation to account for the post–cold war strategic environment.

The scope of the strategic relationship expanded to include cooperation on humanitarian and peacekeeping activities, joint efforts to enforce international sanctions, and Japanese "rear-support," in a noncombat posture, for U.S. forces.[65] A direct comparison of the 1978 guidelines and those from 1997 reveals a significant shift in Japan's security policy over the two decades—including, for example, the operations abroad that Japan began to undertake following the recommendations of the Higuchi Commission in 1994[66]—and prefigures U.S.-Japan cooperation in the Indian Ocean and Japan's membership in the Proliferation Security Initiative. The shift toward a more active foreign policy represents the emergence of a "new realism" in Japan, based on generational change and strategic necessities, that is drawing Japan out of its previously normative and ideological foreign policy structure.[67] North Korea's 2006 nuclear test has pushed Japan toward accepting collective self-defense with the United States and a role as a "normal" country in terms of national security.[68]

In October 2005, the U.S.-Japan Security Consultative Committee met to chart the future of the relationship and produced an agreement entitled Transformation and Realignment for the Future. In their talks, the United States and Japan reaffirmed their dedication to continued cooperation on matters of defense and agreed on a large number of common strategic goals. Targets included strengthening their partnerships with India and Australia through increased economic and diplomatic cooperation with both and through security cooperation with Australia; denuclearizing the Korean Peninsula; encouraging China to be a responsible stakeholder in the international system; and supporting reconstruction in Iraq and Afghanistan.[69] The list marked the first time that Japan had directly identified North Korea and China as strategic concerns.[70] This so-called "2+2" document often is given by the Chinese as an example of the U.S. lack of trust of China. The talks also focused on increased interoperability in ballistic missile defense and on the relocation of U.S. forces to other bases in Japan away from politically sensitive areas.[71]

The United States has been a primary supplier of military equipment to Japan since the end of World War II. All of Japan's primary fighter aircraft (F-15, F-4, and F-2) are either U.S.-built or joint projects of Japanese and U.S. companies. Even in Japanese-built systems—such as the Kongo-class destroyers—U.S.-designed and -built systems and munitions play a central role. The fact that Japan's self-defense forces use U.S. equipment greatly increases interoperability, since U.S. forces are already familiar with the operating systems and can provide technical assistance wherever necessary. Japan also has expressed interest in purchasing the F-22 Raptor, the most advanced U.S. fighter aircraft, but as of mid-2008 U.S. law bans export of the F-22.[72] Missile-defense components and unmanned aerial vehicles (UAVs) constitute a significant percentage of U.S. arms sales to Japan in recent years, with a $458 million sale of SM-3 missile interceptors since 2006 and the ongoing delivery of U-125A unarmed surveillance aircraft.[73]

INDIAN, CHINESE, AND JAPANESE MARITIME DEVELOPMENTS

India and China have pursued their maritime outreach in starkly divergent ways. While China has pursued maritime issues largely on a bilateral basis with countries in the Indian Ocean, India has sought to build multilateral frameworks in the region that serve to gently assert India's status as the naturally dominant state in the region.[74] Japan's role has been more restricted, but over time that could change.

INDIA'S MARITIME ROLE

While the Indian navy has never been the most powerful in the Indian Ocean, eclipsed first by the British navy and then by the U.S. navy, it has always aspired to control the body of water that bears its country's name. Indian strategists have suggested since the 1940s that India should aim to control the Indian Ocean and secure its vital sea-lane chokepoints such as the Andaman Islands, the shipping route off Sri Lanka, and Mauritius with individual, independent fleets.[75] India considers the security of the entire Indian Ocean region—from the Cape of Good Hope to the Horn of Africa and the Strait of Malacca and as far south as Antarctica—to be of interest, with the Arabian Sea, the Bay of Bengal, and the Gulf having primary importance.[76] Historically, India has not possessed the economic or military clout to back up its interests, but with a growing economy and an aggressive plan to modernize its navy, things are beginning to change. India hopes to "establish herself as an acknowledged maritime power" and a provider of security in a region beset by a variety of localized conflicts.[77]

While the Indian navy has consciously and publicly stated its will to be the dominant power in the Indian Ocean, it has taken care to demonstrate its increasing capability in a manner that neither challenges the other powers operating in the region nor threatens the smaller states of the Indian Ocean littoral. Its strategy is predicated on the idea that the Indian navy is not seeking solely to build a "sea denial" or "sea control" naval force with purely military utility but a navy that is capable of providing regional security and that seeks to do so in cooperation with other regional navies. The Indian navy created an office dedicated to international cooperation in 2005. Over the past few years, it also has worked to demonstrate its commitment by undertaking humanitarian and security operations as well as by engaging the nations of the Indian Ocean littoral and Southeast Asia in port visits, international forums, and joint military exercises.[78]

Deployments.   In recent years, the Indian navy has displayed a capability for conducting security and humanitarian operations that it previously did not possess. In June 2003, the INS Ranjit and INS Suvarna provided security for a meeting of the African Union at Maputo, the capital of Mozambique. The month-long deployment of the ships, more than 3,500 nautical miles from India, was an impressive display of India's naval capabilities.[79] The Indian navy also guarded U.S. ships passing through the Strait of Malacca in 2003 and provided humanitarian assistance to Sri Lanka in mid-May 2003 when significant floods struck the southern and central districts of the country.[80] Even more impressive, in 2006 the Indian navy conducted simultaneous humanitarian operations in both Lebanon and Fiji.[81]

While Indian naval forces have been venturing far abroad for port visits for many years, it is only recently that the navy has been considered a direct vehicle of diplomacy. In the 1970s and 1980s the Indian navy's port stops outside the Indian Ocean often involved the delivery of newly acquired vessels, with some exceptions in Southeast Asia.[82] In 2002, twenty-six ships of the Indian navy visited twenty-four foreign ports and ventured west into the Mediterranean Sea and as far east as Japan in 2003.[83] Since 2000, Indian warships have visited Japan, the Philippines, Singapore, and Indonesia on a biennial basis. Beginning in 2004, one can see a deliberate attempt by India to engage Middle Eastern nations, with port visits to Iran, the United Arab Emirates, Saudi Arabia, Oman, and Israel. The trend continued in 2005, when Indian ships visited the Persian Gulf and also traveled as far abroad as the Mediterranean, South Africa, and the South China Sea.[84] In 2006, one of India's new frigates even traveled as far east as Australia, New Zealand, and Fiji.[85] In 2007, the navy visited China, Singapore, Qatar, Oman, Bahrain, Saudi Arabia, Japan, South Korea, the Philippines, and Djibouti. Those visits are clear evidence of a trend—that over the past five years the Indian navy has been seeking to establish "bridges of friendship" with its neighbors.[86] India also began formal naval staff talks with the UAE in 2007, formalizing annual visits that began in 2004.[87]

Exercises.   India also has used bilateral and multilateral naval exercises to quietly demonstrate its increased strategic reach, capability, and outreach to other nations. In 2000, a group of Indian naval surface forces—which provide combat-ready ships and stations to the navy and ensure that they are supplied with the leadership, personnel, and equipment needed—sailed into the South China Sea, provoking a rebuke from China.[88] Since that incident, the Indian navy has greatly increased its interaction with foreign navies while also working carefully not to alienate its neighbors. India began annual exercises with France and Singapore in 2001 (VARUNA and SIM-BEX respectively), the United States and Russia in 2002 (MALABAR and INDRA), and the British navy (KONKAN) in 2006. The exercises, especially MALABAR, have grown in complexity with each passing year.[89] For example, the MALABAR series began with just a handful of participants from each side, but in 2005 the exercises featured an aircraft carrier from both India and the United States and in 2007 they expanded to incorporate ships from Singapore and Australia.[90] India and Iran held naval exercises in 2003 and 2004.[91] The Indian navy also held search-and-rescue maneuvers with China in 2005 before beginning full naval exercises near Qingdao, China, in 2007.[92] In 2007, the Indian navy conducted joint patrols with Indonesia, Vietnam, and Thailand and for the first time held joint naval exercises with Oman, Bahrain, Saudi Arabia, and Kuwait.

The Indian naval command has demonstrated an adept sense of diplomacy in conducting naval exercises. For example, in 2007 the Indian navy held joint exercises with the United States and Japan in the northern Pacific Ocean. The exercises were significant for two reasons; first, previous naval exercises with the United States had been conducted in the Arabian Sea and second, the format and location had the potential to draw the ire of both China and Russia.[93] India responded to this potential concern by conducting independent parallel exercises with both China and Russia. Such an approach is typical of the Indian navy's overall strategy of displaying its increasing capability and reach while engaging regional actors to allay any fears about its intentions.[94]

Regional Forums.   Another step that the Indian navy has taken to demonstrate its benign intent and interest in cultivating ties with other countries'

STRATEGIC ISSUES AND THE MARITIME ENVIRONMENT

navies was the founding of two regional engagement forums, MILAN and IONS. The Indian navy began the MILAN gathering in 1995. MILAN, whose name comes from a Hindi word for "meeting," occurs biennially; India invites not only the navies of India's South and East Asian neighbors, including states like Myanmar and Thailand, but also those further removed from India's immediate neighborhood, such as the Philippines, Australia, and New Zealand. MILAN events include passing exercises, seminars on topics like pollution control, and social and sporting events.[95] India held another MILAN in 2008 in which the head Indian delegate focused on security and discussed the effectiveness of joint patrols in the Malacca Strait.[96] India has expressed a willingness to assist in protecting the strait from piracy and terrorism, but Malaysia and Indonesia typically have been wary of such suggestions.

The Indian navy also hosted the inaugural IONS (Indian Ocean Naval Symposium) in February 2008. The symposium includes the chief naval or maritime officials of all of the Indian Ocean littoral states including those on the eastern coast of Africa. The overall objectives of the gathering are to promote mutual understanding, develop mechanisms to confront common security problems, and improve interoperability of defense mechanisms in humanitarian situations.[97] Thirty nations participated in the initial gathering, twenty-six of which sent their naval chiefs.[98] India also has broached the idea that IONS could grow into a loose body dedicated to ensuring safe passage in the Indian Ocean that would meet biennially under a rotating leadership.[99]

Indian Fleet Development.   India's navy began as an inherited postcolonial force and grew on a sea-denial pattern under Soviet tutelage during the cold war. Sea denial is the practice of preventing a hostile navy from gaining access to the nation's coastal waters. Economic difficulties in the late 1980s and early 1990s stymied India's modernization plans; however, over the last decade India has been conducting an ambitious modernization program. In 2007, India's defense budget allocated 18 percent to the navy, indicating the country's drive to become a maritime power and develop its domestic ship-building capabilities.[100] Although exact estimates vary, most Indian analyses consider roughly 200 ships an optimal fleet size, a figure based on what India sees as the geographical and practical necessity of having two fleets divided into three battle groups. Under those plans, India would have one fleet and carrier each for the Arabian Sea and Bay of Bengal, while the third carrier would be under refit and repair. That fleet estimate would also incorporate around eight fleet tankers—implying a much wider strategic reach than the current force of three allows—approximately twenty-four diesel submarines, and a handful of nuclear submarines that could provide a nuclear deterrent.

India has also set ambitious procurement targets for its surface and submarine forces. The government recently approved Undersea, a massive 30-year plan to build twenty-four additional submarines by about 2030.[101] Included in the plan is the purchase in the next few years of six French-designed Scorpene-class advanced diesel submarines to add to its current fleet of sixteen diesel submarines.[102] India is especially keen on expanding its fleet of conventionally powered submarines—much harder to detect than nuclear submarines at the low speeds required for navigation in the Indian Ocean.[103] In addition, Russian defense sources have indicated that India will receive two Akula-class (Type 971) nuclear submarines from Russia on a ten-year lease in 2010. The Russian-made subs reportedly will come equipped with the multi-role, nuclear-capable 3M-54 Klub missiles, which have a range of 300 kilometers.[104] The acquisition of the missiles would fulfill the Indian navy's goal of acquiring a credible sea-based minimum nuclear deterrent.[105]

On July 26, 2009, India launched its first nuclear-powered submarine, the INS *Arihant*.[106] India hopes to field three nuclear-powered ballistic missile subs by 2015.[107] The subs will carry the Sagarika missile, which is capable of carrying a 500-kilogram nuclear warhead up to 1,500 kilometers.[108] The navy also purchased the INS *Jalashwa*—formerly the USS *Trenton* LPD (landing platform dock)—from the United States in 2007. The *Jalashwa*, which is an amphibious transport warship that can transport up to 1,500 troops, represents a substantial increase in India's amphibious power projection capacity.[109] Plus, the navy is building roughly twenty surface combatant ships (ships built to fight other ships, submarines, or aircraft that can carry out other missions, including counternarcotics operations and maritime interdiction) and plans to procure at least three more Talwar-class advanced stealth missile frigates from Russia.[110] Each of the three Talwar-class frigates that India currently possesses is armed with 200-kilometer-range missile systems. In addition to the Talwar-frigate, India also has upgraded its Rajput-class destroyers with the supersonic anti-ship BrahMos missile and is reported to be looking into obtaining three more BrahMos-equipped frigates.[111] The supersonic Barak anti-ship missile system, which India currently is developing in collaboration with Israel, should further enhance the navy's offensive capabilities.[112] The former Indian chief of naval staff, Admiral Madhvenra Singh, estimated that by the late 2020s, India should aim to possess twenty frigates and twenty destroyers; the current stock includes eleven of each.[113]

Carrier Ambitions. The Indian navy has long wanted to have a substantive carrier capability. Despite having a checkered operational history because of maintenance problems, carriers remain the focal point of India's future maritime plans. It is the only regional navy to possess aircraft carriers, and it keeps one operational.[114] India plans to acquire one carrier from foreign suppliers to replace the *Viraat*. The first component is the planned acquisition of the retrofitted former Russian carrier *Admiral Gorshkov* (to be renamed INS *Vikramaditya)* and an air wing of MiG-29K fighter aircraft. The procurement of the *Gorshov*, with its range of 22,530 kilometers—much greater than the 8,050-kilometer range of the INS *Viraat*—will significantly enhance India's offensive capability at sea. Although delays and cost overruns have plagued the retrofit, delivery of the *Gorshkov* is expected by 2013, around the same time the INS *Viraat* is set to be retired.[115]

India also is building two domestically designed air defense ships, the first of which is expected to be complete by 2012,[116] although some estimates say as late as 2015, and the second, by 2017. The ships are planned to operate an air wing similar to that of the foreign carrier (most likely MiG-29K fighters and a mix of helicopters). It will displace about 38,000 tons—slightly smaller than the U.S. Wasp-class helicopter carriers.[117]

Modernization Challenges. Over the next ten years, India intends to double its number of frigates and destroyers and triple its number of carriers, but it faces pressure to replace other combatants in the short term. India's former chief of naval operations, Madhvendra Singh, estimated that the Indian navy has five frigates that need to be replaced immediately and three more that need to be replaced in the next two to seven years. The submarine force faces a similar predicament, as the replacement of four outdated diesel submarines is already overdue and practically the entire current submarine fleet is due to be retired between 2015 and 2025.[118]

In the longer term, the Indian navy's expansive modernization and procurement plan could be derailed by any of three factors. First, shipbuilding plans require continued and consistent political will at home to ensure that long-term procurement projects operate on schedule. Second and related, any significant downturn in India's economy would likely cause a downsizing of plans because they are based on the most recent projections of at least 6 percent GDP growth a year and a growing share of budget allocations to naval defense (from 17 percent to 20 percent).[119] Third, India could find it difficult to procure foreign warships if domestic shipyards cannot meet their needs. Russia historically has been and continues to be India's primary source for imported naval vessels, but a strain in the relationship could spell trouble. Recent retrofit contracts for key naval systems like the *Admiral Gorshkov* and missile modernization on Kilo/Sindhughosh-class subs have run into serious cost overruns, and delays and increases could sour their long-standing relationship.[120] Supply difficulties would be limited primarily to surface combatants, however, as India has multiple potential suppliers for its submarine and aviation needs, including Germany, Russia, France, Spain, and the United Kingdom.

CHINA'S MARITIME STRATEGY

Historically, China has been considered primarily a land power, focused on deterring invaders from the north and aiming to expand its influence to the south. The voyages of Admiral Zheng He's massive fleets in the fifteenth century were a notable exception.

The People's Liberation Army Navy (PLAN), the naval forces of the People's Republic of China, played a role secondary to that of the army throughout the cold war, but it took an important part in planning to defend against the invasion that Chinese leaders expected the United States to undertake in the 1950s or 1960s. The PLAN force structure of the cold war focused on brown-water (or coastal- and inland-water) operations as a means of preventing invasion, a strategy clearly unsuited to protecting Chinese interests in the far reaches of the South China Sea and the deep waters of the western Pacific. Accordingly, in the 1990s China pursued a "green water active defense strategy" that called for the PLAN to defend an area forming an arc from Vladivostok in the north to northern Indonesia in the south and out to the first island chain containing Okinawa at the eastern edge of the East China Sea.

That doctrine changed in the late 1990s under the influence of Liu Hua-qing—then the ranking officer of China's Central Military Commission and a student of Admiral Sergey Gorshkov of the Soviet Union, who was a great proponent of a submarine- and destroyer-based sea-denial strategy.[121]

China's naval modernization currently is focused on Taiwan in the near term and resource disputes with Japan in the East China Sea and South China Sea in the medium term. China's strategy regarding Taiwan has centered on contingencies for possible U.S. intervention and strategies to limit the access of U.S. forces to a conflict zone surrounding Taiwan. For decades now, China has been conducting exercises enacting an amphibious invasion of Taiwan, taking into account possible U.S. intervention.[122] Since the late 1990s, the PLAN has sought to expand its reach to the second island chain—including the Bonins, Guam, the Marianas, and the Palau Islands.[123] Some Chinese analysts see the islands as essential to ensuring China's security, since they are close to its economically developed coastal areas, which are dependent on maritime trade.[124] Any international attempt to contain China militarily will ostensibly depend on securing the waters between those islands, making it vital for China to prepare for their defense.

In the long term, Beijing's maritime interest lies in protecting the sea lines of communication carrying Chinese oil supplies through the Middle East, with an eye on the Malacca Strait in particular.[125] China's dependence on foreign oil and the continued naval superiority of the United States, especially in the Gulf region, has rendered Chinese energy supplies and SLOCs increasingly vulnerable to a U.S. blockade should the two ever come into conflict. China is equally dependent on securing its maritime access to foreign markets for its manufactured products (although without exports, China needs much less energy).

Such fears have led China in recent years to develop closer ties to states in Africa and South America as a means of diversifying its energy resources. Beijing realizes, however, that such contracts—no matter how fruitful—will not suffice as a long-term solution to China's growing energy needs. In order to protect its access to Middle Eastern oil, China will have to develop a strategic presence in the region.[126] These goals—and the experience of being unable to deter the U.S. deployment of two carrier groups to the Taiwan Strait in 1996—have encouraged the aggressive modernization drive for the PLAN.[127]

A String of Pearls?   Among the China watchers who worry about China's long-term potential to pose a strategic challenge to both the United States and other Asian powers, a particular scenario, which can be termed the String of Pearls Narrative, deserves mention. It refers to Chinese maritime activities that could provide China with a much greater presence in

Southeast Asia and the Indian Ocean. It must be noted that scenarios that depict "worse cases" in terms of future trends are the bread and butter of strategic analysts, especially those who work for or support countries concerned about China's rise, and that is especially true for Indian analysts. Nevertheless, the narrative itself is interesting.

China is investing in port facilities from Gwadar in western Pakistan—near the Strait of Hormuz—to China's own Hainan Island. Those ports, which make up the "string of pearls," would allow China access to the region for trade, intelligence, and, potentially, warship berthing (see map 7-3).[128] The easternmost pearl is the Sanya naval base on Hainan Island—an advanced port featuring extensive berth space and an underground submarine base.[129] There is speculation that a recently discovered set of tunnels—estimated to be 60 feet high—on the south tip of the island could conceal up to twenty nuclear submarines from satellite detection. The location of the island provides easy access to deep water, which would allow the PLAN to launch its submarines on short notice while completely avoiding detection.[130] Hainan Island also provides a base from which Chinese naval aircraft could cover most of the South China Sea.[131]

Intermittent reports suggest that Beijing has isolated stations in the Paracel and Spratly island chains. China is assisting Myanmar with the development of its deep-water port at Sittwe and has acquired an intelligence station in the Coco Islands. China also is assisting with port development in Chittagong and Mongla in Bangladesh and Hambantota in Sri Lanka.[132] The facilities will provide the infrastructure for increased trade in the Indian Ocean. They also suggest the potential for a Chinese naval presence. India has taken notice and in a recent maritime strategy speaks of the need to "wean" away littoral states from "the increasingly pervasive influence of states hostile to Indian interests."[133] The pearl with the most significance is the Gwadar complex, which is located in Pakistan, India's fiercest rival.

China and Pakistan are collaborating in building a large deep-water port and naval base at Gwadar (see chapter 4) that eventually will have a modern air-defense unit, a garrison, and an international airport that can accommodate jumbo jets.[134] Located only 250 miles from the Strait of Hormuz—through which nearly 40 percent of the world's oil flows—Gwadar's potential as a strategic port has long been clear to Pakistan. Pakistan's government requested U.S. assistance to build the port in the 1970s, but the project was left unrealized until China agreed to provide 79 percent of the $500 million needed for construction in exchange for what Indian

MAP 7-3

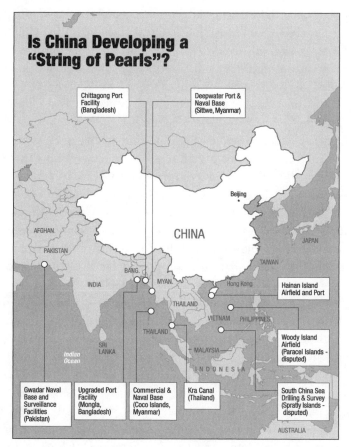

Is China Developing a "String of Pearls"?

commentators have called "sovereign guarantees to the port facilities."[135] China, however, is usually very respectful of other nations' sovereignty. It seems unlikely, based on all other Chinese foreign policy pronouncements and practices, that it would seek to coerce another country to give it some form of "sovereign" rights on that country's territory or any other form of extraterritoriality.

The complex has the potential to greatly enhance China's reach in the region both as a trade port and in strategic terms. Gwadar could provide a base for Chinese surface forces and nuclear submarines in the Arabian Sea, astride the Middle Eastern oil trade route. It also is likely that once China develops the ability to deploy a multiple carrier fleet it would want to place an aircraft carrier off Gwadar—a strategic move that would allow China to project power into the Persian Gulf, protect its SLOCs, and block critical supply lines, thereby complicating U.S. naval planning in the Gulf and raising the stakes in the Taiwan dispute.[136] According to Indian press reports, China has already established an intelligence post in Gwadar, allowing it to monitor ship traffic through the Strait of Hormuz and in the Arabian Sea.[137] Gwadar's new international airport could also serve as a base for Pakistani or—in a less likely scenario—Chinese aircraft.

No public evidence exists at this time that China intends to base aircraft at Gwadar, a move that would require impressive shifts in Pakistan's relationships with both the United States and China. Yet hypothetically, Gwadar could serve the same role for China in the Arabian Sea that Sanya or Hainan does in the South China Sea—as a base for aircraft to cover the surrounding waters. Gwadar's proximity to the Strait of Hormuz would allow aircraft to reach the strait and the northern Arabian Sea quite easily. China has not stated its intent to base naval or air assets in Gwadar—and many have argued that doing so is not in China's interest—but Gwadar and the other "pearls" clearly provide China room to grow in the Indian Ocean.

Gwadar also strengthens China's position vis-à-vis India in that it bolsters the Pakistani navy. A traditionally weak naval power compared with its Indian rival, Pakistan has recently begun to focus more on its naval forces. In 2006, the Pakistani navy commissioned its third French-made Agosta-90B class submarine, giving it the only submarine in the Arabian Sea with an AIP system, which allows the submarine to operate without surfacing for oxygen.[138] The Pakistani navy is likely to add more Agosta submarines in the future, and it has ordered four F-22P frigates from China, with delivery slated between 2009 and 2013.[139]

Those upgrades, however, will have little strategic impact on the Gulf because India remains the focus of Pakistan's military strategy—a strategy in which the development of Gwadar and the strengthening of Pakistan's ties with China will play a central role. In the past, Pakistan's navy operated primarily out of the port at Karachi. Karachi would be vulnerable to blockade in a war with India, leaving the smaller Pakistani navy bottled up and unable to receive supplies by sea.[140] Gwadar makes such an effort much more difficult. Previously India would have needed to set up only a 200-mile blockade incorporating Karachi and Omara; basing operations in Gwadar, on the other hand, would require India to cover Pakistan's entire 400 miles of coastline. Likewise, a Pakistan-backed trade corridor could circumvent the Strait of Malacca and give China a land-based oil import route during a blockade. Furthermore, Pakistan's relative lack of airpower and vulnerability to India's BrahMos-capable destroyers pose a serious threat to Pakistan's improving navy.[141] An increased Chinese military presence at Gwadar—most important, the deployment of an aircraft carrier—would provide Pakistan with an additional level of deterrence and protection from possible Indian aggression.

Stressing the strategic importance of Gwadar and other far-flung Chinese maritime developments gives scope for much speculation about long-term maritime rivalries. However, it must be emphasized that there are more benign explanations for China's activities and Pakistan's eagerness to develop Gwadar. China's forays into islands in the Indian Ocean and ports like Gwadar are typical of a large economic power that increasingly depends on freedom of the seas to ensure its access to the imports that it needs to sustain its industry and the exports that it must ship to customers worldwide. From Pakistan's perspective, the horrendous overcrowding at Karachi and the vulnerability of the port to an array of domestic threats, as well as India, provides a strong case for seeking a second major port on the Indian Ocean. India, China, and all other maritime powers have reasons to worry about threats to commerce from non-state actors. Because of that, when China or India sends warships to patrol and interdict pirates off the coast of Somalia, that action can be interpreted as either a benign, necessary policing operation or, seeing a more sinister motive, as evidence of their expansion of their maritime reach.

Despite such scenarios, there has been maritime cooperation between India and China. Their warships conducted a rare joint exercise in November 2005, the first time that Chinese forces joined in military exercises in Indian territory.[142] Appointed in 2006 as the commander-in-chief of the People's Liberation Army Navy, Admiral Wu Shengli was projected to take overseas trips to between one and four countries and to host an average of three to six counterparts each year.[143]

China also has carried out exercises with Pakistan in the Arabian Sea. In March 2007, two PLAN Jianghu-class frigates, the *Sanming* and the *Lianyungang*, took part in AMAN 07, a multinational naval exercise with a focus on maritime counterterrorism operations hosted by the Pakistani navy.[144] Ships that participated included those of the United States, the United Kingdom, France, and Malaysia. Interestingly, representatives of Qatar, the UAE, and Saudi Arabia also were in attendance, acting as observers of the exercises.[145] The PLAN has participated in similar exercises in the past, notably in November 2005, when it carried out naval maneuvers with both India and Pakistan in two separate exercises—China-India Friendship 2005 and China-Pakistan Friendship 2005, which was held in the Arabian Sea.[146] Both Friendship exercises focused on nonconventional security practices, with the Luhai-class destroyer *Shenzhen* and the Qiandaohu-class depot ship *Weishanhu* carrying out search-and-rescue drills with both navies as a means to increase preparedness for post-disaster humanitarian assistance. The exercises are a clear indication that the Chinese have been involved in the Arabian Sea from both a commercial and military perspective and will no doubt carry on with such activities as they continue to expand their sphere of influence.

Fleet Modernization.   The PLAN's modernization has been a product of China's improving economy and evolving national strategy. The effort has had three distinct facets—first, the decommissioning of outdated surface combatants, submarines, and aircraft; second, the integration of Western technology to improve the PLAN's capability and sustainability; and third, increased emphasis on the training of officers and enlisted personnel.[147] The PLAN has acquired vessels and technology from a number of countries—chiefly Russia, but also France and Israel.[148]

All aspects of the modernization effort reflect the PLAN's sea-denial strategy, which focuses on destroyers and submarine forces. The navy has acquired a number of modern destroyers since the late 1990s, including Sovremenny-class guided missile destroyers. China also has been building a number of domestically designed destroyers. In total, China incorporated ten new destroyers into the PLAN in 2006.[149] As of 2006 the PLAN had twenty major surface combatants capable of warfare in a twenty-first-century environment and another forty that could provide limited sea-lane protection against surface threats.[150] According to the International Institute for Strategic Studies (IISS), the PLAN's submarine force remains the backbone of its fleet.[151] China possesses twenty-four quiet diesel attack submarines—twelve Kilo-class, ten Song-class, and two Yuan-class—which are extremely effective in short-range, shallow-water environments such as those immediately off China's coast but unsuitable for longer-range deployments.[152] A handful of nuclear submarines are operating in the navy's northern fleet, including older Han-class and newer Shang-class nuclear submarines.[153] The International Institute for Strategic Studies estimates that China eventually will deploy five Type-094 nuclear submarines, each capable of carrying multiple warhead missiles with intercontinental range.[154]

The PLAN does not currently have an aircraft carrier. However, China has openly declared its desire to develop a carrier fleet, which is seen as indispensable for protecting its interests at sea.[155] While China's carrier program focuses on domestic production of its carriers, Chinese technicians also are working to reverse-engineer an old Soviet-era carrier purchased from Ukraine. Russian press reports of Chinese interest in acquiring Su-33 carrier-borne fighters indicate that China may not be far from turning its carrier ambitions into reality.[156] Estimates on how many carriers the PLAN expects to have operational by the end of the next decade are unclear— ranging from two[157] to six[158]—but it is plausible that the PLAN will have one carrier by 2010 and two by 2011.[159]

China's current expansion program can be clearly tied to its near- and medium-term goals in relation to Taiwan and the contested islands in the South and East China Sea. However, how China will handle its "Malacca dilemma"—the potential for a blockade of the Malacca Strait—is an open question. China has a number of options, including overland pipelines. Bernard Cole has argued that instead of trying to develop a naval force to police far-reaching SLOCs, "Beijing seems to be concentrating on forming supportive relationships with the nations bordering those routes, from the Philippines to Saudi Arabia."[160] Cole is skeptical that China will drastically expand the PLAN for ventures in force into the Indian Ocean. He doubts that China's military paradigm will change from being army-centered to being navy- or air force–centered and suggests that funds for naval expansion will follow from economic expansion, not from a massive reordering of budgetary priorities that benefits the navy.[161]

JAPAN'S MARITIME ROLE

Japan's status as an island nation fundamentally leaves the country two strategic options—isolation or oceanic trade and regional integration. Japan has pursued the latter course since the mid-nineteenth century, and its geography—which includes 17,000 miles of coastline (three times that of India) and maritime territories spread over an area the size of continental Europe—has compelled maritime forces to play a central role in its overall strategy.[162] Japan's navy was a critical factor in its growth as a major power in the early twentieth century—it was a naval victory at the Tsushima Strait in 1905 that proved crucial in the Russo-Japanese War and marked Japan's arrival as a world power. In the early 1940s, the imperial Japanese navy controlled much of the Pacific, as far west as the Malacca Strait, but it was decimated over the course of World War II by U.S., British, and Australian forces. Throughout the cold war, the United States facilitated the growth of Japan's maritime forces, which by the 1980s were able to take a primary role in ensuring Japan's defense and to patrol a significant stretch of sea-lanes in the western Pacific.[163] In the wake of the cold war, Japan has sought to contribute to international maritime security through peacekeeping and humanitarian operations. However, provisions of the Japanese constitution have limited Japan's growth as a maritime power.

Following its defeat in World War II, Japan adopted a pacifist constitution that imposed strict limits on the Japanese military. Article 9 of the 1946 constitution declares that Japan "renounce(s) war as a sovereign right . . . and the threat or use of force to solve international disputes." Some have interpreted that provision as banning Japan from possessing any military, but the prevailing view since the mid-1950s has been that Article 9 allows for solely defensive forces. Japan's maritime force, therefore, is called the maritime self-defense force (MSDF).[164] According to the prevailing interpretation of Article 9, Japan's forces may possess advanced defensive weapons but they cannot possess overtly offensive systems such as aircraft carriers. Article 9 remains a hotly contested issue in Japanese politics. Some conservative groups in Japan wish to further revise Article 9 to give the armed forces more latitude, but changing it directly would require a two-thirds majority in each house of Japan's legislature and the passage of a national referendum—quite a high bar politically.[165]

Deployments.   Japan began wider deployment of its maritime forces in the early 1990s. The first evidence of the shift was Japan's dispatch of a flotilla of four ships—including three newly built, state-of-the-art mine-sweepers and a supply ship—to the Gulf after hostilities in the 1991 Gulf War ceased. Japan also deployed a battalion of peacekeepers to Cambodia in 1992 and sent air transports to assist with UN efforts in Mozambique in 1994. Japan cooperated in anti-piracy operations in 2000 and deployed an Osumi-class transport to East Timor in 2002 to supply UN peacekeeping operations.[166] International peacekeeping operations became increasingly important to Japanese government strategists throughout the 1990s, offering a venue in which the U.S.-Japan relationship could move forward in new directions. The recommendations of the Higuchi Commission in 1994 led

to passage of the International Peace Cooperation Law in 2002, which gave
Japanese forces more latitude in overseas deployment. Subsequently, the
Araki report recommended that "'international peace cooperation" should
be made "a core objective of Japanese security policy."[167]

Japan also has deployed maritime forces in the Indian Ocean to support U.S.-led actions in Iraq and Afghanistan. In November 2001, Japan
dispatched two destroyers and a tender in support of U.S.-led operations in
Afghanistan and by 2005 had supplied coalition warships with more than
4 million liters of fuel.[168] One of Japan's Osumi-class transports deployed
to Iraq in 2003 to deliver noncombatant Japanese troops to the region. In
addition, Japan deployed nearly 1,000 troops on three ships to assist relief
efforts following the Indian Ocean tsunami in 2004.[169]

Japan has been an active member in the U.S.-led Proliferation Security
Initiative, dispatching MSDF and Japanese coast guard ships to participate
in drills and operations.[170] Daniel Kliman has described the shift toward
international engagement since 1992—and especially Japan's actions since
2001—as evidence of a "new realism." Kliman ascribed the shift to the
desire to strengthen Japan's alliance with the United States and the ascen-
sion of a younger generation to leadership in Japan.[171]

The MSDF's foreign deployments are sometimes overlooked because of
their size, but Japan has increased its maritime reach and involvement significantly over the last two decades. While most of the MSDF's deployments
in the Indian Ocean have been small, Japan clearly has the ability—barring domestic legal restrictions—to deploy small but effective groups to
the Indian Ocean as far as the Arabian Sea. Considering Japan's historical
tendency to act in coordination with, or alongside, the United States, that
capability should not be discounted.

Fleet Modernization.   Japan currently has the second-most-advanced
navy in the Pacific and has world-class capabilities in certain niche operations, especially minesweeping. The bulk of the MSDF comprises forty
guided-missile destroyers. Five use the U.S. Aegis system—the most advanced
seaborne radar and air-defense system in the world. Four of Japan's Aegis-
equipped destroyers, the Kongo class, boast a more formidable weapons
package than some frontline U.S. warships. The MSDF also operates sixteen
advanced diesel attack submarines equipped with anti-ship missiles, and it is
preparing to induct a new class of diesel subs fitted with ultra-quiet air independent propulsion that allows for a longer deployment range. In addition,

the MSDF operates five supply and replenishment oilers that are crucial to Japan's ability to project naval power. The Japanese coast guard operates more than eighty ocean-going patrol vessels more than 200 feet in length, twenty-four of which accommodate helicopters.[172] The coast guard participates in protecting shipping in connection with the Proliferation Security Initiative.[173] Japan also possesses three Osumi-class flat deck transport ships that can accommodate helicopters.

While building a Japanese carrier capacity was considered as early as the Korean War, it has been a touchy political issue in Japan because Article 9 of the postwar Japanese constitution forbids Japan's possession of offensive forces like carriers. The MSDF's perceived need for carrier-like vessels has been linked to protecting shipping against enemy submarines, which has been a central MSDF role since its inception. During the Korean War, the U.S. navy considered leasing Japan a flat-deck 7,000-ton "escort carrier" for helicopter operations tracking Russian submarines, but the Japanese political environment precluded it. In 1960 the MSDF floated a plan for construction of an 11,000-ton ship capable of carrying eighteen helicopters, but the proposal was shelved, again because of domestic political concerns.[174] Instead, the MSDF focused on procurement of maritime patrol aircraft. Today the P-3 Orion aircraft is one of the key components of Japan's maritime forces. Some observers see the MSDF's three Osumi-class transports, which Japan cites as necessary for peacekeeping and relief operations, as a carrier precursor because of its flat deck and side-mounted superstructure, yet the transports are configured to operate helicopters as a secondary function and their decks are too thin for full flight operations.[175]

Japan's Hyuga-class "helicopter destroyer," however, is a slightly different matter. The 13,500-ton *Hyuga,* which was commissioned on March 18, 2009, is larger than Thailand's lone light carrier, but it is roughly a third of the size of the U.S. Wasp-class helicopter carriers and India's planned carriers. The *Hyuga* will be able to carry eighteen helicopters, allowing it to concurrently conduct antisubmarine operations and amphibious or relief operations.[176] In 2005, a Japanese strategic paper suggested that Japan would need ship-launched vertical-take-off-and-landing (VTOL) aircraft like the Harrier or F-35 in a potential conflict with China over offshore island chains; accordingly, the *Hyuga* has been noted as a candidate to be modified to carry such aircraft.[177] Yet, like that of the *Osumi, Hyuga*'s deck may not be thick enough to accommodate the nonvertical landing of fixed-wing aircraft.[178] While it would provide lessons in carrier construction, the

Hyuga is better suited for noncombat applications like humanitarian assistance; according to Daniel Kliman, it "would not be an effective tool of aggression."[179]

Japan's recent and planned naval procurement certainly represents an increase in MSDF capability, but most analysts do not believe that it portends a change in overall strategy.[180] The refitting of Japan's Aegis-equipped destroyers to allow for missile defense roles represents a response to North Korea's missile arsenal, but it does not provide any new offensive capability. Similarly, the Hyuga-class destroyers expand Japan's transport, humanitarian, and peacekeeping capabilities, but they do not suggest a more aggressive expeditionary posture, as advocated by some Japanese strategists such as Jun Kitamura.[181] Furthermore, while the MSDF's most recent procurement plan expects "sizable" acquisitions of equipment in the near future, the overall defense budget is projected to shrink. Cost offsets, therefore, would have to be found elsewhere to ensure the sustainability of even the current force.[182]

U.S. NAVAL COOPERATION INITIATIVES

In a September 2005 speech to the Seventeenth International Sea Power Symposium, Admiral Michael Mullen, then the U.S. chief of naval operations, outlined a vision for a "thousand ship navy." That vision should not be understood in literal terms. Rather, Mullen presented the case for a "global network of maritime nations" composed of various international navies, merchant vessels, and port officials working together to meet maritime security needs.[183] The proposed network is intended to counteract a vast range of threats to maritime security, including piracy, smuggling, terrorist acts, and illegal weapons shipments of all types. Because the U.S. navy cannot, and does not wish to, police all the world's oceans, Mullen said, the United States and other countries are seeking a cooperative effort to enhance maritime security across the globe.

The term "thousand ship navy" has been revised by the U.S. navy to "Global Maritime Partnership Initiative" (GMPI). In his speech at the Seventeenth International Sea Power Symposium, Mullen described the concept of the "thousand ship navy" as a "global network that focuses on making the maritime domain safe for everyone's use, in most every nation's self-interest, by leveraging the unique capabilities that all your organizations bring, no matter how large or small."[184] He went on to say that the GMPI would be modeled on the decentralized, voluntary structure of the Proliferation Security Initiative and cited joint humanitarian, construction, and riverine anti-drug operations as examples of potential GMPI actions. The GMPI represents an attempt to foster international cooperation against all maritime security concerns. Implied in the initiative is the notion that each nation would act in its desired capacity on problems relevant to its interests. Thus, one nation's coast guard might assist by stepping up patrols and sharing information about its own national waters; another country might participate by playing a part halfway around the globe. GMPI, as proposed, would also include merchant vessels' provision of information on nearby ships through commercial systems such as an automatic identification system that "enables users to track the location and communicate with all other ships in range."[185]

Despite the inclusive and multilateral tone of the initiative, some nations have concerns about the underlying intent of the United States in proposing the GMPI, and others have been reluctant to embrace the initiative, which they see as a repackaging of other unpopular U.S. initiatives. Furthermore, some have suggested that the structure of the GMPI, or the lack thereof, will inevitably prevent it from achieving any real success.

From an analytical perspective, the GMPI appears to have grown out of the same milieu as other recent international initiatives of the United States, which was seeking a new security paradigm after the 9/11 attacks. That drive resulted in a set of international initiatives proposed by the Bush administration, including the Container Security Initiative (CSI) and the Proliferation Security Initiative (PSI). The CSI, which began in 2002, aims to screen cargo containers in their ports of departure; membership is voluntary and the services offered are reciprocal in nature. By 2008, fifty-eight ports worldwide were involved in the initiative.[186] The PSI, however, has been much more controversial.

The PSI, which began in 2003, aimed to prevent WMD materials from moving between countries, especially by sea. Its implementation called for at-sea inspections and the boarding of suspect vessels, which many nations, including India and China, considered a breach of international law.[187] The PSI currently has ninety-one members, but it does not include important states in the Southeast Asian and Indian Ocean littoral such as China, Pakistan, Indonesia, or India.[188] The U.S. Pacific Command also suggested a Regional Maritime Security Initiative with the cooperation of ASEAN that would have included U.S. marines patrolling in small boats to help prevent

WMD shipments through the Strait of Malacca. That idea was stillborn, as the littoral nations thought the action would have represented a breach of their sovereignty.[189] The newer Global Maritime Partnership Initiative, based on Admiral Mullen's idea of the "thousand ship navy," aims to incorporate the goals of the CSI and, to a lesser degree, the PSI as well as other maritime security goals.

International reception of the GMPI has primarily been positive, but the voluntary and decentralized nature of the GMPI and the thousand ship navy concept make it difficult to directly determine both the initiative's impact and its future shape and purpose. A number of U.S. allies, including Australia, Canada, the United Kingdom, Japan, Korea, and Bulgaria, have already indicated their support.[190] Important regional naval powers such as China, India, and Indonesia have been cautiously supportive of the project, especially on issues along the lower end of the spectrum, such as counter-piracy operations.

The United States has invited China to participate in the GMPI but has yet to receive a formal reply. China's concern with the GMPI falls primarily into two categories: first, that it represents a "utilitarian repackaging" of the same old power politics aimed at U.S. naval hegemony and second, that it is really a cover, with some additions, for the previously controversial PSI.[191] Yang Yi, a retired Chinese admiral, argued that for China to be involved in the GMPI, it would have to focus on "sovereignty of territory, non-traditional security threats . . . including national separatism" and that it would be difficult for China to participate in activities involving "sensitive issues like maritime interception, blockage, or embargo."[192] Put succinctly, under the new informal auspices, China is happy to continue to do what it already is doing. Any Taiwanese participation would be a major stumbling block, and if the GMPI became conflated with the PSI and its efforts to prevent North Korea from illegally selling missile and nuclear material, for example, that also could prove to be an obstacle to Chinese involvement.

Some in India have similar reservations about the GMPI, considering it to be "PSI by other means," but because the GMPI also provides for assistance and information sharing with regard to local concerns and environmental issues, the Indian government has responded favorably.[193] It is worth noting that India's primary objection to the PSI is not its goal of preventing the spread of WMDs but rather its method, maritime interdiction, which New Delhi considers to be questionable under international law.[194] India therefore observes PSI meetings and exercises but does not participate.[195] The overall spirit of the GMPI is consistent with India's maritime policy of encouraging cooperation in the Indian Ocean—for example, through joint patrols with Indonesia and the MILAN and IONS regional engagement forums.

The U.S. Navy's effort to encourage cooperative efforts to meet nontraditional maritime security challenges through the GMPI can be traced to both stretched and declining U.S. resources and increased understanding of the effect of regional maritime disputes on broader U.S. interests. While some have argued that the GMPI is another vehicle for U.S. initiatives like the PSI, the GMPI goes beyond the PSI in endeavoring to cover the entire range of maritime issues, not just those of interest to the United States. Whether countries that are uncomfortable with PSI-type activities will be comfortable with the possible conflation of those activities under GMPI over the long term is a valid question.

The United States also facilitated the creation of another maritime cooperation organization in the Indian Ocean—SARPSCO (South Asia Regional Port Security Cooperative)—although it will not be a member. The organization, which began in May 2008, includes Bangladesh, Comoros, India, Madagascar, the Maldives, Mauritius, Oman, Pakistan, and Sri Lanka; it aims to promote cooperation on the low end of the spectrum of maritime security threats, such as smuggling, human trafficking, illegal fishing, and port security.[196]

THE PROBLEM OF UNRESOLVED ASIAN CONFLICTS

While the many elements of cooperative security described previously are encouraging, it must be remembered that the Asian agendas include a number of unresolved conflicts that inevitably color their attitudes toward each other, their bilateral relations with the United States, and their willingness to contemplate a truly multilateral cooperative security concept such as the NATO alliance.

Those conflicts could, under certain circumstances, influence both how the Asian powers view their roles in the Middle East and how they relate to U.S. and Middle Eastern efforts to engage them in an effective regional security condominium to protect their mutual interests. For instance, if relations between China and India deteriorate, the role of Pakistan could become a crucial factor, influencing how both countries regard their interests and commitment in the Middle East. If Japan and China become more hostile toward each other, that could affect how both countries see their relationship with the United States and influence their relations with important powers such as Iran and Saudi Arabia. Most ominous, a future conflict over Taiwan would embroil the United States and China. China's dependency on sea-borne energy supplies from the Middle East would then become a strategic factor of great importance, and it would clearly influence how China behaves toward both the United States and the key Middle Eastern countries that supply it with oil and natural gas.

Any analysis of the strategic attitudes of the Asian players must take into account their experiences with Western imperialism and intra-Asian wars. Each of the countries has at one time or another suffered humiliation through confrontation with Western powers. The past has not been forgotten and memories persist, although at different levels of intensity, and that fact remains central in their relations with the West. Equally important, within Asia itself, China has, in the past, been humiliated by Japan, and India has been humiliated by China. One cannot discount the impact that these various events have had on the national psyche.

China's narrative is replete with anguish about "the century of national humiliation," which refers to the period from the Opium War of 1840 to the Communist Revolution in 1948. India's humiliation as part of the British Empire included the Indian Mutiny in 1857 (or as the Indians refer to it, the First War of Independence) and the agonies of independence in 1947, which resulted in the dissolution of British India and the partition of the subcontinent and the creation of Pakistan in the majority Muslim region. Japan, having launched a preemptive strike against the United States in 1941, suffered the ultimate degradation in nuclear attacks, unconditional surrender, and the occupation of its homeland in 1945.

While the United States currently has good relations with China and excellent relations with India and Japan, there are a number of ways in which this foursome could become less stable and potentially more dangerous.

China-India-Pakistan

Potential catalysts for conflict between India, China, and Pakistan concern disputes over weapons, borders, and Tibet. The first two issues involve all three states; the other issue is more specific to the Sino-Indian relationship. Relations have been further complicated by what some have termed China's overbearing attitude toward India and its culture.[197] While less than a decade ago India cited China as the reason behind its nuclear ambitions, today the Sino-Indian relationship is not an imminent threat to regional security. Both countries, however, do present a possible threat to each other's territorial integrity, economic growth, and national dignity.[198]

The Arms Balance.   India has for years been concerned about Chinese arms sales to Pakistan; similarly, Pakistan and China are troubled by increased U.S.-Indian military cooperation, including arms sales. The fact that all three countries have expanding nuclear arsenals intensifies concerns. A February 2003 Congressional Research Service report stated that Beijing's support to Islamabad is "widely understood to have included WMD-related transfers."[199] One such example was the 1994–95 Chinese sale of 5,000 ring magnets—used to enrich uranium—to Pakistan. In addition, Pakistan allegedly acquired its short- and medium-range missiles from China and North Korea.[200] A report to Congress by the Central Intelligence Agency supports that proposition. It revealed that "Chinese and North Korean entities continued to provide assistance to Pakistan's ballistic missile program during the first half of 1998. Such assistance is critical for Islamabad's efforts to produce ballistic missiles."[201] Chinese weapons transfers have been less visible in recent years in part because the United States also is supplying Pakistan with new weapons because of its cooperation in the U.S. war on terror.

Pakistan and China have been watching uneasily as India and the United States have solidified their military relations. India and the United States conduct naval, ground, and air exercises and the United States is an important provider of arms to India. In 2002, for example, the United States sold India $190 million worth of counterbattery radar sets alone. In addition, India has bought $29 million worth of counterterrorism equipment and purchased a refitted U.S. amphibious transport for $50 million in 2007.[202] Although Pakistan observes U.S.-India military cooperation with suspicion, the United States—which also sells high-technology arms to Pakistan, including F-16 fighters with advanced avionics packages and P-3 maritime patrol aircraft—maintains that it does not intend to disrupt the regional strategic balance.[203]

Border Disputes.   The most volatile border dispute, which dates back to 1947, involves the Kashmir region of northwest India. Pakistan, which controls the northern areas of Kashmir, also lays claim to the Indian-controlled regions of Jammu and southern Kashmir, which have a Muslim majority. Each country considers the region essential to its raison d'être. India wants to validate its claim to being a secular nation by having non–Hindu majority states. Pakistan, the Islamic breakaway from India, wants to embrace Kashmir as a majority-Muslim state.[204] The dispute over Kashmir has led to numerous military clashes and wars between India and Pakistan, and currently it is the most militarized territorial dispute in the world.[205]

Despite six decades of tension and three wars between India and Pakistan, the past five years have seen much greater cooperation. In 2004, New Delhi and Islamabad rejuvenated efforts to resolve their border disputes and alleviate tension.[206] Those efforts were put at risk following Prime Minister Singh's claim in October 2006 that his country's intelligence had "credible evidence" that Pakistan was involved in the July 11, 2006, Mumbai train bombing.[207] Despite that accusation, a month later, India hosted Riaz Khan, Pakistan's foreign secretary. Although they did not settle the border disputes, the two emissaries expounded on previous proposals to cooperate on antiterrorism measures.

Relations have improved most in areas of mutual interest, such as culture, travel, and trade.[208] In mid-2007 Ramesh Thakur, assistant secretary-general of the United Nations, stated that "relations between India and Pakistan are poised to be the most hopeful in decades."[209] The Pakistan People's Party (PPP)-led Pakistani government elected in February 2008 has shown a desire to improve the relationship, but recently tensions have increased. In the first half of 2008, altercations on the line of control in Kashmir increased in frequency and even involved small skirmishes between the border forces. While the general trend is away from armed conflict and possibly toward a diplomatic improvement, significant tensions and the potential for miscalculation and limited conflict remain. However, the very attempt at improving ties with Pakistan will make it easier for the states of the Middle East to deepen their strategic partnerships with New Delhi.[210] Unfortunately, the terrorist attacks in Mumbai over November 26–29, 2008, which almost certainly were orchestrated by groups operating out of Pakistan, have made compromise over Kashmir less likely.

Afghanistan is another point of contention between India and Pakistan, the root of which is a border disagreement between Afghanistan and Pakistan. The international border between the two countries—the Durand Line—was created by an agreement between a British civil servant and an Afghan king in 1893. Under the agreement the Afghan king leased parts of western Pakistan to the British for a 100-year period expiring in 1993. Pakistan is concerned that Afghanistan may try to reassert a claim to the region in regional forums.[211] Pakistan and Afghanistan have never agreed on the border, and it has proven quite porous historically due to mountainous terrain and the fact that it divides Pashtun tribes between the two countries.

This dispute led to close cooperation—described by Frédéric Grare as a "quasi-alliance"—between India and Afghanistan from India's independence in the late 1940s until the late 1970s. India supported every Afghan government until 1992 and assisted the Baloch insurgency in Pakistan in the 1970s.[212] Under Zia-ul-Haq in the late 1970s through 1988, Pakistan responded to Afghan attempts to promote Pashtun nationalism by emphasizing Islam over nationalism.[213] Pakistan responded to the Soviet invasion of Afghanistan in a similar vein, using Pashtun and Islamist proxies to fight the Soviets.

In recent years, the India-Pakistan conflict has been playing out by proxy in Afghanistan, first in the 1990s, when India supported a segment of the Northern Alliance against the Pakistan-backed Taliban.[214] Since the U.S. and NATO intervention in Afghanistan, however, India's support has taken a different form. India has taken a leading role in Afghan reconstruction—especially in infrastructure development—and has been a leading donor, contributing roughly $1.2 billion.[215] India also has opened consulates in Kandahar and Jalalabad. Pakistan views those acts, and India's ties with Iran, as a less-than-benign attempt to encircle Pakistan and has portrayed the consulates as cover for intelligence operations intended to destabilize Pakistan.

Both India and Pakistan likely have a strong intelligence presence in Afghanistan, but it is difficult to prove or disprove any malicious actions by either side.[216] The Afghan government and Indian national security adviser M. K. Narayanan both claimed that Pakistan's Inter-Services Intelligence (ISI) had a role in the early July 2008 bombing of the Indian embassy in Kabul.[217] While it is not clear that the proxy war is escalating, both sides believe that Afghanistan is essential to their security. In Pakistan's view, Afghan territorial claims threaten the integrity of the state, and the prospect of a firmly pro-India government, while a fact of life in the past, is difficult to accept.[218] India's primary interest lies in the stability of Afghanistan, which would allow for trade and help prevent the spread of radical Islam in Central Asia. While Indo-Pakistani conflict in Afghanistan presents a lower risk than that in Kashmir, it will likely prove intractable barring greater progress in the broader Indo-Pakistani relationship.

China and India also have had unresolved border disputes since their 1962 war. Although the situation is not as volatile as that in Kashmir, the disputes have hindered relations between the two countries. India also accuses China of occupying 15,000 square miles of Indian territory in Aksai

Chin, and China claims rightful ownership of the majority of India's northeastern state of Arunachal Pradesh.[219] The disputes remain unresolved.

However, conflict between China and India appears even less likely than war between India and Pakistan, and economics is the reason. Bilateral trade increased from a paltry $2.3 billion in FY 2001 to $25.7 billion in FY 2007.[220] Furthermore, both nations recognize the need to maintain stability in order to attract foreign investment.[221] Since 1981, India and China have held thirty-one rounds of peace talks. In April 2005 alone, India and China agreed on eleven new accords and agreed to a "strategic partnership." In 2006, called the Year of India-China Friendship, that partnership progressed as the two economic powers agreed to secure oil resources and reopened the Nathu La border; in addition, the Chinese premier visited India.[222] Furthermore, recent discussions and confidence measures between India, China, and Pakistan have decreased tensions over Kashmir. Nevertheless, low-level tension remains over the border dispute in Arunachal Pradesh and the fact that India harbors Tibet's government in exile.

Tibet.   Confrontation could also erupt over differences vis-à-vis Tibet, a territory administered by China but susceptible to destabilization by India. The Sino-Indian disagreement over Tibet began in the late 1950s, when India granted the Dalai Lama sanctuary while China was trying to crack down on Tibetan protests. India is home to 130,000 Tibetans, some of whom are actively involved in Free Tibet movements.[223] Moreover, India expresses sympathy for the Tibetans who seek religious freedom.[224] China fears that an independent Tibet would create a cascade of quests for independence among its various non-Han ethnic groups. China and India have held thirteen rounds of talks since 2003, as both sides continue to maneuver militarily and diplomatically in attempts to consolidate territorial gains and probe for weaknesses. This strictly Indian-Chinese dispute, compounded by other factors, could lead to conflict.

CHINA AND JAPAN

There may be a greater chance of conflict between China and Japan than between China and India. China and Japan could find themselves in conflict over societal grudges, perceived threats, offshore disputes, and differences over policies on Taiwan. Moreover, the buildup of the Japanese military could heighten their differences from mere diplomatic disagreements to more confrontational actions.

Societal Grudges.   Although economic relations between the two states are good, the same cannot be said about public opinion vis-à-vis the other state. Both states harbor historical resentments. Two key issues that impair relations are "comfort women" and the Nanjing Massacre. "Comfort women" were both Japanese and foreign nationals from countries occupied by Japan during World War II who most historians and analysts agree were coerced into sexual slavery by Japan. Japan, however, denies having taken a direct role in any coercion. A similar historical issue is the 1937–38 Nanjing Massacre. While China claims that Japan ordered the killing of approximately 300,000 Chinese civilians in Nanjing and the raping of about 20,000 Chinese women, the Japanese government officially recognizes the deaths of only a few hundred Chinese, all supposedly killed in military combat.[225]

Perceived Threats.   Japan still depends on the United States for security but new developments—specifically, Japan's Law on Special Antiterrorism Measures, involvement in Iraq, participation in the Proliferation Security Initiative, and constitutional amendment efforts—signify Japan's reevaluation of the role of its military.[226] All of those developments have allowed Japan to further develop its conventional military capabilities. Furthermore, Japan could easily develop nuclear weapons—it has the necessary scientists, plutonium, and nuclear energy capability.[227] As former U.S. secretary of state Henry Kissinger once noted, "It will come as no surprise if Japan goes nuclear someday."[228] That would be most likely to happen if efforts to contain and roll back North Korea's nuclear capabilities fail. China is watching developments in Japan closely and evaluating their potential as strategic threats.

And Japan is watching the evolution of China's military. In a 2005 defense white paper, Japan's Ministry of Defense expressed concern over China's modernization of its military, defense buildup, and elusiveness.[229] China's January 2007 anti-satellite test (ASAT) test "raised concerns about the peaceful use of space."[230] Although the first official comment about the test by a Chinese official attempted to calm the international community, Japan is still apprehensive. The ASAT test is just one example of China's increasing military capabilities. On March 4, 2007, Beijing announced a $17.8 billion increase in military spending.[231] The vagueness of the reasons for the budget increase, as well as other ambiguous military-related issues, concerns Japan. Japan's chief cabinet secretary, Yasuhisa Shiozaki, called on China to "improve transparency on its national defense, including military spending."[232] Japan fears that China is following the advice of its former leader Deng Xiaoping, who encouraged China to "hide our capacities and bide our time; be good at maintaining a low profile."[233] Japan's trade minister even brazenly called China a "scary country."[234]

Offshore Dispute. China, Taiwan, and Japan have disputes over rights to the uninhabited Senkaku-shoto (Diaoyu Tai) islands, which lie in the East China Sea 255 miles west of Okinawa, 130 miles from the northern point of Taiwan, and 220 miles from the Chinese coast. China does not recognize Japan's definition of the international demarcation lines in the East China Sea.[235] Because of China's intrusion into Japanese territorial waters in the East China Sea between April and September 2005, Japan deployed its self-defense forces thirty times trying to intercept Chinese aircraft.[236] An incident that involved the detection by the Japanese coast guard of a Chinese research ship violating the two nations' 2001 agreement to obtain permission to enter each other's exclusive economic zones (EEZ) resulted in strong diplomatic exchanges.[237] After failing to give a satisfactory explanation of its actions to Japan's Foreign Ministry, China went even further, denying that the territory was Japanese. That incendiary remark compelled Japan to express its anger at China's refusal to give "an honest response."[238] That incident typifies territorial disputes between China and Japan in the East China Sea.

Likewise, China views some of Japan's escapades in the East China Sea as threatening. Japan's oil drilling operations, for example, arouse Chinese ire. Japan has been drilling in disputed territory since 2003; Chinese foreign ministry spokesman Liu Jianchao has stated that "if Japan persists in granting drilling rights to companies in disputed waters it will cause a serious infringement of China's sovereign right."[239] Nonetheless, as the head of strategic research at China's Academy of Military Sciences, Major General Yao Youzhi, asserted,

> As long as the East China Sea issue is concerned, we will by no means tolerate Japan's behavior, neither will we give way to Japan's behavior. China will deal with the issue from the height of peace in East Asia and world peace, and will not bring the contradiction up to the level of military conflict in the short term.[240]

Despite Yao's reassurances, analyst Susan Craig suggests that in the long term, the East China Sea could be the setting of direct engagement between China and Japan: "The real dispute over territory and resources in the East

China Sea provides a venue for all the other unresolved problems and emotions that taint the Sino-Japanese relationship to come into play."[241]

Taiwan. Another contentious issue between China and Japan is Taiwan. Taiwan and Japan have both a historic relationship and modern commonalities that bind them together. Historically, Taiwan was a Japanese colony from 1895 until 1945; however, in accordance with Beijing's one-China policy, Japan cut diplomatic ties with Taiwan in 1972.[242] In the face of current regional relations, however, Japan's policy is shifting. At the beginning of 2006, Japan's foreign minister, Taro Aso, referred to Taiwan as a "country" twice within a two-month span.[243]

Japan's modern interactions with Taiwan have increased in economic, political, and cultural terms. With respect to politics, Japan has a de facto embassy, the Interchange Association, in Taipei. With respect to economics, Japan is Taiwan's biggest trading partner.[244] On the cultural front, the two nations exchange 2.3 million tourists a year. Such political, economic, and cultural interaction could undermine future Chinese efforts in Taiwan.

Japan and Taiwan may cooperate on security issues as well. Taiwan's former president, Chen Shuibian, stated that "Japan has a requirement and an obligation to come to the defense of Taiwan" because "the peace and stability of the Taiwan Strait and security of the Asian Pacific region are the common concerns for not only Taiwan, but also Japan and the United States."[245] The potential threat to Japan alluded to by Chen Shuibian is very real. If China were to take over Taiwan, then Chinese missiles would be a mere 66 miles from Japanese territory and Japan's sea access to Middle East oil would be extremely vulnerable.[246] Accordingly, for the first time, the United States and Japan announced in 2005 that Taiwan is a "common strategic objective."[247] China took great offense at their unprecedented joint statement, claiming that it undermined Chinese sovereignty by meddling in domestic Chinese affairs.[248] China fears that it is a precursor to future solidified Taiwanese-Japanese-U.S. relations. The concern is that the statement commits Japan to support U.S. military intervention in the event of a conflict with China over Taiwan—for example, by allowing the United States to use Japanese bases—and possibly even to deploy Japanese forces for joint antisubmarine operations and exercises.

Of the potential Asian conflicts considered here, that between China and Japan is the most dangerous. In 2005 *New York Times* journalists Norimitsu Onishi and Howard W. French observed that "the elements are in place for a showdown over Taiwan between Beijing and Tokyo. No one is predicting war, but Taiwan poses a permanent and unpredictable potential crisis."[249]

CONCLUSION

This review of the emerging maritime environment shows that the littoral states of the Persian Gulf and Indian Ocean as well as China, Japan, and the United States have many common interests that should encourage greater security cooperation among them.[250] Threats from piracy, terrorism, and nuclear arms proliferation encourage consensus among the major powers, as does the overriding need to ensure the security of energy supplies from the Gulf to the rest of the world. However, no matter how rational and logical it is to talk about mutual cooperation and common interests among major powers that have interests in the stability of the Middle East and the Indian Ocean region, nationalism and historic resentment are still alive and strong in Asia. Intensifying competition among China, Pakistan, and India and growing U.S. concerns over China's military buildup mean that the chances for miscalculation and accidental confrontation are higher than before.[251] For that reason, caution is necessary when advocating grandiose schemes for regional security. Perhaps the best way to ensure regional security is for the Gulf states to encourage a balance of power wherein no one power has complete hegemony, no power is excluded, and all have a deep interest in maintaining the status quo.[252] However, as long as Asia itself remains a source of inter-state conflict and as long as the key powers, especially China, retain deep suspicion of U.S. motives regarding cooperation, the possibility exists that conflict between the United States and key Asian countries or conflict among the Asian powers themselves could influence the geopolitics of the Middle East and the stability of the region. The biggest challenge in the Indian Ocean is to balance the need for greater cooperation on threats such as piracy, which requires the presence of many Asian navies, against the fear that Sino-Indian-Japanese maritime rivalry could become a significant reality, especially if the United States reduces its presence.

It is not easy to determine in any systematic fashion how potential inter-Asian and U.S. decisionmakers are perceived by the Gulf countries since all of them, including Iran, have gone out of their way not to become directly embroiled in the quarrels outlined above. Iran would be too proud to look to China or India to be a guardian of the Gulf because it thinks that the job should be left to the Gulf states themselves and that Iran should be their leader. The Arab Gulf states are far too dependent on the United States for protection to side with any Asian state against the United States. But there are voices in the Gulf that raise the question in a more indirect way and speculate about alternatives if the United States itself were to decide to reduce its responsibilities. Under those circumstances India and Pakistan are more frequently mentioned as defense collaborators than China, although over the years that could change. Much will depend upon how the global economic, political, and strategic environment evolves. As the final chapter shows, a number of alternative scenarios driven by a number of "wild card" developments can be envisioned, making it difficult to predict the future. What is clear is that a great deal will depend on the development and behavior of India and China and how those two giants interact with Japan and, most important, the United States.

CHAPTER EIGHT

ALTERNATIVE SCENARIOS
AND UNCERTAINTIES

THE GROWING TIES BETWEEN Asia and the Middle East will have a significant influence on the geopolitics of the vast region that stretches from the eastern Mediterranean to East Asia. India and China will become important actors. Pakistan, Japan, South Korea, and the Central and Southeast Asian countries also will play significant roles. The momentum that is pulling these two regions together is driven primarily by economic factors, especially Asia's need for the Middle East's fossil fuels. But that very momentum may have within it the seeds for greater competition and conflict rather than harmony and cooperation. History suggests that even the strongest economic ties between countries are seldom sufficient to mollify the forces of nationalism, ideology, ethnicity, and religion, which are the primary causes of most wars and unresolved conflicts. If economic rationality were the determining factor in international relations, the deep-rooted conflicts in the Middle East, Asia, and elsewhere would have been resolved long ago.

The Middle East itself provides examples of the dangers of overconfidence. During the early 1990s, following the 1990–91 Gulf War, the 1991 Madrid Peace Conference, and the 1993 Oslo Agreement between Israel and the Palestinians, a new era of cooperation and prosperity was predicted. High-level economic summits took place in Morocco, Jordan, and Egypt and grandiose plans for trade between Israel and its neighbors—including tourism and joint infrastructure projects—were presented in glossy handbooks. The problem was that key states including Syria, Iraq, and Iran were not part of the process, and in 1995 Israel's prime minister, Yitzhak Rabin, was assassinated. Within months a new era of Israeli-Palestinian violence had begun. The case of India and Pakistan illustrates the fragility of relations in the region. In the waning months of the Musharraf regime, after months of secret—and evidently very productive—negotiations, Indian and Pakistani interlocutors reached a number of key decisions on the future of Kashmir. But then came the Muslim terrorist attacks in Mumbai in November 2008, which were perpetrated by Pakistan-based extremists who wanted to prevent reconciliation between the two countries. Although the government of India displayed great caution in refraining from any military retaliation against the radicals, the negotiations on Kashmir were put on hold.

This volume reaffirms the great economic and political benefits of closer ties between Asia and the Middle East and why such ties are in the interest of the wider international community, especially the United States, which is reluctant to be perpetual guardian of the Gulf and Indian Ocean unless there is a commensurate sharing of the burdens by local powers. The supporters of the U.S. presence, including most of the Arab countries, would argue that in the absence of a U.S. military presence, anarchy, chaos, terrorism, and interstate war would increase. The result would be a high risk of disruption of oil and natural gas supplies that would deny the producers income while causing a spike in world energy prices that would not serve the interests of the major energy consumers, including the United States. Any surge in prices that suddenly added between $30 and $50 or more to the price of a barrel of oil would have a profound impact on the U.S. growth rate and could precipitate another recession. The assumption is that bad things would happen if the United States were not present. The counter-narrative, heard most vocally in Tehran and among anti-American politicians in many Muslim countries, argues that the large U.S. military presence in the area provokes tension and conflict and thereby spurs the rearmament programs that already are under way in the region.

India, China, and Japan are very aware of the dilemmas that they face in becoming more dependent on Middle East fossil fuels. In their own ways, they are seeking alternatives to limit their exposure to disruption of supplies from the region. Japan has long-term plans to reduce oil imports; China is diversifying its sources, seeking oil in Africa, Latin America, and Russia. India, too, seeks diversification and increased supplies from its neighborhood. But if long-term projections of their oil and natural gas needs are correct, there is little chance that they can avoid becoming increasingly dependent on the Middle East for at least the next two decades. That means that the energy factor will become a key agenda item in their discussions with each other and with the United States on the security of supplies.

In the last resort, energy security cannot be decoupled from other vital issues, such as Iran's quest for nuclear capabilities. India, China, and Japan all see Iran as an important future source for oil and natural gas, but they are also aware that until the nuclear issue is resolved, the United States will pressure them to reduce their projects in the Iranian energy sector. If the nuclear issue is resolved and the United States and Iran restore diplomatic and economic relations, the Asian countries will be net beneficiaries, and it will serve U.S. and Western interests too, since it could open up additional fuel supplies in a tight market.

Concerning Middle East stability, there is agreement that Islamist radicalism is a threat, that further nuclear proliferation is dangerous, that a resolution of the Arab-Israeli conflict would be an important breakthrough, and that Iraq should be a united country that poses no threat to its neighbors. But on more specific policy questions, including how to contain radicalism and Iranian nuclear proliferation, how to unite Iraq, and how to solve the Arab-Israeli crisis, strong differences of opinion emerge. China and India are more willing to challenge U.S. policy in the region than Japan, but because all three want to consummate energy deals with Tehran, all are reluctant to use preemptive strategies against Iran that invoke the use of force. Thanks to intense U.S. diplomatic lobbying during the Clinton administration, China stopped most of its nuclear dealings with Iran, but since then it has upgraded its investments in the Iranian energy sector and continues to provide some weapons to the regime. Japan has been responsive to U.S. pressure on diminishing its stake in Iran's energy sector, but it would like to do more business in that area if political circumstances were to change. India has been critical of Iran's nuclear program, to which it provides no assistance, but a big issue with the United States concerns its plans with Pakistan to build a gas pipeline from Iran through Pakistan to its northern cities. Although such energy cooperation makes sense for all three parties, it works against U.S. efforts to hamper Iran's long-term energy programs.

In the long run, the most difficult and potentially contentious question relates to possible security agreements between the Asian countries and the United States and bilateral relations between the United States and the big three Asian countries and the countries of the Gulf. Aside from the United

States, only India has direct military ties with the Gulf states, and those ties are presently low-key in scope and purpose. China has close links to Pakistan but as yet has only dabbled in Gulf security issues, most specifically in arms sales to Iran and anti-piracy patrols off the coast of Somalia. Japan, which has the most minor military presence, does not seek a direct relationship in the Gulf defense establishments. Therefore, it is difficult to see, based on current trends, any Asian military role that would supplement, let alone supplant, the current dominant position of the United States.

Could that pattern change? If so, how and under what circumstances? Pressure for U.S. withdrawal will not come from the Arab countries or from Pakistan, India, China, or the other Asian countries, with the exception of Iran and North Korea. A drawdown of U.S. military capabilities would leave them vulnerable to threats that they currently have no capability to deter or stop. Neither India, China, nor Japan has any wish to "replace" or substitute for U.S. power in the region. Over time, that attitude could change; a weakened United States would stimulate further competition between China, India, and Japan, given their list of unresolved quarrels. While U.S. support will facilitate India's drive to become the dominant Asian power in the Indian Ocean, it also is likely to serve as a catalyst for China's continued expansion of its offensive naval capabilities.[1]

Some have portrayed India as a rising power seeking to expand its influence through a practical mix of engagement-based diplomacy backed up by increasing economic clout and military capability.[2] In the period of the British Raj, much of the Indian Ocean region was governed from Bombay and Simla, and many Indians wish to reclaim such a regional leadership role. Despite positive trends in their relationship, India and China are likely to remain competitors over the long term, although that will play out primarily to India's east. Potential competition with China can be seen as the reason for India's recent diplomatic initiatives with Singapore and a number of ASEAN states. In the long run, India probably will play the role of integrator in the Indian Ocean region, helping to bring widely separated littoral nations together through trade and diplomacy.

China's power projection capability in the region is still being developed, and potential conflict with India would be unlikely to arise from issues emanating out of the Persian Gulf. That said, the India-China border dispute could result in India or the United States seeking to restrict the flow of oil to China from the Persian Gulf. However, some U.S. China experts argue that an oil embargo would be difficult to impose and that any such scenario is vastly overblown and highly unlikely.[3] Others argue that inherent distrust among Asian governments pushes them to accommodate China but also to band together to hedge against China's power. In other words, Chinese pressure serves in some ways to increase U.S. influence in Asia.

For all those reasons, it would be unwise to make specific forecasts regarding the path that this huge region is likely to take in the years ahead. However, it is useful to suggest a number of different scenarios that could play out, depending on which of the key regional factors outlined in the analysis predominates and how the global economy evolves in the coming years. Four scenarios are presented, followed by a more detailed survey of uncertainties and "wild cards" that could influence the future of Middle East–Asian relations.

Under the first scenario, termed Growth and Prosperity, the best-case analysis for the region turns out to be the winner. Strong economic growth in Asia resumes after the global recession of 2008–09, with China and India leading the way. That means greater demand for fossil fuels and a subsequent rise in energy prices. Under these circumstances, the energy-producing countries—especially in the Arab Gulf—are able to continue their huge expansion projects and the Gulf becomes a real world center for tourism, sports, and cultural activities. In parallel, the land infrastructure projects in Central Asia and new undersea communications cables make access between East, Central, and South Asia and the Middle East easier and cheaper. While a number of unresolved political conflicts remain, the crises that have overwhelmed the region in recent years—notably Iraq, Afghanistan, and Pakistan—are likely to be brought under control and the risk of major military operations significantly reduced. Under this scenario, a slow but systematic drawdown of the ubiquitous U.S. presence will be both possible and desirable since the regional powers will have sufficient wealth to take more responsibility for their own security and the maritime traffic on which they are so dependent. It is, of course, an outcome that the United States and the Western world welcome, since it suggests a more stable international environment and less need for Western intervention in faraway places.

The second scenario, called Mayhem and Chaos, is the opposite of the first scenario; everything that can go wrong does go wrong. The world economic situation weakens rather than strengthens, and India, China, and Japan suffer a major reduction in their growth rates, further weakening the global economy. As a result, energy demand falls and the price of fossil fuels plummets, leading to a financial crisis for the energy-producing states, which are forced to cut back dramatically on expansion programs and social welfare. That in turn leads to political unrest and nurtures different radical groups, including, but not limited to, Islamic extremists. The internal stability of some countries is challenged, and there are more "failed states." Most serious is the collapse of the democratic government in Pakistan and its takeover by Muslim extremists, who then take possession of a large number of nuclear weapons. The danger of war between India and Pakistan increases significantly. Iran, always worried about an extremist Pakistan, expands and weaponizes its nuclear program. That further enhances nuclear proliferation in the Middle East, with Saudi Arabia, Turkey, and Egypt joining Israel and Iran as nuclear states. Under these circumstances, the potential for nuclear terrorism increases, and the possibility of a nuclear terrorist attack in either the Western world or in the oil-producing states may lead to a further devastating collapse of the world economic market, with a tsunami-like impact on stability. In this scenario, major disruptions can be expected, with dire consequences for two-thirds of the planet's population.

A third scenario, Asian Balance of Power, assumes that while economic growth on a global level resumes and India, China, and Japan continue to show economic strength, the overall prosperity of the Western world—particularly of the United States—weakens. That leads to increasing domestic pressures for the United States and Europe to pay less attention to security problems in the Middle East and Asia, given the high price that they already paid for intervention in the 1990s and the first decade of the twenty-first century. While the Western world still has an interest in stable energy markets, there is less inclination to intervene and play the role of policeman. In the United States, there is an equivalent of the East of Suez debate that took place in Britain in the 1960s, when Britain decided to draw down its military presence in both the Indian Ocean and the Gulf. With the unilateral decision by the United States to draw down its presence, the major Asian powers—given that they continue to have unresolved problems among themselves—expand their own military forces, particularly their nuclear and maritime capabilities, ultimately leading to a triangular Asian arms race among India, China, and Japan. Under those circumstances, Japan is likely to obtain nuclear weapons, especially if the crisis on the Korean peninsula remains unresolved, and the security of the region ultimately will be in the hands of the Asian powers themselves. The sorts of alliances and arrangements that they make with the Gulf states and other Middle East countries would be uncertain. In all probability, India would play a key role, particularly in the Gulf. Indeed, India would be most assertive if it felt that China was encroaching on a region in which India believes that it should have hegemonic control.

A fourth scenario, International Cooperation, assumes that while the world economic situation may not be as rosy as outlined in the first scenario, there nevertheless remains a strong interest on the part of all the major industrial powers in ensuring secure energy supplies; as a result, the price of energy is kept at a reasonable level. The United States does not go through an East of Suez moment and continues to play a responsible and significant role in the maritime peacekeeping operations in the region. However, there is more pressure on the regional powers to share more of the burden and to participate in joint security operations ranging from sea control missions to cooperative ventures to curb terrorism, proliferation, and radicalism. Under these circumstances, the presence of the United States is seen as beneficial and reduces the tendency of the Asian powers to compete among themselves. While the U.S. commitment is not open ended, it serves long-term U.S. interests, in much the same way that the U.S. presence in Europe today continues to serve U.S. national interests. In this cooperative environment, local conflicts are easier to manage since it is in the interests of the all major powers to resist the forces of radicalism and proliferation—particularly nuclear terrorism.

CRITICAL UNCERTAINTIES

Which of the many uncertainties and drivers are the most important? While this volume assumes that the growing links between Asia and the Middle East are driven primarily by economic realities, linear economic growth, whether global or regional, is rarely sustained. Any number of events can disrupt it, as the 2008 financial crisis so amply demonstrates. Even if sustained growth resumes and perhaps even accelerates, growth can pose a series of challenges for the countries involved. The rapid growth of Dubai, the muddle and confusion that followed, and its unique vulnerability to market downturns is a case in point.

More generally, the economies of the Middle East and Asia are all susceptible to internal and external traumas that can come in different forms. Most dramatic is the possibility of a major terrorist event in one of the super-rich Gulf states, which would have an instant and highly disruptive impact on the financial sector and would put a serious damper on the high-value tourism that several Gulf states are counting on to pay for their extraordinary outlays in infrastructure and facilities such as hotels, sports arenas, universities, and museums. Within the Gulf, other disruptive events could include sustained labor unrest and ethnic and religious conflict. Any number of unresolved interstate quarrels over boundaries, offshore islands, and oil and gas fields could lead to violent conflict.

To the north of the Gulf, the Caspian region and Central Asia—which this book suggests could be an important gateway to the Middle East as well as an important source of energy for Asia—is a region replete with unresolved conflict, authoritarian and corrupt governments, and growing radical Islamic movements. Those factors could put on hold many of the most promising infrastructure and energy projects. It is worth remembering that in the wake of the Soviet Union's exit from Afghanistan in 1989, there was great enthusiasm and support for the construction of a pipeline to bring natural gas from Turkmenistan to Pakistan. An agreement was signed in 1995 between the two countries and the American company UNOCAL to start construction. But the pipeline was abandoned as the civil war in Afghanistan escalated, leading to the eventual triumph of the Taliban a year later. When the Taliban were defeated by U.S. forces in 2001 for their complicity in the 9/11 attacks, the hope was that new pipeline options could be developed. However, the resurgence of the Taliban and the continuing conflict in the country rule out any such project for the foreseeable future.

Beyond the possible contingencies in the Gulf and Caspian, two sets of events—or "wild cards"—could radically change the Middle East–Asia dynamic. They have been briefly noted in the preceding four scenarios, but they warrant repeating. The first set relates to developments within and between the key Asian countries themselves; the second set concerns U.S. politics and foreign policy in the aftermath of the wars in Iraq and Afghanistan and the nuclear crisis with Iran.

In the second and third scenarios it was suggested that beyond economic downturns, some of the Asian wild cards include the radicalization of Pakistan; an enhanced arms race between China, India, and Japan; and further nuclear proliferation in the Middle East and East Asia. It is possible to imagine many more dire events that could lead to radically different paths of development. The most extreme would be a political implosion within China, leading to chaos and violent class warfare. Such an implosion could have many different causes, the most obvious being collapse of the Chinese economy resulting in severe unemployment, but beyond that there remain major unresolved ethnic tensions, particularly on China's borders, with the Muslim Uighurs and Tibet. The unresolved conflict with Taiwan also could get out of hand and lead to a war that might even draw in the United States. Other possible crises include conflict with Japan over offshore territories, trade wars with the United States and Europe, and regional border crises with China's neighbors, including Vietnam and North Korea. A major health pandemic would put China and all the major countries on a precarious track and set back development, as could natural disasters such as earthquakes, hurricanes, soil erosion, and freshwater shortages. A similar set of possibilities arises in the case of India, which in many respects has more internal conflicts than China and an economy that may be more fragile. Certainly, India is equally vulnerable to environmental and meteorological disasters. Of special concern is the growing demand for fresh water and fears that the Himalayan glaciers, which supply water to the great rivers of South Asia, are melting, though at what rate is unknown.

In East Asia, a full-blown crisis on the Korean Peninsula could draw in China, the United States, South Korea, and Japan. The collapse of North Korea would carry with it major risks for instability. On the other hand, a more peaceful unification of the two Koreas could lead to a country with formidable economic, political, and military potential within East Asia, which could upset the regional balance of power. Likewise, a more assertive and nationalistic Japan is not out of the question, given the tensions with neighbors that still persist. All those scenarios add a further caveat to the prediction that Asia's rise will continue and will be the key factor in international politics in the twenty-first century.

The second set of events concerns changes in U.S. politics. Aside from economic turmoil, perhaps the most serious development would be the failure of the United States to secure a stable situation in Afghanistan after a period of intense conflict that resulted in high U.S. casualties. That would be a repeat of the U.S. experience in Vietnam and would leave Americans disillusioned about continued engagement in Asia, which has brought them great misery since the early 1960s. Under those circumstances, especially if accompanied by economic hardship, the growth of neo-isolationism on the political right and the left could precipitate an East of Suez moment for the United States, leading to a drawdown of capabilities that would have far-reaching consequences for the entire region. The capacity of the U.S. public to support endless military commitments in the Middle East and Asia is finite, and given the long list of domestic challenges that need to be met, including unemployment, health care, infrastructure, and the environment, such a gloomy scenario is possible.

Given the different events that could occur, is there any sure route for the analyst to take in projecting the future? There is not, but even a cautious analyst would have to anticipate that the rise of Asia will be an inevitable feature of the twenty-first century, just as the rise of the United States was the dominant event of the twentieth century. Progress will not be linear; there will be ups and downs and setbacks, and wild cards such as those described above could come into play. However, with respect to foreign policy, whether U.S., Middle Eastern, or Asian, the growing ties between Asia and the Middle East will become increasingly important. They will not directly undermine or threaten U.S. power, but they will erode the pre-eminence of the United States. In many ways a growing Asian presence in the Middle East will bring a welcome breath of fresh air to a region left with the bitter historical legacies of European dominance and character-ized by contemporary antagonism toward the hegemonic role of the United States. As suggested throughout this volume, the major Asian players in the Middle East have not been colonizers or occupiers and they have far less of an emotional stake in the Arab-Israeli conflict. On the one hand, that means that they approach political issues and unresolved conflicts with what some would argue is a cynical, laissez-faire attitude, perhaps exempli-fied by China's initial indifference to human rights abuses in Sudan. How-ever, the upside is that the Asians do not interfere directly in Middle East politics and therefore enjoy good relations with most states. How long they can sustain their hands-off approach is questionable if, by virtue of their economic dominance and their own strategic stakes in the region, they get drawn into the messiness of Middle East politics at a time when the United States becomes disillusioned by the burdens of hegemony.

SINGAPORE, INDONESIA, AND MALAYSIA IN THE MIDDLE EAST

SINGAPORE, INDONESIA, AND MALAYSIA have emerged as leaders in promoting political, economic, and social cooperation between Southeast Asia and the Middle East. One indicator of the growth of collaborative multilateralism is the Asia–Middle East Dialogue (AMED), initiated by Singapore in 2005. At the inaugural session, the nations involved in the dialogue said that "[because] profound political, economic and social developments are taking place in both Asia and the Middle East . . . [there are] considerable opportunities for greater cooperation between the two regions."[1] The objectives of AMED are threefold: first, to increase understanding on a person-to-person as well as government level to help foster cooperation among Middle Eastern and Asian countries; second, to produce policy recommendations on political, economic, and social policy that can enhance relations; and third, to give voices of moderation a platform to promote tolerance and interfaith understanding and dialogue.[2]

The two AMED conferences held so far have focused on promoting interregional cooperation on security and on economic and cultural issues. In addressing the ever-present concern of terrorism, AMED affirmed that a broad coalition of like-minded countries is necessary to contain the threats posed by Islamic radicalism. While AMED saw the U.S.-led military operation in Afghanistan as an essential part of the confrontation with extremists, it considered a more local approach by the Asian nations a necessary corollary. Goh Chok Tong made this point in his keynote address:

Relations between the Middle East and the West have been historically difficult. But there are no deep historical, cultural, religious, or ideological barriers preventing better relations between the Middle East and Asia. On the contrary, the links between our regions are ancient; the historical influences on each other profound. It was only in the last century or so, with colonialism and the Cold War, that we neglected each other. But the ancient links are now being re-established. We should encourage and facilitate this process of mutual rediscovery.[3]

That "mutual rediscovery," however, must be comprehensive, including more than just international dialogue on security issues. The participating nations at AMED also recognized that "sustainable economic development requires a sound political environment between the two regions and a strong foundation of mutual interests."[4] The economic foundation, undoubtedly, is oil. AMED thus acknowledged the growing need for the free flow of Middle East fuels to Asia.[5]

SINGAPORE

Singapore, in particular, has emphasized the need for greater economic collaboration with the Middle East. Located on the strategic Singapore Strait, the city-state sits at a chokepoint of maritime transportation between Asia and the Indian Ocean region. Because of its small size and vulnerability to hostility from its larger neighbors, Singapore has cultivated a strong economic and military relationship with India. The two have acted closely together as leaders on anti-piracy patrols in the greater Malacca Strait region and have conducted joint military exercises.[6] Singapore, a Buddhist nation, differs from Indonesia and Malaysia in that it has formal diplomatic ties with Israel; in fact, Israel and Singapore have had strong relations since 1968, especially in areas such as business, technology, health care, and defense. Singapore has similarly established growing economic ties with many Arab states. In fact, Singapore first pioneered the sovereign wealth fund (SWF) in the 1950s. Though initially intended to insulate governments from volatility in the exchange rate market, SWFs today are one of the primary investment tools used by wealthy Arab Gulf states like Saudi Arabia, the UAE, and Kuwait.[7]

INDONESIA

Indonesia also has ties with the Middle East. As a significant exporter of oil, Indonesia's links with Middle Eastern nations are based less on economic factors than religious ones. With a population of more than 240 million people, almost 90 percent of which is Muslim, Indonesia is the world's most populous Muslim country. Notably, the practice of Islam in Indonesia has evolved differently from its practice in the Arab world due to Indonesia's historical interactions with Hindu and other Asian religions.[8] Nevertheless, their common religious background creates a natural cultural and religious link between Indonesia and the land of Islam's origin.

Indonesia has also led the way in calls for moderation and multinational cooperation, especially on security issues. The nation, which has produced a significant number of radical groups, has endured several major terrorist attacks on its soil in the past decade.[9] Even as Jakarta seeks to address internal security problems, it hopes to capitalize on its historically strong relations with the West and take a greater role in peacemaking in the Middle East. Indonesia's democracy has been strong since Suharto's fall in 1998, and it has promoted its newfound liberal democracy abroad by supporting reconciliation between Hamas and Fatah. Regarding Iraq, Indonesia supports "reconciliation among factions in Iraq, replacement of American forces by a Muslim-dominated coalition under United Nations auspices, and reconstruction."[10]

MALAYSIA

While maintaining trade with its traditional economic partners in Europe and East Asia, Malaysia has also increased trade and investment with the Middle East, especially in the area of Islamic finance. Islamic banks based in the Gulf states have been rapidly increasing their asset holdings in Kuala Lumpur and other Malaysian cities. Islamic loans and mortgages, which forbid the earning of profit through interest payments, provide a competitive alternative to the more traditional, Western-dominated financial markets. For its part, the Malaysian government has provided numerous incentives to encourage foreign businesses to invest in the niche Islamic banking system. Malaysian officials have said that they hope to have 20 percent of all national banking assets in Islamic financial institutions by 2010.[11]

Malaysia also has played a role in Middle East–related security issues. Like Indonesia, Malaysia has no diplomatic relationship with Israel, claiming that no relationship is possible until a peace settlement is signed. On broader security issues like terrorism, however, Malaysia has been a more constructive partner for the United States. Kuala Lumpur has taken an active role in jailing terrorists and giving a voice to Islamic moderation.[12]

Undersea Cable Networks in the Middle East and Asia

International communications between the Middle East and Asia have improved dramatically in the past few years. Most of the progress has come from the decision to shift from communications satellites to undersea fiber-optic cable networks that carry Internet and telecommunications traffic. Deregulation and huge demand, specifically in the Middle East, has helped to open up the market to private interests, and each of the major cable systems laid in recent years has been achieved through the work of private companies.[1]

Two of the undersea fiber-optic networks were facilitated under Flag Telecom, a fully owned subsidiary of Reliance Communications, an Indian telecommunications company. The first system, which was announced in 1997, is known as FLAG Europe-Asia (FEA). FEA connects Europe to Asia through the Middle East, and the cable comes ashore in key landing sites such as Egypt, Jordan, Saudi Arabia, the United Arab Emirates, India, China, South Korea, Malaysia, Thailand, and Japan. FEA became the first independent cable system as well as the longest privately funded undersea cable.[2]

Also initiated in 1997 was another major fiber-optic network, the Southeast Asia–Middle East–Western Europe (SEA-ME-WE) network, which operates two lines, SEA-ME-WE3 and SEA-ME-WE4. Supported by a consortium of sixteen international telecommunications companies, it now provides Internet, telephone, and broadband capabilities throughout the Middle East and Asia, with landing sites in key locations such as Hong Kong,

243

China, Taiwan, South Korea, Japan, Singapore, Malaysia, Thailand, Bangladesh, India, Sri Lanka, Pakistan, the United Arab Emirates, Saudi Arabia, and Egypt. In March 2008, Alcatel-Lucent announced that it was planning to double the network's capacity in order to support growing traffic.[3]

FALCON, the second network laid by Flag Telecom, was announced in 2004. The major function of FALCON is to give broadband access to a number of previously unserved countries in the Middle East, such as Bahrain, Qatar, Oman, Kuwait, and Yemen and to connect them to India. FALCON was completed and the inaugural call was made in September of 2006. This system is especially significant because it was the first in the Middle East to provide a protective self-healing loop, a function that can be critical to the everyday operation of a cable system.

Through all these improvements and introductions, the general trend in the region throughout the past 10 years has been to increase the capacity, quality, and number of landing sites of the cable networks throughout the Middle East and Asia to both reach and better serve more areas.

Despite the progress that has been made, the cable networks in the Middle East and Asia face a number of vulnerabilities. There have been two major instances of damaged undersea cables, one in the Taiwan Strait in 2006, the other off the coast of Egypt in 2008. In Taiwan, the cuts came as a result of an earthquake that damaged many of the existing lines, while in the Middle East the cuts were the result of a ship anchor unintentionally cutting the lines.

In general, damage to undersea cables across the globe is fairly common. Along most of the Atlantic and the Pacific Ocean cable networks, the cutting of cables, while frequent, is not very noticeable because there are a number of other cable lines and routes as well as satellite systems that provide back-up in the event of any failure. However, in the Red Sea, the Persian Gulf, and the Indian Ocean, geography plays a role: these regions have narrow straits that limit the number of cables that can be laid, seabeds that lie along fault lines, and uneven ocean floors that are unsuitable for cable systems.

The 2008 cuts were especially damaging because the undersea cables are laid along one narrow route.[4] Two of the major cables that were damaged, FLAG Europe-Asia and SEA-ME-WE, lay parallel to each other, leaving little or no margin for error if one system was damaged. That problem could be addressed by developing alternative, less direct routes so that back-up systems are available; unfortunately, doing so would be very costly and therefore is unappealing to both consumers and companies in the region.[5]

Each cable system has its own maintenance authority, usually the company or companies that built the network. After the 2006 events, it took almost 50 days to repair the overwhelming damage found along the lines. In 2008, however, all damage was repaired within 14 days of being reported.

The cable cuts in 2008 in the Middle East raised questions about the vulnerability of these systems in general. "If two unwitting captains could cripple Persian Gulf communications for a week," communications consultant Richard Gasparre asked, "what would happen if disgruntled or corrupt officers—or more likely teams of dedicated pirates or saboteurs—were actually trying to cause damage?"[6] Because the cable networks are privately owned, they are not the responsibility of any national government or military force. Despite the fact that disruption of certain cables could be a major national security threat, they remain largely underprotected. It should be noted that communication lines have long been viable targets during wartime. According to a Department of Defense report on maritime law, "Undersea cables, including those connecting belligerents with neutrals, have been interfered with during all naval wars since the Spanish-American War, as Article 15 of the 1884 Convention for the Protection of Undersea Cables exempts belligerents."[7]

The reality is that there are a number of potential problems that leave global cable systems vulnerable to both intentional and accidental damage. The foremost reason that certain areas are unprotected is that it is not logistically possible, not to mention cost-effective, to physically patrol or survey the entire length of the cable routes. Even if there was surveillance across the world's oceans, terrorist or belligerent vessels would adapt to their environment and hide among or disguise themselves as normal vessels. Gasparre notes that "seaborne terrorists could use merchant ships or small coastal boats for cover and transportation,"[8] which would make the task of identifying and protecting against threats far more difficult.

The numerous landing sites where undersea cables come ashore are another major point of vulnerability. According to a study done by the International Capital Group, it is easy to access information about the location of cables and landing sites: "A simple search on 'submarine cable landing' will produce a list of international submarine communications cables as well as 983 locations where undersea cables come ashore, most all of them in rural to remote areas."[9] Furthermore, the areas where cables come ashore are not monitored by armed guards protecting the networks but by small teams of technicians monitoring standard operating progress.

Cable protection and vulnerability becomes vitally important because 95 percent of international telecommunications traffic is carried over the global network of undersea cables, which has taken over the role once played by satellites. The most direct effect of cable damage is that it can severely reduce Internet availability to large numbers of people in a region or across the globe. After the cuts off the coast of Egypt in December 2008, well over 50 percent of people with Internet access lost their connection in Egypt and India. In this case, if one more cable had been cut, the entire Middle East could have suffered a full Internet blackout. Because many of the cable systems hit in 2008 originate in Europe and pass through the Middle East on the way to Asia, many European nations lost their connectivity with Asia and the Middle East as well.

Another effect may be felt by international companies that have chosen to outsource or operate in the Middle East and Asia, specifically in India: the loss of Internet service slows down and can stop the everyday functioning of business ventures in those regions.[10] Fortunately, there are some options for circumventing the problem when it arises; for example, according to spokeswoman Linda Laughlin, "Verizon Communications Inc. . . . rerouted traffic for its Verizon Business customers making calls to the Middle East by siphoning it to Europe and the U.S. and then down through Asia." However, connections will not have the same strength or quality when the network is overloaded; in that case, "the rerouting slowed some traffic to about half its normal speed."[11]

The most critical concern is that cable damage can have a significant impact on national security. Defense departments depend on cable networks for communication; if cables are cut, military commanders cannot reach their units to give orders, intelligence capability can be lost, and a number of other potentially disastrous consequences can occur. The recent direction of the U.S. military has been toward warfare in which communications networks play an integral role. Network-centric warfare requires coordination and cooperation among a number of different military units so that the military can act as a cohesive unit; a lack of effective communications would cripple this new system.[12]

A number of solutions to these challenges have been proposed, and some are in the process of development. China has made a special effort to guarantee the safety of an especially vulnerable stretch of cable. According to the People's Daily Online, they have created a new police force charged with the task of patrolling the restricted area where the cable is laid to prevent activities that could damage the cable.[13] Although this is a small-scale program, it could be used in other key areas, such as the chokepoints in the Middle East where other cables have been affected.

There also have been technological developments that should facilitate surveillance of the ocean depths. The U.S. Navy has begun to use unmanned undersea vehicles (UUVs) that eliminate the problem of physically surveying the length of the ocean. Availability of this technology currently is limited, and so far it has been used only for short-range operations, but it has the potential to protect undersea cables spanning the length of the ocean floor.[14] There are reports that China's navy also has been working to develop the technology for UUVs as part of its program to modernize its naval capabilities.[15]

Military establishments also rely on back-up systems of satellites and alternative cables to prevent a full blackout from disabling their operations. The U.S. Navy has developed a program known as FORCEnet that will integrate a number of communications methods (radio, infrared, microwave, fiber, cable, and so forth) to allow for more efficient, effective, and decentralized operations.[16] It also will allow certain nodes in the system to function independently of others to avoid widespread consequences in the event of accidental or intentional damage to any part of the system. Another function of FORCEnet will be to target any actions by hostile actors that threaten the system: "The goal is not only to detect, locate, identify, and target, but also to infer capabilities and intentions."[17] The last function of FORCEnet is information assurance, which will include protection from attack, ability to identify hostile actions and counter them, and ability to mitigate the effects of possible attacks, all while operating autonomously.[18]

Besides innovation in military technology, there also have been cooperative efforts, particularly in Asia, to develop a regional maritime security regime to secure shipping routes, communication lines, and other components of maritime security from, for example, the growth of maritime terrorism. One example is SARPSCO, the South Asia Regional Port Security Cooperative, which brings together a number of states surrounding the Indian Ocean, including Bangladesh, Comoros, India, Madagascar, the Maldives, Mauritius, Oman, Pakistan, and Sri Lanka. The formation of SARPSCO sends a clear warning to terrorists and criminals in the South Asia and Indian Ocean region that they will be detected, they will be interdicted, and their activities will not be tolerated. It has yet to be seen, however, whether this regional cooperative will be successful, specifically in terms of protecting against damage to undersea telecommunications cables.

NOTES

CHAPTER ONE

1. A number of organizations, including the UN and the Indian and Chinese foreign policy establishments, regard the term "Middle East" as Eurocentric and instead refer to the region as West Asia. The term "Middle East" is usually attributed to American strategist Alfred Thayer Mahan, who was one of the key geopolitical thinkers of the nineteenth century. At that time British diplomats presiding over their huge empire distinguished the Near East from the Far East. Mahan suggested the term "Middle East" to refer to the Persian Gulf, the region in between. Today, the term is used to cover a wider area, although some debate just what its parameters are. For a more detailed discussion, see Geoffrey Kemp and Robert E. Harkavy, *Strategic Geography and the Changing Middle East* (Brookings, 1997).

2. As the financial crisis of 2008–09 demonstrates, there is nothing inevitable about such projections: natural or man-made disasters, including prolonged global recession or internal upheavals, could derail China's and India's march to power and wealth. As late as 1993, a flurry of books and articles appeared in the United States warning of Japan's unstoppable growth. Yet at that very time, Japan's bubble economy was entering into a recession from which it has still to fully emerge.

3. Central Intelligence Agency, *World Factbook* (www.cia.gov/library/publications/the-world-factbook/index.html).

4. "India to Keep Existing Troops in UNIFIL for 'Time Being,'" *Muslim World News,* August 29, 2006.

5. Yitzhak Shichor, "Silent Partner: China and the Lebanon Crisis," *China Brief* 6, no. 17 (August 16, 2006).

6. "China to Increase Peacekeeping Force in Lebanon to 1,000," Xinhua News Agency, September 18, 2006 (http://news.xinhuanet.com/english/2006-09/18/content_5105874.htm).

7. Energy Information Administration (EIA), "World Proved Reserves of Oil and Natural Gas: Most Recent Estimates," March 3, 2009 (www.eia.doe.gov/emeu/international/reserves.html).

8. EIA, "World Total Liquids Production by Region and Country," *International Energy Outlook 2007* (http://tonto.eia.doe.gov/FTPROOT/forecasting/0484(2007).pdf).

9. International Energy Agency, *World Energy Outlook 2006*, p. 119 (www.iea.org/textbase/nppdf/free/2006/weo2006.pdf).

10. "Migration in the Asia-Pacific Region," Migration Policy Institute, July 2009 (www.migrationinformation.org/Feature/display.cfm?id=733).

11. Brian Bremner and Assif Shameen, "The Ties That Bind the Middle East and Asia," *Business Week,* May 17, 2007.

12. Data taken with permission from United Nations Conference on Trade and Development (UNCTAD) (www.unctad.org). Generalized data on FDI flows and stocks can be obtained from UNCTAD's *World Investment Report 2009* (www.unctad.org/wir). For more detailed information, contact Masataka Fujita, officer-in-charge, Investment Analysis Branch, Division on Investment and Enterprise, UNCTAD (fdistat@unctad.org).

13. Heather Timmons, "The Middle East Is Buying into Asia," *International Herald Tribune,* November 30, 2006.

14. "Arabian Travel Market Confirms the Address for 2010," *Arabian Travel Market,* May 4, 2008 (www.arabiantravelmarket.com/page.cfm/T=m/Action=Press/PressID=24).

15. Shakir Husain, "Mideast Tourism Likely at $3 Trillion Investment by 2020," *Gulf News,* May 3, 2007 (http://gulfnews.com/business/tourism/mideast-tourism-likely-at-3tr-investment-by-2020-1.176643).

16. Manal Alafrangi, "Study Abroad or Not: That Is the Question," *Gulf News,* September 27, 2005 (http://gulfnews.com/news/gulf/uae/general/study-abroad-or-not-that-is-the-question-1.302192).

17. "Saudi Arabia Looks Eastwards for Higher Education," *AMEInfo,* March 30, 2006 (www.ameinfo.com/81824.html).

18. Hubert Védrine, "To Paris, U.S. Looks Like a 'Hyperpower,'" *New York Times,* February 5, 1999.

19. "Beware the Beijing Model," *The Economist,* May 26, 2009.

20. See Fareed Zakaria, *The Post-American World* (W. W. Norton, 2009); Jon Alterman and John Garver, *The Vital Triangle: China, the United States, and the Middle East* (Washington: Center for Strategic and International Studies, 2008); Teresita Schaffer, *India and the United States in the 21st Century: Reinventing Partnership* (Washington: Center for Strategic and International Studies, 2009).

21. Charles Krauthammer, "The Unipolar Moment," *Foreign Affairs* (Winter 1990/91).

CHAPTER TWO

1. "India," *Encyclopaedia Britannica*, 2006.
2. Ibid, p. 353.
3. C. Raja Mohan, "India's Strategic Challenges in the Indian Ocean and Gulf," in *India's Growing Role in the Gulf: Implications for the Region and the United States* (Dubai: Gulf Research Center, November 2008), p. 56 (www.nixoncenter.org/Monograph-Indias-Growing-Role-in-the-Gulf.pdf).
4. Address by Shri Kamal Nath, India's minister of commerce and industry, to the Second India-GCC Industrial Conference in Muscat, March 25, 2006 (www.kuwaitsamachar.com/press/march27gcc.htm).
5. Samir Pradhan, "India's Economic and Political Presence in the Gulf: A Gulf Perspective," in *India's Growing Role in the Gulf* (www.nixoncenter.org/Monograph-Indias-Growing-Role-in-the-Gulf.pdf).
6. "India Top Receiver of Migrant Remittances in 2007, Followed by China and Mexico" (Washington: World Bank, March 19, 2008); Pradhan, "India's Economic and Political Presence in the Gulf"; Muzaffar A. Chishti, "The Phenomenal Rise in Remittances to India: A Closer Look," Migration Policy Institute Policy Brief, May 2007 (www.migrationpolicy.org/pubs/MigDevPB_052907.pdf).
7. Jason DeParle, "Fearful of Restive Foreign Labor, Dubai Eyes Reforms," *New York Times*, August 6, 2007 (www.nytimes.com/2007/08/06/world/middleeast/06dubai.html).
8. "A New Look at Neutralism," *Time,* October 24, 1960 (www.time.com/time/magazine/article/0,9171,871750,00.html).
9. For an excellent overview of U.S.-Indian relations, see Teresita Schaffer, *India and the United States in the 21st Century: Reinventing Partnership* (Washington: Center for Strategic and International Studies, 2009).
10. J. Mohan Malik, "India's Response to the Gulf Crisis," *Asian Survey*, September 1991, p. 847.
11. Chishti, "The Phenomenal Rise in Remittances to India: A Closer Look"; "Indian Workers' Gulf Remittances Exceed $2.2 B," United Press International, April 26, 1994; S. Venkat Narayan, "2,100 Indians Died in Gulf Last Year," *Moneyclips*, May 13, 1994; John Eckhouse, "Migrant Workers' Economic Impact," *San Francisco Chronicle*, July 1, 1991.
12. Randall Palmer, "Arab Ban on Planes, Ships Isolates Indians in Gulf," *Reuters European Business Report*, September 29, 1994; Malik, "India's Response to the Gulf Crisis," p. 847.
13. Pradhan, "India's Economic and Political Presence in the Gulf."
14. International Monetary Fund, "World Economic Outlook 2009 Update: Contractionary Forces Receding but Weak Recovery Ahead," July 8, 2009 (www.imf.org/external/pubs/ft/weo/2009/update/02/index.htm).
15. Jennifer Asuncion-Mund, "India Rising: A Medium-Term Perspective," Deutsche Bank special report, May 2005 (www.dbresearch.com/PROD/DBR_INTERNET_DE-PROD/PROD0000000000187531.PDF).

16. Office of the United States Trade Representative, "Countries and Regions: India" (www.ustr.gov/countries-regions/south-central-asia/india).

17. Bibek Debroy, "Who Are the Middle Class in India?" *Indian Express,* March 24, 2009 (www.indianexpress.com/news/who-are-the-middle-class-in-india/438429/).

18. Central Intelligence Agency (CIA), *World Factbook,* "India" (2007 and 2000).

19. Ibid.

20. Carl Haub and O. P. Sharma, "India's Population Reality: Reconciling Change and Tradition," *Population Bulletin* 61, no.3 (Population Reference Bureau, September 2006) (www.prb.org/pdf06/61.3IndiasPopulationReality_Eng.pdf).

21. Sudeep Chakravarti, "The Middle-Class: Hurt but Hopeful," *India Today,* April 15, 1995.

22. Ibid.

23. "India Manages to Clock 6.7 Percent Growth in 2008–2009," *The Hindu,* May 30, 2009 (www.thehindu.com/2009/05/30/stories/2009053054191300.htm).

24. "India's GDP Growth to Dip Sharply to 5.6 Percent: Economist Intelligence Unit," *Business Standard,* January 29, 2009 (www.business-standard.com/india/news/india%5Cs-gdp-growth-to-dip-sharply-to-56-economist-intelligence-unit/347432/).

25. Manjeet Kripalani, "India's Economy Hits the Wall," *Business Week,* July 1, 2008 (www.businessweek.com/globalbiz/content/jul2008/gb2008071_743900.htm).

26. Sharif D. Rangnekar and Manich Sharma, "The State of India's Economy," *Far Eastern Economic Review,* December 8, 2008 (www.feer.com/economics/2008/december/The-State-of-Indias-Economy).

27. CIA, *World Factbook,* "India."

28. Government of India, Central Electricity Authority, "Monthly Review of Power Sector: Executive Summary," September 30, 2009 (www.cea.nic.in/power_sec_reports/executive_summary/2009_09/28-34.pdf).

29. "India Sees Solar Energy as an Option to Reduce the Energy Crisis," *Economic Times* (India), October 8, 2008 (http://economictimes.indiatimes.com/News/PoliticsNation/India-sees-solar-energy-as-an-option-to-reduce-the-energy-crisis-/articleshow/3572770.cms).

30. Venkataraman Krishnaswamy and others, *Prospects and Potential for Energy Trade in the South Asian Region* (Washington: World Bank, Sustainable Development Department, June 2007), p. 31.

31. Kirit S. Parikh, "Energy Needs, Options, and Environment Sustainability" (http://scid.stanford.edu/events/PanAsia/Papers/Parikh.pdf).

32. Ibid., p. 62.

33. U.S. Energy Information Administration (EIA), *International Energy Outlook 2006* (Washington: National Energy Information Center, 2006).

34. Kristi McCabe, "Asia's Thirst for Oil," *Wall Street Journal,* May 5, 2004 (www.iags.org/wsj050504.htm).

35. Ministry of Coal, Government of India, "Coal: Choice for Indian Energy" (http://coal.nic.in/welcome.html).

36. S. Raghotham, "What Are These Strategic Compromises For, After All? Part II," *India's National Interest,* August 10, 2006.

37. EIA, "India," Country Analysis Briefs (www.eia.doe.gov/emeu/cabs/India/Oil.html).

38. EIA, *International Energy Annual 2004* (Washington: National Energy Information Center); EIA, *Short-Term Energy Outlook 2007* (Washington: National Energy Information Center).

39. EIA, *International Energy Outlook 2007*, pp. 87, 187.

40. Ibid.

41. Ibid. The figure varies 1 to 2 percent if one uses data from the Reference Case (p. 86) of the International Energy Agency's *2006 World Energy Outlook* instead.

42. Raghotham, "What Are These Strategic Compromises For, After All? Part II."

43. EIA, "India," Country Report, January 2007.

44. Ibid.

45. Indrani Bagchi, "India Keen to Be Part of Turk Pipeline Plan," *Times of India*, July 29, 2008 (http://timesofindia.indiatimes.com/india/India-keen-to-be-part-of-Turk-pipeline-plan/articleshow/3299314.cms).

46. Raghotham, "What Are These Strategic Compromises For, After All? Part II."

47. Government of India, Central Electricty Authority, "Monthly Review of Power Sector: Executive Summary," December 31, 2007 (www.cea.nic.in/power_sec_reports/executive_summary/2007_12/24-30.pdf).

48. Krishnaswamy and others, *Prospects and Potential for Energy Trade in the South Asian Region*.

49. Ministry of Road Transport and Highways, Government of India (www.morth.nic.in/index1.asp?linkid=63&langid=2).

50. "India Transport Sector," World Bank (http://siteresources.worldbank.org/INTSARREGTOPTRANSPORT/2723688-1154429552731/21011357/PresentationbyNirmaljitSingh_NHAI.pdf).

51. Jason Overdorf, "The Boom from the Bottom," *Newsweek,* January 19, 2009 (www.newsweek.com/id/178814/page/2).

52. Aastha Rao, "Golden Quadrilateral to Be Reality Soon," UTVi, June 25, 2008.

53. CIA *World Factbook*, Country Comparisons, "Railways" (www.cia.gov/library/publications/the-world-factbook/rankorder/2121rank.html).

54. B. S. Chauhan, "Indian Railways: Life-Line of Economy," press release, Press Information Bureau, Government of India, August 5, 2005 (http://pib.nic.in/release/rel_print_page.asp?relid=10995).

55. "Development of Metro, Non-Metro, and Greenfield Airports in India," Government of India, Ministry of Civil Aviation, 2006–07, p.1 (http://infrastructure.gov.in/pdf/brochure_airports.pdf).

56. "Saudi Arabia: International Religious Freedom Report 2008," U.S. Department of State (www.state.gov/g/drl/rls/irf/2008/108492.htm).

57. Waiel Awwad, "Saudi King's Visit Will Herald a New Era," *Rediff India Abroad*, January 24, 2006 (http://us.rediff.com/news/2006/jan/24guest.htm?q=np&file=.htm).

58. Indian Embassy, Riyadh, "Indo Saudi Relations" (www.indianembassy.org.sa/Pages/IndiaSaudi/FirstPage.htm).

59. Shamsur Rabb Khan, "Needed: A Strategic Partnership with Saudi Arabia," Institute of Peace and Conflict Studies, New Delhi, May 6, 2008 (www.ipcs.org/article_details.php?articleNo=2560).

60. Indian Embassy, Riyadh, "Indo-Saudi Relations" (www.indianembassy.org.sa/Pages/IndiaSaudi/FirstPage.htm).

61. Consulate General of India, Jeddah, Saudi Arabia, "Indo-Saudi Economic and Commercial Relations" (www.cgijeddah.com/cgijed/COMM/bilateral/ISBER.htm).

62. Ibid.

63. Indian Embassy, Riyadh, "Indo-Saudi Relations" (www.indianembassy.org.sa/Pages/IndiaSaudi/FirstPage.htm).

64. Subhash Kapila, "India-Saudi Arabia: The Strategic Significance of the Delhi Declaration," South Asia Analysis Group, March 2006 (www.saag.org/papers18/paper1734.html).

65. Delhi Declaration, January 27, 2006 (www.cgijeddah.com/cgijed/KingsVisit/DD.pdf).

66. Arshi Khan, "Indo–Saudi Arabian Relations: Toward a Strategic Partnership," Media Monitors Network, January 26, 2006 (http://usa.mediamonitors.net/Headlines/India-Saudi-Arabia-Relations-towards-Strategic-Partnership).

67. "It's Business Unusual: India, Saudi Arabi Ink Four Pacts to Give Trade Its Due," *Financial Express* (India), January 26, 2006 (www.financialexpress.com/news/It%92s%20business%20unusual:%20India,%20Saudi%20Arabia%20ink%20four%20pacts%20to%20give%20trade%20its%20due%20/61318/).

68. "India, Saudi Arabia Sign MoU to Cooperate in Health Care Sector," *Web India 123*, November 23, 2006 (http://news.webindia123.com/news/articles/Health/20061121/513732.html).

69. M. Ghazanfar Ali Khan, "Manmohan's Visit in May," *Arab News*, February 11, 2007 (www.arabnews.com/?page=1&section=0&article=92007&d=11&m=2&y=2007&pix=kingdom.jpg&category=Kingdom).

70. Government of Saudi Arabia, Ministry of Foreign Affairs, "HRH Prince Saud Al-Faisal Visits India April 23, 2008" (www.mofa.gov.sa/Detail.asp?InNewsItemID=76317); M. Ghazanfar Ali Khan, "India Seeks to Strengthen Links with Saudi Arabia," *Arab News*, April 20, 2008 (www.arabnews.com/?page=1&section=0&article=109136).

71. "India, Saudi Arabia Plan Multi-Entry Visas for Businessmen," *Economic Times* (India), April 21, 2008 (http://economictimes.indiatimes.com/articleshow/2966356.cms).

72. "Indian Oil Imports from Middle East Up 11 PC, Says Govt.," *Financial Express*, August 7, 2008 (www.financialexpress.com/news/indian-oil-imports-from-middle-east-up-11-pc-says-govt/345891/).

73. Interview with Shri Pranab Mukherjee, external affairs minister, *Asharq Alawsat* (Arabic daily), during his visit to Saudi Arabia, April 4, 2008 (http://164.100.17.21/interview/2008/04/20in01.htm).

74. Consulate of India, Jeddah, Saudi Arabia, "Indo-Saudi Economic and Commercial Relations."

75. Michel Cousins, "India's Economic Revolution Changed Everything," Arab-News.com, January 26, 2006 (www.arabnews.com/?page=23&section=0&article=76848&d=1&m=2&y=2006).

76. Atul Aneja , "Saudi Arabia May Set Up India Investment Fund," *The Hindu*, May 6, 2008 (www.thehindu.com/2008/05/06/stories/2008050660541200.htm).

77. "India, Saudi Arabia Discuss Energy Investments," Yahoo News (http://in.news.yahoo.com/050105/43/2iumz.html).

78. Atul Aneja, "Saudi Arabia May Set Up India Investment Fund."

79. Consulate General of India, Jeddah, Saudi Arabia, "General Information" (www.cgijeddah.com/cgijed/index.htm).

80. Pradhan, "India's Economic and Political Presence in the Gulf," p.11.

81. "India and Saudi Arabia Sign New Bilateral Air Service Agreement," *India Aviation*, January 25, 2008 (http://indiaaviation.aero/news/airline/6962/59/India-and-Saudi-Arabia-sign-new-bilaternal-air-service-agreement).

82. Huma Siddiqi, "India-GCC Free Trade Agreement Is Not Far-Off Dream," *Financial Express,* September 11, 2009 (www.financialexpress.com/news/indiagcc-freetrade-agreement-is-not-a-faroff-dream/515524/).

83. "India-GCC: Petrochem Industry Fears Free Trade with the Gulf," *Indo-Asian News Service*, December 28, 2007 (www.bilaterals.org/article.php3?id_article=10816).

84. "India-Saudi Arabia Two-Way Trade to Touch $7 Billion by 2010," *Hindustan Times,* January 23, 2006.

85. Prabeer Hazarika, "India Faces Secret Saudi-Pakistan Defense Alliance," *India Daily*, March 23, 2005 (www.indiadaily.com/editorial/2001.asp).

86. Indian Navy, "Indian Navy: Reaching Out to Maritime Neighbours 2005" (http://indiannavy.nic.in/events2005.pdf).

87. Kapila, "India-Saudi Arabia: The Strategic Significance of the Delhi Declaration."

88. "India, Saudi Arabia Agree Cooperation in Counter-Terrorism, Energy," PTI News Agency (India), January 27, 2006 (BBC Monitoring South Asia: Political).

89. Pradhan, "India's Economic and Political Presence in the Gulf," p. 8.

90. Human Rights Watch, *"Bad Dreams": Exploitation and Abuse of Migrant Workers in Saudi Arabia*, July 14, 2004, E1605 (www.unhcr.org/refworld/docid/412ef32a4.html).

91. Sunita Menon, "Central Agency to Supply Indian Labour," Gulfnews.com, May 7, 2006 (http://gulfnews.com/news/gulf/uae/employment/central-agency-to-supply-indian-labour-1.235935).

92. Devirupa Mitra, "Coming Soon, Amendment to Emigration Act of 1983," *India e-News*, March 26, 2008 (www.indiaenews.com/nri/20080326/106641.htm).

93. "India, Saudi Arabia Agree Cooperation in Counter-Terrorism, Energy," PTI News Agency (India).

94. Siraj Wahab, "For Saudi Students, India Is a Favorite Destination," *Arab News*, December 14, 2007 (www.arabnews.com/?page=15&section=0&article=10 4654&d=27&m=3&y=2009).

95. Kapila, "India-Saudi Arabia: The Strategic Significance of the Delhi Declaration."

96. Harsh V. Pant, "Saudi Arabia Woos China and India," *Middle East Quarterly* (September 2005), pp. 45–52.

97. Harsh V. Pant, "Looking beyond Tehran: India's Rising Stakes in the Gulf," in *India's Growing Role in the Gulf: Implications for the Region and the United States* (Dubai: Gulf Research Center, November 2008), p. 49 (www.nixoncenter.org/ Monograph-Indias-Growing-Role-in-the-Gulf.pdf).

98. "India, Saudi Arabia Sign Delhi Declaration," *People's Daily Online*, January 28, 2006 (http://english.people.com.cn/200601/28/eng20060128_239019.html); Arshi Khan, "Indo-Saudi Arabian Relations: Toward a Strategic Partnership," Media Monitors Network, January 26, 2006.

99. "UAE-India Non-Oil Trade Worth over $44 Bn, says Tharoor," Indo Asian News Service (IANS), October 9, 2009 (www.thaindian.com/newsportal/business/ uae-india-non-oil-trade-worth-over-44-bn-says-tharoor_100258516.html).

100. Shri Pranab Mukherjee, "India's Foreign Policy and India-Gulf Relations: Meeting the Challenges of the 21st Century," speech at the Emirates Centre for Strategic Studies and Research (ECSSR), Abu Dhabi, May 12, 2008 (http://indembkwt. org/press/12may08.htm); Aroonim Bhuyan, "Energy, Infrastructure New Bases of India-Gulf Ties: Pranab," *South Asia Monitor*, May 2008 (www.southasiamonitor. org/2008/May/news/13news11.shtml#).

101. Indian Embassy, Muscat, "India Oman Relations" (www.indemb-oman.org/ india_oman_relation.shtml).

102. Ibid.; U.S. Department of State, Oman (www.state.gov/r/pa/ei/bgn/35834.htm).

103. Indian Embassy, Muscat, "India Oman Relations" (www.indemb-oman.org/ india_oman_relation.shtml).

104. "Oman, India Must Fight Threats from the Sea," *Gulf News*, March 7, 2006.

105. CIA, *World Factbook*, "Oman"; Indian Embassy, Oman, "Indian Community in Oman" (www.indemb-oman.org/Indian_community_Oman.asp).

106. Indian Embassy, Oman, "India Oman Economic Relations" (www.indemb-oman.org/commercial_services_eco_relations.shtml).

107. Sandeep Dikshit, "India, Oman Still Studying Undersea Pipeline," *The Hindu*, October 30, 2009 (www.thehindu.com/2009/10/30/stories/2009103060541000.htm).

108. Statistics from the Indian Department of Commerce's System on Foreign Trade Performance Analysis. Petroleum estimates are based on a comparison of 2007 numbers that included but do not itemize petroleum trade and 2006 figures that do not include petroleum trade.

109. "India Keen to Boost Ties with Oman on Pharmaceuticals, Metals, IT," PTI news agency (New Delhi), January 30, 2006 (www.nexis.com).

NOTES TO PAGES 45–47

110. Indian Embassy, Muscat, Oman, "Bulletin Board: 4th Meeting of the India-Oman Joint Commission" (www.indemb-oman.org/news_bulletionboard1.shtml).

111. Official website of Amir of Qatar (Amiri Diwan), "History of Qatar" (www.diwan.gov.qa/english/qatar/Qatar_History.htm).

112. Faculty of Nursing, University of Calgary, Qatar, "History" (www.ucalgary.ca/UofC/faculties/NU/qatarnursing/about/history.htm).

113. Indian Embassy, Doha, "Qatar Foreign Relations" (http://meaindia.nic.in/foreignrelation/qatar.pdf).

114. Indian Embassy, Doha, "Indo-Qatar Bilateral Economic Relations" (www.indianembassy.gov/qa/economics.htm).

115. Indian Embassy, Doha, "Indian Qatar Bilateral Relations" (www.indianembassyqatar.org/bilateralrelations.html)

116. Indian Embassy, Doha, "Qatar Foreign Relations."

117. Indian Embassy, Doha, "Indo-Qatar Bilateral Economic Relations."

118. Government of India, Central Electricity Authority, "Monthly Review of Power Sector—Executive Summary," September 2009 (www.cea.nic.in/power_sec_reports/executive_summary/2009_09?28-34.pdf).

119. Indian Embassy, Doha, "Qatar Foreign Relations."

120. U.S. Department of State, "Country Profile: Qatar," October 2006 (www.mea.gov.in/foreignrelation/qatar.htm).

121. Indian Embassy, Doha, "Qatar Foreign Relations."

122. Sandeep Dikshit, "Qatar to Invest $5 Billion in India," *The Hindu*, November 20, 2008 (www.hindu.com/2008/11/12/stories/2008111261371200.htm).

123. "New Summit Group Meets in Thailand," *BBC News*, June 19, 2002 (http://news.bbc.co.uk/2/hi/asia-pacific/2052460.stm).

124. Indian Embassy, Doha, "Qatar Foreign Relations."

125. Indian Embassy, Doha, "Indo-Qatar Bilateral Economic Relations."

126. "Qatar Gives Indians Wage Pact to Smile," *The Peninsula*, November 21, 2007 (www5.zawya.com/Story.cfm/sidZAWYA20071123083121/SecMain/pag Homepage/chnAll%20Regional%20News/obj2A17E941-F5E0-11D4-867D00D 0B74A0D7C/).

127. "India, Qatar to Sign Labor Pact" (http://news.webindia123.com/news/articles/India/20070122/570945.html).

128. Indian Embassy, Doha, "Indo-Qatar Relations" (www.indianembassy.gov.qa).

129. "Qatar Seeks Indian Investment in Healthcare, IT," Indo-Asian News Service, January 21, 2006 (www.indiablitz.com/11004/Qatar-seeks-Indian-investment-in-healthcare-IT.htm).

130. "Qatar, India Sign Air Services Pact; Keen to Better Trade Ties," *The Hindu Business Line*, April 15, 2005 (www.thehindubusinessline.com/2005/04/15/stories/2005041501721400.htm).

131. Indian Embassy, Abu Dhabi, "Bilateral Relations" (www.indembassyuae.org/induae_bilateral.phtml).

132. Ibid.

133. Wisconsin Project on Nuclear Arms Control, "United Arab Emirates Transshipment Milestones," *The Risk Report* 11, no. 4 (July-August 2005) (www.wisconsin project.org/countries/dubai/transshipment-milestones.html).

134. Indian Embassy, Abu Dhabi, "Bilateral Relations."

135. Shri Pranab Mukherjee, "India's Foreign Policy and India-Gulf Relations: Meeting the Challenges of the 21st Century," speech at Emirates Centre for Strategic Studies and Research (ECSSR), Abu Dhabi, May 12, 2008 (http://indembkwt.org/press/12may08.htm).

136. Atul Aneja, "India Faces Uphill Task," *The Hindu*, June 3, 2008 (www.the hindu.com/2008/06/03/stories/2008060354780900.htm); *UAE Yearbook 2008*, p. 56.

137. Statistics from the Indian Ministry of Commerce's System on Foreign Trade Performance Analysis (http://commerce.nic.in/ftpa/default.asp).

138. Pradhan, "India's Economic and Political Presence in the Gulf: A Gulf Perspective," p.12.

139. Statistics from the Indian Ministry of Commerce's System on Foreign Trade Performance Analysis.

140. Indian Embassy, Abu Dhabi, "Bilateral Relations."

141. Ibid.

142. Pradhan, "India's Economic and Political Presence in the Gulf: A Gulf Perspective."

143. Government of India, Department of Planning (http://dipp.nic.in/fdi_statistics/india_fdi_index.htm). India's number one source of investment in this period was Mauritius, which likely represents a causeway for foreign funds for tax purposes.

144. Atul Aneja, "India Seeking UAE Investment for Industrial Corridor," *The Hindu*, April 25, 2008 (www.thehindu.com/2008/04/25/stories/2008042555721300.htm).

145. "Deyaar Set for $5 Bn India Township Deal," Arabianbusiness.com, November 6, 2007 (www.arabianbusiness.com/property/article/503422-deyaar-set-for-5bn-india-township-deal).

146. Vimala Vasan, "India, GCC States May Sign Economic Pact Next Year," March 28, 2006 (www.thehindubusinessline.com/2006/03/28/stories/2006032803241800.htm).

147. Indian Embassy, Abu Dhabi, "Indian Community in UAE" (www.indembassy uae.org/induae_community.phtml).

148. Indian Embassy, Abu Dhabi, "Bilateral Relations."

149. "Indian Airlines to Introduce Daily Dubai-Mumbai Flights," Gulfnews.com, March 23, 2006.

150. "UAE, India Sign MoU on Flight Services," *UAE Interact*, February 12, 2008 (http://uaeinteract.com/docs/UAE,_India_sign_MoU_on_flight_services/28581.htm).

151. Indian Embassy, Abu Dhabi, "Bilateral Relations."

152. "India and the Gulf: Convergence of Interest," *CSIS South Asia Monitor*, No. 113, December 4, 2007.

153. Indian Embassy, Abu Dhabi, "India-UAE Bilateral Relations" (www.ind embassyuae.org).

154. Ibid.

155. Indian Embassy, Abu Dhabi, "Bilateral Relations."

156. Vinay Kumar, "A Milestone in India-UAE Ties," *The Hindu*, December 10, 2002; Pant, "Looking beyond Tehran: India's Rising Stakes in the Gulf," p. 7.

157. Government of Pakistan, Board of Investment, "Pakistan Economy: Foreign Investment" (www.pakboi.gov.pk/forign-invest.htm).

158. "Partners in Progress," Gulfnews.com, May 19, 2008.

159. Ibid.

160. "UAE Signs MoU with Pakistan," Gulfnews.com, May 3, 2009 (http://gulfnews.com/news/gulf/uae/employment/uae-signs-mou-with-pakistan-1.153245).

161. American International School, Kuwait, "History of Kuwait" (www.aiskuwait.org/q8history.html).

162. Indian Embassy, Kuwait, "India—Kuwait Cultural Relations" (www.indembkwt.org/jan/ind-kwtculturalrelation.php).

163. Indian Embassy, Kuwait, "Indo-Kuwait Bilateral Ties" (www.indembkwt.org/indkuwait-bilateral.htm); "India, Kuwait Airfares Go down 20–30 Percent," *Times of India*, March 30, 2006.

164. Indian Embassy, Kuwait, "Indo-Kuwaiti Agreements" (www.indembkwt.org/bilateral.php#4a).

165. Indian Embassy, Kuwait, "Indo-Kuwait Bilateral Visits" (www.indembkwt.org/indkuwait-visits.htm).

166. Indian Embassy, Kuwait, "Embassy of India, Kuwait" (www.indembkwt.org/june19.htm).

167. Statistics from the Indian Ministry of Commerce's System on Foreign Trade Performance Analysis (http://commerce.nic.in/ftpa/default.asp).

168. "India-Kuwait Sign Extradition Treaty" (http://sify.com/news_info/fullstory.php?id=135524440).

169. Indian Embassy, Kuwait, "Indo-Kuwait Bilateral Relations."

170. "Commercial Relations" (www.kuwait-info.com/sidepages/indoku_commercialrel.asp).

171. Arabnews.com, June 14, 2006 (http://arabnews.com/?page=4&section=0&article=833744&d=14&m=6&y=2006).

172. Pradhan, "India's Economic and Political Presence in the Gulf: A Gulf Perspective," p. 9.

173. Indian Embassy, Bahrain, "About the Embassy, Embassy in Bahrain" (www.indianembassybahrain.com).

174. Indian Embassy, Bahrain, "India Bahrain Bilateral Relations" (www.indianembassybahrain.com); CIA, *World Factbook*, "Bahrain—Economy."

175. Indian Embassy, Bahrain, "Indian Community" (www.indianembassybahrain.com/Indian_Community.html).

176. Christine Fair, "Indo-Iranian Relations: Prospects for Bilateral Cooperation Post–9-11," in *The "Strategic Partnership" between India and Iran,* edited by Robert Hathaway, Asia Program Report No. 120 (Washington: Woodrow Wilson Center, 2004), p. 8.

177. Kashif Mumtaz, "Changing Patterns of India-Iran Relations" (Islamabad: Institute for International and Strategic Studies, 2006).

178. David Temple, "The Iran-Pakistan-India Pipeline: The Intersection of Energy and Politics" (New Delhi, Institute for Peace and Conflict Studies, April 2007), p.10.

179. Mumtaz, "Changing Patterns of India-Iran Relations."

180. Christine Fair, "Indo-Iranian Ties: Thicker than Oil," *The Middle East Review of International Affairs* 11, no.1 (March 2007).

181. Jalil Roshandel, "The Overdue 'Strategic' Partnership between Iran and India," in *The "Strategic Partnership" between India and Iran,* edited by Robert Hathaway, Asia Program Report No. 120 (Washington: Woodrow Wilson Center, 2004), p. 17

182. B. Raman, "India's Strategic Thrust in S.E. Asia—Before and After 9/11," South Asia Analysis Group, Paper No. 2643, March 26, 2008.

183. Mumtaz, "Changing Patterns of India-Iran Relations."

184. Fair, "Indo-Iranian Ties: Thicker than Oil."

185. "Energy Statistics: Oil Production, Thousand Barrel Daily (Most Recent) by Country," Nationmaster.com (www.nationmaster.com/graph/ene_oil_pro-energy-oil-production).

186. Pant, "Looking beyond Tehran: India's Rising Stakes in the Gulf," p. 44.

187. "US Opposition to Iran Deal Import of Gas Imperative to Meet Domestic Demand," *Business Recorder* (Pakistan), January 9, 2006, accessed through Nexis (www.nexis.com).

188. Pant, "Looking beyond Tehran: India's Rising Stakes in the Gulf," p. 44.

189. "Analysis: Iran-India Pipeline Uncertain," United Press International, February 6, 2006 (www.nexis.com).

190. Temple, "The Iran-Pakistan-India Pipeline: The Intersection of Energy and Politics," p. 11.

191. Ibid., p.38.

192. Siddharth Srivastava, "Price Imbroglio Stymies Iran Pipeline," *Asia Times,* July 27, 2006 (www.atimes.com/atimes/South_Asia/HG27Df02.html).

193. "Turkey Offers Alternative to Iran Pipeline," *Times of India*, February 10, 2008 (http://timesofindia.indiatimes.com/India/Turkey_offers_alternative_to_Iran_pipeline/articleshow/2770237.cms).

194. "Pakistan, Iran Finally Sign Gas Pipeline Accord," Dawn.com, May 24, 2009 (www.dawn.com/wps/wcm/connect/dawn-content-library/dawn/news/business/09-iran-pakistan-sign-gas-pipeline-deal-media-szh--07).

195. "India Takes New Look at IPI," UPI.com, July 21, 2009 (www.upi.com/Science_

News/Resource-Wars/2009/07/21/India-takes-new-look-at-IPI/UPI-99411248 190920/).

196. Christine Fair, "India and Iran: New Delhi's Balancing Act," *Washington Quarterly*, Summer 2007, p. 149.

197. Pant, "Looking beyond Tehran: India's Rising Stakes in the Gulf," p. 43

198. "Iran Seeks $1 Bn 'Advance' for LNG Supplies," *Indian Express*, November 16, 2009(www.expressindia.com/latest-news/Iran-seeks--1-bn--advance--for-LNG-supplies/542181/).

199. Fair, "Indo-Iranian Ties: Thicker than Oil."

200. Ibid.

201. Sudha Ramachandran, "India Rules Its Troops out for Iraq," *Asia Times*, July 15, 2003 (www.atimes.com/atimes/South_Asia/EG15Df03.html).

202. Fair, "Indo-Iranian Ties: Thicker than Oil."

203. Ibid.

204. Sultan Shahin, "Iran, Nukes and the South Asian Puzzle," *Asia Times Online*, August 30, 2003 (www.atimes.com/atimes/South_Asia/EH30Df02.html).

205. Donald L. Berlin, "India Iran Relations: A Deepening Entente" (Honolulu: Asia-Pacific Center for Security Studies, October 2004).

206. Fair, "Indo-Iranian Ties: Thicker than Oil."

207. Christine Fair, "Indo-Iranian Relations: Prospects for Bilateral Cooperation Post 9-11."

208. Sunil Dasgupta, "Pakistan Responds to New Ties between Iran and India" (Washington: Woodrow Wilson Center, 2004).

209. Shah Allam, "Iran Pakistan Relations: Strategic and Political Dimensions" (New Delhi: Institute for Defence Studies and Analysis, October 2004).

210. Dasgupta, "Pakistan Responds to New Ties between Iran and India."

211. Allam, "Iran Pakistan Relations: Strategic and Political Dimensions."

212. Sultan Shahin, "Iran, Nukes and the South Asian Puzzle," *Asia Times Online* (www.atimes.com/atimes/South_Asia/EH30Df02.html).

213. C. Raja Mohan, "India's Strategic Challenges in the Indian Ocean and the Gulf," p. 9.

214. Amit Baruah, "India's IAEA Vote was Decided In Advance," *The Hindu*, September 26, 2005 (www.thehindu.com/2005/09/26/stories/2005092606971100.htm); Fair, "Indo-Iranian Ties: Thicker than Oil."

215. Pant, "Looking beyond Tehran: India's Rising Stakes in the Gulf," p. 45.

216. Briefing by Foreign Secretary Shri Shivshankar Menon on visit of President Ahmadinejad of Iran to India, April 29, 2008 (www.meaindia.nic.in/press briefing/2008/04/29pb01.htm).

217. "Inaugural Address by National Security Adviser Shri Brajesh Mishra at the ORF Conference on 'Iran: Twenty-Five Years after the Revolution,'" July 2004 (http://meaindia.nic.in/speech/2004/03/07ss01.htm).

218. Temple, "The Iran-Pakistan-India Pipeline: The Intersection of Energy and Politics," p. 38.

219. Shebonti Ray Dadwal, "Re-Energising India-Iran Ties," *IDSA Strategic Comments* (New Delhi: Institute for Defence Studies and Analyses, May 2, 2008) (www.idsa.in/idsastrategiccomments/ReenergisingIndiaIranties_SRDadwal_020508).

220. Pant, "India and Iran: Hype vs. Substance."

221. Fair, "India and Iran: New Delhi's Balancing Act."

222. Pant, "India and Iran: Hype vs. Substance."

223. Ibid.; Bruce Riedel, "Israel & India: New Allies," May 7, 2008 (www.brookings.edu/opinions/2008/0321_india_riedel.aspx).

224. Mohan, "India's Strategic Challenges in the Indian Ocean and the Gulf," p. 64.

225. Comment at IISS-Citi India Global Forum, Indo-Asian News Service, April 20, 2008 (www.iiss.org/whats-new/iiss-in-the-press/april-2008/india-says-treat-iran-with-respect-ahead-of-ahmadinejad-visit/).

226. "India's Northern Exposure," Council on Foreign Relations, December 5, 2007 (www.cfr.org/publication/14969/).

227. David C. Mulford, "Speeches & Remarks, 2006: Afghanistan Has Made a Remarkable Transition," U.S. Embassy, New Delhi (http://newdelhi.usembassy.gov/ambfeb092006.html).

228. Jayshree Bajoria, "The Troubled Afghan-Pakistani Border," Council on Foreign Relations, March 20, 2009 (www.cfr.org/publication/14905/).

229. Amin Tarzi, "Afghanistan: Kabul's India Ties Worry Pakistan," Radio Free Europe (www.rferl.org/content/article/1067690.html).

230. Uzbek Embassy, "Uzbekistan's Foreign Policy" (www.uzbekembassy.in/govt/objectiveofuzbekistan.htm); "Uzbekistan and Its Civilization" (www.eurasianet.org/resource/uzbekistan/links/uzbkcivi.html).

231. Indian Embassy, "Political Uzbekistan" (http://indembassy.uz/english/uzbekistan/polit).

232. Uzbek Embassy, "Indo-Uzbek Relations" Uzbek Embassy (www.uzbekembassy.in/about_uzbekistan/indo_uzbek_relation/indo_uzbekrelation.htm).

233. Ibid.

234. Uzbek Embassy, "Uzbekistan's Foreign Policy"; Ministry of External Affairs, Government of India, "Fact Sheet: Uzbekistan," February 2008.

235. "India, Uzbekistan Must Fight Terrorism Together: Manmohan," *The Hindu*, April 27, 2006 (www.hinduonnet.com/2006/04/27/stories/2006042714990100.htm).

236. Rajat Pandit, "Indian Forces Get a Foothold in Central Asia," *Times of India*, July 17, 2007 (http://timesofindia.indiatimes.com/Indian_forces_get_foothold_in_central_Asia/articleshow/2208676.cms).

237. "India, Uzbekistan to Fight Terror," *The Hindu*, April 6, 2005.

238. Ministry of External Affairs, Government of India, Foreign Relations Briefs, "Fact Sheet: Uzbekistan" (http://meaindia.nic.in/).

239. Uzbek Embassy, "Indo-Uzbek Relations."

240. Mohan, "India's Strategic Challenges in the Indian Ocean and the Gulf."

CHAPTER THREE

1. Harsh V. Pant, "Saudi Arabia Woos China and India," *Middle East Quarterly* (Fall 2006), pp. 45–52.

2. There is a huge literature on China's foreign policy. See, of many useful publications, "China's Foreign Policy: 'Soft Power' in South America, Asia, and Africa," prepared for Committee on Foreign Relations, U.S. Senate, by the Congressional Research Service, Library of Congress, April 2008; Kerry Dumbaugh, "China's Foreign Policy: What Does It Mean for U.S. Interests?" (Washington: Congressional Research Service, July 18, 2008).

3. For more details on how China's Middle East relations affect U.S. policy, see John Alterman and John W. Garver, *The Vital Triangle: China, the United States, and the Middle East* (Washington: CSIS, 2008).

4. U.S. Energy Information Administration (EIA), "International Energy Outlook 2004: World Oil Markets" (Washington: National Energy Information Center, 2004).

5. Institute for the Analysis of Global Security, "Fueling the Dragon: China's Race into the Oil Market" (www.iags.org/china.htm).

6. EIA, "China: Coal" (www.eia.doe.gov/emeu/cabs/China/Coal.html).

7. Ibid.

8 EIA, "World Proved Reserves of Oil and Natural Gas: Most Recent Estimates" (www.eia.doe.gov/emeu/international/reserves.html).

9. EIA, "China: Oil" (www.eia.doe.gov/emeu/cabs/China/oil.html).

10. International Crisis Group, "China's Thirst for Oil,"*Asia Report* 153, June 9, 2008, p. 3.

11. EIA, "World Petroleum Consumption: 1980–2007" (www.eia.doe.gov/emeu/international/oilconsumption.html).

12. EIA, "International Energy Outlook 2006" (Washington: National Energy Information Center, 2004), pp. 87, 187; International Energy Agency (IEA) "World Energy Outlook 2006" (Paris: OECD/IA, 2006), pp. 86, 112.

13. International Crisis Group, "China's Thirst for Oil," p. 40.

14. EIA, "China: Oil."

15. Figure derived from EIA, "International Energy Outlook 2007: World Oil Consumption by Region: Reference Case, 1990–2030" (www.eia.doe.gov/oiaf/archive/ieo07/pdf/0484(2007).pdf). The figure varies 1 percent if one uses data from the reference case (p. 86) of the International Energy Agency's "2006 World Energy Outlook" instead.

16. EIA, "China: Natural Gas" (www.eia.doe.gov/emeu/cabs/China/NaturalGas.html).

17. EIA, "International Natural Gas Reserves: Most Recent Estimates" (www.eia.doe.gov/emeu/international/gasreserves.html).

18. EIA, "China: Natural Gas."

19. International Energy Agency (IEA), "2006 World Energy Outlook," pp. 112, 119.

20. EIA, "China: Natural Gas."

21. EIA, "China: Electricity" (www.eia.doe.gov/emeu/cabs/China/Electricity.html); EIA, "China: Profile" (www.eia.doe.gov/emeu/cabs/China/Profile.html); "Beyond Three Gorges Dam," *International Water and Power and Dam Construction*, January 10, 2007 (www.waterpowermagazine.com/story.asp?storycode=2041318); "Largest Hydropower Station on Yellow River Starts Operation," Chinaview.com, May 18, 2009 (http://news.xinhuanet.com/englsh/2009-05/18/content_11395672.htm).

22. EIA, "China: Electricity."

23. Ira Kalish, "China and India: The Reality beyond the Hype" (Deloitte Research, 2006); "Chinese Highways for Fast Traffic Add up to 65,000 km," Xinhua, January 15, 2010 (http://news.xinhuanet.com/english/2010-01/15/content_12817685.htm).

24. World Bank, "An Overview of China's Transport Sector: 2007" (http://site resources.worldbank.org/INTEAPREGTOPTRANSPORT/34004324-118918269 2007/21600796/07-12-19_China_Transport_Sector_Overview_.pdf).

25. Ibid.

26. Calum MacLeod, "China's Highways Go the Distance," *USA Today*, January 29, 2006.

27. World Bank, "An Overview of China's Transport Sector: 2007."

28. Ibid., p. 22.

29. Ibid., p. 23.

30. "Beijing-Tianjin High-Speed Train Service Launched," *China Briefing*, August 1, 2008 (www.china-briefing.com/news/2008/08/01/beijing-tianjin-high-speed-train-service-launched.html).

31. World Bank, "An Overview of China's Transport Sector: 2007."

32. U.S. Department of Commerce, "Transportation Overview" (www.buyusa.gov/china/en/transportation.html).

33. Airports Council International, "Passenger Traffic 2008" (www.airports.org/cda/aci_common/display/main/aci_content07_c.jsp?zn=aci&cp=1-5-54-55_666_2__).

34. World Bank, "An Overview of China's Transport Sector: 2007."

35. Ibid.

36. Mark Drury, "Achaemenid Persia: A History Resource" (http://members.ozemail.com.au/~ancientpersia/).

37. Silk Road Project, "The Silk Road: An Historical Overview" (www.silkroadproject.org/silkroad/overview.html).

38. Iran Chamber Society, "History of Iran: The Contribution of Ancient Iranian Civilization to the Silk Road" (www.iranchamber.com/history/articles/contribution_iranian_civilization_silkroad.php).

39. Ray Gonzales, "The Geography of the Silk Road" (www.humboldt.edu/~geog309i/ideas/raysilk.html).

40. Frank Wong, "Pirooz in China," *The Iranian*, August 11, 2000 (www.iranian.com/History/2000/August/China/).

41. Ray Gonzales, "The Geography of the Silk Road."

42. John W. Garver, *China and Iran: Ancient Partners in a Post-Imperial World* (University of Washington Press, 2006), pp. 6–7.

43. Ibid, pp. 7–8.

44. Ibid, p. 8.

45. John Calabrese, *China and Iran: Mismatched Partners* (Washington: Jamestown Foundation, August 2006), p. 3.

46. Ibid, p. 28.

47. International Trade Centre, "Trade Statistics for International Business Development" (www.intracen.org/menus/countries.htm); American Enterprise Institute, "China-Iran Foreign Relations" (www.irantracker.org/foreign-relations/china-iran-foreign-relations#_ftn14).

48. Robin Wright, "Deepening China-Iran Ties Weaken Bid to Isolate Iran: Tehran Increasingly Important in Beijing's Energy Quest," *Washington Post*, November 18, 2007, p. A12.

49. "China Soaks up Iran Crude as Japan, Korea Cut Back," Reuters, June 5, 2006.

50. "Sino-Iran 2007 Trade Volume Exceeds $20US Bln," China Knowledge Newswire, January 31, 2008.

51. American Enterprise Institute, "China-Iran Foreign Relations" (www.iran tracker.org/foreign-relations/china-iran-foreign-relations#_ftn14).

52. Kamal Nazer Yasin, "Iran and China: Unlikely Partners," Eurasianet, May 4, 2006 (www.eurasianet.org/departments/business/articles/eav040406_pr.shtml).

53. Sudha Ramachandran, "China's Pearl in Pakistan's Waters," *Asia Times*, March 4, 2005.

54. "Sinopec Taps Oil Block in Iran," *People's Daily*, November 11, 2001 (http://english.people.com.cn/english/200101/11/eng20010111_60163.html).

55. "China to Develop Iran Oil Field," *BBC News*, November 11, 2004 (news vote.bbc.co.uk/mpapps/pagetools/print/news.bbc.co.uk/2/hi/business/3970855.stm).

56. China Institute (University of Alberta), "Sinopec and ONGC Set to Develop Iran's Yadavaran Field" (www.uofaweb.ualberta.ca/chinainstitute/nav03.cfm?nav03 =50609&nav02=43873&nav01=43092).

57. "Four National Oil Projects to Go on Stream: Nozari," *Zawya*, May 5, 2009 (www.zawya.com/story.cfm/sidZAWYA20090505042403/Four%20national%20 oil%20projects%20to%20go%20on%20stream:%20Nozari).

58. Taleh Ziyadov, "Iran and China Sign Agreement to Explore Oil in the Caspian Sea," *Eurasia Daily Monitor*, February 1, 2006.

59. Robert Lowe and Claire Spencer, *Iran, Its Neighbors, and the Regional Crises* (London: Chatham House: 2006) (www.chathamhouse.org.uk/files/3376_iran0806.pdf).

60. Harsh V. Pant, "Alternative Superpowers and the Middle East," LFI Policy Focus (London: Labour Friends of Israel, Summer 2008), p. 4.

61. Ibid.

62. Ibid.

63. Jephraim P. Gundzik, "The Ties That Bind China, Russia, and Iran" (http://atimes.com/atimes/printN.html); Kamal Nazer Yasin, "Iran and China: Unlikely Partners."

64. Monterey Institute of International Studies, "China's Nuclear Exports and Assistance to Iran," September 23, 2003 (www.nti.org/db/china/niranpos.htm).

65. China Institute (University of Alberta), "China Defends Nuclear Cooperation with Iran" (www.uofaweb.ualberta.ca/CMS/printpage.cfm?ID=46360).

66. Sharif Shuja, "China's Energy Needs and Central Asia," *National Observer* 67 (Summer 2006), pp. 56–65.

67. Jephraim P. Gundzik, "The Ties That Bind China, Russia, and Iran."

68. Farhang Jahanpour, "Iran's Nuclear Threat: Exploring the Politics," *Payvand's Iran News*, May 7, 2006 (www.payvand.com/news/06/jul/1041.html).

69. "Six Months to an Iranian Bomb?" *Foreign Policy*, June 2008 (http://blog.foreignpolicy.com/node/9122).

70. "Enough Time to Address Iran Bomb Concern: IAEA Head," Reuters, February 2, 2009 (www.reuters.com/article/worldNews/idUSTRE5111S520090202).

71. "IAEA Defends Iran against Misinformation," *PressTV*, February 3, 2009 (www.presstv.ir/detail.aspx?id=84515&sectionid=351020104).

72. "1st Sino-Arab Cooperation Forum Ministerial Meeting Held," Xinhua News Agency, September 15, 2004 (www.china.org.cn/english/2004/Sep/107188.htm).

73. "The Sixth Official Meeting for China-Arab Cooperation Forum," *Global Times*, June 23, 2009 (www.china.globaltimes.cn/diplomacy/2009-06/439120.html).

74. Ibid.

75. "Sino-Arab Cooperation Forum Focuses on Energy," *People's Daily*, April 14, 2005 (www.english.people.com.cn/200504/14/eng20050414_181041.html).

76. Ibid.

77. "Sino-Arab Forum Agrees to Seek Doubling of Trade Volume within 5 Years," *First Maroc*, June 6, 2006 (www.1stmaroc.com/actuuk/archivesuk/resultat.php?id=605).

78. "Sino-Arab Civilization Dialogue Concludes with Call for Enhanced Ties, Communications," Xinhua News Agency, May 13, 2009

79. "Sino-Arab Forum Agrees to Seek Doubling of Trade Volume within 5 Years," *First Maroc*.

80. Ibid.

81. "Sino-Arab Forum Ends with Final Document," *China Daily*, June 7, 2007 (www.chinadaily.com.cn/china/2007-07/06/content_911081.htm).

82. "The Sixth Official Meeting for China-Arab Cooperation Forum," *Global Times*.

83. John Calabrese, "Saudi Arabia and China Extend Ties beyond Oil," *China Brief 5*, no. 20 (2005).

84. "Energy, Trade Deals Inked as Hu Visits Saudi," *Dalian News*, April 23, 2006 (http://english.dl.gov.cn/info/157270_207841.htm).

85. "Chinese President Continues Visit to Saudi Arabia," Xinhua News Agency, February 12, 2009 (http://news.xinhuanet.com/english/2009-02/12/content_1080 6785.htm).

86. "China-Saudi Relations at Best Stage Ever," *China View*, June 21, 2008 (http://news.xinhua.com/english/2008-06/21/content_8412145.htm).

87. Michele Markey, "Update on China," Apache Corporation, July 24, 2006 (www.apachecorp.com/Explore/Weekly_Energy_Perspective/Topic_Report/).

88. It should be mentioned that China's state economic planners and oil importers have focused on acquiring sources of sweet crude, a more productive source of gasoline, demand for which has increased exponentially along with Chinese automobile ownership. Traditionally there has been less demand for high-sulfur oil in China; houses are normally heated by electricity or coal furnaces, while electricity production is generated most often by domestic coal-fired plants rather than oil-burning ones.

89. Pant, "Saudi Arabia Woos China and India," pp. 45–52.

90. Edward Lanfranco, "Signs of Warming Sino-Saudi Ties," United Press International, March 31, 2006 (www.upi.com/Business_News/Security-Industry/2006/03/31/Signs-of-warming-Sino-Saudi-ties/UPI-50091143813258/).

91. Cindy Hurst, *China's Global Quest for Energy*, report prepared for the Institute for the Analysis of Global Security (January 2007) (www.iags.org/chinasquest0107.pdf).

92. "Energy, Trade Deals Inked as Hu Visits Saudi," *China Daily*, April 23, 2006 (www.chinadaily.com.cn/china/2006-04/23/content_574320_2.htm).

93. Chris Dobson, "Refining Sino-Saudi Relations," *South China Morning Post*, September 23, 2006.

94. Saudi Arabian General Investment Authority, "Actual Inflows and Stocks of Foreign Direct Investments in KSA by Country and Sector 2006" (www.sagia.gov.sa/%7Ecssgrey/sagia/english/downloads/Summary%20Report%20on%20Actual%20FDI%20&%20SAGIA%20Licenses%20up%20to%202006_4.2.4.pdf).

95. "Makkah Metro Contracts Signed," *Railway Gazette International*, June 24, 2009 (www.railwaygazette.com/news/single-view/view//makkah-metro-contracts-signed.html).

96. China Institute, University of Alberta, "China Preparing to Build Underground Oil Storage Facility" (www.uofaweb.ualberta.ca/chinainstitute/nav03.cfm?nav03=47921&nav02=43610&nav01=43092).

97. Myra P. Saefong, "China and Saudi Arabia: Interesting SPR Team Up?" *MarketWatch*, June 23, 2006 (www.marketwatch.com/News/Story/Story.aspx?guid=%7BBDDC6EA6-C0E8-4F33-9B51-28314C17EDEC%7D&siteid=mktw&dist=nwhwk).

98. Therefore, China will most likely look for more deals with West African nations that ship sweet crude. China Institute, University of Alberta, "China to Look Abroad to Fill Strategic Oil Reserves" (www.uofaweb.ualberta.ca/chinainstitute/nav03.cfm?nav03=47849&nav02=43610&nav01=43092).

99. "Exxon Mobil, Saudi Aramco Enter China Oil Markets," *MarketWatch*, February 25, 2007 (www.marketwatch.com/story/exxon-mobil-saudi-aramco-enter-china-oil-markets).

100. AME Info, "Saudi Arabia Plans Huge Refinery Investments," July 23, 2006 (www.ameinfo.com/64680.html).

101. Khaled Almaeena, "Kingdom, China Sign Landmark Energy Pact," *Arab News*, January 24, 2006 (www.arabnews.com/?page=1&section=0&article=76724 &d=24&m=1&y=2006).

102. "Qingdao Refinery Takes First Arabian Crude," *Saudi Aramco News*, June 11, 2008 (www.aramcoexpats.com/Articles/Pipeline/Saudi-Aramco-News/Dhahran-Media/3181.aspx).

103. Ibid.

104. "Energy, Trade Deals Linked as Hu Visits Saudi," *China Daily* (www.china daily.com.cn/china/2006-04/23/content_574320_2.htm).

105. Ibid.

106. "Saudi SABIC, Sinopec Agree $2.5 Bln China Petchem JV," Reuters, June 23, 2008 (http://uk.reuters.com/article/oilRpt/idUKPEK23790720080623).

107. "Energy, Trade Deals Inked as Hu Visits Saudi," *China Daily*.

108. Stockholm International Peace Research Institute, "Saudi Arabia Country Profile," November 12, 2009 (www.sipri.org/research/disarmament/nuclear/researchissues/past_projects/issues_of_concern/saudi_arabia/saudi_arabia_default).

109. Richard Russell, "China's WMD Foot in the Greater Middle East's Door," *Middle East Review of International Affairs* 9, no. 3 (September 2005).

110. Stockholm International Peace Research Institute, "Saudi Arabia Country Profile."

111. Thomas Woodrow, "The Sino-Saudi Connection," *China Brief* 2, no. 21 (2002).

112. John Calabrese, "Saudi Arabia and China Extend Ties beyond Oil."

113. Stephen Pollard, "How China's Secret Deals Are Fueling War," *The Times*, August 8, 2006.

114. Thomas Woodrow, "The Sino-Saudi Connection."

115. G. Parthasarathy, "Axis of Evidence," *Indian Express*, November 14, 2003.

116. Thomas Woodrow, "The Sino-Saudi Connection."

117. People's Republic of China, Ministry of Commerce, "China and GCC Cosponsored in Riyadh FTA Talk," June 30, 2009 (http://english.mofcom.gov.cn/aarticle/newsrelease/significantnews/200906/20090606367914.html).

118. "Chinese FM Says Confident in Free Trade Talks with GCC," *People's Daily*, May 22, 2008 (http://english.people.com.cn/90001/90776/6415868.html).

119. "Oman History," Inoman.com (www.inoman.com/history.htm).

120. Oman Information Center, "Oman History" (www.omaninfo.com/oman/history.asp).

121. "Oman Willing to Further Ties with China," *Sina*, September 20, 2005 (http://english.sina.com/china/1/2005/0920/46686.html).

122. "Omani Ambassador Treasures Cooperation with China on 25th Anniversary of Diplomatic Ties," China.org, May 23, 2003 (www.china.org.cn/english/international/65237.htm).

123. "Oman: Partnerships with China," *APS Review Downstream Trends*, February 13, 2006.

124. "China Tops Oman Crude Oil Import," *Khaleej Times Online*, July 9, 2005 (www.khaleejtimes.com/DisplayArticle.asp?xfile=data/business/2005/July/business_July173.xml&section=business&col).

125. "Omani Ambassador Treasures Cooperation with China on 25th Anniversary of Diplomatic Ties," China.org.

126. "China Signs Oil/Gas Deal with Oman," *World Tribune*, August 30, 2004 (www.worldtribune.com/worldtribune/WTARC/2004/ea_china_08_30.html).

127. "China Gas Wins Rare Import/Export License," *Platts Oilgram News*, December, 14, 2006.

128. "China Gas, Oman Oil in JV to Supply China; Company Aiming to be Major Asian Energy Importer and Producer," *Platts Oilgram News*, May 24, 2007.

129. Oman Oil Company, "Oman Oil Company to Purchase 8 Percent Share in China Gas Holdings" December 5, 2005 (www.oman-oil.com/newsdetails.asp?id=58).

130. "Qatar Seeks LNG Sales to China," *Khaleej Times*, May 13, 2005 (www.khaleej times.com/displayArticle.asp?col=&section=business&xfile=data/business/2005/May/business_May250.xml).

131. Embassy of Qatar, *Trade* (www.qatarembassy.net/trade.asp).

132. Qatar Airways, "Qatar Airways' China Week Hailed Huge Success," April 29, 2008 (www.qatarairways.com/global/en/newsroom/archive/press-release-19Apr08.html).

133. "Qatar Airways Celebrate First Anniversary of Beijing Route with Extra Capacity," *China Travel News*, November 29, 2005 (www.chinatravel.com/china-travel-guides/china-travel-news/china-travel-news-2005/china-travel-news-2005-11/qatar-airways-celebrates-.shtml).

134. "China Cuts Military Deals in Qatar," *World Tribune*, June 22, 2006 (www.worldtribune.com/worldtribune/06/front2453909.15.html).

135. "China Urges United Arab Emirates to Stop Official Contacts with Taiwan," *China Daily*, October 1, 2005 (www.chinadaily.com.cn/english/doc/2005-10/01/content_482321.htm).

136. Embassy of the People's Republic of China in the United Arab Emirates, "China and the United Arab Emirates" (http://ae.china-embassy.org/eng/sbgx/t150466.htm).

137. "What to Do in Dubai: Dubai Dragon Market," *Dubai City Travel Guide*, August 30, 2007 (www.dubaicity.com/what_to_do_in_dubai/dubai_dragon_mart.htm).

138. Embassy of the People's Republic of China in the State of Kuwait, "China and Kuwait" (http://kw.china-embassy.org/eng/sbgx/t580302.htm).

139. "History: The Roots of Kuwait" (http://members.tripod.com/~kuwaitq8/history.html).

140. Embassy of the People's Republic of China in the United States, "China, Kuwait Stress UN's Role in Iraq," July 7, 2004 (www.china-embassy.org/eng/xw/t142319.htm).

141. "China Begins Free Trade Talks with GCC," *China Daily*, July 7, 2004 (www.chinadaily.com.cn/english/doc/2004-07/07/content_346014.htm).

142. People's Republic of China, Ministry of Foreign Affairs, "Kuwait: Bilateral Relations" (www.mfa.gov.cn/eng/wjb/zzjg/xybfs/gjlb/2838/).

143. Ibid.

144. Embassy of the People's Republic of China in the United States, "China, Kuwait Stress UN's Role in Iraq," July 7, 2004 (www.china-embassy.org/eng/xw/t142319.htm).

145. "China Begins Free Trade Talks with GCC," *China Daily* (www.chinadaily.com.cn/english/doc/2004-07/07/content_346014.htm).

146. AMEinfo.com, "Kuwait, $720 Million Deal," September 25, 2006 (www.ameinfo.com/97267.html).

147. "China Encourages Kuwaiti Investment," *Kuwait Times*, May 8, 2007 (www.kuwaittimes.net/read_news.php?newsid=MTE1OTczMDcwOA).

148. "Kuwait Seeks to Strengthen Oil Ties with China," Xinhua News Agency, April 4, 2005 (http://news.xinhuanet.com/english/2005-04/04/content_2782591.htm).

149. "China, Kuwait to Expand Economic Trade Cooperation," *People's Daily*, February 27, 2002 (http://english.people.com.cn/200407/07/eng20040707_148729.html); EIA, "Kuwait: Oil" (www.eia.doe.gov/cabs/Kuwait/Oil.html).

150. "Kuwait Set to Expand in China," *International Herald Tribune*, December 22, 2005.

151. China Institute, University of Alberta, "Sinopec-KPC $5 Billion Refinery Gets Early Go-Ahead" (www.uofaweb.ualberta.ca/chinainstitute/nav03.cfm?nav03=48642&nav02=43875&nav01=43092).

152. Ibid.

153. "Sinopec-KPI Refinery JV Deal Not Yet in Hand," *Platts Oilgram Price Report* 87, no.89 (2009), p. 14.

154. Niklas Swanstrom, Nicklas Norling, and Zhang Li, "China," in *The New Silk Roads: Transport and Trade in Greater Central Asia*, edited by S. Frederick Starr (Central Asia–Caucasus Institute and Silk Road Studies Program, 2007) (www.silkroadstudies.org/new/docs/publications/GCA/GCAPUB-12.pdf).

155. Charles E. Ziegler, "Competing for Markets and Influence: Asian National Oil Companies in Eurasia" *Asian Perspectives* 32, no. 1 (2008), pp. 129–63.

156. Ibid.

157. Central Intelligence Agency (CIA), *World Factbook*, "Natural Gas: Proved Reserves" (www.cia.gov/library/publications/the-world-factbook/rankorder/2179rank.html).

158. Eric Hyer, "Central Asia–China Relations," in *Encyclopedia of Modern Asia,* vol. 3, edited by Karen Christensen and David Levinson (Charles Scribner's Sons, 2002), pp. 183–84.

159. N. T. Tarimi, "China-Uzbek Pact Bad News for Uighurs," *Asia Times*, June 30, 2004 (www.atimes.com/atimes/Central_Asia/FG30Ag01.html).

160. Ahmed Rashid, *Jihad: The Rise of Militant Islam in Central Asia* (New York: Penguin Books, 2003).

161. Tarimi, "China-Uzbek Pact Bad News for Uighurs."

162. John C. K. Daly, "SCO to Host 'Peace Mission 2007' Anti-Terrorist Drill in August," *Eurasia Daily Monitor* 4, no. 146, July 27, 2007.

163. International Crisis Group, *Uzbekistan: The Andijon Uprising* (Brussels: May 25, 2005).

164. "China, Uzbekistan Vow to Promote Bilateral Co-op to Higher Level," Xinhua News Agency, November 3, 2007 (http://news.xinhuanet.com/english/2007-11/03/content_7002328.htm).

165. Eurasianet.org, "Uzbekistan: Tashkent Strives to Diversify Its Trade Partners," March 19, 2008 (www.eurasianet.org/departments/insight/articles/eav031908.shtml).

166. Ibid.

167. Environmental Justice Foundation, "Trade in Uzbek Cotton" (www.ejfoun dation.org/page147.html).

168. Swanstrom, Norling, and Li, "China."

169. Ibid.

170. Ziegler, "Competing for Markets and Influence: Asian National Oil Companies in Eurasia."

171. "China Eximbank to Lend 79.3m Dollars to Uzbekistan," *UzReport*, December 5, 2007 (http://finance.uzreport.com/other.cgi?lan=e&id=40477).

172. "Uzbek Joins CNPC in Pipeline Deal," *Upstream*, April 14, 2008 (www.upstreamonline.com/incoming/article152400.ece).

173. Ibid.

174. Alisher Illkhamov, "Profit, Not Patronage: Chinese Interests in Uzbekistan," *China Brief* 5, no. 20 (October 23, 2005).

175. Sebastien Peyrouse, "The Growing Trade Stakes of the Chinese-Kyryz-Uzbek Railway Project," Central Asia–Caucus Institute (March 2009) (www.caci analyst.org/?q=node/5058).

176. CIA, *World Factbook*, "Kazakhstan" (www.cia.gov/library/publications/the-world-factbook/geos/kz.html).

177. Rashid, *Jihad: The Rise of Militant Islam in Central Asia.*

178. Ziegler, "Competing for Markets and Influence: Asian National Oil Companies in Eurasia."

179. Ibid.

180. "China, Kazakhstan in 13 Cooperation Deals, Pledge to Develop Strategic Partnership," *People's Daily*, December 21, 2006 (http://english.people.com.cn/200612/21/eng20061221_334553.html).

181. Bruce Pannier, "China/Kazakhstan: Forces Hold First-Ever Joint Terrorism Exercises," Radio Free Europe, August 24, 2006 (www.rferl.org/content/article/1070801.html).

182. Roger McDermott, "Kazakhstan's Armed Forces Look for Western 'Approval,'" *Eurasia Daily Monitor* 5, no. 115 (2008).

183. European Commission, "Kazakhstan: EU Bilateral Trade and Trade with the World," October 9, 2009 (http://trade.ec.europa.eu/doclib/docs/2006/september/tradoc_113406.pdf).

184. People's Republic of China, "China, Kazakhstan Start to Build Tax-Free Trade Center," June 3, 2006 (www.gov.cn/english/2006-06/03/content_299483.htm).

185. "Tax-Free Trade Center to Open at China-Kazakhstan Border," *China Daily*, May 13, 2006 (http://english.peopledaily.com.cn/200605/13/eng20060513_265219. html).

186. Ibid.

187. "China, Kazakhstan Sign Joint Communiqué on Promoting Relations and Trade," *People's Daily*, February 18, 2007 (http://english.people.com. cn/90001/90776/6242980.html).

188. Ziegler, "Competing for Markets and Influence: Asian National Oil Companies in Eurasia."

189. PetroKazakhstan owns the entire stake in the Kumkol South oil field and has a 50 percent stake in the Kumkol North and KazGermunai fields, all of which are in south-central Kazakhstan. Lukoil holds the other 50 percent in Kumkol North, and German companies have minority shares in KazGermunai. In 2004 PetroKazakhstan produced 12 percent of the Kazakh output or 151,000 barrels. This source claims that the assets go up to 550 million tons of oil. Vladimir Socor, "Implications of China's Takeover of PetroKazakhstan," *Eurasia Daily Monitor* 2, no. 165 (2005).

190. James Fishelson, "From the Silk Road to Chevron: The Geopolitics of Oil Pipelines in Central Asia," *Journal of Russian and Asian Studies* 7 (Winter 2007).

191. China Institute, University of Alberta, "U.S. Exerts Pressure to Hinder Opening of China-Kazakhstan Oil Pipeline" (www.uofaweb.ualberta.ca/chinainstitute/nav03.cfm?nav03=47452&nav02=43871&nav01=43092).

192. EIA, "Kazakhstan" (www.eia.doe.gov/emeu/cabs/Kazakhstan/Full.html).

193. "China, Kazakhstan Sign Deal on Gas Pipeline," *Pipeline and Gas Journal*, December 1, 2007.

194. "China Adds Transport Routes to Kazakhstan," *Xinhua*, June 11, 2006 (www. gov.cn/misc/2006-06/11/content_307075.htm).

195. World Bank, "Kazakhstan and World Bank Agree on a Plan for a $2.5 Billion Road Project," June 23, 2008.

196. "New Rail Line to Link China and Germany," *Railway Age*, July 1, 2004.

197. U.S. Department of State, "Turkmenistan" (www.state.gov/r/pa/ei/bgn/35884.htm).

198. Embassy of Turkmenistan in the United States, "Culture, Traditions, and History" (www.turkmenistanembassy.org/turkmen/history/hist_cult.html).

199. U.S. Department of State, "Background Notes: Turkmenistan."

200. "Jiang's Turkmenistan Visit to Deepen Bilateral Relations," *People's Daily*, June 26, 2000 (http://english.people.com.cn/english/200006/26/eng20000626_43998.html).

201. Kathleen J. Hancock, "Escaping Russia, Looking to China: Turkmenistan Pins Hopes on China's Thirst for Natural Gas," *China and Eurasia Forum Quarterly* 44, no. 3 (2006).

202. CIA, *World Factbook*, "Turkmenistan" (www.cia.gov/library/publications/the-world-factbook/geos/tx.html).

203. EIA, "Background Notes: Turkmenistan" (http://tonto.eia.doe.gov/country/country_energy_data.cfm?fips=TX).

204. Hancock, "Escaping Russia, Looking to China: Turkmenistan Pins Hopes on China's Thirst for Natural Gas."

205. Rashid, *Jihad: The Rise of Militant Islam in Central Asia.*

206. EIA, "Background Notes: Turkmenistan."

207. Cen Karpat, "Tired of Russia, Turkmenistan Is Due to Chose China," *Axis Information and Analysis*, August 30, 2005 (www.axisglobe.com/article.asp?article=356).

208. China Institute, University of Alberta, "Turkmenistan to Strengthen Ties with China" (www.uofaweb.ualberta.ca/chinainstitute/nav03.cfm?nav03=56323&nav02=45061&nav01=0).

209. Hancock, "Escaping Russia, Looking to China: Turkmenistan Pins Hopes on China's Thirst for Natural Gas."

210. People's Republic of China, Ministry of Foreign Affairs, "Bilateral Relations," October 10, 2003 (www.fmprc.gov.cn/eng/wjb/zzjg/dozys/gjlb/3245/default.htm).

211. Hancock, "Escaping Russia, Looking to China: Turkmenistan Pins Hopes on China's Thirst for Natural Gas."

212. Karpat, "Tired of Russia, Turkmenistan Is Due to Chose China."

213. "Turkmen Gas Deal Extends Chinese Influence," *Downstream Today*, July 25, 2007 (www.downstreamtoday.com/news/article.aspx?a_id=5015).

214. "China, Turkmenistan Sign Landmark Gas Deal," *News Central Asia*, July 17, 2007 (www.newscentralasia.net/Regional-News/129.html).

215. "CNPC Starts Building Turkmenistan-China Gas Pipeline," *News Central Asia*, August 30, 2007 (www.newscentralasia.net/Regional-News/160.html).

216. "China, Turkmenistan Agree on Pipeline," *China Daily*, April 4, 2006 (www.chinadaily.com.cn/china/2006-04/04/content_559250.htm).

217. "Turkmenistan to Open Gas Pipeline to China," United Press International, October 1, 2009 (www.upi.com/Science_News/Resource-Wars/2009/10/01/Turkmenistan-to-open-gas-pipeline-to-China/UPI-13241254433294/).

Chapter Four

1. See Appendix A for a brief overview of Southeast Asia's role in the Middle East.

2. K. Shankar Bajpai, "Untangling India and Pakistan," *Foreign Affairs* 82, no. 2 (May/June 2003), pp. 119–20.

3. William J. Barnds, "India in Transition," *Foreign Affairs* 46, no. 3 (April 1968), pp. 548–61.

4. Bajpai, "Untangling India and Pakistan," p. 116

5. Barry Bearak, "Pakistan Is," *New York Times*, December 7, 2003, sec. 6, p. 62.

6. Bajpai, "Untangling India and Pakistan," p. 115.

7. "Mumbai Suspect Trial to Proceed," *BBC News*, July 23, 2009 (http://news.bbc.co.uk/2/hi/8164279.stm).

8. Anatol Lieven, "Can Peace Finally Come to Kashmir," *New York Times*, October 21, 2001, sec. 4, p. 15.

9. Eric Schmitt and Jane Perlez, "Pakistan Objects to U.S. Expansion of Afghan War," *New York Times*, July 22, 2009, sec. 1, p. 1.

10. "Al-Qaeda 'rebuilding' in Pakistan," *BBC News*, January 12, 2007 (http://news.bbc.co.uk/2/hi/south_asia/6254375.stm).

11. Jessica Stern, "Jihad Culture," *Foreign Affairs* 79, no. 6 (November/December 2000), p. 121.

12. Bill Powell and others, "Struggle for the Soul of Islam," *Time* 164, no. 11 (2004) (www.time.com/time/magazine/article/0,9171,995071,00.html).

13. "Arab World, 1946–2006," *Encyclopaedia Judaica* 2, 2nd ed. (Detroit: Macmillan Reference USA, 2006), p. 302.

14. Stern, "Jihad Culture," p. 124.

15. Hussein Haqqani, "Saudis Send Them Packing," *Far Eastern Economic Review* 51, no. 138 (1987), pp. 51–52.

16. "They Know It Well," *The Economist*, August 18, 1990, pp. 24–29.

17. Salamat Ali, "Muddle Mediation: No Takers for Pakistan's Peace Plan," *Far Eastern Economic Review* 6, no. 151 (1991), p. 11.

18. Jay Solomon, "Pakistan Aid Effort Hits Saudi Hurdle," *Wall Street Journal* (eastern ed.), April 15, 2009, p. A10.

19. Bruce Riedel, "If Pakistan Fails," *National Interest* (July/August 2009), pp. 9–18.

20. Haqqani, "Saudis Send Them Packing," pp. 51–52.

21. Abdullah Rasheed, "Expat Numbers Rise Rapidly as UAE Population Touches 6m," *Gulf News*, October 7, 2009 (http://gulfnews.com/news/gulf/uae/general/expat-numbers-rise-rapidly-as-uae-population-touches-6m-1.505602).

22. "Profiles—Pakistan," Mine Action Information Center, James Madison University (http://maic.jmu.edu/JOURNAL/5.1/Profiles/Pakistan/pakistan.htm).

23. "Oman—People—Ethnic Groups," Central Intelligence Agency (CIA), *World Factbook* (www.cia.gov/library/publications/the-world-factbook/geos/mu.html).

24. Robert Kaplan, "Pakistan's Fatal Shore," *The Atlantic Online* (May 2009) (www.theatlantic.com/doc/200905/kaplan-pakistan).

25. "Pakistan, Bahrain Defense Forces Strengthen Relations," United States Navy, January 15, 2008 (www.navy.mil/search/display.asp?story_id=34341).

26. "Qatar, Pakistan Stage Naval Exercise," August 20, 2007 (www.defence.pk/forums/naval-forces/3891-qatar-pakistan-stage-naval-exercise.html).

27. "Pakistan Considering Qatari LNG over Iranian Gas," *Qatar Daily News*, March 4, 2009 (http://news.qatarguidebook.com/pakistan-considering-qatari-lng-over-iranian-gas.html#more-391).

28. "Fresh Pakistan Protest over Power," *BBC News*, July 22, 2009 (http://news.bbc.co.uk/2/hi/south_asia/8162793.stm).

29. Some of these transmission losses are due to the outdated infrastructure, but rampant energy theft is adding to the problem. UPI Asia Online reported, "Power thefts in Karachi and the Federally Administered Tribal Areas cost the country revenue losses of $227.4 million annually" (www.upiasia.com/Energy_Resources/2009/07/24/Pakistans-energy-woes/UPI-76771248474252/).

30. "Pakistan's new leader confronts energy crisis as generating capacity fails to keep up with rising demand," *New York Times*, October 29, 2008 (www.nytimes.com/2008/10/29/business/worldbusiness/29iht-renpak.1.17281565.htm).

31. World Bank, "Macroeconomics and Economic Growth in South Asia: Growth in Pakistan" (http://web.worldbank.org/WBSITE/EXTERNAL/COUNTRIES/SOUTHASIAEXT/EXTSARREGTOPMACECOGRO/0,,contentMDK:20592484~menuPK:579404~pagePK:34004173~piPK:34003707~theSitePK:579398,00.html).

32. "Which Way out for Pakistan's Power Sector?" Reuters U.K., July 22, 2009 (http://uk.reuters.com/article/idUKISL48621320090722).

33. Ibid.

34. "Pakistan's Oil Reserves Will Last Only 6 Days," Indo-Asian News Service (IANS), January 26, 2009 (www.thaindian.com/newsportal/uncategorized/pakistans-oil-reserves-will-last-only-6-days_100147285.html); U.S. Agency for International Development (USAID), Pakistan, "Energy Sector Assessment for USAID/Pakistan," June 2007, p. 9 (www.usaid.gov/pk/downloads/eg/PEDP.pdf).

35. "Qatar Agrees LNG Deal with Pakistan," ArabianOilandGas.com, June 29, 2009 (www.arabianoilandgas.com/article-5772-qatar_agrees_lng_deal_with_pakistan/).

36. "Pakistan, Iran Finally Sign Gas Pipeline Accord," Dawn.com, May 24, 2009 (www.dawn.com/wps/wcm/connect/dawn-content-library/dawn/news/business/09-iran-pakistan-sign-gas-pipeline-deal-media-szh--07).

37. "Hydel, Coal, Renewable Resources Vital to Overcome Energy Crisis," Associated Press of Pakistan, July 28, 2009 (www.app.com.pk/en_/index.php?option=com_content&task=view&id=82480).

38. Ibid.

39. World Bank, "Transportation: Pakistan" (http://go.worldbank.org/7CYYM39VG0).

40. Ibid.

41. World Bank, "Pakistan, Promoting Rural Growth and Poverty Reduction," Report No. 39303-PK (March 30, 2007), p. 84 (http://siteresources.worldbank.org/PAKISTANEXTN/Resources/293051-1177200597243/ruralgrowthandpovertyreduction.pdf).

42. World Bank, "Second Trade and Transport Facilitation Project" (Project Appraisal), Report No. 48094-PK, April 10, 2009, p. 25 (http://go.worldbank.org/1B1R5E7DK0).

43. Ibid.

44. "Lahore-Karachi-Lahore Sindh Express Inaugurated," *Daily Times* (Pakistan), July 25, 2006 (www.dailytimes.com.pk/print.asp?page=2006\07\25\story_25-7-2006_pg7_48).

45. "Kashgar to Become Central Asian Trading Hub, Again," China Briefing, September 11, 2008 (www.china-briefing.com/news/2008/09/11/kashgar-to-become-central-asian-trading-hub-again.html).

46. Government of Pakistan, Infrastructure Project Development Facility, "Facts about Pakistan—Ports," 2008 (www.ipdf.gov.pk/tmpnew/DF_Ports.php).

47. Karachi Port Trust, "Projects in Brief" (www.kpt.gov.pk/Projects/Proj.html).

48. Shah Mahmood Qureshi, foreign minister of Pakistan, speech at Brookings Institution, July 11, 2008, p. 5 (www.brookings.edu/~/media/Files/events/2008/0711_pakistan/0711_pakistan.pdf).

49. Ammad Hassan, "Pakistan's Gwadar Port—Prospects of Economic Revival," master's thesis, Naval Postgraduate School, Monterey, Calif., June 2005 (www.nps.edu/Academics/Centers/CCC/research/StudentTheses/Hassan05.pdf).

50. "Chinese-Assisted Pakistani Gwadar Deep-Water Port Starts Operation," Xinhua News Agency, March 21, 2007 (http://news.xinhuanet.com/english/2007-03/21/content_5874101.htm).

51. Tarique Niazi, "Gwadar: China's Naval Outpost on the Indian Ocean," *China Brief 5*, no. 4 (Washington: Jamestown Foundation, February 2005)

52. "Musharraf: Ties with China Deeper than the Sea," *People's Daily,* March 12, 2007 (www.chinadaily.com.cn/world/2007-03/12/content_824816.htm).

53. Ministry of Foreign Affairs, People's Republic of China, "Pakistan—Reviewing the Bilateral Political Relations," October 23, 2003 (www.fmprc.gov.cn/eng/wjb/zzjg/yzs/gjlb/2757/).

54. Ibid.

55. Ibid.

56. Urvashi Aneja, "Pakistan-China Relations," Special Report 26 (New Delhi: Institute of Peace and Conflict Studies, June 2006), p. 2 (http://ipcs.org/pdf_file/issue/136564802IPCS-Special-Report-26.pdf).

57. Richard R. Fisher, "Musharraf Visits China: Current Issues in Pakistan-China Relations" (Alexandria, Va.: International Assessment and Strategy Center, February 25, 2006) (www.strategycenter.net/research/pubID.92/pub_detail.asp).

58. Aneja, "Pakistan-China Relations," p. 5.

59. Ahmed Rashid, *Descent into Chaos: The United States and the Failure of Nation Building in Pakistan, Afghanistan, and Central Asia* (New York: Viking, 2008), p. 287; Dennis Kux, *The United States and Pakistan, 1947–2000: Disenchanted Allies* (Washington: Woodrow Wilson Center Press, 2001).

60. Rashid, *Descent into Chaos*, p. 287.

61. D. S. Rajan, "Visit of Prime Minister of Pakistan to China—An Assessment," Paper 1199 (New Delhi: South Asia Analysis Group, December 2004) (www.southasiaanalysis.org/papers12/paper1199.html).

62. Ministry of Commerce, People's Republic of China, "China-Pakistan FTA on Trade in Services Comes into Force on Oct. 10," September 13, 2009 (http://english. mofcom.gov.cn/aarticle/newsrelease/significantnews/200909/20090906528543. html).

63. "Pakistan, China Sign Free Trade Agreement," *Daily Times*, November 25, 2006 (www.dailytimes.com.pk/default.asp?page=2006\11\25\story_25-11-2006_pg5_1).

64. Rahimullah Yusufzai, "Zardari's Visits to China," *News International* (Pakistan), September 1, 2009 (www.thenews.com.pk/editorial_detail.asp?id=196091).

65. Raviprasad Narayanan, "Musharraf in China: Economic Benefits of an "All Weather Friendship," IDSA Strategic Comments (New Delhi: Institute for Defence Studies and Analyses. April 22, 2008) (www.idsa.in/idsastrategiccomments/MusharrafinChina_RNarayanan_220408).

66. Fazal-Ur-Rehman, "Prospects of Pakistan Becoming a Trade and Energy Corridor for China," *Strategic Studies* (Pakistan), XXVII (Summer 2007) (www.issi.org.pk/journal/2007_files/no_2/article/a3.htm).

67. Ammad Hassan, "Pakistan's Gwadar Port—Prospects of Economic Revival." The 2,000 km figure refers to 2,500 km from Gwadar against 4,500 from Eastern China.

68. Fazal-Ur-Rehman, "Prospects of Pakistan Becoming a Trade and Energy Corridor for China."

69. "Pakistani Highway Opened," *Washington Post*, June 19, 1978, p. A-21 (www.nexis.com).

70. Fazal-Ur-Rehman, "Prospects of Pakistan Becoming a Trade and Energy Corridor for China."

71. Rajeev Ranjan Chaturvedy, "Interpreting China's Grand Strategy at Gwadar," Institute for Peace and Conflict Studies, February 14 2006 (http://ipcs.org/article/china/interpreting-chinas-grand-strategy-at-gwadar-1939.html).

72. Raviprasad Narayanan, "Musharraf in China: Economic Benefits of an "All Weather Friendship." Also "China, Pak to Join to Build Nuke Plants," ExpressIndia. com, May 9, 2008 (www.expressindia.com/latest-news/China-Pak-to-join-to-build-nuke-plants/307419/).

73. Narayanan, "Musharraf in China: Economic Benefits of an "All weather Friendship."

74. Hassan, "Pakistan's Gwadar Port—Prospects of Economic Revival," p. 25.

75. Rashid, *Descent into Chaos*, p. 284.

76. Ibid., p. 283

77. Ibid.

78. Niazi, "Gwadar: China's Naval Outpost on the Indian Ocean."

79. Rashid, *Descent into Chaos*, p. 285.

80. Ibid., pp. 286–87; Niazi, "Gwadar: China's Naval Outpost on the Indian Ocean."

81. Syed Fazl-e-Haider, "Pakistan Port Opens New Possibilities," *Asia Times Online*, March 22, 2007 (www.atimes.com/atimes/South_Asia/IC22Df02.html)

82. Syed Fazl-e-Haider, "Forgotten Pledges Revived," Dawn.com, December 7, 2009 (www.dawn.com/wps/wcm/connect/dawn-content-library/dawn/in-paper-magazine/economic-and-business/forgotten-pledges-revived).

83. B. Rahman, "The Blast at Gwadar," Paper 993 (New Delhi: South Asia Analysis Group, May 2004) (www.southasiaanalysis.org/%5Cpapers10%5Cpaper993.html).

84. B. Rahman, "The Blast at Gwadar."

85. Tarique Niazi, "China, Pakistan, and Terrorism," *Foreign Policy in Focus*, July 16, 2007 (www.uyghuramerican.org/forum/showthread.php?6463-China-Pakistan-and-Terrorism).

86. Gilles Boquerat, "Sino-Indian Relations in Retrospect," *Strategic Studies* (ISSI Pakistan), XXVII (Summer 2007) (www.issi.org.pk/journal/2007_files/no_2/article/a1.htm).

87. "A Shared Vision for the 21st Century of the Republic of India and the People's Republic of China," Joint Declaration, January 14, 2008 (www.chinaconsulatesf.org/eng/xw/t399545.htm).

88. Christopher W. Hughes and Ellis S. Krauss, "Japan's New Security Agenda," *Survival* 49, no. 2 (Summer 2007), p. 157.

89. "Japan Eyes Military Missile Threat," *USA Today*, August 1, 2006 (www.usatoday.com/news/world/2006-08-01-japan-military_x.htm).

90. "Japan Wary of China's Growing Military," *International Herald Tribune*, August 2, 2005 (www.iht.com/articles/2005/08/02/news/japan.php).

91. "Japan FM Calls China a Military Threat," *China Daily* (www.chinadaily.com.cn/china/2006-04/03/content_558106.htm).

92. "Indo-Japan Trade Relations," *Economy Watch*, 2005 (www.economywatch.com/world_economy/japan/indo-japan-trade-relation.html).

93. U.S. Energy Information Administration (EIA), "Japan," Country Analysis Briefs, September 2008 (www.eia.doe.gov/emeu/cabs/Japan/Oil.html).

94. Japan Ministry of Finance, Trade Statistics (www.customs.go.jp/toukei/info/index_e.htm).

95. Michael Penn, "The Battle of Azadegan: Japan, Oil and Independence," *Japan Focus 1590*, August 27, 2005 (http://japanfocus.org/-Michael-Penn/1590).

96. Richard Hanson, "Japan, Iran Sign Major Oil Deal, US Dismayed," *Asia Times*, February 20, 2004 (www.atimes.com/atimes/Japan/fb20dh04.html).

97. Michael Penn, "Japan's Persian Gulf Policies in the Koizumi Era" (Silver City, N.M., and Washington: Foreign Policy in Focus, June 30, 2006) (http://americas.irc-online.org/am/3336/).

98. Ibid. See also, "Japan Vows to Proceed with Oil Deal in Iran," *Financial Times*, August 19, 2003 (http://yaleglobal.yale.edu/content/japan-vows-proceed-oil-deal-iran), and "Iran Weighing Inpex Oil Role," *International Herald Tribune*, October 8, 2006 (www.nytimes.com/2006/10/08/business/worldbusiness/08iht-inpex.3068410.html).

99. Penn, "Japan's Persian Gulf Policies in the Koizumi Era."

100. Mindy L. Kotler, "Unrequited Responsibility: Japan and Iran," *Japan Information Access Project,* January 16, 2006 (www.jiaponline.org/publications/ur_ji.html).

101. Hisane Masaki, "Japan Energy: Goodbye Iran, Hello Iraq," *Asia Times Online,* November 7, 2006 (www.atimes.com/atimes/Japan/HK07Dh01.html).

102. Ministry of Foreign Affairs of Japan, "Joint Statement," July 13, 2004 (www.mofa.go.jp/region/middle_e/kuwait/joint0407.html).

103. "Japan, Kuwait Foreign Ministers Agree on Need for Mideast Reforms," Japan Economic Newswire, July 12, 2004 (www.nexis.com).

104. "Japan PM in Kuwait on Third Leg of Mideast Tour," *Kuwait Times,* May 1, 2007 (http://kuwaittimes.net/read_news.php?newsid=Mzk5mdg5ndm0).

105. EIA, Country Analysis Briefs, "Japan—Background," September 2008 (www.eia.doe.gov/emeu/cabs/Japan/pdf.pdf).

106. "Japan's Trade Deficit with Kuwait Widens First Time in 13 Months," Kuwait News Agency (KUNA), December 21, 2009 (www.kuna.net.kw/NewsAgenciesPublicSite/ArticleDetails.aspx?Language=en&id=2048906).

107. Kuwaiti Embassy, Japan, "Kuwait-Japan Relations" (http://kuwait-embassy.or.jp/E_k-j_01.shtml).

108. Ministry of Foreign Affairs of Japan, "Japan-Kuwait Relations," July 2009 (www.mofa.go.jp/region/middle_e/kuwait/index.html).

109. Ibid.

110. "Japan's Mitsui & Co Secures $1.3 Billion Plant Order from Kuwait," *Wall Street Journal Market Watch,* June 26, 2007 (www.marketwatch.com/story/japans-mitsui-co-secures-13-billion-plant-order-from-kuwait).

111. "Japan, Kuwait Renew Energy Partnership," *Middle East Online,* May 1, 2007 (http://middle-east-online.com/English/kuwait/?id=20553).

112. Ministry of Foreign Affairs of Japan, "Japan Saudi Arabia Relations," October 2008 (www.mofa.go.jp/region/middle_e/saudi).

113. "Premier Abe's Visit to Augment Close Ties," *Arab News,* April 28, 2007 (www.arabnews.com/?page=7&section=0&article=92488&d=28&m=4&y=2007).

114. Ministry of Foreign Affairs of Japan, press conference, February 2, 2001 (www.mofa.go.jp/announce/press/2001/2/202.html#6).

115. EIA, Country Analysis Briefs, "Japan."

116. Japan Ministry of Finance, Trade Statistics (www.customs.go.jp/toukei/info/index_e.htm).

117. Ministry of Foreign Affairs of Japan, "Japan Saudi Arabia Relations."

118. Ibid.

119. Ambassador Faisal H. Trad, "Saudi Arabia National Day Message September 2005," transcript, Royal Embassy of Saudi Arabia, Tokyo (www.saudiembassy.or.jp/En/EmbNews/New/EmbassyNews/NDA.htm).

120. "Under the Patronage of King Abdullah Petro Rabigh Celebrates Its Inauguration," press release, Petro Rabigh, November 2009 (www.petrorabigh.com/en/Press_Releases/press6.aspx).

121. "Japan, Saudi Arabia Agree to Launch FTA Talks with GCC," Japan Economic Newswire, April 6, 2006 (www.bilaterals.org/article.php3?id_article=4329).

122. Hisane Masaki, "New Energy to Japan's Diplomacy," *Asia Times,* May 4, 2007 (www.atimes.com/atimes/Japan/IE04Dh01.html).

123. "Japan Exports Body Reports 41.8% Climb in Trade with UAE," *Gulf News,* May 12, 2009 (http://gulfnews.com/business/economy/japan-exports-body-reports-41-8-climb-in-trade-with-uae-1.68518).

124. EIA, Country Analysis Briefs, "Japan—Background."

125. "Japan-UAE Joint Economic Committee Setup," *Gulf News,* April 30, 2007 (http://archive.gulfnews.com/articles/07/04/30/10121926.html).

126. "Mitsubishi Fuso Opens Parts Distribution Center in Dubai As Middle East and Africa Sales Rise," press release, Mitsubishi Fuso Truck and Bus Corporation, April 17, 2007 (www.mitsubishi-fuso.com/en/press/070417/070417.html).

127. Brian Bremner and Assif Shameen, "The Ties That Bind the Middle East and Asia," *Business Week,* May 21, 2007 (www.businessweek.com/globalbiz/content/may2007/gb20070518_344191.htm).

128. Japanese Embassy, Oman, "Bilateral Relations—History" (www.oman.emb-japan.go.jp/4-001history.htm).

129. Japanese Embassy, Oman, "Bilateral Relations—Culture"(www.oman.emb-japan.go.jp/4-004culture.htm).

130. Japan Ministry of Finance, Trade Statistics (www.customs.go.jp/toukei/info/index_e.htm).

131. "UAE Supplies Japan 26% of Its Oil Need," Emirates News Agency, July 1, 2007.

132. "Omani Exports to Japan Surge 54.2 pc," *Oman Daily Observer,* January 21, 2010 (www.zawya.com/printstory.cfm?storyid=ZAWYA20090702034227&l=034200090702).

133. Japanese Embassy, Oman, "Bilateral Relations—Economy," August 2009 (www.oman.emb-japan.go.jp/4-003economy.htm).

134. Ministry of Foreign Affairs of Japan, "Japan Oman Relations" (www.mofa.go.jp/region/middle_e/oman/).

135. "Japan, Qatar Reaffirm Ties on Energy Supply, Education," *Japan Times,* May 3, 2007 (http://search.japantimes.co.jp/cgi-bin/nn20070503a3.html).

136. "Qatar Seeks Japan's Support for Developing Nuclear Energy," *Forbes,* May 1, 2007 (www.forbes.com/business/feeds/afx/2007/05/01/afx3672966.html).

137. Mai Iida, "Doha Bank to Promote Two-Way Investment between Japan, Qatar," *Japan Times,* February 4, 2007 (http://search.japantimes.co.jp/cgi-bin/nb20070204a3.html).

138. Iida, "Doha Bank to Promote Two Way Investment between Japan, Qatar"; "Update 2—Mitsui to Build $1.3 BN Power Plant," Reuters U.K., June 26, 2007 (http://uk.reuters.com/article/idUKT26886520070626), "Kuwait MEW – Shuaiba North Power and Desalination Plant," Zawya Projects (www.zawya.com/projects/project.cfm?pid=140107102731&cc).

139. "Japan, Qatar Reaffirm Ties on Energy Supply, Education," *Japan Times,* May 3, 2007.

140. "Qatar Committed to Meet World's LNG Demands: Attiyah," *Peninsula Online,* December 8, 2009 (www.thepeninsulaqatar.com/Display_news.asp?section=Business_News&subsection=Local+Business&month=December2009&file=Business_News200912082339.xml).

141. EIA, "OPEC Revenues Fact Sheet," January 2010 (www.eia.doe.gov/emeu/cabs/OPEC_Revenues/Factsheet.html).

142. "South Korean Giants Target Middle East as UAE Leads Recovery for Construction Industry," AMEinfo.com, October 1, 2009 (www.ameinfo.com/210907.html).

143. "Korea, Saudi Arabia Agree to Widen Ties in Energy, IT, Education," *Korea Herald,* March 26, 2007 (www.nexis.com).

144. "Roh, Abdullah Discuss Mideast," *Arab News,* March 25, 2007 (www.arabnews.com/?page=1&section=0&article=94170&d=25&m=3&y=2007).

145. EIA, Country Analysis Briefs, "South Korea," June 2007 (www.eia.doe.gov/cabs/South_Korea/Oil.html).

146. "S. Korea, Saudi Arabia Agree to Widen Relations to IT, Education," Yonhap News Agency, March 24, 2007 (www.nexis.com).

147. Perry Williams, "Oppurtunity Knocks in the Gulf for South Korea," Middle East Economic Digest (MEED), September 9, 2009 (www.meed.com/supplements/opportunity-knocks-in-the-gulf-for-south-korea/3000534.article#at).

148. "Aramco Looks to Boost Ties with Korean Refiners, Universities," *Korea Herald,* December 3, 2009 (www.nexis.com).

149. EIA, Country Analysis Briefs, "South Korea."

150. "Aramco Looks to Boost Ties with Korean Refiners, Universities," *Korea Herald.*

151. "S. Korea, Saudi Arabia Agree to Widen Relations to IT, Education," Yonhap News Agency.

152. "Over eighty Saudi Arabian students to enroll in S. Korean universities in March," Yonhap News Agency, February 22, 2007 (www.nexis.com).

153. "Korea-Arab Friendship Express Caravan to Be Held," Korea.net, October 13, 2008 (www.korea.net/News/News/NewsView.asp?serial_no=20081015007).

154. Parviz Esmaeili, "Bright Outlook for Iran-South Korea Ties," *Tehran Times,* October 16, 2007 (www.tehrantimes.com/index_View.asp?code=154987).

155. Ministry of Foreign Affairs and Trade, Republic of Korea, "Iran: Bilateral Ties" (www.mofat.go.kr/english/regions/meafrica/20070824/1_1355.jsp?board=board&boardid=&key=1).

156. "South Korean Official Regards Iran as a Neighboring Country," *Tehran Times,* May 4, 2009 (www.tehrantimes.com/NCms/2007.asp?code=193781).

157. Esmaeili, "Bright Outlook for Iran-South Korea Ties."

158. "The Republic of Korea and the Iran Nuclear Issue," James Martin Center for Nonproliferation Studies, Monterey Institute of International Studies, February 14, 2006 (http://cns.miis.edu/research/iran/reaction/skorea.htm).

159. "South Korea Tries to Solace Furious Iran," Islamic Republic News Agency (IRNA), November 29, 2003 (www.globalsecurity.org/wmd/library/news/iran/2003/iran-031129-irna02.htm).

160. Ariel Farrar-Wellman, "South Korea–Iran Foreign Relations," American Enterprise Institute, Washington (www.irantracker.org/foreign-relations/south-korea-iran-foreign-relations#at).

161. "South Korea Expresses 'Concern' Over Iran's Nuclear Activity," Yonhap News Agency, January 11, 2006 (www.nexis.com).

CHAPTER FIVE

1. Armand Cucciniello and Pramit Mitra, "India and Israel Move Closer Together," *South Asia Monitor*, No. 63 (Washington: Center for Strategic and International Studies, October 1, 2003) (http://csis.org/files/media/csis/pubs/sam63.pdf).

2. Harsh Pant, "India Israel Partnership: Convergence and Constraints," *Middle East Review of International Affairs* 8, no.4 (December 2004), pp. 60–73, p. 61 (http://meria.idc.ac.il/journal/2004/issue4/pant.pdf); Efraim Inbar, "The Indian-Israeli Entente," *Orbis* (Winter 2004), p. 61 (www.biu.ac.il/SOC/besa/Inbar.pdf).

3. Cucciniello and Mitra, "India and Israel Move Closer Together."

4. Stephen Cohen, *India: Emerging Power* (Brookings, 2001), pp. 247–48. Inbar, "The Indian-Israeli Entente," p. 91; Pant, "India Israel Partnership," p. 61.

5. Subhash Kapila, "India-Israel Relations: The Imperative for Enhanced Strategic Cooperation," South Asian Analysis Group, August 1, 2000 (www.southasiaanalysis.org/%5Cpapers2%5Cpaper131.html).

6. Harsh Pant, "India Israel Partnership," p. 67.

7. "India-Israel: Sharon's Visit: Vow to Jointly Fight Terrorism," *India News Online*, September 15, 2003 (http://news.indiamart.com/news-analysis/india-israel-sharon--773.html).

8. Government of India, Ministry of Defence, "Defence Cooperation" (http://mod.nic.in/ainstitutions/body.htm).

9. Bethany Tindall and Pramit Mitra, "Pakistan and Israel: An Emerging Entente," *South Asia Monitor*, No.88 (Washington: Center for Strategic and International Studies, November 3, 2005) (http://csis.org/files/media/csis/pubs/sam88.pdf).

10. Harsh Pant, "India Israel Partnership," p. 62.

11. Rajesh Rajagopalan, "Restoring Normalcy: The Evolution of the Indian Army's Counterinsurgency Doctrine," *Strategic Affairs,* August 16, 2001 (www.stratmag.com/issue2Aug-15/page07.htm).

12. Harsh Pant, "India Israel Partnership," p. 67.

13. T. S. Subramanian, "Space Launches and the Cost Factor," *The Hindu,* November 16, 2007 (www.thehindu.com/2007/11/16/stories/2007111654451300.htm).

14. Yossi Melman, "Satellite Launch Bolsters Ability to Spy on Tehran," *Haaretz,* January 21, 2008 (www.haaretz.com/hasen/spages/946750.html).

15. Israeli Embassy, New Delhi, "Israeli Experts to Train Indian Professionals on 'International Marketing for Agribusiness,'" MASHAV—International Cooperation: Local Mashav Activities, May 5, 2006 (http://delhi.mfa.gov.il/mfm).

16. "Pawar Signs Agriculture Work Plan with Israel," *The Hindu*, May 12, 2006 (www.hindu.com/2006/05/12/stories/2006051204831500.htm).

17. David Isenberg, "Israel's Role in China's New Warplane," *Asia Times*, December 4, 2002 (www.atimes.com/atimes/China/DL04Ad01.html).

18. Herb Keinon, "Ally in the Making," *Sino-Judaic Institute Points East*, February 3, 2005 (www.sino-judaic.org/pointseast/ally.html).

19. Harsh V. Pant, *Alternative Superpowers and the Middle East*, LFI Policy Focus, Summer 2008, pp. 5–6 (www.lfi.org.uk/files/LFI%20Policy%20Focus%20-%20China%20and%20the%20Middle%20East.pdf).

20. David Isenberg, "Israel's Role in China's New Warplane."

21. Harsh V. Pant, *Alternative Superpowers and the Middle East*, p. 7.

22. Yakov Katz, "Latest Rockets Manufactured in China," *Jerusalem Post*, January 1, 2009. See also Bill Gertz, "Inside the Ring," *Washington Times*, January 29, 2009.

23. "Japan's Koizumi Urges Israel Not to Seek 'Eye for Eye,'" Associated Press, July 12, 2006 (www.foxnews.com/printer_friendly_story/0,3566,203095,00.html).

24. Central Bureau of Statistics (Israel), "Imports by Country of Purchase and Exports by Country of Destination" (www1.cbs.gov.il/shnaton60/st16_03x.pdf).

25. Jeanette Goldman, "Tokyo Hosts Israel-Japan Diamond Trade Seminar," Diamonds.net (www.diamonds.net/news/NewsItem.aspx?ArticleID=16157).

26. Yoni Teltz, "Building Bridges to Japan," *Jerusalem Post*, June 25, 2007 (www.jpost.com/servlet/satellite?cid=118240932094).

27. Yaacov Cohen, "The Improvement in Israeli–South Korean Relations," *Jewish Political Studies Review* 18 (Spring 2006), pp. 1–2 (https://secured4.catom.com/JCPA/Templates/ShowPage.asp?DRIT=5&DBID=1&LNGID=1&TMID=111&FID=625&PID=860&IID=1016&TTL=The_Improvement_in_Israeli-South_Korean_Relations).

28. Israeli Ministry of Foreign Affairs, "FM Livni to Visit South Korea and Japan," January 15, 2007 (www.mfa.gov.il/MFA/About+the+Ministry/MFA+Spokesman/2007/FM+Livni+to+visit+South+Korea+and+Japan+15-Jan-2007.htm).

29. Choi Soung-ah, "Korea, Israel to Push for FTA: Israeli Minister," *Korea Herald*, January 18, 2005 (www.bilaterals.org/article.php3?id_article=1191).

30. Ibid.

31. Yaacov Cohen, "The Improvement in Israeli–South Korean Relations."

32. Israeli Embassy, Singapore, "Bilateral Relations: Historical Overview" (http://singapore.mfa.gov.il/mfm/web/main/document.asp?SubjectID=2010&MissionID=58&LanguageID=0&StatusID=0&DocumentID=-1).

33. Meir Javedanfar, "Israel's Central Asian Power Play," *International Analyst Network*, June 4, 2009 (www.analyst-network.com/article.php?art_id=2965).

34. Joanna Sloame, "The Virtual Jewish History Tour—Azerbaijan," American-Israeli Cooperative Enterprise (www.jewishvirtuallibrary.org/jsource/vjw/Azerbaijan.html#ir).

CHAPTER SIX

1. Kevin Whitelaw, "Dubai Rides the Oil Boom," *U.S. News and World Report*, June 5, 2008 (www.usnews.com/articles/news/world/2008/06/05/dubai-rides-the-oil-boom.html).

2. "Dubai's Building Frenzy Lays Foundation for Global Power," *Sunday Times*, May 21, 2006 (http://business.timesonline.co.uk/tol/business/industry_sectors/construction_and_property/article722549.ece).

3. "A Little Oil, a Lot of Land and 100% Debt," *Haaretz*, December 1, 2009 (www.haaretz.com/hasen/spages/1131630.html).

4. Nakheel, "See What We Are Building: Palm Jebel Ali" (www.nakheel.com/developments/).

5. "Dubai's Palm and World Islands: Progress Update," October 4, 2007 (www.ameinfo.com/133896.html).

6. Nakheel, "See What We Are Building: The Universe" (www.nakheel.com/developments/).

7. Kevin Whitelaw, "6 New Dazzling Dubai Developments," *U.S. News and World Report*, June 5, 2008 (www.usnews.com/articles/news/world/2008/06/05/6-new-dazzling-dubai-developments.html).

8. Emaar Properties PJSC, "Burj Dubai" (www.burjdubai.com).

9. "Dubai International Airport Defies Worldwide Trend," *Gulf News*, December 26, 2009 (http://gulfnews.com/business/aviation/dubai-international-airport-defies-worldwide-trend-1.558055).

10. Ibid.

11. Ibid.

12. Christopher M. Davidson, *Dubai: The Vulnerability of Success* (Columbia University Press, 2008), p. 111. Davidson's prescient book was published before the economic crisis of late 2008 but it remains a sober and thorough analysis of the challenges facing Dubai, whose success is based on global growth and ample sources of credit.

13. National U.S.-Arab Chamber of Commerce, "The East-West Transport Hub," *U.S. Arab Tradeline* 15, no.3 (June 2007), p. 7 (www.nusacc.org/images/stories/Publications/USArabTradeline/trdln0607_uae.pdf).

14. Cathy Buyck, "Big, Bigger, Biggest," *Air Transport World*, November 2007, p. 26 (www.atwonline.com/channels/airlineFocus/article.html?articleID=2114).

15. Patrick Verdonck, "Emirates Airline Executive Shares Success Story That Began '22 Years Ago with Two Planes in the Desert,'" *The Wharton Journal*, November 5, 2007 (www.whartonjournal.com/media/storage/paper201/news/2007/11/05/News/).

16. "Emirates Airlines Orders 4 More Airbus A380 Superjumbos," Associated Press, May 7, 2007 (www.aviationnews.us/articles.php?art_id=2972&start=1).

17. Davidson, *Dubai: The Vulnerability of Success*, p. 110.

18. "Emirates Airline Raises $1.13 Billion," *Wall Street Journal*, December 10, 2009 (online.wsj.com/article/SB10001424052748703514404574587702499896132.html).

19. Flydubai, "Flydubai Makes Low Cost Travel to Dubai a Reality," June 1, 2009, press release (www.flydubai.com/whatsnew.aspx).

20. Anthony Lawler, "Point-to-Point, Hub-to-Hub: The Need for an A380 Size Aircraft," Leeham Company, April 4, 2006 (www.leeham.net/filelib/A380_Lawler.pdf).

21. "World Container Port League 2005 (Top 50)," International Association of Ports and Harbors (www.iaphworldports.org/world_port_info/WorldPortTraffic League(2005).pdf).

22. "Jebel Ali's Container Capacity to Grow 27%," *Gulf News,* January 28, 2008 (www.gulfnews.com/BUSINESS/Shipping/10185601.html).

23. National U.S.-Arab Chamber of Commerce, "The East-West Transport Hub."

24. "Jebel Ali Set to Take over Port Rashid's Cargo Business," *Khaleej Times,* April 27, 2008 (www.khaleejtimes.com/DisplayArticleNew.asp?section=business& xfile=data/business/2008/april/business_april818.xml).

25. Kevin Whitelaw, "Abu Dhabi's Buying Binge," *U.S. News and World Report,* June 5, 2008 (www.usnews.com/articles/news/world/2008/06/05/abu-dhabis-buying-binge.html).

26. "Best Middle Eastern Ports," ArabianBusiness.com, February 26, 2008 (www. arabianbusiness.com/511600-best-middle-eastern-ports).

27. Kevin Whitelaw, "6 New Dazzling Dubai Developments."

28. Dubai Desert Classic (www.dubaidesertclassic.com/).

29. Events in Dubai (www.dubaiholidayspecialists.com/Events_in_Dubai.asp).

30. Dubai World Cup (www.dubairacingclub.com/dubai-world-cup/default.asp).

31. Dubai International Film Festival (www.dubaifilmfest.com/); Dubai Event Calendar 2009 (www.index.ae/event_calendar_2009.php).

32. Dubai Department of Tourism and Commerce Marketing, "DTCM Announces Five Percent Increase in Dubai Hotels' Guests in Q1 2009," May 11, 2009 (www.dubaitourism.ae/PressReleases/PressReleaseList/tabid/183/ctl/Details/ mid/561/ItemID/2596/language/en-US/Default.aspx); "Cruise Tourists Arrive in Dubai 5,076," November 11, 2009 (www.dubaitourism.ae/PressReleases/Press ReleaseList/tabid/183/ctl/Details/mid/561/ItemID/2727/language/en-US/Default. aspx); "Dubai's Department of Tourism Makes a Mark at WTM 2008," November 28, 2008 (www.dubaitourism.ae/PressReleases/PressReleaseList/tabid/183/ctl/ Details/mid/561/ItemID/2487/language/en-US/Default.aspx).

33. Tamara Walid, "Dubai Tourism Takes a Hit as Hotel Occupancy Rate Falls," Reuters, May 19, 2009 (www.zawya.com/Story.cfm/sidDS190509_dsart58Dubai% 20tourism%20takes%20hit%20as%20hotel%20occupancy%20rate%20falls/).

34. Kevin Whitelaw, "Dubai Rides the Oil Boom."

35. U.K. Foreign and Commonwealth Office, Travel Advice by Country: UAE (www.fco.gov.uk/en/travelling-and-living-overseas/travel-advice-by-country/ middle-east-north-africa/united-arab-emirates); Abdul Hameed Bakier, "An Al-Qaeda Threat to the UAE?" *Terrorism Focus* 5, no. 25 (Washington: Jamestown Foundation, July 1, 2008) (www.jamestown.org/single/?no_cache=1&tx_ttnews% 5Btt_news%5D=5025).

36. Andrew England, "Managing Challenges of Soaring Growth," *Financial Times*, May 15, 2008.

37. "Oil boom Triggers Vast Expansion in Gulf Airports," Agence France-Presse, October 7, 2007 (http://afp.google.com/article/ALeqM5iIyU_gz9wJBNmLA7aMs-YkxEi Lnw?index=0).

38. "Celebrity Architects Reveal a Daring Cultural Xanadu for the Arab World," *New York Times*, February 1, 2007 (www.nytimes.com/2007/02/01/arts/design/01isla. html).

39. Ibid.

40. Abu Dhabi Tourism Authority, "Abu Dhabi Population 2001-10" (www. visitabudhabi.ae/en/uae.facts.and.figures/population.aspx).

41. Formula1, "2009 Formula 1 Etihad Airways Abu Dhabi Grand Prix" (www. formula1.com/races/in_detail/abu_dhabi_823/).

42. "Abu Dhabi's US$3.3Bn Desert Island Dream," Asia Times Online, October 20, 2000 (www.atimes.com/reports/BJ20Ai01.html).

43. Ibid.

44. Bryan Walsh, "Renewable Energy: Desert Dreams," *Time*, February 14, 2008 (www.time.com/time/specials/2007/article/0,28804,1712863_1712864,00.html).

45. Ibid.

46. Paul Reynolds, "French Make Serious Move into the Gulf," BBC News, January 15, 2008 (http://news.bbc.co.uk/2/hi/middle_east/7189481.stm).

47. "US-UAE Nuclear Deal to Take Effect Soon-State Dept," Reuters, October 22, 2009 (www.reuters.com/article/marketsNews/idUSN2220155420091022).

48. Ibid.

49. Ibid.

50. Ibid.

51. "A Model Nuclear Power Deal?" *New York Times*, February 3, 2009 (www. nytimes.com/2009/02/03/world/americas/03iht-letter.1.19890840.html?page wanted=1&_r=1).

52. Christopher M. Blanchard and Paul K. Kerr, "The United Arab Emirates Nuclear Program and Proposed U.S. Nuclear Cooperation," Congressional Research Service, March 10, 2009 (http://assets.opencrs.com/rpts/R40344_20090310.pdf).

53. "Oil Boom Triggers Vast Expansion in Gulf Airports."

54. Nick Summers, "Olympics: Will Doha Get the Gold?" *Newsweek*, October 16, 2006 (www.newsweek.com/id/44994).

55. "Doha Fails to Make Olympic Shortlist," *Gulf Times*, June 5, 2008 (www. gulf-times.com/site/topics/article.asp?cu_no=2&item_no=222672&version=1& template_id=57&parent_id=56).

56. "Singapore Ranks Eighth in Accommodation Costs in Asia According to Survey," ECA International, May 22, 2007 (www.eca-international.com/showpress-release.aspx?ArticleID=6467).

57. "The Gleaming Towers of Doha," *fDi Magazine*, October 5, 2006 (www.fd imagazine.com/news/fullstory.php/aid/1828/The_gleaming_towers_of_Doha.html).

58. Ibid.

59. Elsa Baxter, "Supply of Doha Homes Now Exceeding Demand," ArabianBusiness. com, October 4, 2009 (www.arabianbusiness.com/569255-supply-of-doha-homes-now-exceeding-demand#at).

60. Ibid.

61. "Oil Boom Triggers Vast Expansion in Gulf Airports."

62. James Boley, "Cashing in with Kuwait," ConstructionWeekonline.com, October 15, 2009 (www.constructionweekonline.com/article-6594-cashing-in-with-kuwait/).

63. Tom Arnold, "City of Silk," ArabianBusiness.com, August 21, 2008 (www. arabianbusiness.com/528459?newsletter=1).

64. "Oil Boom Triggers Vast Expansion in Gulf Airports."

65. Benjamin Millington, "Bahrain Contractors Facing Squeeze in Downturn," ArabianBusiness.com, October 28, 2009 (www.arabianbusiness.com/571839-bahrain-contractors-facing-squeeze-in-downturn).

66. Bahrain Financial Harbour Media Centre, "Bahrain Financial Exchange to Set up Operations at Bahrain Financial Harbour," August 30, 2009 (www.bfharbour. com/html/mediacentre/latestnews.php?id=51).

67. Bahrain World Trade Center, "About BWTC" (www.bahrainwtc.com/real estate.htm).

68. Oman Airports Management Company, "New Airport" (www.omanairports. com/seeb_newterminal.asp).

69. "Saudi Arabia Attracts $410b in Construction Projects," Middle East North Africa Financial Network, August 16, 2008 (www.menafn.com/qn_news_story_s.asp? StoryId=1093208190).

70. Central Intelligence Agency (CIA), *The World Factbook 2009: Saudi Arabia, UAE, and Qatar* (www.cia.gov/library/publications/the-world-factbook).

71. Barbara Cockburn, "Major Expansion Planned for Saudi Airports," Arabian Business.com, November 7, 2006 (www.arabianbusiness.com/488214?ln=en).

72. Hong Kong Trade Development Council, "Construction Boom in UAE and Saudi Arabia: Opportunities for Hong Kong," August 2, 2007 (www.hktdc.com/info/ mi/a/ef/en/1X006SZP/1/Economic-Forum/Construction-Boom-In-UAE-And-Saudi-Arabia-Opportunities-For-Hong-Kong.htm).

73. United World, "Updating the Rail System," *Our World*, March 29, 2006, p. 15 (www.unitedworld-usa.com/pdf/saudiarabia.pdf); Impact Media Global, "Land Bridge Project," *Saudi Arabia: Climate for Change*, p. 4 (www.washingtonpost. com/wp-adv/specialsales/spotlight/saudiarabia/images/Saudi_Arabia_Climate_For_ Change.pdf).

74. Ibid.

75. "China to Build Mecca Monorail," *Straits Times*, February 12, 2009 (www. straitstimes.com/Breaking%2BNews/Asia/Story/STIStory_337287.html).

76. Conrad Egbert, "Tenders for $4bn Saudi-Egypt Causeway This Year," ArabianBusiness.com, March 1, 2008 (www.arabianbusiness.com/512333-tenders-for-4bn-saudi-egypt-causeway-this-year).

77. Hong Kong Trade Development Council, "Construction Boom in UAE and Saudi Arabia: Opportunities for Hong Kong."

78. Pamela Ann Smith, "Opening the Door to Foreign Investment in the Arab World," *The Middle East*, May 2008, pp. 28–31.

79. UN Conference on Trade and Development, "7.3 Foreign Direct Investment: Inward and Outward Flows and Stocks," *UNCTAD Handbook of Statistics 2009* (http://stats.unctad.org/Handbook/TableViewer/tableView.aspx?ReportId=1923); UNCTAD, *World Investment Report 2009*, pp. 57–58 (www.unctad.org/en/docs/wir2009_en.pdf).

80. Organization for Economic Cooperation and Development, "FDI Flows by Partner Country," OECD.Stat Extracts (http://stats.oecd.org/Index.aspx?DataSet Code=FDI_FLOW_PARTNER).

81. Indian Embassy, Riyadh, "India-Saudi Arabia Business Relations" (www.indianembassy.org.sa/IndiaSaudiRelations.html). Note: All figures are in terms of FDI flows.

82. Martin Reiser and Dennis DeTray, "Uzbekistan," in *The New Silk Roads: Transport and Trade in Greater Central Asia*, edited by S. Frederick Starr (Washington: Central Asia-Caucasus Institute and Silk Road Studies Program, 2007), p. 206.

83. Ibid., p. 207.

84. Ibid., pp. 208–09.

85. Asian Development Bank, "ADB Funds Upgrade of Key 'Silk Road' Highway in Uzbekistan," news release, December 20, 2007 (www.adb.org/Media/Articles/007/12353-uzbekistan-roads-projects/).

86. Transport Corridor Europe-Caucusus-Asia, "FAQ" (www.traceca-org.org/tp/faq.php?l=eng).

87. Gulshan Sachdeva, "India," in *The New Silk Roads: Transport and Trade in Greater Central Asia*, edited by S. Frederick Starr (Washington: Central Asia-Caucasus Institute and Silk Road Studies Program, 2007), p. 358.

88. C. Christine Fair, "Indo-Iranian Ties: Thicker than Oil," *The Middle East Review of International Affairs 11*, no. 1 (2007) (http://meria.idc.ac.il/journal/2007/issue1/jv11no1a9.html).

89. Ibid.

90. Ibid.

91. Government of India, Ministry of External Affairs, "New Delhi Declaration" text, January 25, 2003 (http://meaindia.nic.in/speech/2003/01/25spc01.htm).

92. Niklas Swanstrom and others, "China," in *The New Silk Roads: Transport and Trade in Greater Central Asia*, edited by S. Frederick Starr (Washington: Central Asia-Caucasus Institute and Silk Road Studies Program, 2007), p. 407.

93. Asian Development Bank, "The Status of Regional Trade and Transport," in *Connecting Central Asia: A Road Map for Regional Cooperation* (2006) p. 7 (www.adb.org/Documents/Books/Connecting-Central-Asia-Road-Map/default.asp).

94. Asian Development Bank, *Rebuilding the Silk Road, Encouraging Economic Cooperation in Central Asia: The Role of the Asian Development Bank* (Central

Asian Development Bank Brochures, 2001), p. 18 (www.adb.org/documents/brochures/silk_road/default.asp?p=carcpub).

95. Asian Development Bank, "The Status of Regional Trade and Transport," p. 10.

96. Andrew Maiden, "Iran in the Middle: The Revival of a North-South Trade Corridor Linking Europe with Southern Asia Will Enhance Iran's Influence in the Middle East," *The Middle East*, January 2003, pp. 40–41.

97. "Central Asia/Caucasus: Silk Road Conference Agrees on Eurasian Corridor," Radio Free Europe/Radio Liberty, September 9, 1998 (www.rferl.org/content/article/1089437.html).

98. Vladimir Boyko, "Russia," in *The New Silk Roads: Transport and Trade in Greater Central Asia,* edited by S. Frederick Starr (Washington: Central Asia-Caucasus Institute and Silk Road Studies Program, 2007), pp. 472–73.

99. "India, Pakistan to Discuss IPI, TAPI Pipeline Next Week," *Thaindian News,* April 14, 2008 (www.thaindian.com/newsportal/south-asia/india-pakistan-to-discuss-ipi-tapi-pipeline-next-week_10037933.html).

100. "Uzbekistan Announces Gas Pipeline Project with China," Agence France-Presse, April 14, 2008 (www.energy-daily.com/reports/Uzbekistan_announces_gas_pipeline_project_with_China_999.html).

101. Ibid.

102. "China, Kazakhstan to Press ahead with Pipeline," The Caspian Information Centre, November 8, 2007 (www.caspianinfo.org/news.php).

Chapter Seven

1. See appendix B for more details on undersea cable networks in the Gulf and Indian Ocean.

2. Robert Kaplan, "How We Would Fight China" *Atlantic*, June 2005, pp. 49–64; Robert Kaplan, "America's Elegant Decline" *Atlantic*, November 2007, pp. 104–16; Robert Kaplan, "Lost at Sea," *New York Times*, September 21, 2007, p. A19. Kaplan presents a more nuanced overview of his theme "elegant decline" in a 2009 *Foreign Affairs* essay. He argues that the key role of the United States in the Indian Ocean is to be a "coalition builder supreme, ready to work with any Navy that agrees to cooperate with it." He concludes that the United States remains the vital link to future security but that "indispensability rather than dominance must be the goal." Robert Kaplan, "Center Stage for the Twenty-First Century: Power Plays in the Indian Ocean," *Foreign Affairs* (March/April 2009), pp. 16–32.

3. Robert Farley, "The False Decline of the U.S. Navy," *American Prospect*, October 23, 2007 (www.prospect.org/cs/articles?article=the_false_decline_of_the_us_navy).

4. The revolution in military affairs describes a U.S. military view according to which the future of warfare depends on technological and organizational transformation and total systems integration.

5. International Chamber of Commerce (ICC) International Maritime Bureau, *ICC-IMB Piracy and Armed Robbery against Ships Report— Second Quarter 2007* (London), p. 26.

6. United Nations Peacekeeping, *Monthly Summary of Military and Police Contribution to United Nations Operations* (www.un.org/Depts/dpko/dpko/contributors/).

7. United Nations Conference on Trade and Development (UNCTAD), *World Investment Report 2007: Transnational Corporations, Extractive Industries and Development— Major FDI Indicators* (www.unctad.org/en/docs/wir2007_en.pdf).

8. ICC International Maritime Bureau, *ICC-IMB Piracy and Armed Robbery against Ships Annual Report* (London, 2009), p. 3.

9. Martin N. Murphy, "Contemporary Piracy and Maritime Terrorism: The Threat to International Security," Adelphi Paper 388 (International Institute for Strategic Studies, July 9, 2007), p. 13.

10. Peter Gwin, "Dark Passage." *National Geographic*, October 2007, p. 139.

11. Ibid.

12. Murphy, "Contemporary Piracy and Maritime Terrorism: the Threat to International Security," p. 23.

13. ICC International Maritime Bureau, *ICC-IMB Piracy and Armed Robbery against Ships Report—Second Quarter 2007*, p. 26.

14. ICC International Maritime Bureau, *ICC-IMB Piracy and Armed Robbery against Ships Annual Report* (London, 2008), p. 5.

15. ICC International Maritime Bureau, IMB Piracy Reporting Centre (www.icc-ccs.org/index.php?option=com_content&view=article&id=30&Itemid=12).

16. Gwin, "Dark Passage," p. 134.

17. ICC International Maritime Bureau, *ICC-IMB Piracy and Armed Robbery against Ships Report— Second Quarter 2007*, p. 25.

18. Ibid., p. 26.

19. Data taken from: ICC International Maritime Bureau, *ICC-IMB Piracy and Armed Robbery against Ships Annual Report* (2008), pp. 5–6; ICC International Maritime Bureau, *ICC-IMB Piracy and Armed Robbery against Ships Report for the Record* (2009), pp. 5–6.

20. Catherine Zara Raymond, "Piracy and Armed Robbery in the Malacca Strait: A Problem Solved?" *National War College Review* 62, no. 3 (Summer 2009), pp. 31–42.

21. U.S. Naval Forces Central Command, U.S. Fifth Fleet, "Combined Maritime Forces" (www.cusnc.navy.mil/cmf/cmf_command.html).

22. U.S. Department of Defense, Office of the Assistant Secretary of Defense (Public Affairs), news transcript, Vice Admiral David Nichols, Commander, U.S. Naval Forces Central Command and Commander of the U.S. Fifth Fleet, Defense Department Briefing, September 22, 2005 (www.globalsecurity.org/military/library/news/2005/09/mil-050922-dod01.htm).

23. ICC International Maritime Bureau, *ICC-IMB Piracy and Armed Robbery against Ships Annual Report* (2009), pp. 5–6.

24. International Institute for Strategic Studies, *The Military Balance 2008* (London: Europa, 2008).

25. Kaplan, "America's Elegant Decline."

26. Terror Free Tomorrow: The Center for Public Opinion, "2006 Poll: Humanitarian Relief Sustains Change in Muslim Public Opinion" (www.terrorfreetomorrow. org/articlenav.php?id=82).

27. Mohammad Qodari, "The Tsunami, Humanitarian Aid, and the Image of the United States in the Muslim World," in *One Year after the Tsunami: Policy and Public Perceptions*, Asia Program Special Report No.130, edited by Michael Kugelman (Washington: Woodrow Wilson Center, 2006), p. 9.

28. Drew Thompson, "Tsunami Relief Reflects China's Regional Aspirations," *China Brief 5*, no. 2 (Washington: Jamestown Foundation, January 2005).

29. Ibid.

30. Josy Joseph, "Target Next: Indian Military Bases," *Rediff News*, April 21, 2003 (http://rediff.com/news/2003/apr/21josy.htm).

31. Indian Navy, "Tsunami Relief Operations" (http://indiannavy.nic.in/tsunami. htm).

32. Indian Navy, "'Op Sukoon'—Making 'Sweet Music,'" July 24, 2006 (http:// indiannavy.nic.in/sukoon.pdf).

33. United States Embassy, New Delhi, "U.S.-India Joint Statement: United States and India Complete Civil Nuclear Cooperation Negotiations," July 27, 2007 (http:// newdelhi.usembassy.gov/pr072707.html).

34. U.S. Department of State, "U.S. and India Release Text of 123 Agreement," August 3, 2007 (http://2001-2009.state.gov/documents/organization/90157.pdf).

35. Eric Badger, First Lieutenant USAF, "Cope India 04 Begins," United States Air Force, February 17, 2004 (www.af.mil/news/story.asp?id=123007001).

36. Nellis Air Force Base, "Nellis Air Force Base Flying Operations" (www.nellis. af.mil/library/flyingoperations.asp).

37. U.S. Navy, Seventh Fleet Public Affairs, "Exercise Malabar 07-1 Begins" (www. c7f.navy.mil/news/2007/04-april/10.htm); Rajat Pandit, "Navy Uses Wargames to Win Allies," *Times of India*, March 30, 2007 (http://timesofindia.indiatimes.com/ india/Navy-uses-wargames-to-win-allies/articleshow/1830417.cms).

38. Indian Navy, "Reaching out to Maritime Neighbors" (http://indiannavy.nic. in/events2005.pdf); Col. Rahul K. Bhonsle, "Reliving Legacy of the Cholas," *Boloji*, October 29, 2006 (http://boloji.com/opinion/0262.htm).

39. United States Army, Pacific, "Yudh Abhyas 07-02" (www.usarpac.army.mil/ news/YudhAbhyas0702.asp).

40. Gurpreet Khurana, "Indian Navy's Amphibious Leap: A Little Help from America," *India Defence*, April 7, 2006 (www.india-defence.com/reports-1703).

41. "U.S. Expects Breakthrough in Arms Sales to India," GlobalSecurity.org, May 24, 2007 (www.globalsecurity.org/military/library/news/2007/05/mil-070524-rianovosti03.htm).

42. John E. Carbaugh Jr., "U.S.-India Defense Cooperation Continues to Overcome Obstacles," US-India Friendship.net, June 2, 2003 (www.usindiafriendship.net/archives/viewpoints/carbaugh-062003-1.htm).

43. Steven Donald Smith, "U.S., India Partnership Makes World Safer, Bush Says," American Forces Press Service, March 2, 2006 (www.defense.gov/news/news article.aspx?id=15288).

44. Indian Navy, Integrated Headquarters, Ministry of Defense, "Freedom to Use the Seas: India's Maritime Military Strategy," May 2007, p. 41.

45. Kurt Campbell and Richard Weitz, "The Limits of U.S.-China Military Cooperation: Lessons from 1995–1999," *Washington Quarterly* 29, no. 1 (Winter 2005–06), p. 169.

46. Ibid., p. 181.

47. U.S. Department of Defense, "The United States Security Strategy for the East Asia-Pacific Region: 1998" (www.dod.mil/pubs/easr98/easr98.pdf), p. 31.

48. Campbell and Weitz, "The Limits of U.S.-China Military Cooperation: Lessons from 1995–1999," p. 174.

49. Ibid., p. 175.

50. Ibid., p. 178.

51. Ibid., p. 181.

52. Kathleen T. Rhem, "U.S., China Seek to Resume Military-to-Military Cooperation," American Forces Press Service, December 10, 2002 (www.globalsecurity.org/wmd/library/news/china/2002/prc-021210-dod01.htm).

53. Ibid.

54. Marc Kaufman and Dafna Linzer, "China Criticized for Anti-Satellite Missile Test," *Washington Post*, January 19, 2007, p. A1.

55. Ashley Tellis, "Punching the U.S. Military's 'Soft Ribs': China's Antisatellite Weapon Test in Strategic Perspective," *Policy Brief* 51 (Washington: Carnegie Endowment for International Peace, June 2007), pp. 1–2, 3.

56. "U.S. Defense Chief Optimistic about U.S.-China Military Relationship," Xinhua News Agency, June 2, 2007.

57. Campbell and Weitz, "The Limits of U.S.-China Military Cooperation: Lessons from 1995–1999," p. 172.

58. Christopher W. Hughes, *Japan's Re-Emergence as a "Normal" Military Power* (New York: Routledge, 2006), p. 139.

59. The Avalon Project: Yale University, "Security Treaty between the United States and Japan; September 18, 1951" (http://avalon.law.yale.edu/20th_century/japan001.asp).

60. Ministry of Foreign Affairs of Japan, "Treaty of Mutual Cooperation and Security between Japan and the United States of America" (www.mofa.go.jp/region/n-america/us/q&a/ref/1.html).

61. Peter J. Woolley, *Japan's Navy: Politics and Paradox, 1971–2000* (Boulder, Colo.: Lynne Rienner, 2000), p. 71.

62. Ministry of Foreign Affairs of Japan, "Guidelines for U.S.-Japan Defense Cooperation" (www.mofa.go.jp/region/n-america/us/security/guideline2.html).

63. Woolley, *Japan's Navy: Politics and Paradox, 1971-2000*, p. 71.

64. David Fouse, "Japan's FY 2005 National Defense Program Outline: New Concepts, Old Compromises," *Asia Pacific Center for Security Studies* 4, no. 3 (2005).

65. DefenseLINK News, "Report on the Review of the Guidelines for U.S.-Japan Defense Cooperation," June 7, 1997 (www.fas.org/news/japan/b06071997_bt295-97.htm); Ministry of Foreign Affairs of Japan, "Joint Statement: U.S.-Japan Security Consultative Committee Completion of the Review of the Guidelines for U.S.-Japan Defense Cooperation" (www.mofa.go.jp/region/n-america/us/security/defense.html).

66. Fouse, "Japan's FY 2005 National Defense Program Outline: New Concepts, Old Compromises."

67. Daniel Kliman, *Japan's Security Strategy in a Post-9/11 World: Embracing a New Realpolitik* (Westport, Conn.: Praeger, 2006).

68. Christopher Griffin, "Japan's Quiet Revolution," *Daily Standard*, October 26, 2006.

69. Ministry of Foreign Affairs of Japan, "Joint Statement of the Security Consultative Committee Alliance Transformation: Advancing United States-Japan Security and Defense Cooperation" (www.mofa.go.jp/region/n-america/us/security/scc/joint0705.html).

70. Fouse, "Japan's FY 2005 National Defense Program Outline: New Concepts Old Compromises."

71. Ministry of Foreign Affairs of Japan, "Joint Statement of the Security Consultative Committee Alliance Transformation: Advancing United States-Japan Security and Defense Cooperation."

72. David A. Fulghum and Douglas Barrie, "F-22 Tops Japan's Military Wish List," *Aviation Week and Space Technology*, April 22, 2007.

73. International Institute for Strategic Studies, *The Military Balance 2008*, p. 414.

74. Details of fleet modernization for the Indian, Chinese, and Japanese navies can be found in appendix A.

75. K. B. Vaidya, *The Naval Defence of India* (Bombay: Thacker, 1949), pp. 9, 29; K. M. Panikkar, *India and the Indian Ocean: An Essay on the Influence of Sea Power on Indian History* (London: Macmillan, 1945), pp. 83, 95; Adm. Arun Prakash, "Shaping India's Maritime Strategy—Opportunities and Challenges," speech at National Defence College, November 2005 (http://indiannavy.nic.in/cns_add2.htm).

76. Adm. Arun Prakash, "Shaping India's Maritime Strategy—Opportunities and Challenges"; Adm. AK Chatterjee Memorial Lecture, External Affairs Minister Shri Pranab Mukerjee, "International Relations and Maritime Affairs—Strategic Imperatives," June 29, 2007 (http://meaindia.nic.in/speech/2007/06/29ss01.htm); Indian Navy, "Freedom to Use the Seas: India's Maritime Military Strategy," pp. 59–60.

77. Indian Navy, "Freedom to Use the Seas: India's Maritime Military Strategy," pp. 7, 10.

78. For a balanced overview of India's maritime expectations, see Harsh Pant, "India in the Indian Ocean: Growing Mismatch between Ambitions and Capabilities," *Pacific Affairs* 82, no. 2 (2009).

79. Indian Navy, "Tacking to the Blue Waters" (http://indiannavy.nic.in/events 2003.pdf), pp. 2–3.

80. Josy Joseph, "Target Next: Indian Military Bases."

81. Indian Navy, "'Op Sukoon'—Making 'Sweet Music.'"

82. Vice Admiral G. M. Hiranandani, "Transition to Eminence: The Indian Navy 1976–1990" (http://indiannavy.nic.in/t2t2e/trans2emins/24_goodwill_visits.htm).

83. India Defence Consultants, "Make Indian Navy World Class," January 14, 2003 (www.indiadefence.com/INworldclass.htm); Indian Navy, "Tacking to the Blue Waters," p. 3.

84. Indian Navy, "Reaching out to Maritime Neighbors," pp. 6–7.

85. India Defence, "India, Fiji Conduct Naval Exercises," July 20, 2006 (www.india-defence.com/reports/2240).

86. Indian Navy, "Tacking to the Blue Waters," p. 2; David Scott, "India's Drive for a 'Blue Water' Navy," *Journal of Military and Strategic Studies* 10, no. 2 (2007–08), pp. 29–30; Embassy of India, Abu Dhabi, United Arab Emirates, "Visit of Indian Warships to Abu Dhabi" (www.indembassyuae.org/press37.phtml).

87. Embassy of India, Abu Dhabi, United Arab Emirates, "India-UAE Bilateral Relations" (www.indembassyuae.org/induae_bilateral.phtml).

88. "India Challenges China in South China Sea," *Asia Times*, April 27, 2000 (www.atimes.com/ind-pak/BD27df01.html).

89. On KONKAN: Government of India, Ministry of Defence, "Konkan-2006: Ties on Tides"; on MALABAR: U.S. Navy, Seventh Fleet Public Affairs, "Exercise Malabar 07-1 Begins"; on VARUNA: Indian Navy, "Indo-French Joint Naval Exercise 'Varuna 06'"; in general: Pandit, "Navy Uses Wargames to Win Allies."

90. Indian Navy, "Reaching out to Maritime Neighbors," p. 5; Bhonsle, "Reliving Legacy of the Cholas."

91. Donald L. Berlin, "India in the Indian Ocean," *Naval War College Review* 59, no. 2 (2006), p. 70 (www.usnwc.edu/getattachment/cc7b0300-af3a-47be-99c4-4dd3cb9c801a/India-in-the-Indian-Ocean---Berlin,-Donald-L-).

92. Chinese Military: Open and Transparent, "PLA-Foreign Military Exercises Since 2000" (http://english.chinamil.com.cn/site2/special-reports/2008-02/13/content_1122067.htm).

93. Ramtanu Maitra, "Geostrategic Import of the Coming Bay of Bengal Naval Exercise," *Executive Intelligence Review* 34, no. 29 (2007) (www.larouchepub.com/other/2007/3429bay_bengal_naval.html).

94. Indian Navy, "Tacking to the Blue Waters," pp. 2–4.

95. Indian Navy, Milan 2008, "Friendship across the Seas" (http://indiannavy.nic.in/Milan%202008.htm); Indian Navy, Milan 2008, "Schedule of Events" (http://indiannavy.nic.in/Milan%202008_files/Page1237.htm).

96. MaritimeTerrorism.com, "Maritime Security Conference in India" (www.

maritimeterrorism.com/2008/01/20/naval-delegates-from-12-countries-are-meeting-in-india-to-discuss-maritime-security-threats/).

97. Indian Navy, "Indian Ocean Naval Symposium" (http://indiannavy.nic.in/ion.htm).

98. India Defence, "Delegates Arrive for Indian Ocean Naval Symposium in New Delhi," December 2, 2008 (www.india-defence.com Indian /reports-3732).

99. MarineBuzz.com, "Navy to Host Indian Ocean Naval Symposium—IONS 2008" (www.marinebuzz.com/2008/02/13/indian-navy-to-host-indian-ocean-naval-symposium-ions-2008/).

100. Sabahat Khan, "The Impact of Future Asian Naval Security Policy on the Persian Gulf," Institute for Near East and Gulf Military Analysis (INEGMA), October 15, 2008 (www.inegma.com/?navigation=reports&page=6#).

101. Ibid.

102. Rajat Pandit, "India to Acquire New Undersea Cruise Missiles," *Times of India,* August 4, 2008 (http://timesofindia.indiatimes.com/articleshow/msid-3322388,prt page-1.cms).

103. Khan, "The Impact of Future Asian Naval Security Policy on the Persian Gulf."

104. Ibid.

105. Rediff India Abroad, "India to Get Russian Nuke Submarine Next Year," July 3, 2008 (www.rediff.com/news/2008/jul/03nuke.htm). Note: This is *Akula* according to NATO designation—an attack submarine, not a ballistic missile sub.

106. "India to Purchase Six More Submarines," *Deccan Herald,* May 9, 2008 (http://archive.deccanherald.com/Content/May92008/national2008050967096.asp?section=updatenews); "PM Launches INS Arihant in Visakhapatnam," *Times of India,* July 26, 2009 (http://timesofindia.indiatimes.com/NEWS/City/Hyderabad/PM-launches-INS-Arihant-in-Visakhapatnam/articleshow/4820660.cms).

107. Pandit, "India to Acquire New Undersea Cruise Missiles."

108. Rajat Pandit, "Navy Chief: Russia to Honour Gorchkov Deal," *Times of India,* December 1, 2007 (http://timesofindia.indiatimes.com/India/Navy_chief_Russia_has_to _honour_Gorshkov_deal_/articleshow/2586598.cms); Khan, "The Impact of Future Asian Naval Security Policy on the Persian Gulf."

109. James R. Holmes, Andrew C. Winner, Toshi Yoshihara, *Indian Naval Strategy in the 21st Century* (New York: Routledge, 2009), p. 87; Khurana, "Indian Navy's Amphibious Leap: A Little Help from America."

110. Ibid. Also see Madhvendra Singh, "The Indian Navy in 2020," *Security Research Review* 2, no. 2 (2006) (www.bharat-rakshak.com/SRR/2006/02/56.html).

111. Khan, "The Impact of Future Asian Naval Security Policy on the Persian Gulf."

112. Shov Aroor, "India, Israel Tie up on Next-Gen Barak Missiles," *Express India,* February 7, 2006 (www.expressindia.com/news/fullstory.php?newsid=62510); Khan, "The Impact of Future Asian Naval Security Policy on the Persian Gulf."

113. Singh, "The Indian Navy in 2020," p. 5.

NOTES TO PAGES 203–06

114. "India Builds Aircraft Carrier," *Straits Times*, February 27, 2009 (www.straitstimes.com/Breaking%2BNews/Asia/Story/STIStory_343449.html).

115. "INS Viraat to Be Fully Operational in 2 Months," *Times of India*, August 20, 2009 (http://timesofindia.indiatimes.com/INS-Viraat-to-be-fully-operational-in-2-months/articleshow/4913224.cms).

116. India Defence Consultants, "India's Defense Procurements," April 18, 2005 (www.indiadefence.com/defproc1.htm).

117. India Defence, "Indigenous Air Craft Carrier—Air Defence Ship—to Be Launched by October 2010: Cochin Shipyards," July 6, 2007 (www.india-defence.com/reports-3282).

118. Singh, "The Indian Navy in 2020," p. 5.

119. Ibid.

120. Thaindian News, "Delays in Military Hardware Deliveries Being Addressed," April 16, 2008 (www.thaindian.com/newsportal/business/delays-in-military-hardware-deliveries-being-addressed_10038738.html); Bharat Rakshak, "Sindhughosh Class," October 29, 2008 (www.bharat-rakshak.com/NAVY/Submarines/Active/94-Sindhughosh-Class.html).

121. Richard D. Fisher Jr., "Plan for Growth: China's Surface Fleet Modernization Fits Beijing's Appetite for Sea Power," *Armed Forces Journal* 143 (April 2006), p. 30.

122. Khan, "The Impact of Future Asian Naval Security Policy on the Persian Gulf."

123. Brad Kaplan, "China's Navy Today: Storm Clouds on the Horizon . . . or Paper Tiger?" (www.navyleague.org/seapower/chinas_navy_today.htm).

124. Zhang Wenmu, "Sea Power and China's Strategic Choices," *China Security* (Summer 2006), pp.17–31; Bernard Cole, *Chinese Naval Modernization and Energy Security*, paper prepared for the Institute for National Strategic Studies, National Defense University, 2006 Pacific Symposium, Washington, D.C., June 2006, pp. 2–4 (www.ndu.edu/inss/symposia/Pacific2006/Colepaper.pdf).

125. Wenmu, "Sea Power and China's Strategic Choices"; Cole, "Chinese Naval Modernization and Energy Security," pp. 3, 7, 9, 10; Ian Storey, "China's 'Malacca Dilemma,'" *China Brief* 6, no. 8 (Washington: Jamestown Foundation, April 2006).

126. Khan, "The Impact of Future Asian Naval Security Policy on the Persian Gulf."

127. Fisher, "Plan for Growth: China's Surface Fleet Modernization Fits Beijing's Appetite for Sea Power," p. 30.

128. Christopher J. Pehrson, *String of Pearls: Meeting the Challenge of China's Rising Power across the Asian Littoral*, paper prepared for the Strategic Studies Institute, U.S. Army War College, Carlisle, Pa., July 2006.

129. Jane's Security News, "Secret Sanya—China's New Naval Base Revealed," April 21, 2008.

130. Thomas Harding, "Chinese Nuclear Submarine Base," *Telegraph*, May 6, 2008; Khan, "The Impact of Future Asian Naval Security Policy on the Persian Gulf."

131. Gurpreet Khurana, "Cooperation among Maritime Security Forces: Imperatives for India and Southeast Asia," *Strategic Analysis* 29, no. 2 (April 2005).

132. Ibid.; Brahma Chellaney, "China Covets a Pearl Necklace: Dragon's Foothold in Gwadar," *Asian Age*, April 7, 2007; Sudha Ramachandran, "India Chases the Dragon in Sri Lanka," *Asia Times*, July 10, 2008.

133. Indian Navy, "Freedom to Use the Seas: India's Maritime Military Strategy," p. 87.

134. Tarique Niazi, "Gwadar: China's Naval Outpost on the Indian Ocean," *China Brief* 5, no. 4 (Washington: Jamestown Foundation, February 2005).

135. Ahmed Hassan, "Pakistan's Gwadar Port—Prospects of Economic Revival," Naval Postgraduate School, thesis, June 2005; Fazal-Ur-Rehman, "Prospects of Pakistan Becoming a Trade and Energy Corridor for China," *Institute of Strategic Studies, Islamabad* XXVII, no. 2 (2007); Niazi, "Gwadar: China's Naval Outpost on the Indian Ocean."

136. Khan, "The Impact of Future Asian Naval Security Policy on the Persian Gulf."

137. B. Raman, "The Blast in Gwadar," *South Asia Analysis Group*, August 5, 2004 (www.southasiaanalysis.org/papers10/paper993.html).

138. Naval-technology.com, "SSK Agosta 90B Class Attack Submarine" (www.naval-technology.com/projects/agosta); Khan, "The Impact of Future Asian Naval Security Policy on the Persian Gulf."

139. Khan, "The Impact of Future Asian Naval Security Policy on the Persian Gulf."

140. Pradeep P. Barua, *The State at War in South Asia* (University of Nebraska Press, 2005).

141. Khan, "The Impact of Future Asian Naval Security Policy on the Persian Gulf."

142. "India Studying Chinese Navy's Intentions," Indo-Asian News Service, December 2, 2005.

143. Office of Naval Intelligence, *China's Navy 2007* (Washington, 2007).

144. "Chinese Navy Performs Very Well in Multinational Drill," *People's Daily*, March 13, 2007 (http://english.people.com.cn/200703/13/eng20070313_357121.html).

145. Pakistan Navy, "Multi-National Exercise AMAN 07" (www.paknavy.gov.pk/aman/).

146. Kazumine Akimoto, Tsutomu Inuzuka, and others, "OPRF Monthly Report December 2005," Ocean Policy Research Foundation, p. 17 (www.sof.or.jp/en/monthly/pdf/200512.pdf).

147. Kaplan, "China's Navy Today: Storm Clouds on the Horizon . . . or Paper Tiger?"

148. Ibid.

149. Fisher, "Plan for Growth: China's Surface Fleet Modernization Fits Beijing's Appetite for Sea Power."

150. Cole, *Chinese Naval Modernization and Energy Security*.

151. International Institute for Strategic Studies, *The Military Balance 2008* (London).

152. Ibid.

153. Bernard Cole, "Beijing's Strategy of Sea Denial," *China Brief* 6, no. 23 (Washington: Jamestown Foundation, November 2006).

154. International Institute for Strategic Studies, *The Military Balance 2008*, p. 376.

155. Office of the Secretary of Defense, "Annual Report to Congress: Military Power of the People's Republic of China 2007," p. 4 (www.globalsecurity.org/military/library/report/2007/2007-prc-military-power.htm).

156. Ronald O'Rourke, "China Naval Modernization: Implications for U.S. Naval Capabilities—Background and Issues for Congress," Congressional Research Service, November 23, 2009, p. 10 (www.fas.org/sgp/crs/row/RL33153.pdf); Khan, "The Impact of Future Asian Naval Security Policy on the Persian Gulf."

157. Russell Hsiao, "China Navy Floats Three Carrier Plan," *Asia Times*, January 8, 2008 (www.atimes.com/atimes/China/JA08Ad01.html); Khan, "The Impact of Future Asian Naval Security Policy on the Persian Gulf."

158. DEFENSETECH, "Is China Building Aircraft Carriers?" May 23, 2008 (http://defensetech.org/2008/05/23/is-china-building-aircraft-carriers/); Khan, "The Impact of Future Asian Naval Security Policy on the Persian Gulf."

159. Russian News and Information Agency, "China Plans to Build Its First Aircraft Carrier," July 6, 2007 (http://en.rian.ru/world/20070706/68460904.html); Khan, "The Impact of Future Asian Naval Security Policy on the Persian Gulf."

160. Bernard Cole, "Oil for the Lamps of China—Beijing's 21st Century Search for Energy," McNair Paper 67 (National Defense University, 2003).

161. Cole, *Chinese Naval Modernization and Energy Security*, p. 7.

162. Toshi Yoshihara and James R. Holmes, "Japanese Maritime Thought: If Not Mahan, Who?" *Naval War College Review* 59, no. 3 (Summer 2006), p. 30.

163. Woolley, *Japan's Navy: Politics and Paradox, 1971–2000*, pp. 68–69, 71.

164. National Diet Library, "The Constitution of Japan: Chapter 2: Renunciation of War: Article 9" (www.ndl.go.jp/constitution/e/etc/c01.html#s2); for the pacifist view, see S. Hamura and E. Shiu, "Renunciation of War as a Universal Principle of Mankind—A Look at the Gulf War and the Japanese Constitution," *International and Comparative Law Quarterly* 44 (1995), pp. 430–31; Richard J. Samuels, "Constitutional Revision in Japan: the Future of Article 9," speech, Brookings Institution, Center for Northeast Asian Policy Studies, December 15, 2004 (www.brookings.edu/events/2004/1215japan.aspx).

165. Samuels, "Constitutional Revision in Japan: The Future of Article 9."

166. Woolley, *Japan's Navy: Politics and Paradox, 1971–2000*, p. 143; Yann-Huei Song, "The Overall Situation in the South China Sea in the New Millennium: Before and after the September 11 Terrorist Attacks," *Ocean Development & International Law* 34, no. 3-4, pp. 231, 233–34 (www.southchinasea.org/docs/Song,%20Overall%20situation%20in%20the%20South%20China%20Sea%20after%20 9-11.pdf).

167. Daniel Kliman, *Japan's Security Strategy in a Post-9/11 World: Embracing a New Realpolitik,* p. 26; Yoshihara and Holmes, "Japanese Maritime Thought: If Not Mahan, Who?" pp. 36–37.

168. Kliman, *Japan's Security Strategy in a Post-9/11 World: Embracing a New Realpolitik,* p. 26.

169. Yoshihara and Holmes, "Japanese Maritime Thought: If Not Mahan, Who?" p. 38.

170. Ministry of Foreign Affairs of Japan, "The Proliferation Security Initiative (PSI) Maritime Interdiction Exercise 'Team Samurai 04' (Overview and Evaluation)," October 28, 2004 (www.mofa.go.jp/policy/un/disarmament/arms/psi/overview0410.html).

171. Kliman, *Japan's Security Strategy in a Post-9/11 World: Embracing a New Realpolitik.*

172. International Institute for Strategic Studies, *The Military Balance 2008.*

173. Ministry of Foreign Affairs of Japan, "The Proliferation Security Initiative (PSI) Maritime Interdiction Exercise 'Team Samurai 04' (Overview and Evaluation)."

174. Yoshihara and Holmes, "Japanese Maritime Thought: If Not Mahan, Who?" p. 33.

175. Hughes, *Japan's Re-Emergence as a "Normal" Military Power,* p. 82.

176. Yoshihara and Holmes, "Japanese Maritime Thought: If Not Mahan, Who?" p. 39

177. "Jieitai vs. Chugoku Gun: Jieitai Wa Kakutatakaeri," *Bessatsu Takarajima,* September 1, 2005, as cited in Yoshihara and Holmes, "Japanese Maritime Thought: If Not Mahan, Who?" p. 44.

178. Hughes, *Japan's Re-Emergence as a "Normal" Military Power,* p. 82.

179. Kliman, *Japan's Security Strategy in a Post-9/11 World: Embracing a New Realpolitik,* p. 23; Hughes, *Japan's Reemergence as a "Normal" Military Power,* p. 82.

180. Hughes, *Japan's Re-Emergence as a "Normal" Military Power,* p. 95.

181. Yoshihara and Holmes, "Japanese Maritime Thought: If Not Mahan, Who?" p. 44.

182. Ibid., p. 39.

183. Adm. Michael Mullen, "Address to the 17th International Sea Power Symposium," Naval War College, September 21, 2005 (www.navy.mil/navydata/cno/mullen/speeches/mullen050921.txt).

184. Ibid.

185. Amy Klamper, "The Thousand Ship Navy," *Sea Power,* February 13, 2007 (www.military.com/forums/0,15240,125158,00.html).

186. CBP.gov, "CSI In Brief" (www.cbp.gov/xp/cgov/trade/cargo_security/csi/csi_in_brief.xml).

187. Gurpreet S. Khurana, "'Thousand Ship Navy': A Reincarnation of the Controversial P.S.I.?" IDSA Comment, Institute for Defence Studies and Analyses, December 28, 2006.

188. U.S. Department of State, "Proliferation Security Initiative Participants" (www.state.gov/t/isn/c27732.htm).

189. David Rosenberg, "Dire Straits: Competing Security Priorities in the South China Sea," *Asia-Pacific Journal: Japan Focus*, April 13, 2005 (www.japanfocus.org/-David-Rosenberg/1773).

190. George Galdorisi and Darren Sutton, "Achieving the Global Maritime Partnership: Operational Needs and Technical Realities," *Royal United Services Institute for Defence and Security Studies*, June 2007 (www.rusi.org/downloads/assets/Galdorisi_and_Sutton,_Achieving_the_Global_Maritime_Partnership.pdf).

191. Andrew S. Erickson, "New U.S. Maritime Strategy: Initial Chinese Responses," *China Security* 3, no. 4 (Autumn 2007), pp. 40–61; Eric McVadon, "China and the United States on the High Seas," *China Security* 3, no. 4 (Autumn 2007), p. 11; Christopher J. Gilbertson, Lt. USN, "The Thousand Ship Navy: Creating a Maritime System of Systems," Naval War College, October 5, 2007, p. 5 (www.dtic.mil/cgi-bin/GetTRDoc?AD=ADA470826&Location=U2&doc=GetTRDoc.pdf).

192. Yang Yi, "Engagement, Caution," *China Security* 3, no. 4 (Autumn 2007), p. 39.

193. Khurana, "'Thousand Ship Navy': A Reincarnation of the Controversial P.S.I.?"; Gilbertson, "The Thousand Ship Navy: Creating a Maritime System of Systems," p. 5.

194. Khurana, "'Thousand Ship Navy': A Reincarnation of the Controversial P.S.I.?"

195. A. Vinod Kumar, "The Proliferation Security Initiative: Five Years Later, Losing Its Sheen?" IDSA Comment, Institute for Defence Studies and Analyses, July 7, 2008.

196. Steve Herman, "9 Indian Ocean Nations Partner in Security Cooperative," *Voice of America News*, May 19, 2008 (www.voanews.com/english/2008-05-19-voa17.cfm).

197. Thomas Woodrow, "China Opens Pandora's Nuclear Box," *China Brief* 13, no. 15 (Washington: Jamestown Foundation, December 2003).

198. Susan L. Craig, *Perceptions of Traditional and Nontraditional Security Threats* (Carlisle, Pa.: Strategic Studies Institute, March 2007), p. 97 (www.strategicstudies institute.army.mil/pdffiles/PUB765.pdf).

199. K. Alan Kronstadt, "India-U.S. Relations," Congressional Research Service, February 13, 2007, p. 9 (http://fpc.state.gov/documents/organization/80669.pdf).

200. Kronstadt, "India-U.S. Relations," p. 25.

201. James Martin Center for Nonproliferation Studies, "China's Missile Exports and Assistance to Pakistan—Statements and Developments," February 1999 (http://cns.miis.edu/archive/country_india/china/mpakchr.htm).

202. Khurana, "Indian Navy's Amphibious Leap: a Little Help from America"; International Institute for Strategic Studies, *The Military Balance 2008*, p. 330.

203. Kronstadt, "India-U.S. Relations," p. 23.

204. Ibid., p. 34.

205. Central Intelligence Agency (CIA), *World Factbook*, "India: Transnational Issues: Disputes—International" (www.cia.gov/library/publications/the-world-factbook/geos/in.html).

206. Kronstadt, "India-U.S. Relations," p. 7.

207. Ibid.

208. Ramesh Thurkur, "Hope for Peace between India and Pakistan," UNU Update 30, United Nations University, March–April 2004 (http://update.unu.edu/archive/issue30_4.htm).

209. Ibid.

210. C. Raja Mohan, "India's Strategic Challenges in the Indian Ocean and the Gulf," in *India's Growing Role in the Gulf: Implications for the Region and the United States* (Gulf Research Center, November 2008), pp. 55–69 (www.nixoncenter.org/Monograph-Indias-Growing-Role-in-the-Gulf.pdf).

211. Tarique Niazi, "Afghanistan, Pakistan and the Threat of Talibanization," *Terrorism Monitor* 4, no. 10 (Washington: Jamestown Foundation, May 2006); Barnett R. Rubin, "Saving Afghanistan," *Foreign Affairs* (January/February 2007).

212. Frédéric Grare, "Pakistan-Afghanistan Relations in the Post-9/11 Era," Carnegie Papers no. 72 (Washington: Carnegie Endowment for International Peace, October 2006), p. 11 (www.carnegieendowment.org/files/cp72_grare_final.pdf).

213. S. V. R. Nasr, "Islamic Opposition to the Islamic State: The Jama'at-I Islam, 1977–1988," *International Journal of Middle Eastern Studies* 25, no. 2 (May 1993), pp. 261–83.

214. Rahul Bedi, "India Joins Anti-Taliban Coalition," *Jane's Security News*, March 15, 2001.

215. Soutik Biswas, "India: Afghanistan's Influential Ally," *BBC News*, October 8, 2009; Thaindian News, "Unfazed by Kabul Terror, India Announces Fresh Aid for Afghanistan," August 4, 2008 (www.thaindian.com/newsportal/uncategorized/unfazed-by-terror-india-announces-more-aid-for-afghanistan-second-lead_1007 9909.html).

216. Grare, "Pakistan-Afghanistan Relations in the Post-9/11 Era," pp. 12–13.

217. "India Blames Pakistan for Kabul Embassy Attack," Reuters India, July 13, 2008 (http://in.reuters.com/article/domesticNews/idINBOM7063020080713).

218. Grare, "Pakistan-Afghanistan Relations in the Post-9/11 Era," pp. 3, 16–17.

219. Craig, *Perceptions of Traditional and Nontraditional Security Threats*, p. 95.

220. Data compiled using Indian Department of Commerce, System on Foreign Trade Performance Analysis (http://commerce.nic.in/ftpa/default.asp).

221. Center for Advanced Defense Studies, "US Strategy with China and India: Striking a Balance to Avoid Conflict," August 2006, p. 3 (www.c4ads.org/files/cads_report_usindia_aug06.pdf).

222. Kronstadt, "India-U.S. Relations," p. 10.

223. Craig, *Perceptions of Traditional and Nontraditional Security Threats*, p. 95.

224. Ibid.

225. New Jersey Hong Kong Network, "Basic Facts on the Nanjing Massacre and the Tokyo War Crimes Trial" (www.cnd.org/njmassacre/nj.html).

226. Craig, *Perceptions of Traditional and Nontraditional Security Threats*, p. 77.

227. Ibid., p. 79.

228. Ibid., p. 78.

229. Foreign Press Center Japan, "2005 Defense White Paper and Newspaper Commentaries," August 4, 2005 (http://fpcj.jp/old/e/mres/japanbrief/jb_560.html).

230. James J. Przystup, "Japan-China Relations: New Year, Old Problems, Hope for Wen," *Comparative Connections* 9, no. 1 (April 2007), p. 121 (http://csis.org/files/media/csis/pubs/0701q.pdf).

231. Przystup, "Japan-China Relations: New Year, Old Problems, Hope for Wen," p. 122.

232. Ibid.

233. James L. Schoff, *Realigning Priorities: The U.S.-Japan Alliance & the Future of Extended Deterrence,* a project report by the Institute for Foreign Policy Analysis, Cambridge, Mass., March 2009 (www.ifpa.org/pdf/RealignPriorities.pdf), pp. 10–11; "U.S. Defense Department Says China's anti-Satellite Test Posed Threat," *International Herald Tribune* (www.mre.gov.br/portugues/noticiario/internacional/selecao_detalhe3.asp?ID_RESENHA=341385).

234. "China and Japan Rival Giants: Strategic Balance," *BBC News* (http://news.bbc.co.uk/2/shared/spl/hi/asia_pac/05/china_japan/html/strategic_balance.stm).

235. CIA, *World Factbook,* "China: Transnational Issues: Disputes—International" (www.cia.gov/library/publications/the-world-factbook/geos/ch.html).

236. Craig, *Perceptions of Traditional and Nontraditional Security Threats,* p. 82.

237. Przystup, "Japan-China Relations: New Year, Old Problems, Hope for Wen," pp. 122–23.

238. Ibid.

239. "Japan Stokes China Sea Dispute," *BBC News,* July 14, 2005 (http://news.bbc.co.uk/2/hi/asia-pacific/4681823.stm).

240. Craig, *Perceptions of Traditional and Nontraditional Security Threats,* p. 83.

241. Ibid., p. 84.

242. Ibid.

243. Anthony Faiola, "Japan-Taiwan Ties Blossom as Regional Rivalry Grows: Tokyo, Wary of China, Tilts toward Taipei," *Washington Post,* March 24, 2006 (www.washingtonpost.com/wp-dyn/content/article/2006/03/23/AR2006032301784.html).

244. Ibid.

245. Ibid.

246. Yoshihara and Holmes, "Japanese Maritime Thought: If Not Mahan, Who?" pp. 23–51. The sixty-six-mile figure refers to the distance from the Yilan area of Taiwan to the Japanese island of Yonaguni.

247. "US, Japan: Taiwan a Common Security Issue," *China Daily,* February 20, 2005 (www.chinadaily.com.cn/english/doc/2005-02/20/content_417697.htm).

248. Ibid.

249. Norimitsu Onishi and Howard W. French, "China Deploys Ships to Area Japan Claims," *San Francisco Chronicle,* September 11, 2005, p. A12.

250. Awareness of the need for greater security cooperation between the Gulf countries and Asia can be seen in the success of the Manama Dialogue, initiated in 2005 and organized every December by the International Institute for Strategic

Studies (IISS) with direct support from the government of Bahrain. This occasion brings together high-level defense and foreign policy officials including defense ministers and experts from the Gulf, Asia, Europe, and the United States to discuss common security concerns. The dialogue is modeled on the IISS Shangri-La Dialogue (Asian security summit), which has been held since 2002 in Singapore and is focused on security issues in the Asia-Pacific region.

251. Khan, "The Impact of Future Asian Naval Security Policy on the Persian Gulf."

252. Ibid.

CHAPTER 8

1. Sabahat Khan, "The Impact of Future Asian Naval Security Policy on the Persian Gulf," Institute for Near East and Gulf Military Analysis, October 2008.

2. Donald Berlin, "India in the Indian Ocean," *Naval War College Review* 59, no. 2 (Spring 2006).

3. Dennis Blair and Ken Lieberthal, "Smooth Sailing: The World's Shipping Lanes Are Safe," *Foreign Affairs* 86 (May-June 2007), p. 7.

APPENDIX A

1. "About AMED: Rationale and Objectives," Inaugural Asia-Middle East Dialogue (http://app.amed.sg/internet/amed/AbtAMED.asp).

2. Geoffrey Kemp and Steven Brooke, "Singapore's Asia–Middle East Dialogue: Does It Contribute to the U.S. Goals of Conflict Mitigation in the Muslim World?" unpublished paper (Washington: Nixon Center, 2006).

3. Goh Chok Tong, "Asia and the Middle East: Rediscovering Each Other," keynote speech at the Asia–Middle East Dialogue, June 21, 2005 (http://app.amed.sg/internet/amed/view_press_print.asp?post_id=180).

4. "Declaration of Principles," Asia–Middle East Dialogue II (www.mfa.gov.eg/Amed/English/logistics.html).

5. Notably, Israel, Australia, and New Zealand were not invited to AMED.

6. "Singapore and Indian Navies Conduct Military Exercise," *Thaindian News* (www.thaindian.com/newsportal/south-asia/singapore-and-indian-navies-conduct-military-exercise_10032423.html).

7. Nimrod Raphaeli and Bianca Gersten, "Sovereign Wealth Funds: Investment Vehicles for the Persian Gulf Countries," *Middle East Quarterly* 15, no. 2, pp. 45–53 (http://search.ebscohost.com/login.aspx?direct=true&db=aph&AN=31990356&site=ehost-live).

8. Vincent J. Houben, "Southeast Asia and Islam," *Annals of the American Academy of Political and Social Science*, vol. 588, *Islam: Enduring Myths and Changing Realities* (July 2003).

9. Jemaah Islamiyah, the largest terrorist group operating in Indonesia, is affiliated with al Qaeda.

10. "To Gain among Muslims, Indonesia Offers to Mediate Middle East Disputes," *New York Times*, June 8, 2007.

11. Brian Bremner, "The Ties That Bind the Middle East and Asia," *Business Week*, May 21, 2007.

12. John Gershman, "U.S. and Malaysia Now Best Friends in War on Terrorism," *Foreign Policy in Focus* (Washington: Institute for Policy Studies, May 2002).

Appendix B

1. Namitha Jagadeesh, "Waving the Flag," *Businessworld*, 2006 (www.business world.in/index.php/Waving-The-Flag.html).

2. "No Deal in Sight to Free Up FLAG Bandwidth," *Financial Express* (New Delhi), April 4, 2002 (www.financialexpress.com/printer/news/42298/).

3. "Alcatel-Lucent Helps Double Capacity between Asia and Europe with SEA-ME-WE 4 Upgrade," Alcatel-Lucent press release, March 5, 2008 (www.alcatel-lucent.com).

4. John Borland, "Analyzing the Internet Collapse," *ABC News*, February 5, 2008 (http://abcnews.go.com/Technology/Story?id=4244474&page=1).

5. Ryan Singel, "Fiber Optic Cable Cuts Isolate Millions from Internet, Future Cuts Likely," *Wired*, January 31, 2008 (http://blog.wired.com/27bstroke6/2008/01/fiber-optic-ca b.html).

6. Richard Gasparre, "Into the Deep with Unmanned Undersea Vehicles," *Naval Technology*, May 13, 2008 (www.naval-technology.com/features/feature1940/).

7. Lawrence Greenberg, Seymour Goodman, and Kevin Soo Hoo, *Information Warfare and International Law* (Washington: National Defense University Press, 1998), p. 9 (www.dodccrp.org/files/Greenberg_Law.pdf).

8. Gasparre, "Into the Deep with Unmanned Undersea Vehicles."

9. Gordon Housworth, "Submarine Fiber-Optic Cable Breaks: A Study in Hysteria and Ignorance against Analysis," ICG Intellectual Capital Group, February 10, 2008 (http://spaces.icgpartners.com/apps/discuss.asp?guid=4CB553F71F04440DB3 26F888B2142BF5).

10. "Indian Outsourcing Sector Hit by Internet Outages," Agence France-Presse, January 30, 2008 (http://afp.google.com/article/ALeqM5gadarOY4frbM-XSyXS0_wMfxpHig).

11. Malcom Fried and Lars Klemming, "Severed Cables Cut Power across the Mediterranean," *Washington Times*, December 19, 2008 (www.washingtontimes.com/news/2008/dec/19/severed-cables-cut-power/).

12. David S. Alberts, John J. Garstka, and Federick P. Stein, *Network-Centric Warfare: Developing and Leveraging Information Superiority*, 2nd ed., rev. (Department of Defense, CCRP publication Series, July 27, 2001) (www.dodccrp.org/files/ncw_report/report/ncw_0801.pdf).

13. Yin Zhili, "Special Team to Guarantee Undersea Cable Safety," April 16, 2009 (http://english.peopledaily.com.cn/200103/21/eng20010321_65605.html).

14. Gasparre, "Into the Deep with Unmanned Undersea Vehicles."

15. Andrew Erickson, "PLA Navy Modernization: Preparing for 'Informatized' War at Sea," *China Brief* 8, no. 5, April 17, 2009 (www.jamestown.org/programs/china brief/single/?tx_ttnews[tt_news]=4759&tx_ttnews[backPid]=168&no_cache=1).

16. "FORCEnet: A Functional Concept for the 21st Century"(http://forcenet. navy.mil/concepts/fn-concept-final.pdf).

17. Ibid.

18. Ibid.

INDEX

Abdul Aziz airport (Jeddah, Saudi Arabia), 162

Abdullah bin Abdul Aziz (king; Saudi Arabia), 15, 38, 80–81, 130

Abdullah ibn Abd al-Aziz (crown prince; Saudi Arabia), 125

Abe, Shinzo, (prime minister; Japan), 119, 123

Abu Dhabi (UAE): Asian presence in, 3; economic issues of, 155, 156, 158; energy issues of, 156, 158; film festival in, 25–26; infrastructure in, 151, 156–57; tourism in, 157–58. *See also* Middle East; United Arab Emirates

Abu Dhabi International Airport (UAE), 153

Abu Dhabi National Oil Company (UAE), 125–26

ADB. *See* Asian Development Bank

Admiral Gorshov (carrier; Russia), 203, 204

Advanced technology vehicle (ATV), 202

Afghanistan: Balochistan and, 116; history of, 221–22; India and, 60–61, 62, 221, 222; Japan and, 119, 178, 213; NATO and, 61; Pakistan and, 52, 57, 61, 107, 116, 175, 180, 221–22; Saudi Arabia, 107; Soviet Union and, 38, 57, 104, 116; U.S. and, 17, 24, 57, 104, 107, 175, 180. *See also* Asia; Middle East; Taliban

Africa, 11, 17, 81, 205, 230. *See also* individual countries

African Union, 199

Agreement on Medical and Health Technical Cooperation between the Ministries of Health of China and the United Arab Emirates (*1992*), 87

Agricultural issues, 28, 30, 32, 92, 137

Ahmadinejad, Mahmoud (president; Iran), 54, 59, 60, 122

Air Arabia, 15–16

Airports and air traffic, 154

Airports and air traffic—specific countries and regions: in Bahrain, 161; in China, 72–73, 86, 87; in India, 36–37, 40, 49, 50; in Kuwait, 50, 160; in the Middle East, 174; in Oman, 161; in Pakistan, 109, 110, 206, 208; in Qatar, 86, 159, 164; in Saudi Arabia, 40, 81, 162, 174; in UAE, 49, 87, 150, 153–54, 156–57, 161, 164. *See also* Emirates Airlines; Infrastructure

Akihito (emperor; Japan), 124

Aktobe oil field (Kazakhstan), 96

Al-Abdullah, Sheikh Ahmed (oil minister; Kuwait), 89

Alborz drilling platform (Caspian Sea), 76–77

Alcatel Shanghai Bell (China), 94

Aliyev, Heydar (president; Azerbaijan), 144

Al Kaabi, Ali Bin Abdullah (minister of labor; UAE), 25

307

Gulf Cooperation Council (GCC): China and, 84–85, 88; India and, 25, 38, 40, 42, 48, 49; Japan and, 124, 125, 128; Kuwait and, 88; Qatar and, 108, 128
Gulf News, 50
Gulf States. *See* Middle East; *individual countries*
Gulf War (*1991*), 229; Dubai and, 150; India and, 27, 38, 52, 134; Japan and, 119, 127, 212; Oman and, 127; Pakistan and, 107; U.S. and, 139
Gwadar (seaport; Pakistan): China and, 111–12, 113, 167, 206–08, 209; expressway links to, 109, 165; history of, 107; importance of, 56, 76, 110–12, 115–16, 117, 206, 209; India and, 208, 209; Iran and, 76; Pakistan and, 209; problem of Balochistan and, 115–18; upgrading of, 56

Hainan Island (China), 206, 208
Hamas (Palestinian organization), 80, 136, 140, 141, 180
Han Meyong-Sook (prime minister; South Korea), 142
Hatoyama, Yukio (prime minister; Japan), 119
Hezbollah (Islamist organization), 77, 136, 141, 180
Highways. *See* Roads and highways
Higuchi Commission (Japan; *1994*), 197, 212–13
Hitachi (Japan), 126
Hong Kong, 74
Hotel JAL chain, 15
Hout oil field (Saudi Arabia), 122
Huawei Technologies (China), 94
Hu Jintao (president; China), 15, 79, 80–81, 83
Humanitarian relief missions, 186–87, 196, 197, 199, 215
Hussein, Saddam (president; Iraq), 106, 175
Hydrogen power, 158
Hydropower: in China, 70, 109, 170; in India, 31, 34, 109, 199; in Pakistan, 108, 109, 114–15
Hyuga (destroyer; Japan), 214–15
Hyundai (companies; South Korea), 142

IAEA. *See* International Atomic Energy Agency
Ibn Al Sa'ud (king; Saudi Arabia), 124

ICBC. *See* Industrial and Commercial Bank of China
ICC-CCS. *See* International Chamber of Commerce Commercial Crime Services
IEA. *See* International Energy Agency
IDEX. *See* International Defense Exhibition and Conference
IISS. *See* International Institute for Strategic Studies
IMB. *See* International Maritime Bureau
Immigration. *See* Migration issues
Immigration Act (India; *1983*), 41
IMU. *See* Islamic Movement of Uzbekistan
India: arms sales and, 135, 190, 202, 204, 220; class issues in, 28–30, 32; conflict between India, China, and Pakistan, 219–23; as a democracy, 37; economic issues of, 4, 10, 24, 25, 26, 27–31, 35, 54, 134, 137, 204, 223; education issues of, 41, 44–45; energy issues of, 7–8, 9, 24, 27, 30, 31–34, 54, 59, 173, 188–89, 230; exchange programs in, 16; film industry in, 25–26; Gulf Cooperation Council and, 25, 26, 37; higher education opportunities in, 16, 24; history of, 104, 133–34, 219, 232; humanitarian assistance by, 187, 199; infrastructure projects and, 35–37, 166–67; investment and, 30–31, 121, 164, 166–67; maritime issues of, 176, 177, 178, 186, 187, 190, 191, 198–204, 217, 232; migrant labor of, 25, 27, 63; military, defense, and security issues of, 5, 24, 26, 59, 62, 112, 135–36, 176, 188, 189–90, 232; nuclear issues and, 31, 34, 47, 58, 104, 135, 136, 185, 188–89, 219, 231; political issues of, 24, 58, 138; presence in the Middle East, 4–5, 24, 25–26; security issues of, 24, 26, 198–99; strategic cooperation and, 188–91; tourism and, 15–16, 24; trade and, 12, 13, 14, 24, 27, 28, 30, 31, 48, 52, 61–62, 121, 134, 137, 223; World Wars I and II and, 23. *See also* Asia; Bangladesh; Future scenarios; Kashmir; Mumbai attack; Pakistan; *individual countries below*
India—specific countries and regions: Afghanistan, 60–61, 62, 166–67, 221, 222; ASEAN countries, 42; Bahrain, 25, 42–43, 51; Britain, 23, 24, 27; China, 25, 27, 60, 118–19, 167, 185, 222–23,

Organization of Petroleum Exporting Countries (OPEC), 81, 129
Organization of the Islamic Conference, 38,
41
Oslo Agreement (Israel-Palestinians; *1993*),
229
Ottoman Empire, 23

Pacific Ocean, 181, 187, 200, 204, 212
Pakistan: arms sales and, 105, 107, 113,
220; conflict between India, China, and
Pakistan, 219–23; economic issues, 105,
107, 108–09, 113–18; energy issues,
53, 54, 55, 108, 111, 114–15, 116–17,
170; history of, 103–04, 112–13, 219,
221; infrastructure projects in, 76, 108,
109–12, 114, 116; investment in, 108,
114–15; madrassas in, 105–06; military,
defense, and security issues of, 42, 56,
103, 104–05, 106–08, 112, 113, 176,
191, 208; nuclear issues and, 84, 104,
105, 108, 113, 114–15, 185; Oman
and, 107; political issues of, 24, 103,
170, 221; trade and, 52, 107, 111, 112,
113–14, 115–16, 118. *See also* Asia; Bangladesh; Future scenarios; India; Kashmir
Pakistan—specific countries and regions:
Afghanistan and, 52, 57, 61, 107, 175,
221–22; Bahrain and, 107–08; Central
Asia and, 111; China and, 56, 76, 89,
105, 109, 110–19, 139, 206–08; China-
India-Pakistan conflicts, 219–23; India
and, 27, 38, 41–42, 47, 52, 54, 55, 56,
57–58, 61, 103–05, 107, 112, 113, 117,
134, 135, 138, 185, 208, 221; India-
China-Pakistan conflicts, 219–23; Iran
and, 52, 57–58, 106; Israel and, 106;
Oman and, 107; Qatar and, 108; Saudi
Arabia and, 37, 41–42, 84, 105, 106–07;
UAE and, 49–50, 107; U.S. and, 105,
108, 112, 118, 191, 220
Pakistan People's Party (PPP), 221
Palau Islands, 205
Palestine and Palestinians: Arab-Israeli
conflict and, 180; Arab League and, 80;
China and, 140; India and, 133; Israel
and, 142, 229; Japan and, 141; South
Korea, 142. *See also* Arab-Israeli conflict;
Israel; Middle East
Palestine Liberation Organization (PLO),
134, 142

Palms, The (Dubai, UAE), 152
Paracel Islands, 206
Peaceful rise (China), 66, 67, 187
Peacekeepers and peacekeeping: Bangladesh,
178; China, 5–6, 178, 187; India, 5, 178;
Japan, 196, 197, 212, 214, 215; Kazakh-
stan and, 95; Lebanon, 5–6, 178; Middle
East, 178; United States, 196, 197
People's Liberation Army (PLA; China), 187,
194, 204
People's Liberation Army Navy (PLAN;
China), 204–05, 206, 209, 210–11
People's Republic of China. *See* China
Perry, William (secretary of defense; U.S.),
195
Persian Gulf, 176
Persian Empire, 73. *See also* Iran
PetroKazakhstan (Canadian-based, Chinese
owned), 96
Petroleum. *See* Energy issues; Fossil fuels;
Oil
Petroliam Nasional Berhadis (Petronas;
Malaysia), 93
Petronas. *See* Petroliam Nasional Berhadis
Petronet LNG (India), 45
Petro Rabigh (petroleum complex; Japan-
Saudi Arabia), 125
Pipelines—specific countries and regions:
Asia and Central Asia, 170, 171, 172,
173; Burma, 55; China, 8, 70, 93, 95,
96–97, 99, 100, 114, 170–71; Eurasia,
170, 171, 172, 173; India, 34, 44,
53, 54–55, 58, 108, 117, 170; Iran,
53, 54–55, 58, 60, 76, 108, 117, 171;
Iran-Pakistan-India (IPI), 108, 170,
231; Israel, 55; Japan, 170; Kazakh-
China pipeline, 170; Kazakhstan,
70, 95, 96–97, 170–71; Medstream
pipeline project, 34; Oman, 44; Paki-
stan, 54, 58, 108, 114, 117; Qatar,
45–46, 108; Russia, 99; Turkey, 55;
Turkmenistan, 70, 93, 97, 98, 99, 100,
170–71; Turkmenistan-Afghanistan-
Pakistan-India pipeline (TAPI), 170, 236;
Turkmenistan-Kazakhstan-China pipe-
line, 97; Uzbekistan, 70, 93, 170–71.
See also Fossil fuels
Piracy. *See* Maritime issues
Piracy Reporting Centre (IMB), 183
PKK. *See* Kurdish Workers' Party
PLA. *See* People's Liberation Army

migrant labor in, 47, 48, 49, 50, 107; military, defense, and security issues of, 47–48, 49, 50; nuclear issues in, 158–59, 185; tourism in, 15, 155–56, 157–58; trade and, 47, 48–49, 87, 107, 126. *See also* Abu Dhabi; Dubai

United Arab Emirates—specific countries and regions: China, 86–87; India, 25, 46, 47–50; Japan, 125–26; Pakistan, 49–50, 107; Taiwan, 87; U.S., 159, 175, 185

United Kingdom (U.K.), 16, 78, 175, 217. *See also* Britain; Western powers

United Nations (UN): Bangladesh and, 178; China and, 112, 178; India and, 134, 178; Israel and, 133; Pakistan and, 112, 178; Zionism and, 134

UN Commission on Trade and Development, 163

UN Economic and Social Commission for Asia and the Pacific, 166

UN Emergency Force (UNEF), 5, 178

UNIKOM. *See* UN Iraq-Kuwait Observation Mission

UN Interim Force in Lebanon (UNIFIL), 5–6, 178

UN Iraq-Kuwait Observation Mission (UNIKOM), 178

UNOCAL (U.S.), 236

UN Security Council (UNSC), 62, 78, 119–20, 127

UN Truce Supervision Organization (UNTSO), 178

United States (U.S.): arms embargoes, 139–40; arms sales and, 83, 105, 174, 190, 192, 197–98, 220; economic issues of, 175, 176, 177, 230; education issues in, 16, 159; energy issues and, 32, 34, 68, 169, 170, 188–89, 230, 231, 232–33; humanitarian assistance by, 186–87, 196, 197; infrastructure projects and, 174; maritime issues, 215–18; military, defense, and security issues and, 24, 26–27, 57, 174–77, 187–98, 230, 231–32; nuclear issues and, 136, 159, 185, 188–89, 197; piracy and, 183; security issues and, 231–32; September *11, 2001,* and, 17; as sole superpower, 18; strategic cooperation and, 187–98; strategic oil reserves of, 82; Suez crisis and, 17; trade and, 28. *See also* Future scenarios; Tsunami; Western powers

United States—specific countries and regions: Afghanistan, 17, 24, 57, 104, 107, 175, 222; Asia, 227, 231–32; British–Indian Ocean Territory, 175; China, 66, 67, 77, 85, 101, 112, 139–40, 175, 188, 192–95, 205–06, 231; Djibouti, 175; Egypt, 175; GCC countries, 85; India, 18, 26–27, 28, 34, 56, 58–59, 105, 112, 135, 138, 175, 187–91, 220, 231; Iran, 54, 55, 56, 58, 78, 170, 175, 231; Iraq, 17, 24, 175; Israel, 17, 139–40; Japan, 120, 187, 195–98, 212, 213, 224, 231; Jordan, 185; Kuwait, 88, 174–75, 185; Middle East, 17–18, 188, 227, 228, 231–32; North Korea, 196; Oman, 175; Pakistan, 105, 108, 112, 118, 175, 191; Qatar, 175; Saudi Arabia, 17, 175; Soviet Union, 17; Taiwan, 101, 193; UAE, 159, 175, 185

UNSC. *See* United Nations Security Council

UNTSO. *See* UN Truce Supervision Organization

U.S. *See* United States

U.S. Arms Control and Disarmament Agency, 140

U.S.-Azerbaijan Council, 144

U.S.-China Security Review Commission, 140

U.S.-India Nuclear Cooperation Agreement *(2008),* 58

U.S.-Japan Security Consultative Committee *(2005),* 197

U.S.-Japan Security Treaty *(1952),* 195–96

U.S. Pacific Command, 216–17

USS *Enterprise,* 27

USS *Mercy,* 186

USS *Trenton,* 202

USSR. *See* Union of Soviet Socialist Republics

Uzbekistan: China and, 70, 90–94; energy issues of, 70, 90, 92–93, 170–71; foreign aid to, 93; India and, 60, 61–62; infrastructure projects in, 92, 93–94, 165–66; investment and, 92, 164; Islamic groups in, 90–91; military, defense, and security issues, 90–92; Russia and, 92; trade issues, 92–93, 168–69; uprising in Andijan, 91–92; United States and, 91–92

Uzbekneftegaz, 93, 170

Uzbektelecom, 94